Our Life Together

is for
everyone who enjoys
the special feeling
called 'Love.'

Especially for:

____

Cover design & calligraphy
by Joanne Fink

Illustrations by Rita Marandino

Written and compiled by Joanne Fink

For my wonderful husband, Andy Trattner, with love, — you've made "our life together" better than I could have imagined.

ISBN: 1-56245-018-2

Love
is sharing
all of the
wonderful things
life has to offer
with the
person you care
most about.

Weave
the threads
of your lives
together with
Love.

Anything
is possible
if you do it
together!

THE PERFECT RELATIONSHIP *is more than finding the right person. It's* BEING *the right person.*

A RELATIONSHIP
that grows
from mutual love
and respect,
kindness, understanding
and compassion
is strong enough
to last a lifetime.

The place
to be happy is here.
The time
to be happy
is now.
The way to be happy
is to make
another happy.

AUTHOR
UNKNOWN

Having someone
with whom
to laugh,
talk, cry and dream,
is having
a friend to love.

A caring relationship when nurtured can blossom into Love.

Delight

IN SPENDING

TIME WITH

THE PERSON

YOU LOVE.

Treat

EACH DAY

TOGETHER AS

A GIFT AND

AN ADVENTURE.

THE TEST
OF A LOVING
AND LASTING
RELATIONSHIP
LIES IN
COPING WITH
AND GROWING
FROM WHATEVER
DIFFICULTIES
MIGHT ARISE.

A friend

IS SOMEONE

WHO NOT ONLY

ACCEPTS YOU FOR

WHAT YOU ARE

BUT MAKES YOU

FEEL GOOD ABOUT

BEING YOURSELF.

Take the
time to give
to one another,
to work things
out together,
to talk, to listen and
to appreciate
each other.

AS YOU
WALK DOWN
LIFE'S PATH
TOGETHER,
Share your thoughts
AND UNITE
YOUR SPIRITS
IN Love.

Love is

listening

to words

spoken

and to those

left unsaid.

The one word
that makes
a partnership
successful is
'OURS'

Falling in love
is easy.
Growing in love
must be
worked at with
determination.

Lesley Barfoot

Couples who
Love
each other
tell each other
a thousand
things
without talking.

CHINESE PROVERB

Happy relationships are built on blocks of patience.

HA
PPI
NESS
LOVE
FRIEND
SHIP
PATIENCE

Friendship
is the cement
that holds a
relationship
together.

Author
Unknown

Love
follows
friendship
&
friendship
follows
Love

Never forget

THAT

THE MOST

POWERFUL

FORCE ON

EARTH IS

Love.

Nelson Rockerfeller

TWO HEARTS THAT SHARE ONE LOVE will grow together in JOY.

Lasting love

IS A

PROMISE

that takes a

lifetime

to fulfill.

The best way
to appreciate
a loved one
is to imagine
yourself
without them.

Without rain,
there could
be no
RAINBOWS.
Without
sorrow, JOY
would not be
as sweet.

Most people
are about as
happy as they
make up
their minds to be.

Abraham Lincoln

Two souls
with but a
single thought;
two hearts
that beat as one.

Von Munch Billinghausen

A successful relationship

REQUIRES HONESTY, INTEGRITY, COMMITMENT AND CARING.

Two people
who work
to bring out
the best in
each other
truly have a
committed
relationship.

Love

IS

FRIENDSHIP

that has

caught fire!

Ann Landers

Happiness COMES FROM A LOVE THAT DEEPENS WITH EVERY PASSING DAY.

Like a tree
in the
autumn wind,
it is better
to bend
than to break.

Love
IS
SHARING
A PART OF
YOURSELF
WITH
OTHERS!

JANET HOFFBERG

In DREAMS

and in

Love

there are no

impossibilities.

JANUS ARONY

DREAMS

When you
share a dream
you work
together to
make it happen.

Fairytales
are not
just for
children;

Dreams
really do
come true.

Love
is caring
more about
another person
than you
do about
yourself.

Love
endures only
when lovers
love many things
not merely
each other.

Walter Lippman

Love

makes me

want to sing

the melody

my heart

is playing!

A SMALL HOUSE will hold just as much happiness as a large one.

AUTHOR UNKNOWN

Love

is

a little word.

Those in love

make it big!

AUTHOR UNKNOWN

Love is the master key that opens the gates of Happiness.

Oliver Wendell Holmes

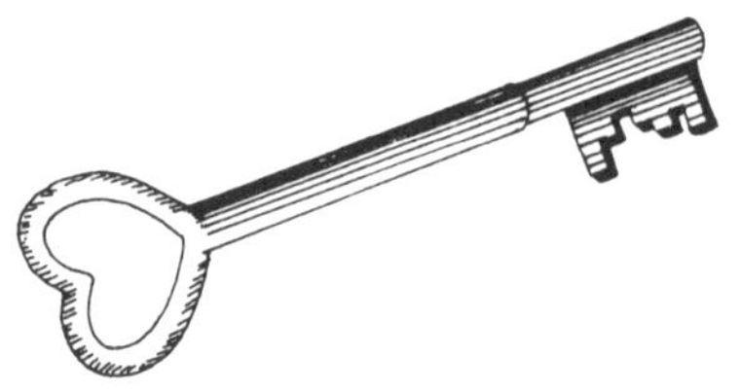

Happiness
is the
feeling
that comes
from
sharing your
Love.

Let there
be spaces
in your
togetherness.

Kahlil Gibran

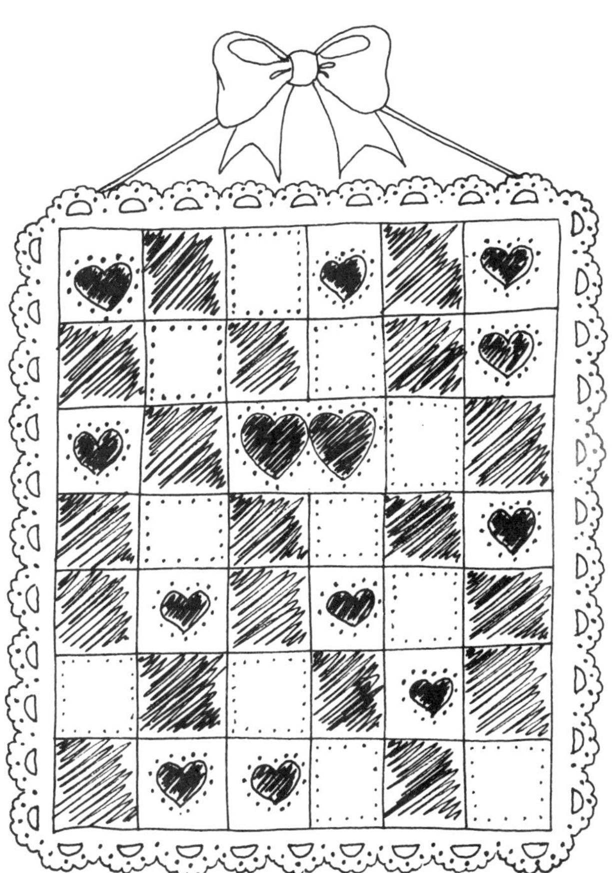

HOPE TOGETHER-

if it were not
for hope,
the heart
would break.

Unknown

Be honest
with each other.
But more
importantly
be honest
with yourself.

LOVE
DOES NOT
CONSIST OF
GAZING AT
EACH OTHER
BUT IN
LOOKING
OUTWARD
TOGETHER
IN THE SAME
DIRECTION

ANTOINE DE SAINT-EXUPÉRY

INDIVIDUALS BRING THEIR OWN UNIQUE COLLECTION OF EXPERIENCES, MEMORIES, THOUGHTS AND IDEALS TO A RELATIONSHIP.

Those who
bring sunshine
into the lives
of others,
cannot keep it
from themselves!

James Barrie

FAITH,

TRUST

AND

FORGIVENESS

can work

wonders.

A HAPPY HOME expresses a couple's love for one another.

The foundation of
a happy home
comes from the
LOVE & TRUST
of the people who
live inside it.

Love is that condition in which the happiness of another person is essential to your own.

ROBERT HEINLEIN

TO LOVE
IS TO
PLACE
OUR
HAPPINESS
IN THE
HAPPINESS
OF ANOTHER·

GOTTFRIED VON LIEBNITZ

You can give without loving, but you can never love without giving.

LOVE CAN FILL
HOMES
WITH SONG
HEARTS
WITH SMILES
AND DAYS
WITH SUNSHINE

There are
so many
ways to love
and each one
has its own
delights!

Sara Teasdale

It takes
imagination
to make a
relationship
flourish.

The sun
S H I N E S
so much
brighter
when
I see
your smile.

Love is
the quiet
understanding
and mature
acceptance
of imperfection.

Ann Landers

Nobody
is perfect.
COMPROMISE
is a necessary
part of any
relationship.

Love
AND
IMAGINATION
make a
house a
HOME.

I love coming home

BECAUSE YOU ARE THERE.

Loving you

IS THE BEST THING THAT EVER HAPPENED TO ME.

Love is a gift and yours is the best present I've ever gotten.

Friendship

IS ONE OF

THE NICEST

KINDS OF

Love!

About the Artist

Joanne Fink is an artist who specializes in lettering and papermaking. Through her studio, CALLIGRAPHER'S INK, in Bellmore, NY, she designs greeting cards, partyware and books, as well as one-of-a-kind commissioned pieces. Her work can be seen in many galleries and museums throughout the country.

When she is not at her drawing board, Joanne can be found teaching workshops on calligraphy and related subjects, studying sign language or scuba diving with her husband.

We hope you have enjoyed this book! We welcome your comments and suggestions. Please send any ideas you may have to the attention of our New Product Department

–The Editor

Other Titles by Great Quotations Publishing Company

COMB BOUND

A Friend Is
A Smile Increases Your Face Value
Aged to Perfection
An Apple A Day
Backfield in Motion
Batter Up
Bedside Manner
Believe and Achieve
Best in Business Humor
Birthday Wishes
Books Are Better
Boyfriends Live Longer Than Husbands
Change Your Thoughts,
Change Your Life
Don't Marry, Be Happy
Double Dribble
Golf Humor
Graduation - Keys To Success
Great Quotes - Great Comedians
Halfway Home (Surviving
the Middle Years)
Harvest Of THoughts
Inspirations
Joy Of Family
Keys To Happiness
Life's Winning Tips
Love, Honor, Cherish
Love, Sex & Marriage
Love On Your Wedding Day
Mothers And Babies
Never Give Up
Our Life Together
Over The Hill Sex
Political Humor
Quotations from African-American
Real Friends
Retirement
Sports Poop
Sports Quotes
Stress
Teachers Inspirations
Thank You
The Quest For Success
Things You'll Learn
Thinking Of You
Thoughts From The Heart
To A Very Special Daughter
To A Very Special Son
To A Very Special Grandparent
To A Very Special Love
To My Mother
To My Father
Unofficial Christmas Survival Guide
Unofficial Executive Survival Guide
Unofficial Stress Test
Unofficial Survival Guide
to Parenthood
Unofficial Vacation Guide
Ordinary Men, Extraordinary Lives
Our Thoughts Are Prayers
What To Tell Your Children
Who Really Said
Wonders & Joys Of Christmas
Words From Great Women

PAPERBACK

199 Useful Things to Do With
A Politician
201 Best Things Ever Said
A Lifetime of Love
A Light Heart Lives Long
A Teacher Is Better Than Two Books
As A Cat Thinketh
Cheatnotes On Life
Chicken Soup
Dear Mr. President
Father Knows Best
Food For Thought
Golden Years/Golden Words
Happiness Walks On Busy Feet
Heal The World
Hooked on Golf
Hollywords
I'm Not Over The Hill
In Celebration of Women
Life's Simple Pleasures
Mother - A Bouquet of Love
Motivation Magic
Mrs. Webster's Dictionary
Reflections
Romantic Rendezvous
Sports Page
So Many Ways To Say
Thank You
The ABC's of Parenting
The Best Of Friends
The Birthday Astrologer
The Little Book of
Spiritual Wisdom
Things You'll Learn,
If You Live Long Enough

PERPETUAL CALENDARS

Apple A Day
Country Proverbs
Each Day A New Beginning
Friends Forever
Golf Forever
Home Is Where The Heart Is
Proverbs
Seasonings
Simply The Best Dad
Simple The Best Mom
Simple Ways To Say I Love You
Teacher"s" Are "First Class!"

Great Quotations Publishing Company
1967 Quincy Court
Glendale Heights, IL 60139-2045
Phone (708) 582-2800
FAX (708) 582-2813

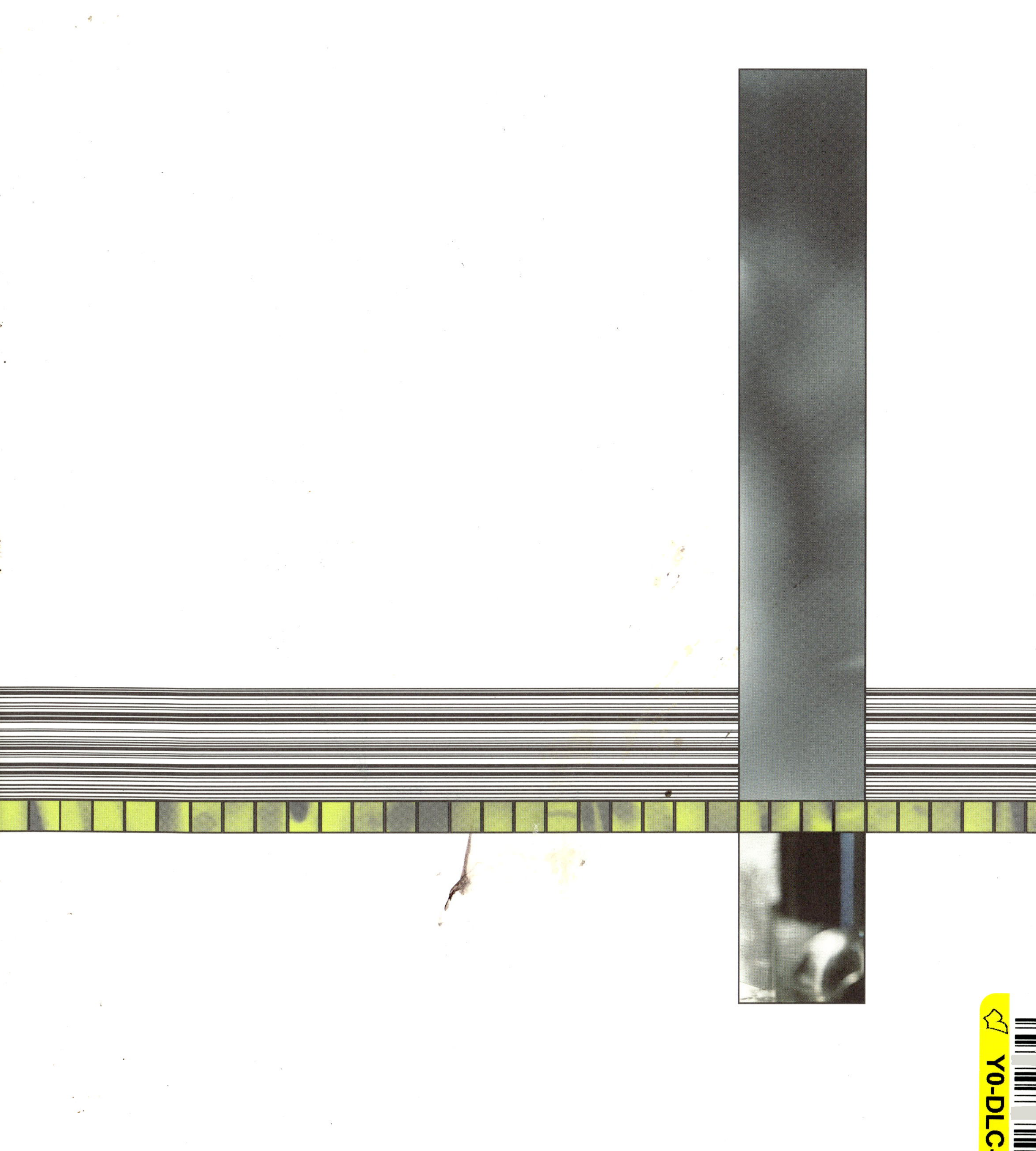

XML

Student Manual

Australia • Canada • Mexico • Singapore
Spain • United Kingdom • United States

XML

VP and GM of Courseware: Michael Springer
Series Product Managers: Caryl Bahner-Guhin, Charles G. Blum, and Adam A. Wilcox
Developmental Editor: Brandon Heffernan
Copyeditor: Robert Tillett
Keytester: Brandon Heffernan
Series Designer: Adam A. Wilcox
Cover Designer: Steve Deschene

For more information contact:

Course Technology
25 Thomson Place
Boston, MA 02210

Or find us on the Web at: www.course.com

For permission to use material from this text or product, contact us by

• Web: www.thomsonrights.com
• Phone: 1-800-730-2214
• Fax: 1-800-730-2215

Trademarks

Disclaimer

ISBN 0-619-20587-3

Printed in the United States of America

4 5 PM 06

Contents

XML

Introduction

After reading this introduction, you will know how to:

A Use Course Technology ILT manuals in general.

B Use prerequisites, a target student description, course objectives, and a skills inventory to properly set your expectations for the course.

C Re-key this course after class.

Topic A: About the manual

Course Technology ILT philosophy

Course Technology ILT manuals facilitate your learning by providing structured interaction with the software itself. While we provide text to explain difficult concepts, the hands-on activities are the focus of our courses. By paying close attention as your instructor leads you through these activities, you will learn the skills and concepts effectively.

We believe strongly in the instructor-led classroom. During class, focus on your instructor. Our manuals are designed and written to facilitate your interaction with your instructor, and not to call attention to manuals themselves.

We believe in the basic approach of setting expectations, delivering instruction, and providing summary and review afterwards. For this reason, lessons begin with objectives and end with summaries. We also provide overall course objectives and a course summary to provide both an introduction to and closure on the entire course.

Manual components

The manuals contain these major components:

- Table of contents
- Introduction
- Units
- Appendices
- Course summary
- Glossary
- Index

Each element is described below.

Table of contents

The table of contents acts as a learning roadmap.

Introduction

The introduction contains information about our training philosophy and our manual components, features, and conventions. It contains target student, prerequisite, objective, and setup information for the specific course.

Units

Units are the largest structural component of the course content. A unit begins with a title page that lists objectives for each major subdivision, or topic, within the unit. Within each topic, conceptual and explanatory information alternates with hands-on activities. Units conclude with a summary comprising one paragraph for each topic, and an independent practice activity that gives you an opportunity to practice the skills you've learned.

The conceptual information takes the form of text paragraphs, exhibits, lists, and tables. The activities are structured in two columns, one telling you what to do, the other providing explanations, descriptions, and graphics.

Appendices

An appendix is similar to a unit in that it contains objectives and conceptual explanations. However, an appendix does not include hands-on activities, a summary, or an independent practice activity.

Course summary

This section provides a text summary of the entire course. It is useful for providing closure at the end of the course. The course summary also indicates the next course in this series, if there is one, and lists additional resources you might find useful as you continue to learn about the software.

Glossary

The glossary provides definitions for all of the key terms used in this course.

Index

The index at the end of this manual makes it easy for you to find information about a particular software component, feature, or concept.

Manual conventions

We've tried to keep the number of elements and the types of formatting to a minimum in the manuals. This aids in clarity and makes the manuals more classically elegant looking. But there are some conventions and icons you should know about.

Convention	Description
Italic text	In conceptual text, indicates a new term or feature.
Bold text	In unit summaries, indicates a key term or concept. In an independent practice activity, indicates an explicit item that you select, choose, or type.
`Code font`	Indicates code or syntax.

`Longer strings of ►`
`code will look ►`
`like this.`
	In the hands-on activities, any code that's too long to fit on a single line is divided into segments by one or more continuation characters (►). This code should be entered as a continuous string of text.

Select **bold item**	In the left column of hands-on activities, bold sans-serif text indicates an explicit item that you select, choose, or type.
Keycaps like ↵ ENTER	Indicate a key on the keyboard you must press.

Hands-on activities

The hands-on activities are the most important parts of our manuals. They are divided into two primary columns. The "Here's how" column gives short instructions to you about what to do. The "Here's why" column provides explanations, graphics, and clarifications. Here's a sample:

Do it!

A-1: Creating a commission formula

Here's how	Here's why
1 Open Sales	This is an oversimplified sales compensation worksheet. It shows sales totals, commissions, and incentives for five sales reps.
2 Observe the contents of cell F4	F4 = =E4*C_Rate
	The commission rate formulas use the name "C_Rate" instead of a value for the commission rate.

For these activities, we have provided a collection of data files designed to help you learn each skill in a real-world business context. As you work through the activities, you will modify and update these files. Of course, you might make a mistake and, therefore, want to re-key the activity starting from scratch. To make it easy to start over, you will rename each data file at the end of the first activity in which the file is modified. Our convention for renaming files is to add the word "My" to the beginning of the file name. In the above activity, for example, a file called "Sales" is being used for the first time. At the end of this activity, you would save the file as "My sales," thus leaving the "Sales" file unchanged. If you make a mistake, you can start over using the original "Sales" file.

In some activities, however, it may not be practical to rename the data file. If you want to retry one of these activities, ask your instructor for a fresh copy of the original data file.

Topic B: Setting your expectations

Properly setting your expectations is essential to your success. This topic will help you do that by providing:

- Prerequisites for this course
- A description of the target student at whom the course is aimed
- A list of the objectives for the course
- A skills assessment for the course

Course prerequisites

Before taking this course, you should be familiar with personal computers and the use of a keyboard and a mouse. Furthermore, this course assumes that you have basic knowledge of World Wide Web (WWW) services and HTML.

Target student

This course is intended to serve the needs of individuals interested in an introduction to XML. The material in this course explains how to create XML documents to describe a wide range of data and how you can use XML in a real-world scenario.

Course objectives

These overall course objectives will give you an idea about what to expect from the course. It is also possible that they will help you see that this course is not the right one for you. If you think you either lack the prerequisite knowledge or already know most of the subject matter to be covered, you should let your instructor know that you think you are misplaced in the class.

After completing this course, you will know how to:

- Describe XML as a metalanguage and a markup language, and discuss the evolution and benefits of XML.
- Define an XML document and use its components.
- Create a DTD, differentiate between internal and external DTDs, create a content model, and create and validate an XML document.
- Describe schema and its components, and create schema.
- Create a CSS style sheet and link an XML document to it.
- Create and modify CSS styles.
- Perform XSLT transformations.
- Create and validate XLinks.
- Describe XML APIs, work with DOM objects, and choose between SAX and DOM.
- Apply data binding, integrate XML data, and work with data source objects.

Skills inventory

Use the following form to gauge your skill level entering the class. For each skill listed, rate your familiarity from 1 to 5, with five being the most familiar. *This is not a test.* Rather, it is intended to provide you with an idea of where you're starting from at the beginning of class. If you're wholly unfamiliar with all the skills, you might not be ready for the class. If you think you already understand all of the skills, you might need to move on to the next course in the series. In either case, you should let your instructor know as soon as possible.

Skill	1	2	3	4	5
Describing XML as markup language and metalanguage					
Discussing the evolution and benefits of XML					
Defining and using XML components: prolog, elements, attributes, and entities					
Creating a DTD, and differentiating between internal and external DTDs					
Creating a content model and adding attribute list declarations					
Creating and validating an XML document					
Understanding schema description, the schema element, namespaces, element types, compositors, attributes, cardinality, simple types, schema structures, and complex type declaration					
Creating a schema					
Creating a CSS style sheet and linking an XML document to it					
Creating and modifying CSS styles					
Understanding XML, XPath, and XSLT and the need to transform XML documents					
Carrying out a simple XSLT transformation					
Defining XML Linking Language					
Creating links with Xlink					
Validating XLinks					
Understanding XML APIs					

Skill	1	2	3	4	5
Working with DOM objects					
Choosing between SAX and DOM					
Applying data binding techniques					
Integrating XML data and using data binding and table repetition agents					
Working with data source objects and creating a component to navigate recordsets					

Topic C: Re-keying the course

If you have the proper hardware and software, you can re-key this course after class. This section explains what you'll need in order to do so, and how to do it.

Computer requirements

To re-key this course, your personal computer must have:

Hardware

- A keyboard and a mouse
- A Pentium II-class processor or faster
- 128MB of RAM
- At least 4GB hard disk space
- 1.44 MB 3½-inch floppy disk drive
- CD-ROM drive supported by Windows 2000
- A monitor capable of a minimum of 256 colors at 800×600 resolution
- Internet access, if you want to download the Student Data files from www.courseilt.com/instructor_tools.html

Software

- Microsoft Windows 2000 Professional
- XML Spy 2004 Professional Edition (available at `www.xmlspy.com`)
- Internet Explorer 5.50 (with SP2) or later
- Netscape 6.1 or later (The latest version of Netscape is available for download at http://channels.netscape.com/ns/browsers/default.jsp)

Setup instructions to re-key the course

Before you re-key the course, you will need to perform the following steps.

1. Install Microsoft Windows 2000 Professional according to the software manufacturer's instructions. You can also use Microsoft Windows XP Professional, although the screen shots in this course were taken using Microsoft Windows 2000 Professional, and your screens might look somewhat different.
2. Install XML Spy 2004 Professional Edition according to the manufacturer's instructions.
3. Install all other software mentioned in the software section as per the manufacturer's instructions.
4. If necessary, reset any defaults that you have changed. If you do not wish to reset the defaults, you can still re-key the course, but some activities might not work exactly as documented.
5. Create a folder called Student Data at the root of the hard drive.

6 Download the Student Data examples for the course. (If you do not have an Internet connection, you can ask your instructor for a copy of the data files on a diskette.)

   a Connect to `www.courseilt.com/instructor_tools.html`.

   b Click the link for XML to display a page of course listings.

   c Click the link for this course.

   d Click the link for downloading the Student Data files, and follow the instructions that appear on your screen.

7 Copy the data files to the Student Data folder.

Unit 1
XML basics

Unit time: 60 minutes

Complete this unit, and you'll know how to:

A Describe XML as a metalanguage and a markup language.

B Discuss the evolution of XML.

C Identify the benefits of XML.

Topic A: Introduction to XML

Explanation

Extensible Markup Language (XML) provides a standard to structure data for transmission across a variety of networks, most notably the World Wide Web. XML is not necessarily intended to replace existing technologies, but to complement them in this increasingly connected, fast-paced, data-dependent world of international commerce and communication.

XML defined

XML can be categorized as both a metalanguage and a *markup* language. The function of a metalanguage is to create a formal description of another language. The function of a markup language (or markup specification language) is to describe information, usually for storage, transmission, or processing by a program. How you categorize XML depends on what you use it for. XML also has a formal definition, as stated in the World Wide Web Consortium's XML 1.0 Recommendation:

"The Extensible Markup Language (XML) is a subset of SGML ... [the goal of which] is to enable generic SGML to be served, received, and processed on the Web in the way that is now possible with HTML. XML has been designed for ease of implementation and for interoperability with both SGML and HTML."

XML as a metalanguage

XML is used to create XML-based languages, which in turn are used to create specific documents (or files) for use by the developer, their organization, or their industry.

XML allows you to create your own customized components that accurately and efficiently describe the physical contents of your documents. In this capacity, XML acts like an alphabet combined with its punctuation and other semantic symbols. An XML document cannot do anything by itself. A program must be developed to interact with it.

XML documents can contain many types of data, such as text, graphics, object metadata, Application Program Interfaces (APIs), equations, and multimedia, among others. All documents contain one or more of these types of information according to a predetermined and deliberate structure. Structured information also indicates what role each bit of content plays. For example, content in an ordinary document does not carry meta-information about itself. A header might be formatted to *look* like a header but there's nothing that semantically defines it as a header. XML describes what each chunk of content is, and how it fits into the overall document structure.

XML as a markup language

XML is also a markup language and is used to mark up text. Markup refers to the insertion of characters or symbols to indicate how the information in a document should appear when it is printed or displayed, or to describe a document's logical structure. Marking up text is a way to add information about your data to the data itself. Consider these real world examples of how you might already be marking up documents:

- Have you ever underlined words or passages, or used a highlighter pen, to indicate their importance?
- Have you ever marked up a rough draft of a report with symbols indicating "new paragraph here," or "bold this," or "remove this"?
- Have you ever made marks on a map indicating where you want to turn left, or hazards to avoid?
- Have you ever numbered bits of information, or steps, in an otherwise unnumbered procedure?

If you have ever performed any of these activities, you were marking up data. Your margin symbols, notes, or highlights indicated the relative importance, order, or other emphasis of the data at hand.

The primary goal of markup is to separate the description of document logic, structure, data, and other content from the description of the final display. In addition, documents that use markup are ASCII (text-based), so they remain independent of platforms and operating systems.

Markup indicators are called *tags* or *tag names*. As an XML document designer, you use tags to describe a document's contents as accurately as possible. Formatting is an automated process that occurs later. You can insert markup in many ways, including:

- Typing all the tag names using a simple text editor (e.g., MS Notepad)
- Using a more advanced text editor and prepackaged markup symbols to save keystrokes (e.g., MS Word)
- Using an Integrated Development Environment editor (IDE) that lets you create the document as you want it to appear (e.g., XML Spy)

Do it!

A-1: Defining XML

Exercises

1 To which of the following computer language categories does XML belong?

A Markup language

B Assembly language

C Fourth generation language

D Metalanguage

2 What are two names given to markup indicators?

A Tags

B Attributes

C Tag names

D Structures

3 The primary goal of markup is to combine the description of document logic, structure, data, and other content with the description of the final display. True or false?

4 The function of a metalanguage is to design ways to describe information, usually for storage, transmission, or processing by a program. True or false?

5 XML cannot do anything by itself; a program must be developed to interact with it. True or false?

Exploring a simple XML document

Explanation

Elements are the basic building blocks of an XML document. Each element represents a piece of data, identified by a tag. The following code shows how a simple XML document looks like:

```
<student>
<name>John Strange</name>
<course id="1">XML</course>
<code>16425</code>
</student>
```

Each element begins with a *start tag* or an opening tag (`<student>`) and, generally, each element ends with an *end tag* or a closing tag (`</student>`). Each tag name is delimited by angle brackets (< and >). In the end tag, the element name is always preceded by a forward slash (/).

Elements can include *attributes*. Attributes specify properties for your elements, and they appear in the form of name-value pairs. In the preceding code, the element `<course>` has an attribute named "id" with a value of "1". Attributes can only be placed in start tags, after the tag name.

You need to follow certain rules when you write an XML document:

- XML is case-sensitive. As a result, the tag name `<student>` is not the same as `<Student>` and is interpreted differently.
- All opening tags must have a corresponding closing tag. The exception to this rule is an *empty tag*, which has a special start tag in place of a closing tag. Empty tags must have a forward slash before the closing angular brace (`<element_name/>`).
- The tags must not overlap. A tag that opens inside another tag must close before the latter. A good way to think of it is, "first to open, last to close".
- All attribute values must be enclosed in double quotation marks.

Do it!

A-2: Exploring an XML document

Exercises

1 Closing tags are not required in XML. True or false?

2 In XML, the tags `<firstname>` and `<fiRstName>` will be interpreted as the same. True or false?

3 ____________ appear in the form of name-value pairs.

A Elements

B Attributes

C Tags

D DTDs

4 In an XML document, all attribute values must be enclosed in double quotation marks. True or false?

Topic B: The evolution of XML

Explanation

The evolution from basic, text description languages to XML has taken almost forty years. A brief review of the evolution of XML and its predecessors can help you understand the principles of XML, and the context and rationale of its development.

GML

In 1973, IBM released their Generalized Markup Language (GML), a product that had been in development since 1969. Prior to GML, each of the separate functions (that is, text composition and editing, data-retrieval, and page composition) required separate and different applications of function-specific markup instructions (that is, each required its own distinct and different procedural markup). Further, those instructions sometimes had to be changed according to the applications used to process the documents.

For example, in Exhibit 1-1, at the beginning of every line there are at least two instructions, one for each applicable function. In addition, enclosing the "list" text in parentheses indicates yet another kind of instruction. The challenge faced by the GML developers was to integrate all the functions to create a common set of markup instructions that they all could interpret.

```
\document class[legalpaper, 14pt]{article}
\begin{document}
\section{simple text}%The Inn He supposed to be a Castle
\begin{enumerate}
\item/textbf{Whereon he spied an inn}
\item/textbf{Which to his grief and Don Quixote's joy}
\item/textbf{Must needs be a Castle}
\end{enumerate}
```

Exhibit 1-1: Sample of an early text-processing document

With GML, IBM separated the specific formatting instructions from the content of the document itself. The markup was based only on the identification of the different types of structural components in a document (for example, heading styles, font treatments, bullet lists, paragraphs, etc.). Using GML, you could assign various tag names to respective sections of text. The tag names came from a predetermined set of symbols available with GML. After the various sections of text were identified, any application could be provided with a separate set of instructions on how to process those sections. Exhibit 1-2 shows a sample of GML markup.

```
:h2.The Inn He Supposed to be a Castle
:01.
:li.Whereon he spied an :hp2.inn:ehp2.
:li.Which to his grief and Don Quixote's joy
:li.Must needs be a :hp2.castle:ehp2
:eol.
:hp1.Cervantes
```

Exhibit 1-2: Sample of IBM's Generalized Markup Language

In Exhibit 1-3, a sample tag name is dissected. As you can see, a tag name in GML is preceded by a delimiter (the colon), which instructs the text formatter to begin processing the tag. Then the tag name itself appears. It is followed by a content separator (the period), which tells the processor to stop processing the tag, and then to process the text that follows according to the specification found in the tag name.

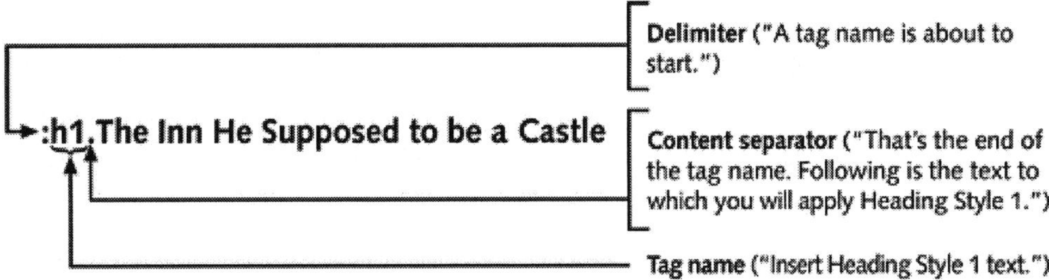

Exhibit 1-3: Sample of a GML tag name

The advantage to GML's generic encoding was that the document became transportable. It could be reprinted in different styles or processed in different ways without making any changes to the original document, and the author did not have to set up the format details to display the document.

Exhibit 1-4 illustrates the advantage of generic encoding. The document has been coded with components such as a basic font, a distinct title/heading, a list of numbered items, bolded text, italicized text, etc. The document displayed on the left indicates that its application interpreted the font code, for example, as Helvetica or Arial. The document on the right has been processed by an application that interpreted the same code in a different base font. The document has two different appearances, but each creates an impact similar to the other. However, the differences in appearance did not occur because of differences in the document's code. They occurred because of the differences between the two applications that processed the code.

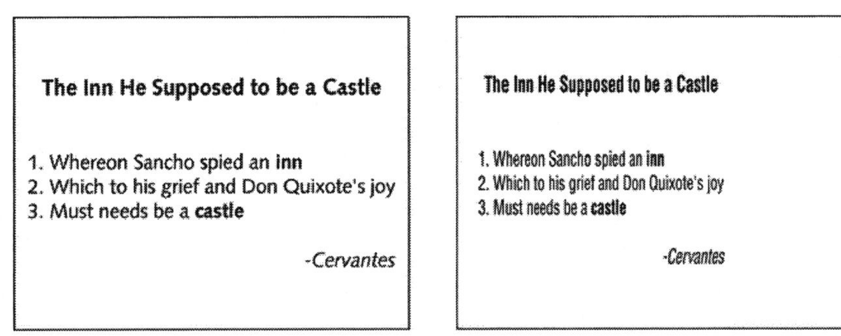

Exhibit 1-4: Generic encoding: one document, two different appearances

The need for standards

The development of GML revealed potential value in creating a universal, machine-independent system of encoding documents. However, as development continued, it became clear that there were other document creation tools being developed by other organizations, and each of those tools had their own respective components and elements—some even included markup principles like GML.

Two crucial points became apparent: for markup languages to be truly useful to many users in several display environments (e.g., hard copy, on screen, etc.), a standard must be developed to list the accepted, valid markup tags, and that such a standard must define what each markup tag means.

Each tag communicates its own specific layout to its respective display environment. In Exhibit 1-2, the `:h2` tags render a Heading Style 2 (i.e., same font, larger font size, bolded, and centered on the line) and the `:hp2` tags render a highlighted phrase (in this case, "same font, same size, but bolded"). Notice that, in Exhibit 1-4, two different display environments (for example, a terminal screen versus a printer) might display the marked up content differently.

The principles behind standard development also included the following assumptions:

- Networks connected many different types of computers, and the information passed among them had to be usable on all of them.
- Information intended for public use could not be restricted to one technology and certainly not to one make, model, or manufacturer of such technology. (That would be the same as giving control of data format to private individuals or organizations, which would be unacceptable.)
- Information should be in a form that could be reused in many different ways, to optimize time and effort.

Thus, proprietary data formats, no matter how well documented or publicized, would simply not be an option due to loss of control, unexpected and unannounced changes, or the institution of exorbitant fees.

Do it!

B-1: Identifying the need for standards

Exercises

1 Which of the following are principles underlying the development of standards?

A Networks connect many different types of computers; the information passed among them has to be usable on all of them.

B Information intended for public use should not be restricted to as few technologies as possible.

C Only standards-related organizations or, if there are no such organizations, national governments should control data formats.

D Data should be in a form that can be reused in many different ways to optimize time and effort.

E All of the above.

2 With the development of ____, IBM separated specific formatting instructions from document content.

SGML

Explanation

The Standard Generalized Markup Language (ISO 8879:1986) was approved in 1986. It is still recognized as the overarching, comprehensive international standard metalanguage. SGML is not simply a document encoding language unto itself, but it facilitates the creation of any number of additional markup/metalanguages. These languages can then be tailored to the specific requirements of any organization or industry, as well as the creation of the respective electronic, machine-readable documents related to those languages.

SGML is an extremely powerful and extensible tool, and has led to the cataloging and indexing of data in many fields such as medical, financial, legal, aerospace, telecommunications, and even the entertainment industry. The following table lists just a few of the hundreds of SGML-based languages developed over the past 15 years:

Language	Description
Extensible Markup Language (XML)	An SGML-based language used to create other industry-specific or organization-specific languages that can be served, received, and processed on the Internet.
Hypertext Markup Language (HTML)	An SGML-based markup language used to create hypertext documents; it has been in use on the World Wide Web since 1990.
Formalized Exchange of Electronic publications (FORMEX)	A European SGML-based standard developed by the Office for Official Publications of the European Communities; it is used for the exchange of electronic publications in the European Union.
Text Encoding Initiative (TEI)	An SGML-based international standard that helps libraries, museums, publishers, scholars, etc., represent texts for online research and teaching.
Air Transport Association (ATA)	Chiefly ATA Spec 2100, an SGML-based specification for the development of manuals and other documents by manufacturers (since 1989).
Telecommunications Industry Markup (TIM)	SGML-based specification for describing information in telecommunications documents.

SGML uses generic descriptive markup, so that document content may be defined in terms that are entirely separate from its processing. The structural basis of SGML is the division of information in a document into elements (titles, paragraphs, part numbers, person names, text, graphics, hypertext links, etc.), which can then be formatted, sorted, or searched.

Using SGML, you can name elements so they can be managed and manipulated in specific ways. The element names (tags) are embedded in the data to identify the beginning and the end of the elements. The resulting tagged data makes the file usable with any conforming software tool running on any operating system. In Exhibit 1-5, everything from the start tag <title> to the end tag </title>, is part of the title element.

Note: End tags can be omitted in SGML. To do this, you need to specify a value of "yes" for the attribute "OMITTAG" in the SGML declaration.

```
<chapter>
<title>Sancho's Complaint</title>
<list>
<item>...it has been nothing but</item>
<item>cudgels and more cudgels,</item>
<item>blows and more blows;</item>
<item>then, as an extra, I get tossed in a blanket...</item>
</list>
<author>Cervantes</author>
</chapter>
```

Exhibit 1-5: Sample of SGML markup

SGML formalizes the concept of a document type and provides for a separate file called a *Document Type Definition* (DTD), which identifies all the elements in its respective document(s), and indicates the structural relationships among them. A simple DTD is shown in Exhibit 1-6.

```
<!Doctype mybook_1.dtd [
<!ELEMENT chapter (title?,item+,author)>
<!ELEMENT title (#pcdata)>
<!ELEMENT item (#pcdata)>
<!ELEMENT author (#pcdata)>
]</mybook_1.dtd>
```

Exhibit 1-6: Sample of a simple DTD

Advantages of SGML

The major advantage to SGML is that any SGML-related language may be customized according to the needs of an individual organization and even across organizations within an industry, provided the organizations cooperate in the development. The language and its documents may then be processed by all participants, without changes or losses, for different purposes and in different forms, using any relevant application that understands SGML. In addition, the relevant documents can be developed for manipulation and display on a variety of platforms: on handheld or laptop computers, on personal computers at work or at home, on more powerful workstations, in print, or through projection, without fear of inadvertent loss of information.

Disadvantages

In spite of its considerable extensibility, which comes from its flexible tagging capability, there are disadvantages to SGML, especially with respect to its application across the World Wide Web. Fully SGML-compliant languages would likely be large, expend a large amount of resources to implement, and be too cumbersome for Web browser-related duties. Therefore, using full SGML to create or view the much smaller and simpler World Wide Web documents is difficult to justify.

The commercial browser manufacturers, who are just now including XML capability, have indicated they do not intend to ever support full SGML. Full SGML systems, therefore, are better suited for large, complex data/document environments that justify the development expense and the installation and administration of the systems needed for development or processing. You're likely to find SGML systems within the internal structures of larger organizations with high-speed intranets.

HTML

Hypertext Markup Language (HTML) is an application profile of the SGML ISO Standard 8879:1986. HTML, like XML, is one of the SGML document types—one of many dialects of the SGML "mother tongue." Any fully conformant SGML system should be able to read HTML documents.

HTML was originally designed at the European Organization for Nuclear Research (CERN), original home of the Web to provide a very simple version of SGML that could be implemented by ordinary users.

HTML combined the advantages of an SGML-based markup with hypertext technologies—the links that provide quick connections between documents. Because HTML was free, simple, and widely supported, its use spread widely and quickly. It became one of the more famous of the computer markup systems. Now, it is the standard markup language on the Web.

HTML markup can represent hypertext news, mail, documentation, and hypermedia; menus of options; database query results; simple structured documents with in-line graphics; and hypertext views of existing bodies of information. HTML defines a simple, fixed type of document with markup designed for common office correspondence or technical reports (e.g., headings, paragraphs, lists, illustrations, etc., and some provision for hypertext and multimedia).

HTML documents are SGML documents with predefined generic markup tags (i.e., predefined semantics) that are appropriate for representing information from a wide range of domains.

Unfortunately, since the inception of HTML, most Web designers have been concerned primarily with the documents' appearance when displayed in a browser. Therefore, although HTML stands for Hypertext Markup Language, it has mostly been applied as a "Hypertext Formatting Language."

All HTML tags are predefined. An HTML author can only use tags that are found in the latest HTML specification. For example, a <b> tag means "bold this text," and its intended meaning does not change. The <ul> tag specifies a rule that tells a browser to begin an unordered list. Exhibit 1-7 shows an example of a simple HTML document that contains some of these predefined elements.

```
<html>
 <head>
  <title>Ingredients</title>
 </head>
 <body>

 <b>Ingredient List</b>
 <ul>
  <li>2 eggs</li>
  <li>Batter</li>
  <li>1tbsp butter</li>
  <li>1/2 cup milk</li>
 </ul>

 </body>
</html>
```

Exhibit 1-7: Sample of HTML markup

Exhibit 1-8 shows the rendered version of the markup in Exhibit 1-7. This rendering is typical of what a browser would return for these markup tags.

Ingredient List

- 2 eggs
- Batter
- 1 tbsp butter
- 1/2 cup milk

Exhibit 1-8: Rendering of HTML markup

Though revised versions of HTML were released in 1994, 1996, and 1997, and individual browser manufacturers augmented HTML with the addition of style sheets and other proprietary extensions, they could not meet the functionality demands of an ever-expanding Internet clientele. The need for greater power and flexibility in markup languages used on the Internet led to a return to the SGML drawing board and to the development of XML.

Do it!

B-2: Discussing SGML and HTML

Exercises

1 A ________ is a separate file, formalized by SGML, which identifies all of the elements in its respective document and indicates the structural relationships between those elements.

A List of elements

B Generalized Markup Language

C Document Type Definition

D XML document

E None of the above

2 HTML was originally intended to denote the structure of hypertext documents, but the desire to create more increasingly sophisticated Web designs resulted in browser companies introducing style-related tags that detracted from the structural integrity of HTML. True or false?

3 __________was designed to provide a universal means to present and link basic documents on the Internet.

4 HTML allows users to arbitrarily create their own specific tags to meet their own specific requirements. True or false?

The evolution of XML

Explanation

In 1996, because of discussions about developing a markup language with the power and extensibility of SGML but with the simplicity of HTML, the World Wide Web Consortium (W3C) decided to sponsor a team of SGML experts to do just that. That team pared away what they considered the nonessential, unused, cryptic parts of SGML to leave a smaller, more easily implemented markup metalanguage, which they named the Extensible Markup Language.

XML, like HTML, is an application profile of SGML. Thus, any fully conformant SGML system is able to read XML documents, too. Like SGML, XML was developed as a public format: it is not a proprietary development of any company.

XML evolved quickly, drawing from the work of its sponsors and the work of other developers who were seeking to solve similar problems. By mid 1997, the W3C's XML Linking Language XLL project was underway, and by the summer of 1997, Microsoft had launched the Channel Definition Format (CDF) as one of the first real-world applications of XML.

The Extensible Markup Language (XML) 1.0 specification was accepted by the W3C as a formal recommendation on February 10, 1998. The XML specification was only a couple dozen pages long, compared to the ISO SGML standard, which was some 200 pages. Nevertheless, all the functionality of SGML deemed useful for the Internet and World Wide Web remained in XML.

Do it!

B-3: Discussing the evolution of XML

Questions and answers

1 XML is not a proprietary development of any company. True or false?

2 XML is an application profile of SGML. True or false?

3 XML was developed to provide a smaller, more efficient markup language that can be implemented more than SGML. True or false?

Topic C: Benefits of XML

Explanation

XML is not only good for transmitting data from a server to a browser, but is also ideal for passing data between applications. The following sections discuss how XML differs from SGML and HTML, and how it overcomes their limitations.

XML is not SGML

XML is an application profile, or Internet/intranet-related, abbreviated version of SGML. XML is designed to make it easier to define XML-related languages for a specific organization or industry. XML is also designed to help programmers create specific document types for those XML-related languages and to help them write applications to handle those documents. By design, XML omits the more complex and less-used parts of SGML, and in return is an easier language in which to write applications, is easier to understand, and is more suited to delivery and interoperability over the Web.

SGML and XML are independent of platforms and software, so the same source files might be used with a wide variety of operating systems, and authoring and publishing environments. A major advantage of XML is that it does not require a system that is capable of understanding full SGML.

XML is a vendor- and technology-independent metalanguage. Users need to create XML-based languages and documents, and then create programs to read them.

XML is not expected to, nor intended to, completely replace SGML. XML is designed to deliver structured content over the Web. Therefore, in many organizations, filtering SGML to XML (that is, using XML as an output format for an SGML installation) would be the standard procedure for Web-based delivery. Nevertheless, XML lacks several features that make SGML a more satisfactory solution for the creation and long-term storage of complex documents or for the use of high-end typesetting applications.

XML is not HTML

XML and HTML are both derived from SGML. Both are text based, and both use tags, elements, and attributes. However, the two languages were designed with different goals. The key concept to remember is that XML was designed to describe data and to focus on what the data actually is. In other words, HTML is about displaying information, XML is about describing information. XML was created so that richly structured electronic documents can be easily shared, especially over the World Wide Web, no matter what software or hardware might be used to access it.

Unlike HTML with its finite number of tags with their predefined semantics, XML allows you to arbitrarily create and name your own elements, to structure and define information that meets your organization's specific needs.

As the WWW continues to develop, it is most likely that XML will be used to structure and describe the Web data, while HTML will still be used to format and display data. So XML will not replace HTML; it will coexist with and complement HTML in many environments.

Exhibit 1-9 illustrates the difference between two documents: one created in HTML and the other created in XML. You can see how the second document, using tag names like `<client>`, `<invamt>`, and `<remark>`, is potentially more flexible and reusable.

<p> ABC Co. owes us <strong>3517.89 dollars. </strong> This account should be monitored. </p>	<text> <client>ABC Co.</client> owes us <invamt>3517.89 dollars. </invamt> <remark>This account should be monitored.</remark> </text>
HTML version	**XML version**

Exhibit 1-9: Comparison of HTML and XML documents

Do it!

C-1: Exploring the limits of HTML

Exercises

1 Which of the following is true? (Choose all that apply.)

A HTML has a finite number of tags and attributes.

B XML allows you to create and name your own tags.

C Both HTML and XML consist of predefined semantics.

D XML is replacing HTML.

2 Like HTML, XML has pre-existing attributes that specify style options. True or false?

3 XML is designed to __________ data, whereas HTML, with its limited semantics, is most often used to merely display data on the Web.

XML benefits

Explanation

XML was developed to overcome the shortcomings of its two predecessors: its parent, SGML, and its sibling, HTML. Although both were successful and popular markup languages, both were flawed in certain ways. XML removes two constraints related to these languages:

- Dependence on a single, inflexible, document markup language (HTML) with a restrictive set of predefined tags and semantics that does not allow arbitrary structure.
- The complexity of full SGML, which requires higher-powered technologies and is not browser-friendly.

The following are other advantages of XML:

- Data exchange
- Extensibility
- Smart searches
- Granular updates

Data interchange

Companies that need to share high volumes of information, especially over the Internet and WWW, use XML. XML provides a structure for storing data in text format, which can be used as a standard format or protocol for data interchange. Several industry-specific markup languages have been created using XML. The following table lists some of the hundreds of XML-based languages that have been developed in recent years:

Language	Description
CDF (Channel Definition Format)	One of the first real-world applications of XML, CDF is an open specification that permits automatic delivery of updated web information (or channels) to compatible receiver programs, (developed by Microsoft).
CML (Chemical Markup Language)	Allows for the conversion of current files into structured documents, including chemical publications, and provides for the precise location of information within files.
EIL (Extensible Indexing Language)	Looks for a particular tag in a document and assigns the content between the tags to a searchable field.
ETD-ML (Electronic Thesis & Dissertation Markup Language)	Converts theses from MS Word, for example, into SGML/XML
FlowML	XML-based format for musical notation; a format for storing audio synthesis diagrams for synthesizers.
ITML (Information Technology Markup Language)	A set of specifications for protocols, message formats, and best practices.
MathML	Mathematical Markup Language is a methodology for describing mathematical notations.
SMIL (Synchronized Multimedia Integration Language)	Designed to integrate multimedia objects into a synchronized presentation.

Language	Description
VXML (Voice Extensible Markup Language)	Allows interaction with the Internet through voice-recognition.
XHTML	Basically, HTML 4.01 written as an XML application.
XSL (Extensible Stylesheet Language)	The style standard for XML; it specifies the presentation and appearance of an XML document.
XSLT (Extensible Stylesheet Language Transformation Language)	Transform (i.e., reformat) XML documents into other types of XML documents.

Extensibility

XML overcomes the major shortcoming of HTML with its extensibility; it allows for author-defined structure. An XML author can develop unique elements that suit the organization's specific needs. Prior to the advent of XML, developers in various fields had to manipulate their data to fit into the HTML document model, which was severely limiting and often impossible. Because XML is a metalanguage and can be used to describe other XML-based markup languages (called XML vocabularies or XML applications), you can interact reliably and predictably within your specialized community.

Although each XML vocabulary is unique and varies widely from others in scope and intent, all vocabularies have two important things in common. First, each is written according to the same XML standards and rules, which makes them members of the same extended markup family and is therefore readable by any XML-compliant browser. Second, each vocabulary represents a markup language designed to describe content specific to an organization or industry.

Smart searches

XML-tagged data can provide high-precision searching in Web environments, and allow users to interchange reusable text over the Internet and through intranets. XML is preferable in environments where the advantages of SGML and XML are desired, but where the features of full SGML that are not supported in XML are unnecessary.

Granular updates

When the data in an XML document needs to be updated, the entire page need not be refreshed. Only the changed elements are downloaded, thus making updates faster. For example, data at stock exchanges is dynamic, and updating the entire page would take a long time. With XML, only the changed information needs to be updated.

The W3C and XML

In October 1994, Tim Berners-Lee, inventor and architect of the WWW, founded the W3C at the Massachusetts Institute of Technology, Laboratory for Computer Science (MIT/LCS). Membership in the W3C has grown to more than 500 organizations from around the world, and the W3C is hosted by three organizations: MIT in the U.S., the French National Institute for Research in Computer Science and Control (INRIA) in France, and Keio University in Japan.

The purpose of the W3C is to develop interoperable technologies (specification, guidelines, software, and tools) to promote the Web as a forum for information, commerce, communication, and collective understanding. Further, the W3C also acts as a referee or even arbiter between or among those who propose or develop standards in the rapidly changing and expanding Web universe.

The first phase of the W3C's XML activity started in June 1996 and culminated in the February 1998 Recommendation "Extensible Markup Language (XML) 1.0." That recommendation was revised in October 2000. Since then, there have been many other XML-related recommendations that have become standards, including XSL and XSLT.

Over the years, additional requirements have been addressed by other specifications; for example, the XML Pointer Language (XPointer) and XML Linking Language (XLink) standards have specified methods to represent links between resources. Several W3C Working Groups are pursuing and publishing additional XML standards.

For the most part, reading and understanding the XML standards and specifications does not require extensive knowledge of SGML or any of the related technologies. Here are some XML-related goals and best practices as set out by the W3C in the W3C Recommendation "Extensible Markup Language (XML) 1.0." For more information, review the actual Recommendation at `www.w3c.org/TR/REC-xml#sec-intro`.

1 It shall be straightforward to use XML over the Internet. Users must be able to view XML documents as quickly and easily as HTML documents. XML shall support a wide variety of applications: authoring, browsing, content analysis, etc.

2 XML shall be compatible with SGML. XML was designed pragmatically, to be compatible with existing standards while solving the relatively new problem of sending richly structured documents over the Web.

3 It shall be easy to write programs that process XML documents. They promote this "first glance" measure: it ought to take about two weeks for a competent computer science graduate student to build a program that can process XML documents.

4 The number of optional features in XML is to be kept to an absolute minimum, ideally zero. Optional features can lead to compatibility problems, confusion, and frustration.

5 XML documents should be legible to humans and reasonably clear. If you don't have an XML browser, you should be able use a text editor to examine XML content.

6 XML design should be prepared quickly. As evidenced by several of these goals, with respect to XML documents and languages, the emphasis is on quicker solutions to problems. Although the final product might be complex, the design stage should proceed with little delay.

7 The design of XML shall be formal and concise.

8 XML documents shall be easy to create. Sophisticated editors are available to create and edit XML content, but it must be possible to create XML documents in other ways, as with a text editor, or with simple scripts, etc.

9 Terseness in XML markup is of minimal importance. While several SGML language features were designed to minimize the amount of typing required, these features are not supported in XML.

Do it!

C-2: Discussing the benefits of XML

Exercises

1 XML allows the developer to define his (or her) own elements and attributes. True or false?

2 The benefits of XML include:

- A Data exchange
- B Extensibility
- C Granular updates
- D Elements are predefined for ease of use
- E All of the above

3 XML-tagged data can provide high-precision searching in web environments. True or false?

4 XML-related specifications include:

- A XSL
- B SMIL
- C XSLT
- D XHTML
- E All of the above

Unit summary: XML basics

Topic A

In this topic, you learned what XML is and how it functions as a **metalanguage** and a **markup language**. You observed a simple XML document and learned what **elements**, **attributes**, and **tags** are. You also learned the basic rules needed to **write a simple XML document**.

Topic B

In this topic, you learned about **GML**, **SGML**, and **HTML** – the predecessors of XML. You learned why there is a **need for standards**, how XML evolved, and how it fits into the landscape of markup languages.

Topic C

In this topic, you learned how XML is different from SGML and HTML. You learned how XML overcomes the shortcomings of SGML and HTML. You also discussed the **benefits of XML**, and the role of the W3C in the development of XML and related specifications.

Review questions

1 A _____________ is used for the formal description of another language.

2 All XML documents contain one or more types of information (e.g., text, graphics, etc.) according to some predetermined and deliberate _____________.

3 Which of the following could be called real-world examples of markup?

A Highlighted words or passages in a book

B A marked up draft report with symbols indicating "new paragraph here," or "bold this," etc.

C Marks on a map indicating where you'll want to turn, stop, etc.

D Numbers inserted into an otherwise un-numbered procedure

E All of the above

4 _____________ is the name of the official international standard describing markup for the structure and content of different types of electronic, machine-readable documents.

5 XML-based markup languages are also known as _____________.

A XML vocabularies

B XML parsers

C XML applications

D XML documents

E All of the above

6 Two types of documents that can be used to augment XML documents are _____________ and XML schemas.

7 All XML vocabularies have two important things in common: they are written according to the same XML standards and rules; and each represents a markup language designed to describe content specific to an organization or industry. True or false?

8 Which of the following are XML-related goals and best practices as set out by the W3C in the Recommendation "Extensible Markup Language (XML) 1.0"?

A XML documents should be legible and easy to create.

B It shall be straightforward to use XML over the Internet.

C The design of XML shall be informal.

D Terseness in XML markup is very important.

9 SGML and XML are _____________ independent and _____________ independent, so the same source files may be used with a wide variety of operating systems, and authoring and publishing environments.

Unit 2

XML components

Unit time: 100 minutes

Complete this unit, and you'll know how to:

A Define an XML document.

B Identify and use components of an XML document.

Topic A: Defining an XML document

Explanation

Some users and developers tend to think of XML documents simply as text documents. However, that is too limiting and draws attention away from XML's major features: its extensibility with respect to data, its straightforward structure, and its human legibility.

Basic concept of XML components

For our purposes, the word "document" refers to textual data documents like this unit, and also to many other data formats such as vector graphics, mathematical equations, and many other kinds of structured information.

The terms essential to your understanding of the basic concepts of XML components are:

- **XML parser (also called an XML processor).** A piece of software that reads XML documents, does front-end screening of the documents on behalf of the application, and then provides access to their content and structure. Many parsers are available, such as AlphaWorks XML for Java, which is used by IBM; Microsoft XML Parser, which is used in Microsoft Internet Explorer; and a parser called Expat, which is used in the Netscape Navigator 6 browser application.
- **Application.** The major processing software module(s) intended for the end users and designers to access and manipulate XML documents. Do not confuse this term with an "XML application," which is a term indicating another markup language that has been created according to XML Recommendation 1.0 concepts and requirements. For example, the well-known Microsoft browser Internet Explorer is an "application" that accesses and displays XML documents. On the other hand, XSLT is an XML-related language—that is, an "XML application"—in that it has been developed by using XML 1.0 constructs.
- **Fatal error.** An error in the document that the XML processor must detect and then report to the application. After a fatal error is detected, the processor might continue processing, but to search only for further errors, which it also must report to the application. When a fatal error occurs, a processor does not continue normal processing.

Do it!

A-1: Exploring XML components

Exercises

1 When an XML parser encounters a fatal error situation, it must detect and report the fatal error to the application, and then it can resume normal processing. True or false?

2 Software that reads XML documents is called an ___________.

A XML interpreter

B XML compiler

C XML reader

D XML parser

3 An ___________ is a program or group of programs intended for the end users and designers to access and manipulate XML documents.

4 The W3C XML 1.0 Recommendation defines XML documents as a class of ___________.

A data objects

B methods

C arguments

D tags

Topic B: Document components

Explanation

The first two components of an XML document are the prolog and the root element.

The prolog

The XML prolog is the first major logical component of an XML document and, because of its content, must be inserted prior to the next major logical component, the root element (also called the document element).

An XML document's prolog can comprise up to five possible components:

- An XML declaration
- Processing instruction(s)
- A Document type declaration
- Comment(s)
- White space

These prolog components facilitate the passing of data and other information to the parser and, thereafter, to the application. The components provide instruction or explanation to the reader. White space can be one or more spaces, tabs, and end-of-line indicators that help to organize the prolog and facilitate human legibility. A simple XML document example is shown in Exhibit 2-1. As you can see, it has a three-line prolog consisting of an XML declaration, a processing instruction, and a comment.

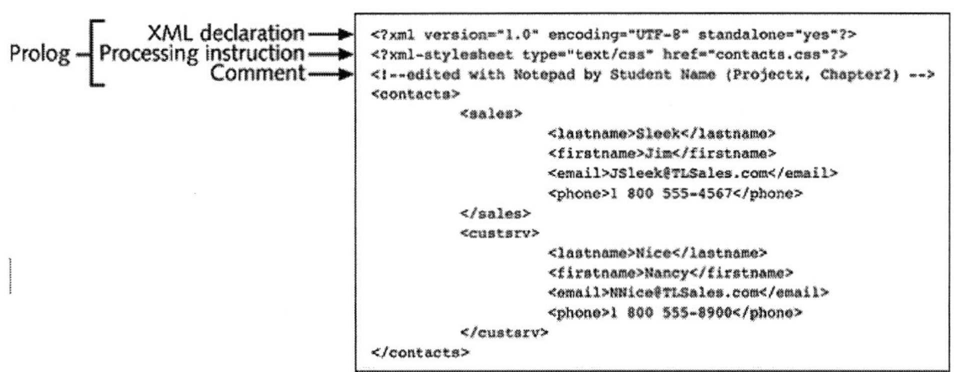


```
<?xml version="1.0" encoding="UTF-8" standalone="yes"?>
<?xml-stylesheet type="text/css" href="contacts.css"?>
<!--edited with Notepad by Student Name (Projectx, Chapter2) -->
<contacts>
        <sales>
                <lastname>Sleek</lastname>
                <firstname>Jim</firstname>
                <email>JSleek@TLSales.com</email>
                <phone>1 800 555-4567</phone>
        </sales>
        <custsrv>
                <lastname>Nice</lastname>
                <firstname>Nancy</firstname>
                <email>NNice@TLSales.com</email>
                <phone>1 800 555-8900</phone>
        </custsrv>
</contacts>
```

Exhibit 2-1: XML document prolog

The W3C XML Recommendation states that a well-formed XML document should begin with an XML declaration. It also states that all prolog components are optional, but if you want to ensure that your XML documents are always well-formed, they should begin with an XML declaration.

The XML declaration

An XML document should begin with a declaration stating that the document is written in XML. The XML declaration (also called the header) should be on the document's first line. Nothing should precede it. The first line in the XML document shown in Exhibit 2-1 is:

```
<?xml version="1.0" encoding="UTF-8" standalone="yes"?>
```

The basic syntax of the declaration is `<?xml ?>`. The `xml` must be written in lowercase letters. There are three attributes defined in the XML declaration: the XML version number ("1.0"), the document's language encoding designation ("UTF-8"), and the standalone specification ("yes").

The `version` attribute refers to the most recent version of the XML Recommendation endorsed by the W3C. It is mandatory to state the current version if you provide an XML declaration statement. Currently, there is only version 1.0, corresponding to the W3C XML Recommendation 1.0.

The second part of the XML declaration is the encoding attribute, which is optional. The choices available to you are: UTF-8, Unicode, UCS-2, UCS-4, and several other character sets. If you do not specify an encoding attribute, UTF-8 is the assumed default.

Note: Visit www.unicode.org or www.cl.cam.ac.uk/~mgk25/ucs/ISO-10646-UTF-8.html for more information about character set encoding.

The third part of the XML declaration, the standalone attribute, is also optional. If the document exists alone—that is, if there is no need to refer to any external physical entities such as DTDs or schemas—the attribute value should be set to "yes". "Yes" is also the default value if the attribute is not specified. However, if external entities are enlisted by the XML document, then specify "no".

The document type declaration

Unlike its predecessor SGML, XML does not require a document type declaration (also called a DOCTYPE definition) in all circumstances. However, when you need to include one, you will follow this basic syntax:

```
<!DOCTYPE rootname options>
```

`DOCTYPE` tells the XML processor that the statement is a document type declaration. The rootname (or class) indicates the type of document according to the author's own specification. In Exhibit 2-2, the rootname specified by the document's author is "contacts" because it was the author's intention that the document contains a list of company contacts and their respective contact information.

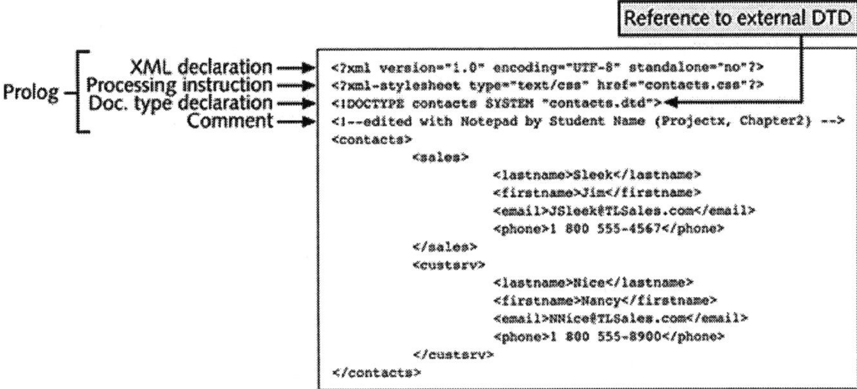

Exhibit 2-2: Referring an external document type declaration (DTD)

The “options” include other specifications, for example, an indication of where DTDs or schemas are located, their own types, etc. This type of declaration states what type the XML document is and to which DTD the document conforms. The declaration might list several elements, attributes, entities or other types of declarations within its own confines (thereby creating an *internal DTD*), or it might provide the name of an external DTD. Although document type declarations are considered optional, one is needed if you intend to refer to an external DTD or schema. To avoid ambiguity, you should always include a document type declaration.

Notice that, in Exhibit 2-2, an external DTD named “contacts.dtd” is designated in the document type declaration statement because the value of the standalone attribute has been set to “no” in the XML version statement.

The W3C Recommendation addresses the reference to the DTD or schema slightly differently: “The document type declaration…points to markup declarations that provide a grammar for (the) class of documents”. The “markup declarations” can be one of four possible types:

- Element-type declaration
- Attribute-list declaration
- Entity declaration
- Notation declaration

Their reference, although oblique in nature (referring to DTDs or schemas as “markup declarations”), is nonetheless correct: DTDs and schemas do contain those markup declarations. The XML document in Exhibit 2-2 must follow the syntax and structure rules found in the DTD called “contacts.dtd” which, because the keyword SYSTEM also appears in the statement, is presumed to be found locally on the server.

In Exhibit 2-3, the value of the standalone attribute is set to “yes” and the XML document contains its own DTD (the DTD, therefore, is called an internal DTD). Please notice that the DTD is contained entirely within the DOCTYPE declaration statement, and consists of an opening square bracket, several ELEMENT declaration statements, and a closing square bracket.

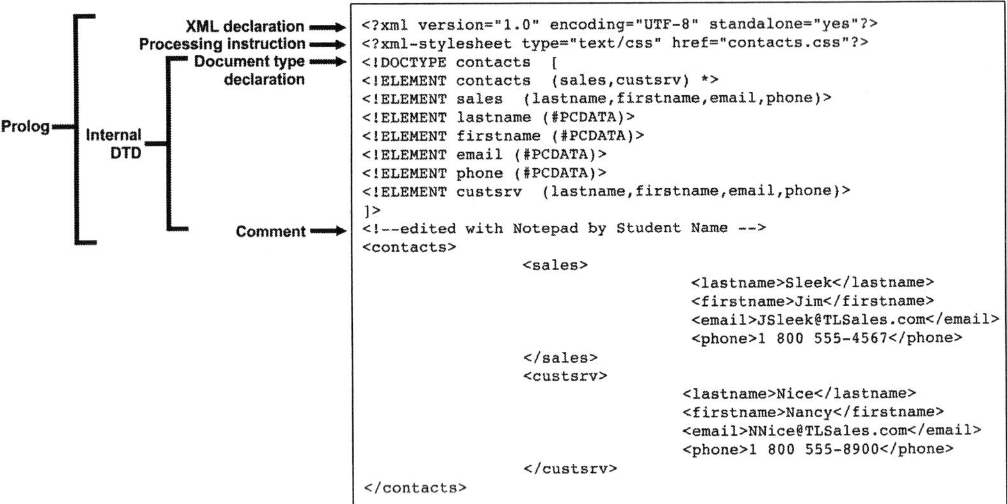


```
<?xml version="1.0" encoding="UTF-8" standalone="yes"?>
<?xml-stylesheet type="text/css" href="contacts.css"?>
<!DOCTYPE contacts  [
<!ELEMENT contacts  (sales,custsrv) *>
<!ELEMENT sales  (lastname,firstname,email,phone)>
<!ELEMENT lastname (#PCDATA)>
<!ELEMENT firstname (#PCDATA)>
<!ELEMENT email (#PCDATA)>
<!ELEMENT phone (#PCDATA)>
<!ELEMENT custsrv  (lastname,firstname,email,phone)>
]>
<!--edited with Notepad by Student Name -->
<contacts>
                <sales>
                                <lastname>Sleek</lastname>
                                <firstname>Jim</firstname>
                                <email>JSleek@TLSales.com</email>
                                <phone>1 800 555-4567</phone>
                </sales>
                <custsrv>
                                <lastname>Nice</lastname>
                                <firstname>Nancy</firstname>
                                <email>NNice@TLSales.com</email>
                                <phone>1 800 555-8900</phone>
                </custsrv>
</contacts>
```

Exhibit 2-3: Internal document type declaration (DTD)

Processing instructions (PIs)

Processing instructions are not textually part of the XML document. They are instructions passed by the XML processor to the application. Processing instruction syntax looks like this:

```
<?piname pidata?>
```

A single question mark appears at the beginning and at the end of the processing instruction. The piname, also called the *PI name* or *PI target*, identifies the PI to the application. Applications should process only the targets they recognize and ignore all other PIs. PI names beginning with the characters XML, xml, or something similar are reserved for future XML standardization by the W3C.

Any pidata options following the PI name facilitate processing by the application. For example, in Exhibit 2-1, Exhibit 2-2, and Exhibit 2-3, the processing instruction is:

```
<?xml-stylesheet type="text/css" href="contacts.css"?>
```

This is a common processing instruction, recognized by MS Internet Explorer and Netscape Navigator, that connects the XML document with a stylesheet; in these examples, it is a cascading stylesheet called "`contacts.css`". This stylesheet contains all the instructions for the presentation of the XML data on the screen that follows in the XML document.

Comments

You add comments to:

- Provide information to someone working on the XML document (i.e., chronicling, modifying, or fixing it).
- Temporarily disable sections of markup and content.

XML uses the same comment syntax as HTML. Any text or markup located between `<!--` and `-->` is invisible to the application processing the document, but is visible to any person reading the document. Comments are not considered part of the text content of an XML document. The XML processor is not needed to pass them along to an application.

Here are a few rules to remember about comments:

- Do not place a comment before the first XML declaration statement (the one containing the XML version, the language encoding, or the standalone designation).
- Do not place a comment inside actual markup statements.
- Do not use the literal string " - - " anywhere in the comment except at the end of it. Otherwise, the XML processor will misinterpret it, thinking that the comment has ended, and will then create errors based on the remaining characters.

In Exhibit 2-1, Exhibit 2-2, and Exhibit 2-3, the comment indicates who worked on the XML document, at what stage the document was created, and the application used to create it.

Do it!

B-1: Exploring the prolog

Exercises

1 A generic identifier is another name for ___________.

2 If you don't specify the language encoding, what is the default?

A UTF-8

B Unicode

C UCS-2

D UCS-4

E Other

3 According to the W3C, how many types of markup declarations are there? What are they?

4 The basic syntax of the XML declaration is ___________.

A `<?xml?>`

B `<!xml!>`

C `<@xml@>`

D `<&xml&>`

5 Another name for the document type declaration is the DOCTYPE definition. True or false?

6 If there is no need to refer to any external physical entities such as DTDs or schemas, the value of attribute "standalone" should be set to ___________.

A "yes"

B "no"

C "true"

D "false"

7 ___________ are not textually part of the XML document; they are instructions passed by the XML processor to the application.

8 Which of the following strings causes a parser to interpret incorrectly and prematurely that a comment has ended?

A ?

B < or >

C !*

D --

E None of the above

9 Which of the following statements is true?

A Comments are not part of the textual content of an XML document. The XML processor is not needed to pass them along to an application.

B Comments are part of the textual content of an XML document. The XML processor is needed to pass them along to an application.

C Comments are part of the textual content of an XML document, but the XML processor is not needed to pass them along to an application.

D Comments are not part of the textual content of an XML document, but the XML processor is still needed to pass them along to an application.

E None of the above.

10 Comments are located between ___________.

A <@ and @>

B <# and #>

C <!-- and -->

D <% and %>

The element hierarchy

Explanation

XML documents must have a logical structure. Each document must contain one or more elements that can be nested within other elements. The boundaries of each element are delimited by start tags and end tags or, for empty elements, by an empty-element tag. You might also give each element a type, also occasionally referred to as its generic identifier (GI), as well as one or more attribute specifications, which are special labels to further describe the contents of the element.

Elements are the basic building blocks of XML and, as such, they have specific properties and functions, and must be combined according to a specific structure. This section briefly discusses three methods of displaying XML documents, and then examines how elements are combined to create the basic structure of a simple XML document.

Displaying XML documents

At the top of Exhibit 2-4 is a small XML document named contacts.xml. contacts.xml is typical with respect to basic XML structure. It consists of a prolog and 11 elements arranged in a prescribed manner to store the names of staff members who serve as contacts for their organization.

Exhibit 2-4 shows three different methods for depicting the structure of XML documents for purposes of design, analysis, or troubleshooting. There is no best style for depicting every document. The choice of style(s) depends on the task at hand and also on personal preference.

The top diagram is a listing of the document contents as you might see in most text editors. Element sequence numbers have been added and indicate the order in which the elements would eventually be encountered and processed by the parser and application. This style of display is sufficient for designing and analyzing simple documents. The advantage to this style is that you can actually see the contents of each element.

The middle diagram is a Venn diagram, consisting of a number of oval and round shapes, one or more within others. Each of the shapes represents a part, usually an element, of the XML document. The largest, all-encompassing oval shape (called contacts.xml) contains the entire document: the prolog plus all the elements. Within the contacts.xml oval is another one, which represents the document's root element, called `<contacts>`. This contains the remaining elements, the names of which correspond to the names listed in the top diagram. Venn diagrams are handy for designing and analyzing fairly simple documents or parts of documents, especially if you need to show relationships between elements. Sequencing might not be easily demonstrated, however.

The bottom diagram is a tree diagram of the same XML document. Tree diagrams are better for displaying entire or parts of larger, more complicated documents. Sequencing is generally indicated left to right and from the top down. However, it is still recommended that you place sequence numbers in or near the element names. As with Venn diagrams, tree diagrams are not usually used to display actual element contents. One style of diagram not shown in Exhibit 2-4 is the typical flow chart. You can use a flow chart to illustrate the relationships among XML documents, parsers, and applications.

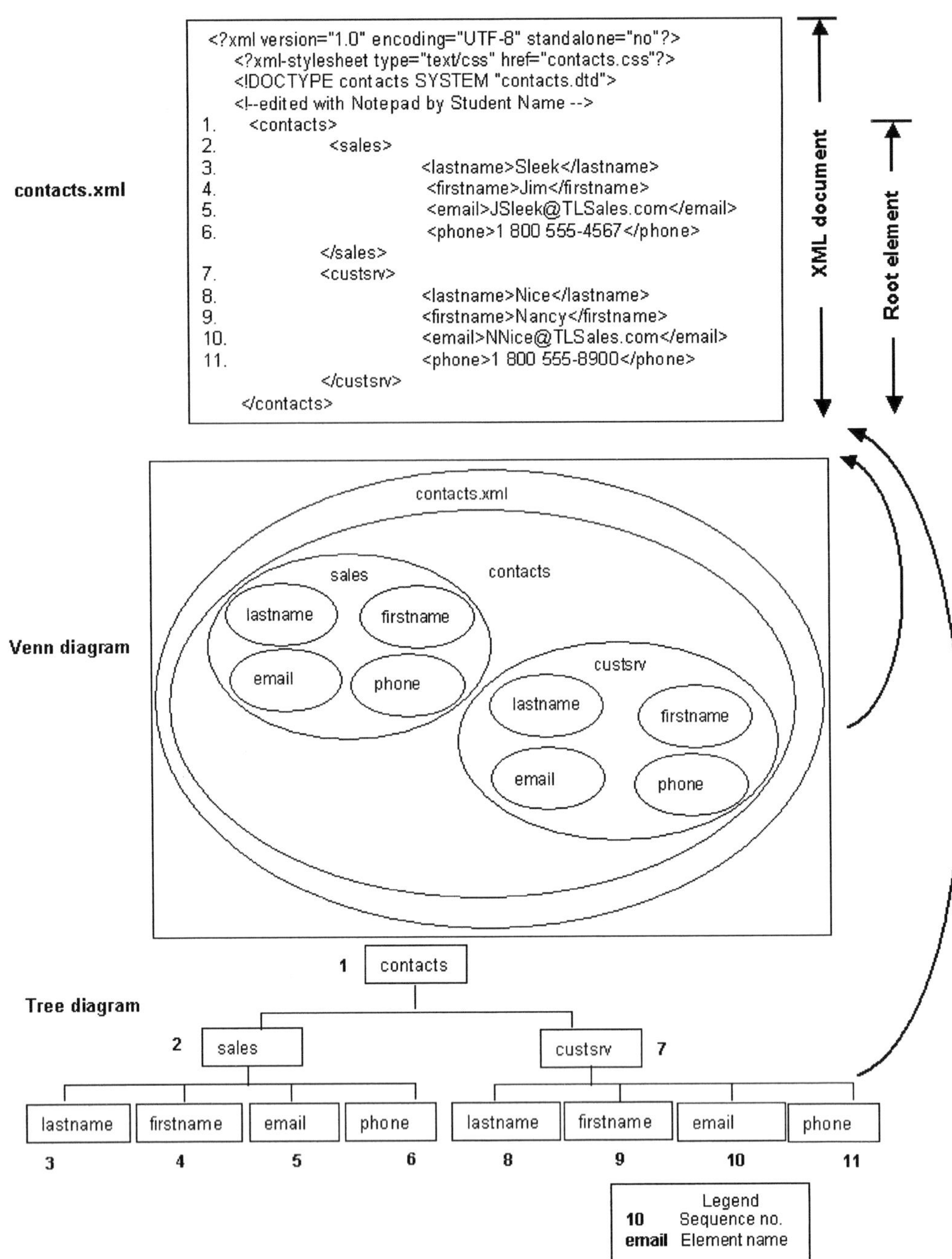

Exhibit 2-4: XML element hierarchy

The root element and document structure

In this example, the XML document contacts.xml stores the names of two staff members who act as contacts for their organization, along with their respective information. The root element of contacts.xml is named `<contacts>`. The *root element* is the parent element of all other elements, because all the elements in the XML document are contained within it. The concept of placing one element within another is called *nesting*. Use Exhibit 2-5 to follow this discussion.

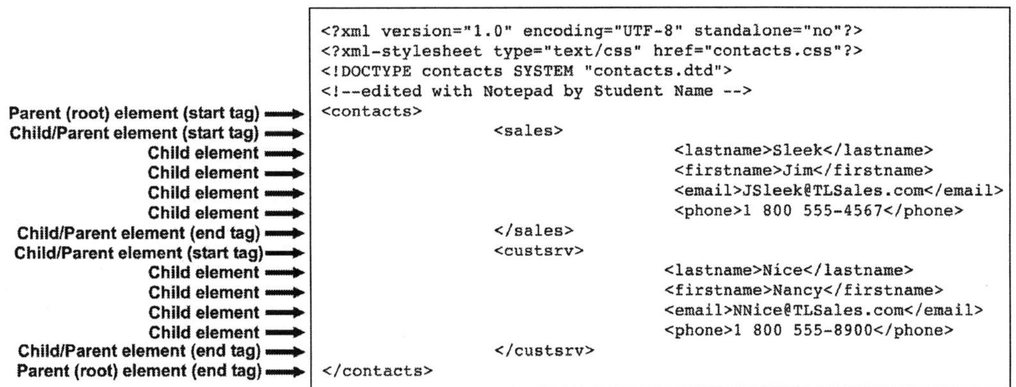


```
<?xml version="1.0" encoding="UTF-8" standalone="no"?>
<?xml-stylesheet type="text/css" href="contacts.css"?>
<!DOCTYPE contacts SYSTEM "contacts.dtd">
<!--edited with Notepad by Student Name -->
<contacts>
        <sales>
                <lastname>Sleek</lastname>
                <firstname>Jim</firstname>
                <email>JSleek@TLSales.com</email>
                <phone>1 800 555-4567</phone>
        </sales>
        <custsrv>
                <lastname>Nice</lastname>
                <firstname>Nancy</firstname>
                <email>NNice@TLSales.com</email>
                <phone>1 800 555-8900</phone>
        </custsrv>
</contacts>
```

Exhibit 2-5: Parent and child elements

In contacts. xml, `<contacts>` is the direct parent of two child elements: `<sales>` and `<custsrv>`, representing the Sales and Customer Service Departments, respectively. The root element does not have a parent of its own. It is the outermost parent element.

Each non-root element in the document has one parent element. As shown in Exhibit 2-5, each child element must be wholly contained within the content of its own parent element, and must not be contained within any other child element that is in the content of the same or any other parent. The latter part is vitally important with respect to the concepts of well-formedness and validity.

To explain the statement by example, look at the `<sales>` element. From beginning to end, `<sales>` is contained within `<contacts>` only. No part of `<sales>` appears outside of `<contacts>` and no part of `<sales>` appears within `<custsrv>`. Thus, `<sales>` does not overlap with other elements; its start and end tags cannot be nested within another element.

The `<sales>` and `<custsrv>` elements are each termed to be *child elements* (also called *subelements*), because each is contained within a parent element, `<contacts>`. However, in this case, `<sales>` and `<custsrv>` are also considered to be parent elements because they, in turn, contain their own child elements.

The `<sales>` and `<custsrv>` elements are also considered *siblings* because they are at the same level and share a parent element. Tree diagrams usually illustrate sibling relationships best. Siblings cannot overlap. Thus, any parent element can have more than one child element within it, but any child can have only one parent and cannot overlap with its sibling element(s).

Note that <sales> contains four child elements: <lastname>, <firstname>, <email>, and <phone>. <custsrv> also contains four children, with identical names to the ones found within <sales>. The child elements found within <sales> are siblings to one another. The child elements within <custsrv> are also siblings to one another. However, the child elements within <sales> are not siblings to the child elements within <custsrv>, because there is no common parent.

XML documents must be well-formed, which means all elements are properly nested to create a sound hierarchical structure.

Do it!

B-2: Exploring the element hierarchy

Exercises

1 When element1 is placed inside element2, element1 is called a _________ element.

2 Two elements that share the same parent and are on the same level are called _________.

A parents

B siblings

C neighbors

D friends

3 Which diagram illustrates sibling relationships best?

A Tree diagram

B Venn diagram

C Flowchart

D Circle

4 What is the root element in the following segment?

```
<student>
<firstname>James</firstname>
<middlename>M</middlename>
<lastname>Jameson</lastname>
</student>
```

5 Which one of the following is inserted before the root element?

A Prolog

B Attribute

C Child element

D <main> tag

Components and properties of an element

Explanation

There are several rules you need to follow when creating elements—rules that are absolutely critical to building valid XML documents.

Tags and tag names

Each element begins and ends with its element name (usually referred to as a tag). Each element begins with a start tag and usually ends with an end tag. Exhibit 2-6 shows a typical generic element.

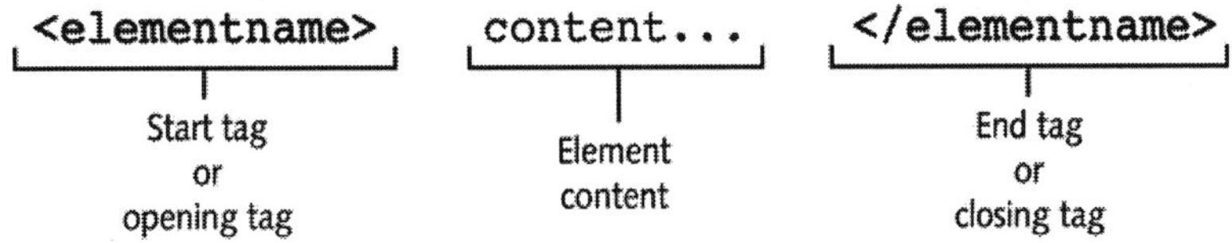

Exhibit 2-6: Generic element

An element that does not require an end tag is called an *empty element.* Empty elements have a special start tag, which contains a forward slash at the end of the tag name, as shown in Exhibit 2-7.

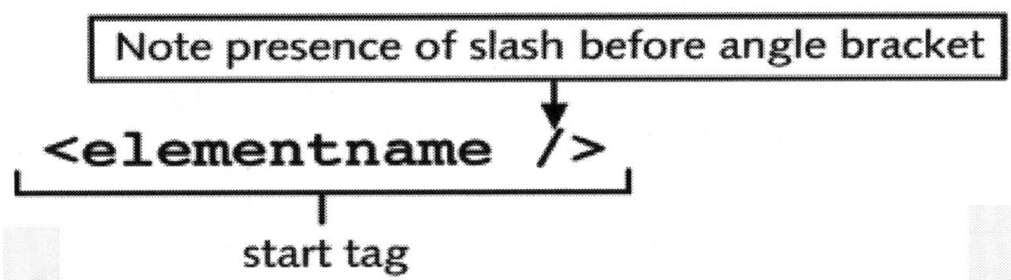

Exhibit 2-7: Generic empty element

If attribute specifications are needed, they must be placed in the start tag, as shown in Exhibit 2-8.

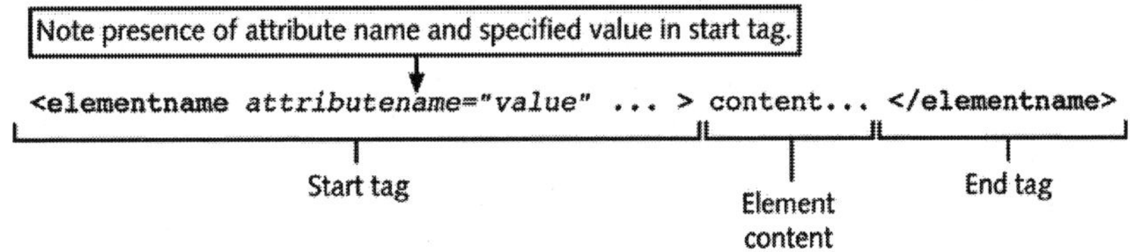

Exhibit 2-8: Generic start tag with attribute (name-value pair)

The rules for tag names are as follows:

- Tag names can begin with a letter, a colon, or an underscore (but not numbers).
- Subsequent characters might include alphanumerics, underscores, hyphens, colons, and periods.
- Tag names cannot contain certain XML-specific symbols, like the ampersand (&), the "at" symbol (@), or the "less than" symbol (<).
- Tag names cannot contain white space.
- Tag names cannot contain parenthetic statements.

Note: When you create element names, choose names that identify or describe the nature of their contents. This practice facilitates the human legibility searchability of the XML document.

The name found in the element's start and end tags is said to specify the element type. The declaration of these element types plays a significant role in DTDs and schemas.

The extent of an element

As shown in Exhibit 2-9, an element extends from the first angle bracket in its start tag through the start tag itself to the last angle bracket in the end tag.

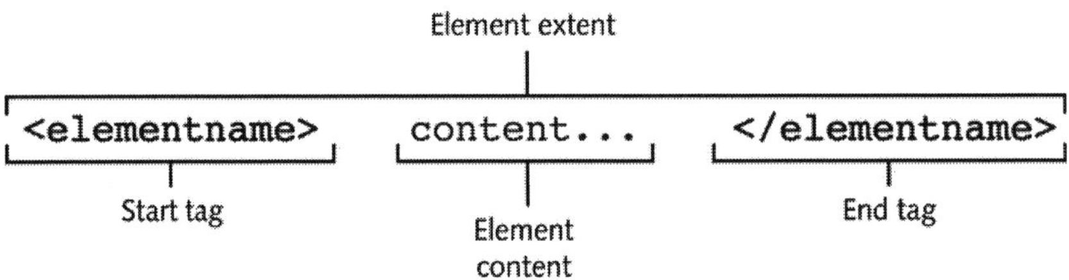

Exhibit 2-9: Extent of a generic element

Elements can be nested within one another. In those cases, each parent element extends from the first angle bracket in its start tag and continues through the child element(s), until the parent element ends with the last angle bracket in its end tag. An illustration of this principle is shown in Exhibit 2-10.

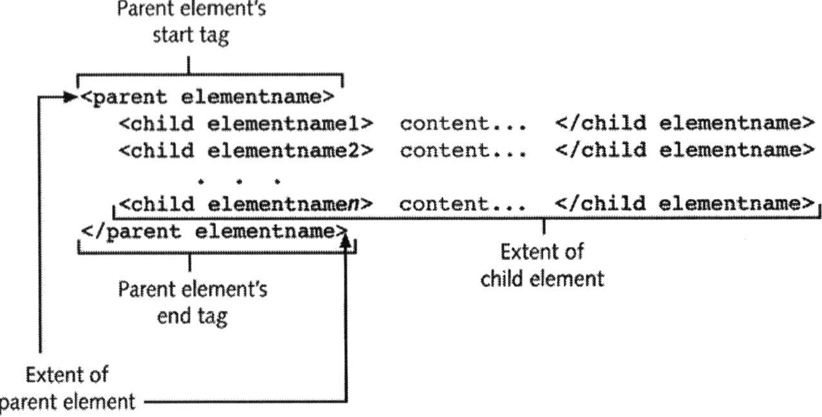

Exhibit 2-10: Extent of a generic parent element

Types of element content

As stated previously, the <contacts> element is the root element of contacts.xml, and the direct parent of two child elements: <sales> and <custsrv>. Because <contacts> contains the <sales> and <custsrv> elements, but no actual data of its own, it is said to have *element content*. The root element is not the only one that can have element content: any element that contains other elements is considered to have element content. The siblings <sales> and <custsrv>, like the root element <contacts>, also have element content, because they each contain child elements of their own.

The child elements <lastname>, <firstname>, <email>, and <phone> are said to have *data content* (not element content) because they contain character strings (e.g., names, phone numbers, email addresses). The data characters are capable of being parsed (that is, checked and appropriately manipulated prior to passing them to the application).

It is also possible for elements to have *mixed content*. An element containing mixed content contains both elements and data. Here's an example of an !ELEMENT declaration specifying an element with mixed content:

```
<!ELEMENT outst_bal (#PCDATA | WARNING)*>
```

This sample declaration specifies properties for an element called outst_bal (in this case, that is intended to mean "outstanding balance on account") that might contain character data or a child element called WARNING. The vertical bar between #PCDATA and WARNING indicates an "or" relationship among the content types, and the asterisk indicates that they are all optional. (They must all be optional in these cases, according to XML rules.) The WARNING tag is used in those cases when a customer, supplier or other party has exceeded some dollar limit, payment period limit, etc.

Elements can also be empty. The W3C XML Recommendation states that an element with no content is said to be *empty*. But empty elements are more complicated than that simplified statement would indicate.

There are two types of empty elements:

- Those elements that, in their respective DTDs or schemas, are declared to be empty.
- Those elements that are declared to be eligible to contain content but do not have any.

With respect to syntax, you've already seen how most elements in a document use start tags and end tags as wrappers around their content. Elements that have been declared empty in their respective DTD or schema have slightly different tag syntax. Empty elements are intended to function as a kind of marker, to indicate a point where, during the course of the execution of the application in question, something specific is supposed to occur. (For example, in HTML, the insertion of a horizontal line when the application encounters an <hr> tag.)

Exhibit 2-11 shows an example of a declared empty element that has been added to the contacts.xml document.

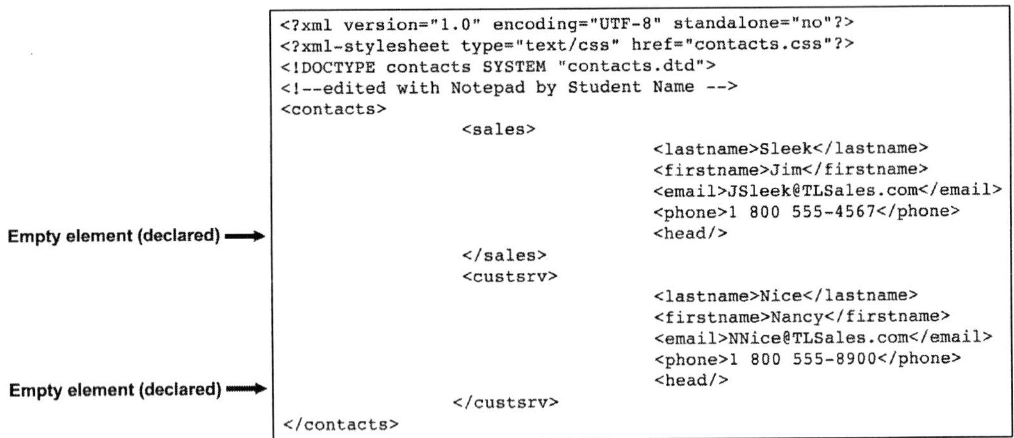

```
<?xml version="1.0" encoding="UTF-8" standalone="no"?>
<?xml-stylesheet type="text/css" href="contacts.css"?>
<!DOCTYPE contacts SYSTEM "contacts.dtd">
<!--edited with Notepad by Student Name -->
<contacts>
        <sales>
                <lastname>Sleek</lastname>
                <firstname>Jim</firstname>
                <email>JSleek@TLSales.com</email>
                <phone>1 800 555-4567</phone>
                <head/>
        </sales>
        <custsrv>
                <lastname>Nice</lastname>
                <firstname>Nancy</firstname>
                <email>NNice@TLSales.com</email>
                <phone>1 800 555-8900</phone>
                <head/>
        </custsrv>
</contacts>
```


Exhibit 2-11: Declared empty elements

In Exhibit 2-11, you can see that Mr. Sleek and Ms. Nice have been appointed as heads of their respective departments, perhaps in anticipation of expanding the staff in those departments. The declared empty element in this case is `<head/>`. When the XML parser encounters a tag with that syntax, it recognizes that tag and does not bother searching for an end tag because it knows that no such end tag exists.

In the contacts.dtd file, there has to be an element declaration similar to the following in order for the document with the `<head/>` tag in it to be considered valid:

```
<!ELEMENT head (EMPTY)>
```

The fact that such a declaration exists is the reason that such elements are termed "declared" empty. Without such a defined rule, it could be impossible for an XML parser to determine whether a tag has deliberately been left empty or whether a mistake has been made.

Consequently, it has become legal in XML to use empty-element tag syntax, such as `<head> </head>`, for elements declared to be empty, and for those elements that are eligible to contain data, but do not at the given time.

If interoperability is a concern, however, the best approach is to reserve empty-element tag syntax (e.g., `<head/>`) for elements that are declared to be empty, and to use only start tag and end tag pairs like `<head> </head>` for those elements that might or might not contain content.

Elements that have a start tag and end tag but do not have content, are termed elements with *no content*, as opposed to declared empty elements. In their respective DTDs, they would be declared as ordinary elements and not as intentional empty elements.

You might have seen electronic forms requesting Social Security Numbers, email addresses, or annual income information. Often those fields are optional and a person might not need to insert any information into them. As a result, the form might have `<ann_income> </ann_income>` elements, which are elements with no content. If the elements are optional on the electronic form, then no error occurs when the application eventually processes the XML document containing the information that you've supplied on the form. In this case, a declared empty syntax (`<ann_income/>`) would be inappropriate.

Do it!

B-3: Modifying an existing XML document

Here's how	Here's why
1 Choose **Programs**, **Accessories**, **Notepad**	You'll learn how to add elements in an XML document.
Open contacts.xml	(From the current unit folder.) Note that one sales contact is already listed in the document.
2 Change the comment line so that it reflects your personal information	
3 Create a new sibling element to <SALES> and name it <CUSTSRV>	
Within <CUSTSRV>, create a <NAME> child element and enter **Nancy Nice** as data	
Create an <EMAIL> element and enter **Nnice@TLSales.com** as its data	
Create a <PHONE> element and enter **1 515 123-4567** as its data	
4 Compare your document with the following code:	
5 Save your changes	

```
<?xml version="1.0" encoding="UTF-8"?>
<-- edited by Student Name-->
<CONTACTS>
  <SALES>
       <NAME>Jim Sleek</NAME>
       <EMAIL>JSleek@TLSales.com</EMAIL>
       <PHONE>1 800 123-4567</PHONE>
  </SALES>
  <CUSTSRV>
       <NAME>Nancy Nice</NAME>
       <EMAIL>NNice@TLSales.com</EMAIL>
       <PHONE>1 515 123-4567</PHONE>
  </CUSTSRV>
</CONTACTS>
```

6 In Internet Explorer, open contacts.xml	From the current unit folder.
7 Try to edit the file	You can open and close the elements by clicking the plus and minus symbols, but you cannot edit the file.
Close Internet Explorer	
8 Open Netscape	
Choose **File**, **Open File**	
Open contacts.xml	From the current unit folder.
Observe the file	Only the unformatted data is visible. No XML tags are shown. This is expected behavior for Netscape.
Close Netscape	
9 In contacts.xml, create a new sibling element to `<SALES>` called `<EMPLREL>`	To add another employee relations contact to the list.
Within `<EMPREL>`, create a `<NAME>` element and enter **Frank Hire** as its data	
Enter **Hire@TLSales.com** as data for the `<EMAIL>` element	
Enter **1 515 123-4568** as data for the `<PHONE>` element	You now have three contacts in the file.
10 Save your changes	
Close Notepad	

11 In XML Spy, open contacts.xml	You'll see a screen that looks similar to the one shown below. This is called Grid view.

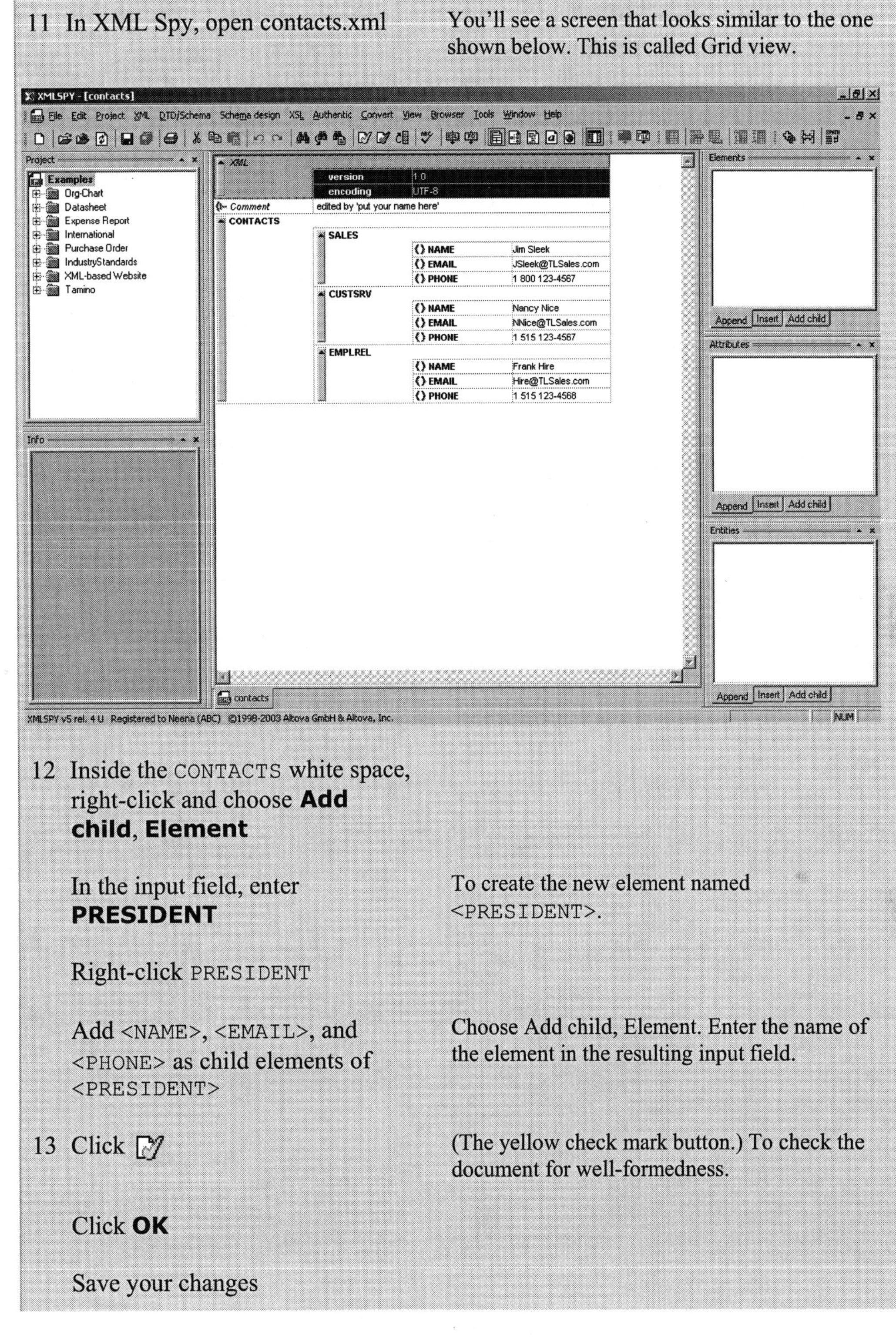

12 Inside the `CONTACTS` white space, right-click and choose **Add child**, **Element**	
In the input field, enter **PRESIDENT**	To create the new element named `<PRESIDENT>`.
Right-click `PRESIDENT`	
Add `<NAME>`, `<EMAIL>`, and `<PHONE>` as child elements of `<PRESIDENT>`	Choose Add child, Element. Enter the name of the element in the resulting input field.
13 Click [check button icon]	(The yellow check mark button.) To check the document for well-formedness.
Click **OK**	
Save your changes	

14 Click **SALES**	
Choose **XML**, **Insert**, **Element**	
15 Type **SALES**	
Right-click **SALES**	
Choose **Add Child**, **Element**	
16 Add two more sales contacts using the following information:	

```
NAME              EMAIL                    PHONE

Anna Gold         Agold@TLSales.com        1 800 123-4567
Terry White       Twhite@TLSales.com       1 800 123-4567
```

17 Click the **SALES** element for Anna	You now have three sales people in the contacts list. You'll use an empty element tag called `<HEAD/>` to indicate that Anna Gold is the head of the sales department.
Right-click and choose **Add Child**, **Element**	
Enter **HEAD**	To declare an empty element named `<HEAD/>`.
18 Check the file for well-formedness	(Click on the yellow check mark in the task bar.)
Save your changes	
In XML Spy, close the file	

Attributes

Explanation

Elements can include *attributes*, which are `name=value` pairs that specify information about an element. Applications can be programmed to look for certain attributes in data documents, and then manipulate only those elements in which the attributes appear. Attributes must be inserted in start tags and placed immediately after the element name. An element can have multiple attributes.

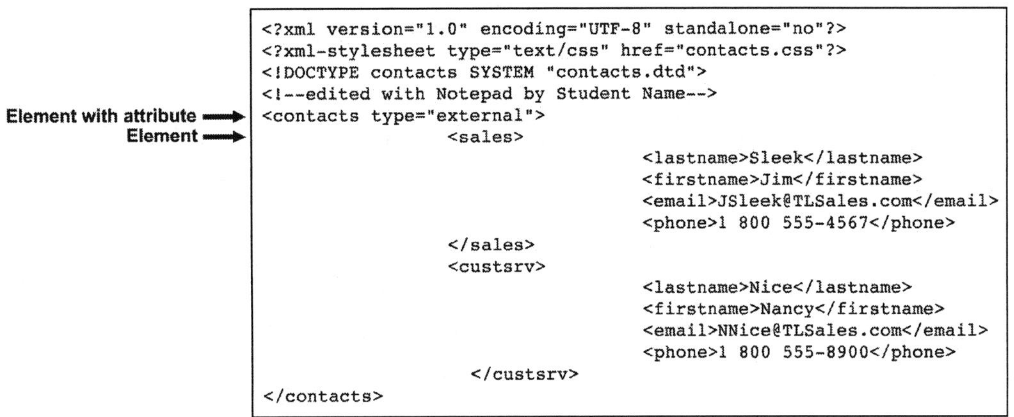


```
<?xml version="1.0" encoding="UTF-8" standalone="no"?>
<?xml-stylesheet type="text/css" href="contacts.css"?>
<!DOCTYPE contacts SYSTEM "contacts.dtd">
<!--edited with Notepad by Student Name-->
<contacts type="external">
        <sales>
                <lastname>Sleek</lastname>
                <firstname>Jim</firstname>
                <email>JSleek@TLSales.com</email>
                <phone>1 800 555-4567</phone>
        </sales>
        <custsrv>
                <lastname>Nice</lastname>
                <firstname>Nancy</firstname>
                <email>NNice@TLSales.com</email>
                <phone>1 800 555-8900</phone>
         </custsrv>
</contacts>
```

Exhibit 2-12: Element with attribute

As shown in Exhibit 2-12, the contacts element has a single attribute:

```
<contacts type="external">
```

Note that the start tag holds the attribute specification: the attribute's name is `type` and its value is set to `external` to indicate that the elements within `<contacts>` contain contact information for staff members who can be contacted from outside the company.

During initial processing, the XML parser reads the attribute specification and passes the data along to the application. If a particular instance of contact information needs to be available to the public, you can use this attribute specification.

The parser used for the XML document might impose a limit on the length of the attributes given to an element (check with the online documentation and reviews), thus requiring you to break the document or one of its elements into smaller elements. Attribute names follow element name rules.

Attribute names:

- Can begin with a letter, a colon, or an underscore (but not numbers).
- Can have subsequent characters that might be alphanumeric, underscores, hyphens, colons, and periods.
- Cannot contain certain XML-specific symbols, like the ampersand (&), the at symbol (@), or the less than symbol (<).
- Cannot contain white space, because white space is used to separate the name-value pairs themselves.
- Cannot contain parenthetic statements (words enclosed in parentheses or brackets).

In any element, attribute names must also be unique. If there are similar attributes, remember that XML is case sensitive. If you are listing products from the fall fashion collection, for example, then an attribute named "SUBCATEGORY" is not considered the same as one named "subcategory," "Subcategory," or "SuBcAtEgOrY."

If you create attributes, you must assign values to them. If you don't, the XML parser treats them as errors. All attribute values must also be quoted (i.e., surrounded by quotation marks). The process of quoting can be complicated at times. First, the most common example, which is straightforward:

```
<CONTACTS type="external">
```

If the value itself needs to include quotation marks, the processor needs to read the end of the value and the end of the quote without any conflict of syntax. To specify a quoted value, you can use single quotes to specify the attribute value. Consider the following example:

```
<WARNING text='From AcctRcv: "Do not extend any more credit to
this customer!"'>
```

Here, the single quotes preserve the value of the attribute, which is a quoted message from Accounts Receivable. In the odd cases where the value contains both single and double quotes, there is still an alternative. You can use the XML-defined entity references for single and double quotation marks. Consider the following example:

```
<DIMENSIONS length="1&apos;3.5&quot;">
```

This value translates to 1 foot, three-and-a-half inches. `'` and `"` are the two entity references for apostrophe and double quotation mark, respectively.

Note: You can find further information regarding character references and for conversion charts can be found at the Unicode Consortium Web site at www.unicode.org/charts/.

Do it!

B-4: Applying XML attributes

Here's how	Here's why
1 Make a copy of contacts.xml	You'll learn how to add attributes to an XML document.
Save the new copy as **attribs**	(Save it in the current unit folder.)
2 In XML Spy, open **attribs**	
3 In `EMPLREL`, right-click **NAME**	To recode the file by converting the child elements into attributes.
Choose **Insert, Attribute**	
Enter **NAME**	
Press TAB	To move to the value field.
4 Type **Frank Hire**	
Repeat the process for Frank's email and phone information	
5 Repeat this process for the other contacts	Occasionally check the file for well-formedness by using the XML, Check well-formedness feature on the menu bar.
6 Save your changes	
Close XML Spy	

Entities

Entities are fragments of an XML document. They range in type and scope from single characters to entire documents identified by their respective entity reference names. Entities can contain either parsed or unparsed data. *Parsed entities* contain text—a sequence of characters—that might represent markup or content data. An *unparsed entity* is a resource whose contents might or might not be text, and which might be in formats other than XML.

Entities can be *text entities*, which are physical storage units that can hold parseable strings or blocks of text, or non-parseable audio files, graphics, and video files. Alternatively, some think of entities as a way of referring to the physical data items. To keep things separate and clear in your mind, think of the entities as the physical storage unit for data, and then think of entity references as the method for referring to them. Entities are basically content management structures.

Some characters have been reserved by XML for use with markup. These are instructions or codes embedded in text to indicate how the text should be processed or to specify what the text represents. Here are some examples of reserved characters in XML:

- The left angle bracket, or "less than" symbol (<)
- The right angle bracket, or "greater than" symbol (>)
- The double quotation mark (")
- The apostrophe, or single quotation mark (')
- The ampersand (&)

If you want to insert these characters in an XML document as content, you must use an alternate way to represent to prevent the XML parser from processing them as entities.

To resolve this potential conflict, XML provides five predefined general entities, one for each of the symbols in the previous list. They are:

- `<`
- `>`
- `"`
- `'`
- `&`

You can also use entities to refer to often repeated or varying text, and to include the content of external files.

There are two kinds of entities: *general entities*, which you can use as content in an XML document; and *parameter entities*, which can be used in a document's DTD. Entities can also be categorized as:

- **Internal.** Those entities that are defined completely within the XML document that references them (in which case, the document itself is considered to become an entity).
- **External.** Entities whose content is found in an external source (e.g., a file); the reference to them usually includes the uniform resource identifier (URI) that points to their location.
- **Parsed.** Entities whose content is well-formed XML text.
- **Unparsed.** Entities whose content is simple text, binary data, or any other form of data you don't want the XML parser to interpret.

Entities in an XML document must first be defined with an entity declaration that assigns a unique name to the entity. Then the entity is referenced by that name in the XML document (for general entities) or in a DTD or schema (for parameter entities).

The five predefined general entities listed previously are the only exceptions to this declaration rule. They are predefined, so you don't need to define them in your document or in a DTD or schema. The XML parsers automatically recognize them and process them accordingly.

The declaration syntax for entities looks like this:

```
<!ENTITY entityname entitydefinition>
```

Here's a simple example. It is a substitution of the current date in a general internal entity named `TODAY`:

```
<!ENTITY TODAY "December 21, 2003">
```

Exhibit 2-13 shows this in action.

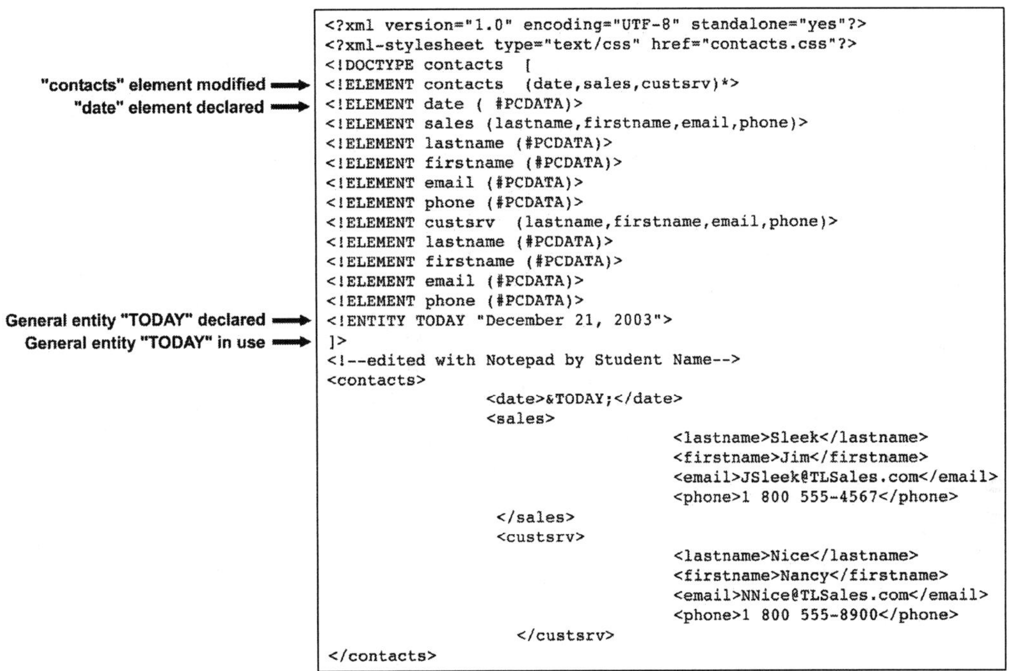


```
<?xml version="1.0" encoding="UTF-8" standalone="yes"?>
<?xml-stylesheet type="text/css" href="contacts.css"?>
<!DOCTYPE contacts  [
<!ELEMENT contacts  (date,sales,custsrv)*>
<!ELEMENT date ( #PCDATA)>
<!ELEMENT sales (lastname,firstname,email,phone)>
<!ELEMENT lastname (#PCDATA)>
<!ELEMENT firstname (#PCDATA)>
<!ELEMENT email (#PCDATA)>
<!ELEMENT phone (#PCDATA)>
<!ELEMENT custsrv  (lastname,firstname,email,phone)>
<!ELEMENT lastname (#PCDATA)>
<!ELEMENT firstname (#PCDATA)>
<!ELEMENT email (#PCDATA)>
<!ELEMENT phone (#PCDATA)>
<!ENTITY TODAY "December 21, 2003">
]>
<!--edited with Notepad by Student Name-->
<contacts>
                <date>&TODAY;</date>
                <sales>
                                  <lastname>Sleek</lastname>
                                  <firstname>Jim</firstname>
                                  <email>JSleek@TLSales.com</email>
                                  <phone>1 800 555-4567</phone>
                 </sales>
                 <custsrv>
                                  <lastname>Nice</lastname>
                                  <firstname>Nancy</firstname>
                                  <email>NNice@TLSales.com</email>
                                  <phone>1 800 555-8900</phone>
                   </custsrv>
</contacts>
```

Exhibit 2-13: Internal general entity

You can also access external general entities. Suppose a file named date.xml exists that contains the current date. You can declare it in the XML document by referencing the external file, as follows:

```
<!ENTITY TODAY SYSTEM "date.xml">
```

You can then access this external entity in the code, as follows:

```
<date>&TODAY;</date>
```

You've seen how a general parameter entity reference begins with an ampersand and ends with a semicolon. Parameter entity references begin with a percent sign (%) and end with a semicolon. Parameter entities are used with DTDs and schemas.

Character references are a special kind of entity reference. You can use them to insert arbitrary Unicode characters from the ISO/IEC 10646 character set—ones that cannot be typed directly on your keyboard—into your document. Characters in the character set are represented by numeric character references, which can be either decimal or hexadecimal.

Decimal references take the following form:

```
&#nnn
```

In the hexadecimal reference form, `nnn` is the decimal number assigned to the character. For example, the decimal character reference for the copyright symbol is `©`. The decimal character reference for the prescription (Rx) symbol is `℞`.

Hexadecimal references take the following form:

```
&#xhhh (or &#Xhhh)
```

In the hexadecimal reference form, hhh is the appropriate hexadecimal number. For example, the hexadecimal reference for the copyright symbol is `©`. The hexadecimal reference for the prescription symbol is `℞`. There is limited support for hexadecimal references in browsers. Decimal references are far more common.

CDATA sections

There will be occasions when you intend to pass the characters that XML normally recognizes as markup characters directly to the application. For example:

```
<NOTE>
All BLACK & WHITE television sets are on sale.
</NOTE>
```

Normally, the XML parser would encounter the ampersand (&), consider it a markup signal, and then interpret it. If the parser does not create an error, then the application would likely create faulty output. To tell the parser to ignore the character and simply pass it and the other characters on to the application, insert a *CDATA section* (Character Data section). For example:

```
<NOTE>
<![CDATA[All BLACK & WHITE television sets are on sale.]]>
</NOTE>
```

There are a few important things to note about CDATA sections:

- You can use CDATA sections to create and maintain areas of program code, as they retain information about white space.
- You cannot nest them. After the parser finds one set of `]]>` indicators, it considers the CDATA section closed.
- Be careful with the syntax. Any minor mistake or typo will create an error.
- Any additional XML markup instructions between the `<![CDATA` and the `]]>`, such as elements, comments, processing instructions, etc. are not recognized by the parser. These characters pass directly to the application as content.

Do it!

B-5: Exploring entities and CDATA sections

Exercises

1 CDATA sections cannot be nested. True or false?

2 To tell the parser to ignore the character and simply pass it and the other characters on to the application, you need to use a ___________.

A element

B attribute

C general section

D CDATA section

3 If you need to place a double quote in a content string, you can use ___________.

A %quot;

B $quot;

C "

D !quot;

4 There are two kinds of entities: general entities and ___________.

Well-formed XML documents

Explanation

Well-formed XML documents are those that meet the following grammatical, logical, and structural rules, as outlined in the W3C's XML 1.0 Recommendation:

- An XML document meets all the well-formedness constraints given in the XML 1.0 Recommendation.
- The document contains one or more elements.
- Each of the parsed entities that is referenced directly or indirectly within the document is (also) well formed.
- An XML document can have only one root element, and all other elements fall within it. No part of the root element (also called a document element) appears in the content of any other element.
- For all the other elements in the document, if the element's start tag is in the content of one element, then the end tag must (also) be within the content of the same element. In other words, the elements, delimited by their respective start and end tags, must nest properly within each other. (Tags cannot overlap, and one element cannot fall within more than one parent).
- Every start tag must have a matching end tag.
- Element names must obey XML naming conventions.

An example of a well-formed document is shown in Exhibit 2-14.

```
<?xml version="1.0" encoding="UTF-8" standalone="yes"?>
<?xml-stylesheet type="text/css" href="contacts.css"?>
<!--edited with Notepad by Student Name (Projectx, Ch. 2) -->
<contacts>
        <sales>
                <lastname>Sleek</lastname>
                <firstname>Jim</firstname>
                <email>JSleek@TLSales.com</email>
                <phone>1 800 555-4567</phone>
        </sales>
        <custsrv>
                <lastname>Nice</lastname>
                <firstname>Nancy</firstname>
                <email>NNice@TLSales.com</email>
                <phone>1 800 555-8900</phone>
        </custsrv>
</contacts>
```

Exhibit 2-14: A well-formed XML document

Note that the root element is called <contacts> and all elements are properly nested within it. Exhibit 2-15 shows the same document with some changes deliberately inserted for illustration.

```
<?xml version="1.0" encoding="UTF-8" standalone="yes"?>
<?xml-stylesheet type="text/css" href="contacts.css"?>
<!--edited with Notepad by Student Name -->
<contacts>
                <sales>
                                <lastname>Sleek</lastname>
                                <firstname>Jim</firstname>
                                <email>JSleek@TLSales.com</email>
                                <phone>1 800 555-4567</phone>

                </sales>
                <custsrv>
                                <lastname>Nice</lastname>
                                <firstname>Nancy</firstname>
                                <email>NNice@TLSales.com</email>
                                <phone>1 800 555-8900</phone>
                </custsrv>
</contacts>
```

Exhibit 2-15: Overlapping elements ("freeform XML")

Note that it is acceptable to put more than one element on one line, because XML parsers, unless specifically instructed, are not concerned with the use of white space. However, within both the <sales> and <custsrv> elements, there are elements that violate one or more of the well-formedness rules (also called well-formedness constraints). There is a clear overlap in the <lastname> and <firstname> elements: the start tag of the second element is encountered before the end tag of the first element. In the <email> and <phone> elements, it appears that the <phone> element content has, in effect, two parents (<email> and <phone>), which is another violation.

Valid XML documents

A valid XML document is a well-formed XML document that also conforms to the declarations, structures, and other rules defined in the document's respective DTD or schema.

If your XML document is well-formed, it's not necessarily valid. A valid XML document must conform to the rules of a DTD or schema.

Exhibit 2-16 illustrates the processing of an XML data object.

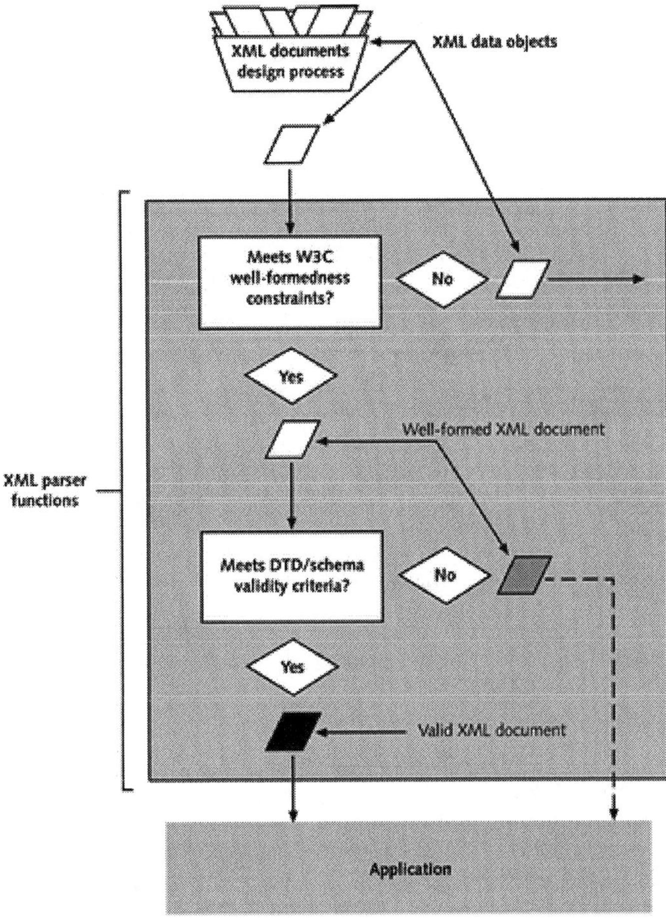

Exhibit 2-16: Process schematic: well-formed and valid documents

The XML data object is considered a well-formed XML document after it has been checked by the XML parser and is deemed to have met the W3C's well-formedness constraints. The XML parser then checks the XML document for validity (by examining its components and structure against the declarations in its DTD or schema). If the XML document proves to be valid, then it is made available for processing by the application. Depending on the application, an XML document need not be valid to be passed for further processing. However, XML documents must be well-formed.

Do it!

B-6: Exploring well-formed and valid XML documents

Exercises

1 What do we call an XML document that meets the W3C's specific grammatical, logical, and structural rules outlined in the W3C's XML 1.0 Recommendation?

A structured

B logical

C well-formed

D correct

2 What do we call a well-formed XML document that also conforms to the rules defined in a DTD or schema?

A structured

B well-formed

C correct

D valid

Unit summary: XML components

Topic A

In this topic, you learned about the **W3C XML 1.0 Recommendations**. These recommendations define XML documents as a class of data objects. You also learned that an **XML processor**, or **parser**, is a piece of software that reads XML documents and provides access to their content and structure. Then, you learned that the **application** is the major processing software module. You also learned that a **fatal error** is an error in the document that the XML processor must detect and report to the application.

Topic B

In this topic, you learned about the **physical structure** of documents. You learned that a document is made up of storage units called **entities** and a logical structure containing a **prolog** section. You also learned that **elements** are the basic building blocks of XML. Then, you learned that the **root element** is the parent of all other elements, and you learned how to use **attributes**, **entities**, and **CDATA sections** in an XML document. Finally, you learned that a **valid XML document** is a **well-formed** XML document that also conforms to the rules defined in a DTD or an XML schema.

Review questions

1 The ____________ is also called the header, which should be on the document's first line, and nothing should precede it.

2 The ____________ indicates the type of document according to the author's own specification.

3 ____________ is an element that contains both elements and data.

4 A ____________ XML document is a well-formed XML document that also conforms to the declarations, structures, and other rules defined in the document's respective DTD or schema.

5 In a ____________ diagram, sequencing is generally indicated left to right and from top to bottom.

6 ____________ are the basic building blocks of XML.

7 The following is the syntax of a ____________ type declaration:

```
<!DOCTYPE rootname options>
```

8 Unparsed entities might be in formats other than XML. True or false?

9 The following is an example of an XML ___________:

```
<?xml-stylesheet type="text/css" href="contacts.css"?>
```

10 An element cannot have both element content and data content. True or false?

11 Which of the following is NOT a good attribute name?

A type

B _1st_time

C 2ndtype

D my:type

E :_._._

12 Take a look at the following code and state the number of elements.

```
<message>
<to>NNice@TLSales.com</to>
<from>Ric@ACME.com</from>
<subject>Orders</subject>
<text>
Your order can be picked up anytime.
</text>
</message>
```

13 Based on the following code, state the number of attributes.

```
<message to="NNice@TLSales.com" from="Ric@ACME.com"
subject="Orders">
<text>
Your order can be picked up anytime.
</text>
</message>
```

14 An item can be included in an XML document by referencing it. Which of the following cannot be legitimately referenced?

A A left-angle bracket

B An entire document

C A collection of DTD definitions

D All of the above

E None of the above

15 Attribute specifications appear in ____________.

A a separate tag

B the start tag

C the end tag

D the closing tag

Independent practice activity

Add a directive to your contacts.xml file to point to a cascading style sheet that can format the unformatted XML data. You'll use a very basic cascading style sheet named "contacts.css". This file is present in your current unit folder. Code a directive statement into your contacts.xml file to use it. Now code a processing instruction (PI) statement into your contacts.xml file to link the contacts.css style sheet to your contacts.xml file. Test the new link using both Internet Explorer and Netscape.

Unit 3

Document type definitions (DTDs)

Unit time: 120 minutes

Complete this unit, and you'll know how to:

A Create a DTD, and differentiate between internal and external DTDs.

B Create a content model and add attribute list declarations.

C Create and validate an XML document.

Topic A: Document modeling and DTDs

Explanation

Each XML vocabulary is unique and can vary significantly from the others in scope and intent, but all vocabularies have two important aspects in common. They all represent a markup language that describes a specific type of content. They are written using XML, which makes all of them members of the same extended markup family, built according to the same standard, and readable by any XML-compliant browser.

Each unique vocabulary must be built to a consistent set of standards and functions, within an exacting set of content rules and structures. XML allows you to create these rules and structures by using a concept called *document modeling*. Documents called document type definitions (DTDs) and XML schemas are the vehicles by which that modeling is conducted. Those documents define or declare all the components that an XML language or document is permitted to contain, as well as the structural relationships among those components.

Document type declarations and DTDs

DTD is the most prevalent type of document model. SGML introduced the concept of a *document type declaration* (the statement within the prolog of an XML document that states what type of document it is and sometimes refers to a document type definition) and provided for the development of DTDs (as an internal subset of an XML document or as a separate external document). XML, as a restricted form of SGML, inherited the DTD concept, complete with its syntax. Anyone can develop his or her own specific XML-related language, documents, and DTDs.

A DTD defines a document type in the following ways:

- The DTD declares a set of permissible elements. You can't use any element names in your related documents other than those that are declared in the DTD.
- The DTD defines the content model for each element. *The content model* is a pattern that indicates what elements or data can be nested within other elements, the order in which the elements or data appear, how many are permitted, and whether they are desired or optional.
- The DTD declares a set of permitted attributes for each of its elements. Each attribute declaration defines the name, datatype, default values (if any), and behavior (desired or optional) of the attribute.
- The DTD includes other mechanisms, such as *entity declarations* (the specifying of a name for an entity plus the definition of what the entity represents) and *notation declarations* (labels generally applied to specific types of non-parsed binary data and occasionally to text data), to facilitate content management. (For example, to facilitate the importing of data from an external file.)

As shown in Exhibit 3-1, the DTD consists of at least four kinds of declarations: element declarations, attribute list declarations, entity declarations, and notation declarations. The "Other content" consists of comments, prologs, and other statements, if applicable. The various sets of declarations help to define and clarify the components and structures of an XML-related language and its related XML documents.

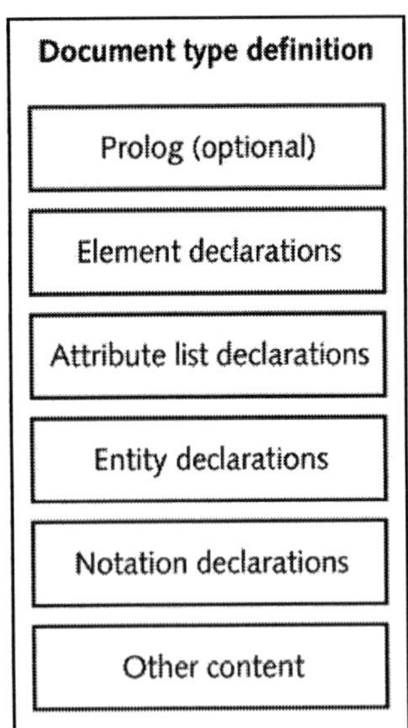

Exhibit 3-1: Basic DTD schematic

The declarations allow a DTD and its documents to communicate *metainformation* about their content to the XML processor. Metainformation includes the type, frequency, sequencing and nesting of elements, attribute information, the various entities employed, the names and types of external files that might be referenced, and the formats of some external (non-XML) data that might also be referenced.

A typical element declaration is shown in Exhibit 3-2. The combination of the start indicator (<!) and the uppercase keyword is called the *declaration identifier*. There is no white space permitted in the declaration identifier between the start indicator and the keyword; the start indicator cannot be separated from the keyword.

When composing DTDs, pay attention to the ordering of the declarations. If you include the same declaration more than once, the first one takes precedence over any others.

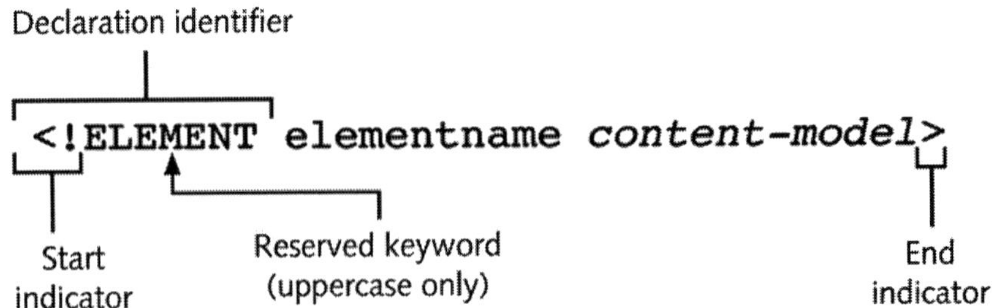

Exhibit 3-2: Typical DTD declaration syntax

XML content can be processed without a document type declaration and without a DTD. However, in many instances, a DTD is absolutely required:

- **Default attribute values.** If an XML document or language relies on any kind of default attribute values, at least part of the declaration must be processed to obtain the correct default values.
- **Handling of white space.** The semantics associated with white space in element content (where it is of little consequence) differs from the semantics associated with white space in mixed content (the interspersing of text with elements) where it might be significant. Without a DTD, there is no way for the processor to distinguish between these cases.
- **Authoring environments.** Most authoring environments need to read and process document type declarations in order for authors to comply with the content models of the document, especially their publishers' models.
- **Authoring methods.** In situations where people compose or edit data regularly, a DTD is desired if any structure is to be created, understood, and maintained.

Do it!

A-1: Discussing document type declarations and DTDs

Exercises

1 What two things do all XML-related vocabularies have in common?

2 DTDs predate SGML. True or false?

3 How many kinds of declarations are there in a typical DTD? What are they?

4 White space is permitted in the declaration identifier between the start indicator and the keyword. True or false?

Internal DTDs versus external DTDs

Explanation

The structure of a conforming XML document consists of two major components: the prolog and the root element. A document type declaration statement (also called a DOCTYPE definition) should always be included in the prolog. That declaration states what class or type the document is and might refer to a DTD to which the document should adhere.

Within its document type declaration statement, the document might actually contain an internal DTD (also called an internal subset), or it might provide the name and location of an external DTD (also called an external subset), or it might have both.

Internal DTDs

Exhibit 3-3 shows an XML document that contains an internal DTD. The standalone document declaration, (i.e., `standalone="yes"`) occurs in the XML declaration. The value "yes" indicates that only internal declarations need to be processed, that no external DTD or schema needs to be processed. A value of "no" indicates that both the internal and any external declarations must be processed.

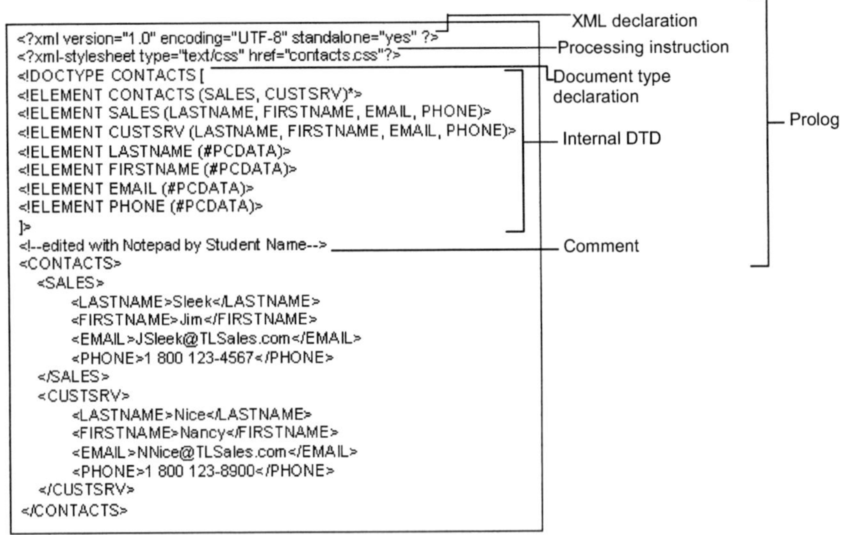

```
<?xml version="1.0" encoding="UTF-8" standalone="yes" ?>
<?xml-stylesheet type="text/css" href="contacts.css"?>
<!DOCTYPE CONTACTS [
<!ELEMENT CONTACTS (SALES, CUSTSRV)*>
<!ELEMENT SALES (LASTNAME, FIRSTNAME, EMAIL, PHONE)>
<!ELEMENT CUSTSRV (LASTNAME, FIRSTNAME, EMAIL, PHONE)>
<!ELEMENT LASTNAME (#PCDATA)>
<!ELEMENT FIRSTNAME (#PCDATA)>
<!ELEMENT EMAIL (#PCDATA)>
<!ELEMENT PHONE (#PCDATA)>
]>
<!--edited with Notepad by Student Name-->
<CONTACTS>
  <SALES>
      <LASTNAME>Sleek</LASTNAME>
      <FIRSTNAME>Jim</FIRSTNAME>
      <EMAIL>JSleek@TLSales.com</EMAIL>
      <PHONE>1 800 123-4567</PHONE>
  </SALES>
  <CUSTSRV>
      <LASTNAME>Nice</LASTNAME>
      <FIRSTNAME>Nancy</FIRSTNAME>
      <EMAIL>NNice@TLSales.com</EMAIL>
      <PHONE>1 800 123-8900</PHONE>
  </CUSTSRV>
</CONTACTS>
```


Exhibit 3-3: XML document with internal DTD

In the document type declaration statement, the internal DTD reference is introduced after the opening square bracket ([ ), the keyword `DOCTYPE`, and the class specification `CONTACTS` (because the document is a contact list for TLSales). The internal DTD consists of the next several `ELEMENT` declarations, and concludes at the closing square bracket ( ]).

Private external DTDs

The DTD portion of the document doesn't always have to be stored inside the related XML document. Instead, it can be saved in a file for reference by one document or by several different documents.

As shown in Exhibit 3-4, "standalone" has been set to "no" in the XML version statement, which indicates that an external DTD or schema as well as all internal declarations must be processed. In this case, the external DTD is a file named "contacts.dtd," as designated in the document type declaration statement. In this case, contacts.dtd is located locally on the server, in the same directory as the XML document itself. (Note that the keyword `SYSTEM` appears after the class specification `CONTACTS`, and no additional directories are specified.)

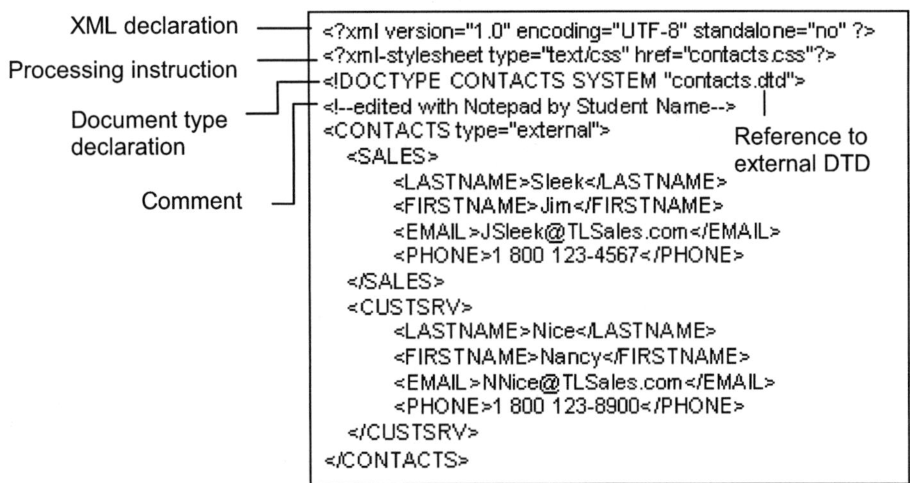

```
<?xml version="1.0" encoding="UTF-8" standalone="no" ?>
<?xml-stylesheet type="text/css" href="contacts.css"?>
<!DOCTYPE CONTACTS SYSTEM "contacts.dtd">
<!--edited with Notepad by Student Name-->
<CONTACTS type="external">
  <SALES>
      <LASTNAME>Sleek</LASTNAME>
      <FIRSTNAME>Jim</FIRSTNAME>
      <EMAIL>JSleek@TLSales.com</EMAIL>
      <PHONE>1 800 123-4567</PHONE>
  </SALES>
  <CUSTSRV>
      <LASTNAME>Nice</LASTNAME>
      <FIRSTNAME>Nancy</FIRSTNAME>
      <EMAIL>NNice@TLSales.com</EMAIL>
      <PHONE>1 800 123-8900</PHONE>
  </CUSTSRV>
</CONTACTS>
```


Exhibit 3-4: XML document with external DTD reference

This XML document must follow the syntax and structure rules found in contacts.dtd. The contacts.dtd DTD is termed private, because it is available only to the user of the system or to those who are able to access the system over a local network.

External DTDs with different URLs

Exhibit 3-5 shows another example of an XML document with an external DTD. In this case, the document refers to an external DTD that is located on the same Web site, but in a different file directory from where the XML document is located. Its specific Universal Resource Locator (URL) identifies the Web site, and a path to the specific directory is appended to the URL.

When the XML processor reads the document type declaration statement, it accesses the DTD through the Web site directory, and continues processing the XML document according to the specifications in the DTD.

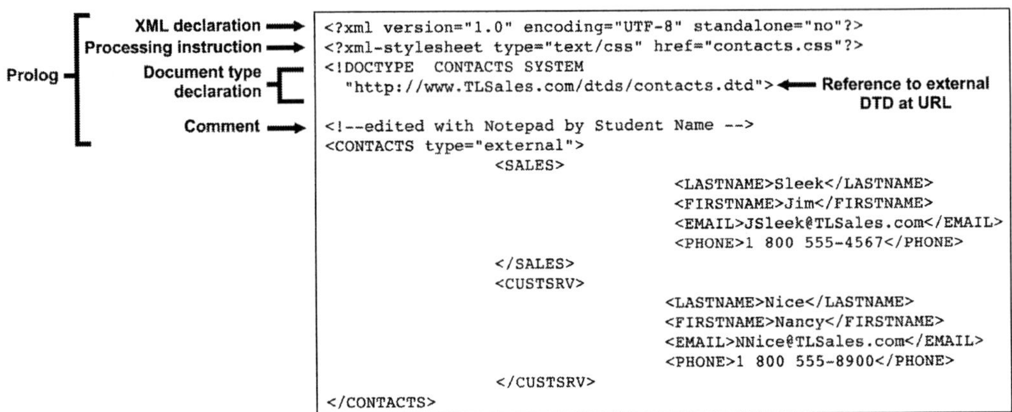

Exhibit 3-5: XML document with external DTD URL reference

External public DTDs

If a DTD is intended for public use, you need to refer to it differently. Exhibit 3-6 shows an example of this type of reference. The generic syntax for a public DTD reference is:

```
<!DOCTYPE root_elementname PUBLIC FPI URL>
```

Note that the keyword `PUBLIC` has replaced the previous keyword `SYSTEM`. The coding immediately after the `PUBLIC` keyword is called the *formal public identifier* (FPI). An example of a public DTD is shown in Exhibit 3-6. The hyphen (-) in the first field of the FPI indicates that the DTD is defined by a private individual or organization, not one approved by a non-standards body (in which case, you would use a plus sign (+).) or by an official standard (in which case, you would reference the relevant standard itself, such as ISO/IEC 10646).

The text "TLSales" in the second field is a unique name that indicates the owner and maintainer of the DTD. The text "Contacts.dtd Version 2.0" in the third field indicates the type of document, along with a unique identifier (the version number, presuming versions are updated periodically). The two-letter specification "EN" in the fourth field indicates that the document is written in English.

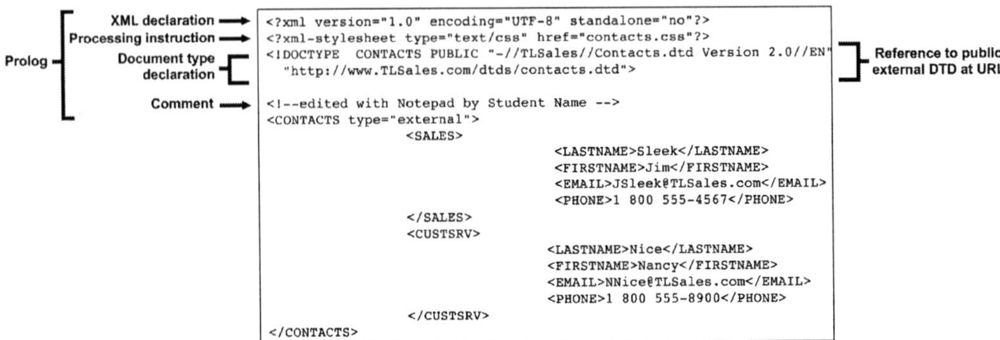

Exhibit 3-6: XML document with public external DTD reference

Combining internal and external DTDs

Exhibit 3-7 shows an example of an XML document that provides an internal DTD and refers to an external DTD.

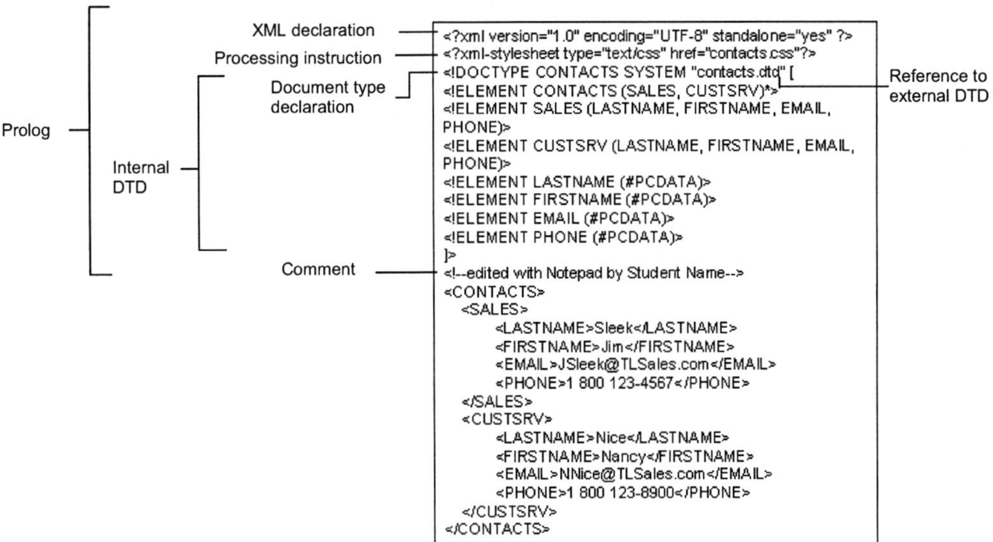

Exhibit 3-7: XML document with internal and external DTDs

If there is an internal DTD and an external DTD, then the declarations in the internal DTD are added to the declarations in the external DTD. If there are declarations in the internal DTD that directly contradict those in the external DTD, then processing stops with an error. Some manuals state that the internal declarations prevail over the external declarations due to precedence, but that is not always the case.

Do it!

A-2: Comparing internal and external DTDs

Exercises

1 The following is a reference to an external DTD. True or false?

```
<!DOCTYPE CONTACTS SYSTEM "contacts.dtd">
```

2 An XML document can have an internal and an external DTD at the same time. True or false?

3 In terms of location, what kinds of DTDs are there? (Choose all that apply.)

A Public internal

B Internal

C Private external

D Public external

E All of the above

4 If an XML document has an internal and an external DTD, and there are declarations in the internal DTD that directly contradict those in the external DTD, then the declarations in the external DTD take priority over those in the internal DTD, and processing continues. True or false?

5 From the following document type declaration statement, what kind of DTD is referenced?

```
<!DOCTYPE CONTACTS SYSTEM
"http://www.TLSales.com/dtds/contacts.dtd">
```

A Public access external DTD

B Private external DTD

C Private internal DTD

D Public internal DTD

E Internal DTD, plus external DTD

6 A value of ________ for the `standalone` attribute indicates that the internal and any external declarations must be processed.

7 The "EN" in the following indicates that ________.

```
"-//TLSales//Contacts.dtd Version 2.0//EN"
```

A The document is written in English.

B The document is in a directory named EN.

C This is the end of the document.

D 2.0//EN is the name of the version.

DTDs and valid XML

Explanation

As mentioned earlier, valid XML languages and their documents are well-formed XML documents that contain both a document type declaration (that refers to a proper DTD or XML schema) and that conform to the constraints of that DTD or schema. The W3C Recommendations for XML and XML schemas identify all of the criteria in detail.

To determine if a document is valid, the XML processor must read the entire document type declaration (including both internal and external subsets). For some applications, however, validity might not be required, and it might be sufficient for the processor to read only the internal subset.

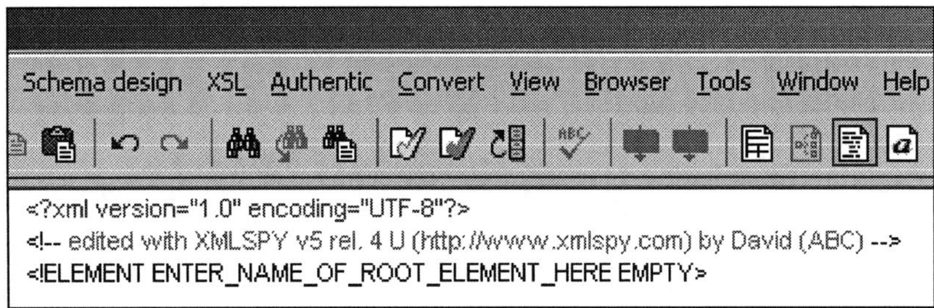

Exhibit 3-8: Default DTD created by XML Spy

Do it!

A-3: Creating a DTD in XML Spy

Here's how	Here's why
1 Launch XML SPY	
2 Choose **Project**, **New project**	The project pane is activated.
3 Choose **Project**, **Save Project**	To open the Save As dialog box.
Click the **Save in** list arrow	
Navigate to the current unit folder	
4 In the File name text box, enter **company**	To specify the project file name.
Click **Save**	To create a new project named "company."
5 Choose **File**, **New...**	To create a new DTD and add it to the company project. The Create new document dialog box appears. It contains a list of document types.
Locate and select **dtd Document Type Definition**	
Click **OK**	

6 Choose **File**, **Save As...**	To open the Save As dialog box.
In the File name text box, enter **company**	To specify the DTD file name.
Click **Save**	
7 In the Project pane, right-click the **DTD/Schemas** folder	You will add the DTD to the DTD/Schemas folder in the Project window.
Click **Add Files...**	To open the Open dialog box; the company.dtd file in the project directory is listed.
Double-click **company.dtd**	To add this file to the company project.
8 Click in the **company.dtd** window	
Choose **View**, **Text view**	To view the source code of the company.dtd file.
9 Examine the code in the window	When you created the DTD, XML Spy created a default DTD document similar to the one shown in Exhibit 3-8.
	The first line contains the XML declaration with two attributes: the version and the document's language encoding. The second line is a comment containing the name and version of the XML application that created the file and the author's name. The third line is the default root element and is declared as empty.
10 Save your changes	

Topic B: Declarations

Explanation

Element declarations, also called *element type declarations*, specify the names of elements and the nature of their content. Each declaration statement can define only one element. The DTD must contain as many element declarations as there are elements. For example, if there are six elements, then there must be six element declarations in the DTD.

Exhibit 3-9 expands the element declaration to show that element declarations are made up of element declaration identifiers, element names, and the content model. As in other declarations, the keyword is the reserved uppercase word `ELEMENT`. The keyword combines with the start indicator to form the element declaration identifier.

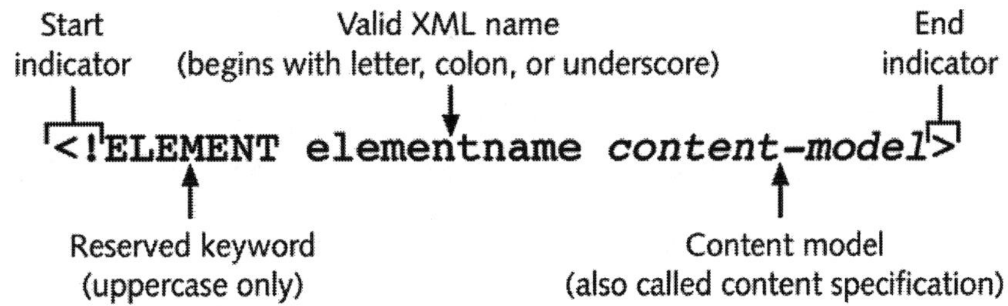

Exhibit 3-9: Element declaration syntax

Element names

The element name must adhere to the following XML naming conventions:

- It must begin with a letter, a colon, or an underscore (no numbers).
- Subsequent characters might be alphanumerics, underscores, hyphens, colons, and periods.
- It cannot contain certain XML-specific symbols, such as the ampersand (&), the at symbol (@), or the less than symbol (<).
- It cannot contain white space.
- It cannot contain parenthetic statements.

Note: All names specified under the other declarations—that is, the attribute list declarations, entity declarations, and notation declarations—also follow these XML name conventions.

It is a good idea to develop a style convention for your names and conform to it throughout the XML document. Some developers and authors suggest that element names should be lowercase, which is mandatory for XHTML. Although this is acceptable, it can occasionally create confusion when attributes are involved. Some developers use title case, where the first letter is uppercase but the subsequent letters are lowercase; some adopt the Java-related convention of capitalizing the second word of an element name consisting of two or more words.

Element names usually appear in uppercase in this text, except when basic syntax is presented and discussed.

If you specify an element name in title case in the DTD, then that element must be written in title case in your XML document. Otherwise, the document will not pass a validity test against its DTD. Whatever you adopt as your style convention, you must consistently maintain it to avoid parsing and application errors.

Do it!

B-1: Discussing elements names

Exercises

1 XML allows you to create and name your own elements. True or false?

2 Element names can begin with a letter, a colon, or an underscore, but not a number. True or false?

3 The DTD must contain as many element declarations as there are elements. True or false?

4 Element names can contain XML-specific symbols, such as ampersand (&). True or false?

The content model

Explanation

The content model (or content specification) defines what an element might contain. There are several content types that you can specify.

Elements containing parsed character data only

An element that contains parsed character data only has the following syntax:

```
<!ELEMENT elementname (#PCDATA)>
```

The reserved uppercase keyword/symbol combination "#PCDATA" indicates that the element contains *parsed* (or *parseable*) *character data*, which means that the characters comprising the content of the element will be checked by the XML parser. The parser checks for entity references and then replaces the reference with the actual entity values.

Character data refers to plain text with no markup symbols (such as <, &, ;, or "). The term "character data" is general. There is no reference to whether the content is alphabetic or numeric. By contrast, XML schemas provide for additional, more precise specifications such as integers, date format, floating-point decimals, and others.

Elements containing element content

Elements that contain only other elements are said to have element content. An element that only contains one or more child elements has the following syntax:

```
<!ELEMENT elementname (child_elementname)>
```

or

```
<!ELEMENT elementname (child_elementname1, …
child_elementnamen)>
```

Here, the name of the child element(s) follows the parent element name and is placed in parentheses. If there is more than one child element, all the names are sequenced within the one set of parentheses and each name is separated from the others by a comma. It is mandatory to give an element declaration for each child element listed in the parent element declaration.

It's a good idea to declare child elements in the same order as they appear in the parent element declaration, but it's not mandatory. However, if child elements are declared out of order in the DTD and a related XML document is eventually tested for validity against that DTD, the related XML document will still be valid.

You can also specify the exact order of appearance of child elements. A content model that contains more than one element name uses specific operator symbols to indicate order of appearance and frequency.

Elements containing mixed content

Elements that contain both character data and child elements are said to contain *mixed content*. A mixed content element declaration has the following syntax:

```
<!ELEMENT elementname (#PCDATA | child_elementname1 |
child_elementname2 | etc. …. )*>
```

If you want an element to contain mixed content, you must specify #PCDATA in the parentheses (to declare that the element might contain parseable data), and then add the names of all the relevant child elements permitted to appear as alternatives to data. You separate child element names with vertical lines, also called *pipes* or *pipe characters*.

Note: When you use a mixed content declaration, you can't use the operator symbols, which are available with "element content only" declarations and are inside the parentheses. You also cannot specify the number of occurrences or the order of appearance of the child elements. For these reasons, avoid mixed content declarations when possible. They are of limited use to most developers, and are commonly used only to translate simple documents into XML.

Empty elements

Empty elements do not hold content. To add a declaration for empty elements, you insert the reserved uppercase keyword `EMPTY` after the name of the element, as follows:

```
<!ELEMENT elementname EMPTY>
```

Declared empty elements function as markers to indicate that some action might take place. For example, a search might be executed on the data and, based on the presence of an empty element or based on the empty element's attributes; its parent element(s) might be selected for display or other manipulation. Exhibit 3-10 shows an example of declared empty elements.

```
<?xml version="1.0" encoding="UTF-8" standalone="no" ?>
<?xml-stylesheet type="text/css" href="contacts.css"?>
<!DOCTYPE CONTACTS SYSTEM "contacts.dtd">
<!--edited with Notepad by Student Name-->
<CONTACTS type="external">
  <SALES>
      <LASTNAME>Sleek</LASTNAME>
      <FIRSTNAME>Jim</FIRSTNAME>
      <EMAIL>JSleek@TLSales.com</EMAIL>
      <PHONE>1 800 123-4567</PHONE>
      <HEAD/>            Empty element (declared)
  </SALES>
  <CUSTSRV>
      <LASTNAME>Nice</LASTNAME>
      <FIRSTNAME>Nancy</FIRSTNAME>
      <EMAIL>NNice@TLSales.com</EMAIL>
      <PHONE>1 800 123-8900</PHONE>
      <HEAD/>            Empty element (declared)
  </CUSTSRV>
</CONTACTS>
```

Exhibit 3-10: Declared empty elements

Exhibit 3-10 shows that Mr. Sleek and Ms. Nice have been designated as the heads of their departments by the insertion of the empty `<HEAD/>` tag. Later, the application might search for and list the company's department heads. The document would not be valid unless the DTD contains the following empty element declaration:

```
<!ELEMENT HEAD EMPTY>
```

Although these elements do not hold any actual content, you can still assign attributes to them.

Elements with no content restrictions

An ANY declaration indicates to an XML validator that it doesn't have to perform a check on the specified element's content. There are no content restrictions on these elements. You declare elements with any content as follows:

```
<!ELEMENT elementname ANY>
```

Use this specification when you are building and testing an XML vocabulary or document. You can save time and processor resources when content doesn't need to be validated all the time.

Note: Avoid using the ANY element declaration in a production environment because it disables all content checking for its element.

Operators used with element content

A content model that contains more than one element name uses specific operator symbols to indicate appearance, order, and frequency. These operators include the comma (,), the vertical line (|), the question mark (?), the plus sign (+), and the asterisk (*). You can use these symbols singly or in combination. When using elements in combination, use parentheses to nest them.

The comma

You can use the comma to specify a desired sequence of child elements. It also serves as an "and" operator. The use of a comma in an element content declaration is shown in the following example:

```
<!ELEMENT FAMILY (MOM, DAD, ELDER_CHILD, YOUNGER_CHILD)>
```

The literal translation of this syntax is: "There is an element named <FAMILY> that consists of one element named <MOM>, one element named <DAD>, one element named <ELDER_CHILD>, and one element named <YOUNGER_CHILD>, in that order."

The pipe character

You can use the vertical line, or the pipe, to specify a list of candidate child elements. When the element appears in the respective XML document(s), only one of those child elements can appear within the parent element. Thus, the pipe also serves as an "or" operator, as shown in the following example:

```
<!ELEMENT TROUBLE (ELDER_CHILD | YOUNGER_CHILD)>
```

The literal translation is: "There is an element named <TROUBLE> that consists of either an element named <ELDER_CHILD> or an element named <YOUNGER_CHILD>."

The question mark

To specify a child element as optional, you use a question mark. A question mark is used in the following example:

```
<!ELEMENT MORE_TROUBLE (DOG?)>
```

The literal translation is: "There is an element named <MORE_TROUBLE> that might or might not contain an element named <DOG>."

The plus sign

You use the plus sign to specify that at least one (i.e., not zero) of the child element(s) is essential. However, there is no restriction on the number of times that any of the specified child elements can appear within the parent element in the XML document. There is also no restriction on the order of their appearance. The plus sign is used in the following example:

```
<!ELEMENT ON_SALE (CHEVY | FORD | NISSAN | VW)+>
```

The literal translation is: "There is an element named `<ON_SALE>` that contains at least one `<CHEVY>, <FORD>, <NISSAN>`, and/or `<VW>`." The child elements within the `<ON_SALE>` element, could be just one `<VW>`, or a collection like `<CHEVY> <VW> <CHEVY> <FORD> <NISSAN> <VW> <FORD> <NISSAN> <NISSAN>`, or more.

The asterisk

You use the asterisk to specify that zero or more of the child element(s) might appear. There is no maximum or minimum. The asterisk is used in the following example:

```
<!ELEMENT ON_SALE (#PCDATA | CHEVY | FORD | NISSAN | VW)*>
```

You might recognize this as an example of the mixed content element declaration. Its literal translation is: "There is an element named `<ON_SALE>` that might or might not contain a child element. If it does, then the child element is parsed character data interspersed with one or more `<CHEVY>, <FORD>, <NISSAN>`, or `<VW>` child element(s)." Thus, there might not be any child elements in the `<ON_SALE>` parent, or there might be just one `<VW>`, or there could be a collection like `<CHEVY> <VW> <CHEVY> <FORD> <NISSAN> <VW> <FORD> <NISSAN> <NISSAN>`, or more. There might be some character data by itself, or there might be character data combined with one or more of the `<CHEVY>, <FORD>, <NISSAN>, or <VW>` child elements.

Complex declarations

Element declarations can be complex. Imagine that you're designing an order form for TLSales that looks like Exhibit 3-11.

TLSales, Inc.

Order

No. xxxxxx-xxxxx-xxx

Customer Name
Street Address
City State Country Zip
Phone Contact Name email

Order taken by Date

Part No. or Description	Each	Qty	Disc	Total-BTax	Tax	Total-ATax
			Totals			

Order filled by Date
Carrier Shipping Date
Comments

Exhibit 3-11: Complex declaration – an order form

This example focuses on the middle section of the order form; the one that describes the item(s) being ordered. Notice that several pieces of information are needed per item (consider an item to be equivalent to the completion of one row of the tabulation in the middle of the order form) for the order to be processed. The corresponding section of the related XML document is shown in Exhibit 3-12. It is referred to as a draft simply because its DTD has not yet been developed; this example is intended to give some insight into one aspect of its design.

The middle portion of Exhibit 3-12 shows how the `<ITEM>` element and its child elements might appear after an item has been properly ordered. All the item information from the form will be inserted into the `<ITEM>` element and its child elements.

Also note that there's information that does not appear on the form itself, but that has been obtained by the TLSales staff member who took the order. This information helps TLSales to better fill the order. The `<ITEM>` element and all its child elements—even ones with information that does not appear on the physical order form—are given here. This also helps the author of the DTD to create the appropriate declarations for the various elements.

```
<ORDER>
        <ODR_NO>123456-78901-234</ODR_NO>
         <CUSTOMER>
                <NAME>Acme, Inc. </NAME>
                <ST_ADDR>123 Any Dr. </ST_ADDR>
                <CITY>MyTown</CITY>
                <STATE>MO</STATE>
                <COUNTRY>USA</COUNTRY>
                <ZIP_CODE>644444-444</ZIP_CODE>
                <PHONE>613-555-1213</PHONE>
                <CT_NAME>B. Jones</CT_NAME>
                <EMAIL>bjones@acme477.com</EMAIL>
         </CUSTOMER>
         <ITEM>
                <DATE>03-21-03</DATE>
                <ODR_TKR> D.Wilson</ODR_TKR>
                <DESC>
                        <PT_NO>7746-56-34-23</PT_NO>
                </DESC>
                <EACH>12.99</EACH>
                <QTY>2</QTY>
                <DISCOUNT>10</DISCOUNT>
                <TTL-BTAX>23.38</TTL-BTAX>
                <TX_ST>08</TX_ST>
                <TTL-ATAX>25.26</TTL-ATAX>
                <RUSH/>
                <NOTE>Stainless steel. Net 30 days</NOTE>
            </ITEM>
   .
   .
   .
</ORDER>
```

Exhibit 3-12: Sample data in the order form's XML document

Drawing upon the information in the following table, as well as the order form itself plus the draft <ITEM> element and child elements, the DTD author might create a declaration for the <ITEM> element that resembles Exhibit 3-13.

Element	Description	Other specifications
<ITEM>	One or more items ordered by entry on order form	The parent element, consisting of several child elements; at least one of these elements must appear.
<DATE>	Date of order	Mandatory; must appear.
<ODR-TKR>	Name of staff member who took order (i.e., filled in order form)	Mandatory.
<DESC>	Description of item being ordered	Mandatory; mixed content: contains character data or PT_NO element.
<EACH>	Price of each item	Mandatory.
<PT_NO>	Part number corresponding to item	One of the optional inputs for the <DESC> element.
<QTY>	Number of items being ordered	Mandatory.
<DISCOUNT>	Amount of discount from regular price	Optional; percentage of regular price.
<TTL-BTAX>	Total cost before taxes are applied	Mandatory.
<TX-ST>	State tax applied against item	Might or might not be applied; percentage of regular price.
<TX-OTHER>	Other taxes applied against item	Might or might not be applied; percentage of regular price.
<TTL-ATAX>	Total cost after taxes are applied	Mandatory.
<RUSH>	Indicates whether delivery of item should be expedited (i.e., ASAP)	Empty element; optional.
<NOTE>	Any special notes or instruction (e.g., specifications, billing, features, etc.)	Zero or more might be inserted.

The notations in Exhibit 3-13 indicate how the declaration addresses the descriptions and specifications. The <ITEM> element is an example of a complex element declaration. As a content model, it contains several of the content types (e.g., mixed, element) and element content operators (the asterisk, the plus sign, the question mark, etc.).

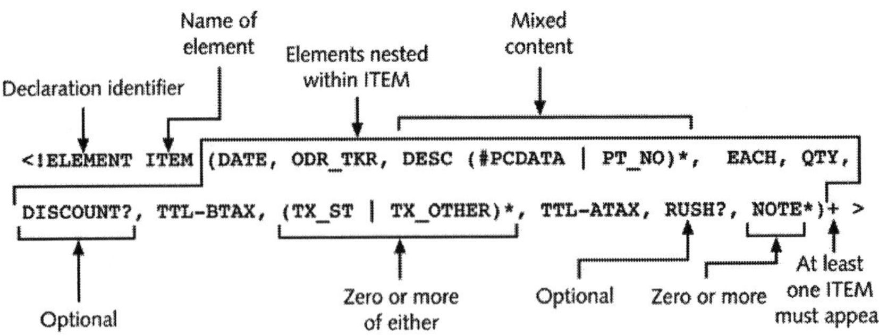

Exhibit 3-13: Order form – DTD declaration

Do it!

B-2: Creating a content model

Here's how	Here's why
1 Replace the default root element text with the name **Company**	(In company.dtd.) To create the content model.
Add the following child elements **(Name, Department+)**	The company will have only one name, but it can have one or more departments. The + (plus sign) following the `Department` child element denotes a cardinality of one-or-more. The cardinality refers to the number of times a child element can appear within a parent element, meaning that a company can have one-or-more departments. By default, the cardinality of a child element is one-and-only-one.
	The root element should now appear as follows:

```
<!ELEMENT Company (Name, Department+)>
```

Here's how	Here's why
2 On the line below the Company element, type:	To add the Name element. This element is declared as containing parseable character data and will be used to represent simple names. Note the relationship between the Company and Name elements—the Name element is a child of the Company element.

```
<!ELEMENT Name (#PCDATA)>
```

3 On the line below the Name element, type:

```
<!ELEMENT Department (Name, Employee*)>
```

Here's how	Here's why
	To declare a Department element. Note that Department also has a Name child element. The Name child elements of both Company and Department refer to the same declaration. In this example, a department can have zero or more staff. The * (asterisk) indicates a cardinality of zero-or-more.
4 On the line below the Department element, type:	To declare an employee element.

```
<!ELEMENT Employee (FirstName, LastName, EmpID)>
```

5 On the next line, type:

```
<!ELEMENT FirstName (#PCDATA)>
<!ELEMENT LastName (#PCDATA)>
<!ELEMENT EmpID (#PCDATA)>
```

To add child elements of Employee. The code should now appear as follows:

```
<?xml version="1.0" encoding="UTF-8"?>
<!-- edited with XMLSPY v2004 rel. 2 U
(http://www.xmlspy.com) by [your name] -->
<!ELEMENT Company (Name, Department+)>
<!ELEMENT Name (#PCDATA)>
<!ELEMENT Department (Name, Employee*)>
<!ELEMENT Employee (FirstName, LastName, EmpID)>
<!ELEMENT FirstName (#PCDATA)>
<!ELEMENT LastName (#PCDATA)>
<!ELEMENT EmpID (#PCDATA)>
```

6 Save your changes

Attribute list declarations

Explanation

Although you can freely add attributes to your XML vocabularies and documents, those vocabularies and documents are not valid unless their attributes also have been defined in the respective DTDs. Attributes are defined in DTDs by attribute list declarations.

Syntax for attribute list declarations in a DTD

Exhibit 3-14 shows the basic syntax of an attribute list declaration (ATTLIST).

Reserved keyword (uppercase only)

```
<!ATTLIST elementname
      attributename1 att_type defaultvalue1
      attributename2 att_type defaultvalue2
      . . .
      . . .
      attributenamen att_type defaultvaluen>
```

Start indicator

End indicator

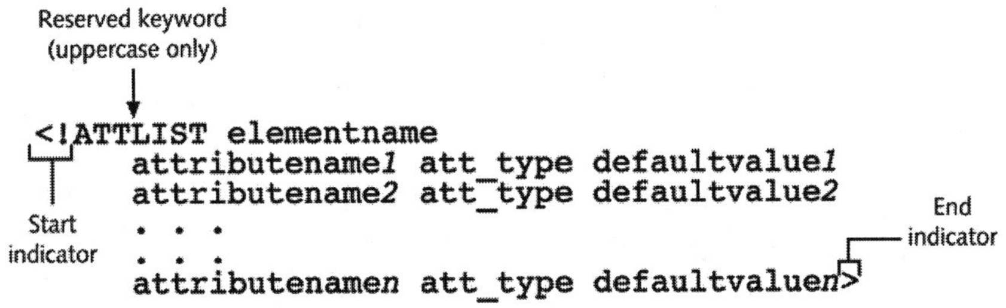

Exhibit 3-14: ATTLIST declaration syntax

Here's a simple one-attribute example of an attribute list declaration:

```
<!ATTLIST CONTACTS type CDATA #REQUIRED>
```

Each attribute list declaration identifies an element that has attributes, and then describes the nature of the attributes for that element. In this example, the element is named `<CONTACTS>`, the name of its attribute is type, the type of values the attributes might hold is `CDATA`, and the default value for the attribute is `#REQUIRED`.

By definition, `#REQUIRED` indicates that no default value exists. During initial processing, the XML parser reads this attribute specification and passes the specification data along to the application.

Attribute types and default values

In the previous example, the type of attribute was specified as `CDATA`, which is one of XML's ten possible attribute types. The following table lists these 10 attributes:

Attribute type	Description
CDATA	The attribute's value is a simple character string. Any text is permitted except that which is used for markup, such as <, “, or &, for example. (For them, use the <, ", and & entity references, respectively.) This use of CDATA is not to be confused with the entity-related concept called CDATA sections.

ENTITY	The attribute's value must be the name of a single entity. The entity must be declared in the DTD. For example:
	
	`<!ATTLIST warning symbol ENTITY #IMPLIED>`
	`<!ENTITY skullxbones SYSTEM "images/poison.jpg">`
	`<warning symbol="skullxbones">`

ENTITIES	The attribute's value might be multiple entity names, separated by white space.

Attribute type	Description
ID	The attribute's value is a proper, unique XML name (a unique identifier). All of the ID values used in a document must be different. IDs uniquely identify individual elements in a document. Elements can have only a single ID attribute. For example: <!ATTLIST CUST cust_no ID #REQUIRED> <CUST cust_no="20021031-37">
IDREF	The attribute's value must be the value of a single ID attribute on some element in the document, usually an element to which the current element is related. For example: <!ATTLIST EMPLOYEE empl_no ID #REQUIRED dept_no IDREF #IMPLIED> allows <EMPLOYEE empl_no = "20021345"> and <EMPLOYEE empl_no = "20021447" dept_no = "200114">
IDREFS	The attribute's value might contain multiple IDREF values, separated by white space.
List of names (*enumerated*)	The attribute's value must be taken from a specific list of names. This is also called because the possible values are all explicitly enumerated in the declaration. For example: contractor= (YES | NO) Alternatively, you can specify that the names must match a notation name.
NMTOKEN	Name token attributes are a restricted form of string attribute (they begin with a letter). In general, an NMTOKEN attribute must consist of a single word or string with no white spaces within it, but there are no additional constraints on the word. It doesn't have to match another attribute or declaration. For example: company="Thomson."
NMTOKENS	The attribute's value might contain multiple NMTOKEN values, separated by white space. For example: company="Thomson Learning."
NOTATION	Consists of a sequence of name tokens, but matches one or more notation types (instructions for processing formatted or non-XML data).

The following table describes four possible default value specifications for attributes:

Default value	Explanation
#REQUIRED	The attribute must have an explicitly specified value for every occurrence of the element in the document.
#IMPLIED	The attribute value is not desired, and no default value is provided. The user might supply one if they choose to do so. If a value is not specified, the XML processor must proceed without one.
value	Any legal value can be specified as the attribute's default. The attribute value is not required for each occurrence of the element in the document. If a value is not specified explicitly, then the attribute for this element is given the specified default value.
#FIXED *value*	An attribute declaration might specify that an attribute has a fixed value. In this case, the attribute is not desired, but if it occurs, it must have that specified value. If it is not present, the element is treated as though it has specified default value for that particular attribute.

The description of the `#REQUIRED` default value indicates that whenever the element `<CONTACTS>` appears, a value for the attribute named type must be specified. In the example, the type attribute in `<CONTACTS>` was given the value "external." It is presumed that, at some point in the application, there is a need for a list of TLSales.com staff members whose contact information can be made available to the public (that is, externally). The `<CONTACTS>` element and its attribute specification `type="external"` is used at that point.

Handling white space

You can use white space (i.e., spaces, tabs, carriage returns, and blank lines) to organize a document and improve legibility. Consider the following code:

```
<contacts type="external">
<sales>
<lastname>Sleek</lastname>
<firstname>Jim</firstname>
<email>JSleek@TLSales.com</email>
<phone>1 800 555-4567</phone>
<head/>
</sales>
</contacts>
```

By default, the XML parser will not preserve the white space (in this case, line breaks after each closing tag). However, it might be important to preserve white space for some documents (e.g., performance scripts, meeting minute translations, long product descriptions, poetry and song writing, etc.). In cases like this, where "significant" white space must be preserved in the delivered version of the document, you can use a special attribute named `xml:space`, as follows:

```
<TITLE xml:space="preserve">The Congo</TITLE>
```

There are two possible values for `xml:space`; `default` and `preserve`. In a DTD, the `XML:space` attribute must be declared as an "enumerated" type with only those two values as choices. Generally, white space is considered significant in mixed content (the interspersing of text with elements) and is insignificant in element content.

Finally, with respect to white space in parsed text, XML processors need to normalize all end-of-line markers to a single-line feed character (`&#A;`). This can eliminate some cross-platform portability issues.

Language identification

Many document processing applications (for example, Web browsers) can benefit from information about the natural language in which the content and attributes of a document are written. XML provides the attribute `XML:lang` to specify the language, by using the values as:

- The two-letter language codes found in ISO 639, titled "Code for the representation of the names of languages"
- Language identifiers registered with the Internet Assigned Numbers Authority (IANA), listed in Request for Comments 1766, and found at http://www.ietf.org/rfc/rfc1766.txt.
- Language identifiers of your own design, as long as the identifiers begin with "x-" or "X-"

For example:

```
<MERCH_US xml:lang="EN-US">Green shirts</MERCH_US>
```

or

```
<PRODUCTS_FRANCE xml:lang="fr">Chemisesverts</PRODUCTS_FRANCE>
```

Note the inclusion of the two-letter language subcode "US" with the language code "EN" in the first example. For some languages, there are dialect or regional dialect subcodes available. This example specifies American English.

Attribute value normalization

The XML processor performs all attribute value normalization on attribute values. The referenced character(s) replace their respective references, and both entity references and white space are resolved.

Do it!

B-3: Adding attribute list declarations

Here's how	Here's why
1 From the DTD, delete **<!ELEMENT EmpID (#PCDATA)>**	(In company.dtd.) To convert the EmpID element into an attribute of Employee.
Delete the **EmpID** child element from the Employee declaration's element list	
2 On a line below the Employee element, type the following code:	

```
<!ATTLIST Employee EmpID ID #REQUIRED>
```

Here's how	Here's why
	To add an attribute specification to the Employee element. The employee ID attribute, EmpID, is now defined as a required and unique attribute of Employee. Every Employee must have a unique EmpID value within an XML document using this DTD.
	The Employee element and attribute should appear as follows:

```
<!ELEMENT Employee (FirstName, LastName)>
<!ATTLIST Employee EmpID ID #REQUIRED>
```

Here's how	Here's why
3 At the end of the child element list for the Employee element, type **(PartTime | FullTime)**	To add a choice element.
The element declaration should appear as follows:	

```
<!ELEMENT Employee (FirstName, LastName, (PartTime |
FullTime))>
```

4 At the end of the DTD, type:

```
<!ELEMENT PartTime EMPTY>
<!ATTLIST PartTime HourlyRate CDATA "$9.75">
```

Here's how	Here's why
	To add the PartTime element and its attribute. Note that the PartTime element is an empty element; it has neither child elements nor parsed character data (#PCDATA). It has one attribute, HourlyRate, which has a default value equal to a hypothetical minimum wage. If the HourlyRate attribute is omitted in an XML document, the validating parser will automatically add the attribute with the default value "$9.75."

5 After the PartTime attribute list, type:

```
<!ELEMENT FullTime (StockOptionGrant*)>
<!ATTLIST FullTime Salary CDATA #REQUIRED BenefitPkg (Tier1
| Tier2 | Tier3) "Tier1">
<!ELEMENT StockOptionGrant EMPTY>
<!ATTLIST StockOptionGrant TotalOptions CDATA #REQUIRED
StrikePrice CDATA #REQUIRED>
```

To add the FullTime element. Note that the FullTime element has a single child element and two attributes. The asterisk in the declaration of FullTime indicates that the element may contain zero or more StockOptionGrant child elements. Also note that the second attribute, BenefitPkg, restricts the possible values to a selection within the enumerated list, and declares a default value of "Tier1."

The DTD should now appear as follows:

```
<?xml version="1.0" encoding="UTF-8"?>
<!-- edited with XML Spy v5 rel. 4 U (http://www.xmlspy.com)
by [your name] -->
<!ELEMENT Company (Name, Department+)>
<!ELEMENT Name (#PCDATA)>
<!ELEMENT Department (Name, Employee*)>
<!ELEMENT Employee (FirstName, LastName, (PartTime |►
FullTime))>
<!ATTLIST Employee EmpID ID #REQUIRED>
<!ELEMENT FirstName (#PCDATA)>
<!ELEMENT LastName (#PCDATA)>
<!ELEMENT PartTime EMPTY>
<!ATTLIST PartTime HourlyRate CDATA "$9.75">
<!ELEMENT FullTime (StockOptionGrants*)>
<!ATTLIST FullTime Salary CDATA #REQUIRED BenefitPkg (Tier1►
| Tier2 | Tier3) "Tier1">
<!ELEMENT StockOptionGrants EMPTY>
<!ATTLIST StockOptionGrants TotalOptions CDATA #REQUIRED►
StrikePrice CDATA #REQUIRED>
```

6 Save your changes

Entity declarations

Explanation

Entities are defined as storage units that hold strings or blocks of parsed data such as text entities, and unparsed data such as graphics, audio files, or video files, among others. Entities are DTD and content management tools. All entities used in an XML language or document must first be defined with an entity declaration in an internal or external DTD. The *entity declaration* specifies a name for the entity and defines what the entity represents (a string of text or an external file, etc.).

General entities are references that are expanded by the parser and then passed along to the application. The following example is a general internal entity representing a specific date:

```
<!ENTITY DATE "January 1, 2003">
```

The next example is a general external entity representing a file that contains a graphic:

```
<!ENTITY PIX SYSTEM "picture04.tif">
```

You can use the entity references, in the form `&entity name;`, as content between the tags in an element in the XML document. The following example shows how each of these entities might be referred to in their respective XML documents:

```
<NEW_FISC_YR>&DATE;</NEW_FISC_YR>
<FIGURE04>&PIX;</FIGURE04>
```

Parameter entities are different from general entities and are not used within the XML documents or languages. They are used only in the DTDs for those documents or languages. Their declaration syntax is similar to that for general entity declarations, but their syntax is also reminiscent of the syntax for attribute type specifications. Exhibit 3-15 shows typical declaration syntax.

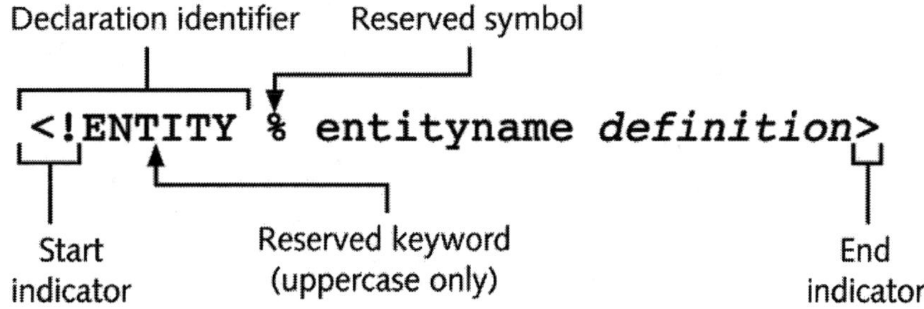

Exhibit 3-15: Parameter entity declaration syntax

To use the parameter entity reference, insert `% entityname;` into an element declaration, as shown here:

```
<!ELEMENT % ENTITYNAME;>
```

The parameter entity references are expanded as the XML processor reviews the DTD. In this way, the data contained in the entity itself is brought into the process as the XML document or language is being validated and not later, when the XML processor passes the document to the application (as is the case with general entities).

Internal parameter entities

Exhibit 3-16 and Exhibit 3-17 show the application of an internal parameter entity. In Exhibit 3-16, the `<SALES>` and `<CUSTSRV>` elements are composed of the same child elements: `<LASTNAME>`, `<FIRSTNAME>`, `<EMAIL>`, and `<PHONE>`. The element declarations are also identical: only one of each of these elements occurs, and they occur in the same order in both `<SALES>` and `<CUSTSRV>`. This is an ideal situation in which to use a parameter entity reference.

Prolog

Internal DTD

Document type declaration

```
<?xml version="1.0" encoding="UTF-8" standalone="yes"?>
<?xml-stylesheet type="text/css" href="contacts.css"?>
<!DOCTYPE CONTACTS [
<!ELEMENT CONTACTS (SALES, CUSTSRV)*>
<!ELEMENT SALES (LASTNAME, FIRSTNAME, EMAIL, PHONE)>
<!ELEMENT CUSTSRV (LASTNAME, FIRSTNAME, EMAIL,
PHONE)>
<!ELEMENT LASTNAME (#PCDATA)>
<!ELEMENT FIRSTNAME (#PCDATA)>
<!ELEMENT EMAIL (#PCDATA)>
<!ELEMENT PHONE (#PCDATA)>
]>
<!--edited with Notepad by Student Name-->
<CONTACTS>
        <SALES>
                <LASTNAME>Sleek</LASTNAME>
                <FIRSTNAME>Jim</FIRSTNAME>
                <EMAIL>JSleek@TLSales.com</EMAIL>
                <PHONE>1 800 123-4567</PHONE>
        </SALES>
        <CUSTSRV>
                <LASTNAME>Nice</LASTNAME>
                <FIRSTNAME>Nancy</FIRSTNAME>
                <EMAIL>NNice@TLSales.com</EMAIL>
                <PHONE>1 800 123-8900</PHONE>
        </CUSTSRV>
</CONTACTS>
```

Exhibit 3-16: Before use of internal parameter entity

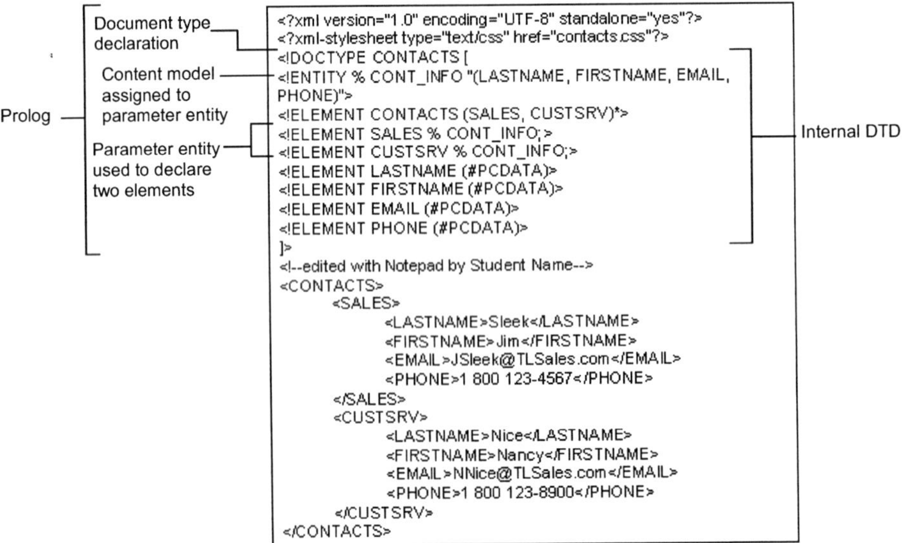


```
<?xml version="1.0" encoding="UTF-8" standalone="yes"?>
<?xml-stylesheet type="text/css" href="contacts.css"?>
<!DOCTYPE CONTACTS [
<!ENTITY % CONT_INFO "(LASTNAME, FIRSTNAME, EMAIL,
PHONE)">
<!ELEMENT CONTACTS (SALES, CUSTSRV)*>
<!ELEMENT SALES % CONT_INFO;>
<!ELEMENT CUSTSRV % CONT_INFO;>
<!ELEMENT LASTNAME (#PCDATA)>
<!ELEMENT FIRSTNAME (#PCDATA)>
<!ELEMENT EMAIL (#PCDATA)>
<!ELEMENT PHONE (#PCDATA)>
]>
<!--edited with Notepad by Student Name-->
<CONTACTS>
        <SALES>
                <LASTNAME>Sleek</LASTNAME>
                <FIRSTNAME>Jim</FIRSTNAME>
                <EMAIL>JSleek@TLSales.com</EMAIL>
                <PHONE>1 800 123-4567</PHONE>
        </SALES>
        <CUSTSRV>
                <LASTNAME>Nice</LASTNAME>
                <FIRSTNAME>Nancy</FIRSTNAME>
                <EMAIL>NNice@TLSales.com</EMAIL>
                <PHONE>1 800 123-8900</PHONE>
        </CUSTSRV>
</CONTACTS>
```

Exhibit 3-17: After insertion of internal parameter entity

In the "After" scenario, shown in Exhibit 3-17, a parameter entity called `CONT_INFO` is declared to be composed of references to the `<LASTNAME>`, `<FIRSTNAME>`, `<EMAIL>`, and `<PHONE>` elements. Later, the declarations of `<SALES>` and `<CUSTSRV>` include the parameter entity `CONT_INFO`.

One of the distinct advantages of using parameter entity references is that you do not need to repeat a number of similar element declarations. Also, if a number of parameter entities have been created for your elements and those entities are not satisfactory or you want to experiment, then you only need to modify the parameter entities or create new ones. You don't have to alter the original elements themselves.

External parameter entities

In a manner similar to the internal parameter entity, parameter entities can be added to external DTDs wherever they are: in the same directory as the XML document, in a private DTD at another Web site, or in a public DTD at another Web site. The advantages listed for internal parameter entities are multiplied if you are using external DTDs, especially if several XML documents access each DTD. Another use of the external parameter entity is to use it to reference public standards, like the W3C's XHTML 1.0 transitional DTD, and then to combine it with the some of your own elements.

In the respective DTD, add the following entity declaration:

```
<!ENTITY % XHTML1-trans-DTD PUBLIC "-//W3C//DTD XHTML 1.0
Transitional//EN" SYSTEM
"http://www.w3.org/TR/xhtml1/DTD/xhtml1-transitional.dtd">
```

After this reference is inserted, you only need to refer to it by its parameter entity name "`%XHTML1-trans-DTD;`" in the DTD.

Notation declarations

XML handles unparsed data, or non-XML data, such as audio, video, other graphics, etc., by using *notation declarations*. Notation declarations apply labels to specific types of non-parsed binary data, but they can also play a role with text data, too. You can use notation declarations to label text data that has specific formats (for example, date formats). After being labeled, the data can be passed directly to the application that processes it according to its coded instructions. A typical notation declaration is shown in Exhibit 3-18.

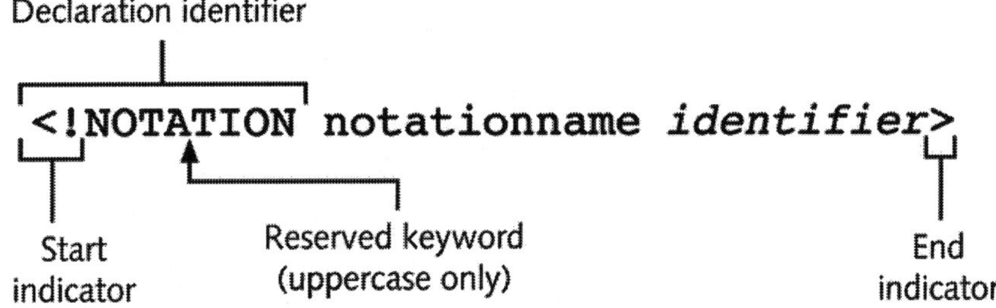

Exhibit 3-18: Notation declaration syntax

Whatever takes the place of the generic term "identifier" in Exhibit 3-18 is presumed to mean something to the application. If these notation declarations are to be used, then it is up to the application developers to communicate what the application interprets and uses.

The declaration syntax creates a label that's used in conjunction with attribute or unparsed external entity declarations. Unparsed entities import non-parsed data. The declaration syntax for such unparsed entities is shown in Exhibit 3-19.

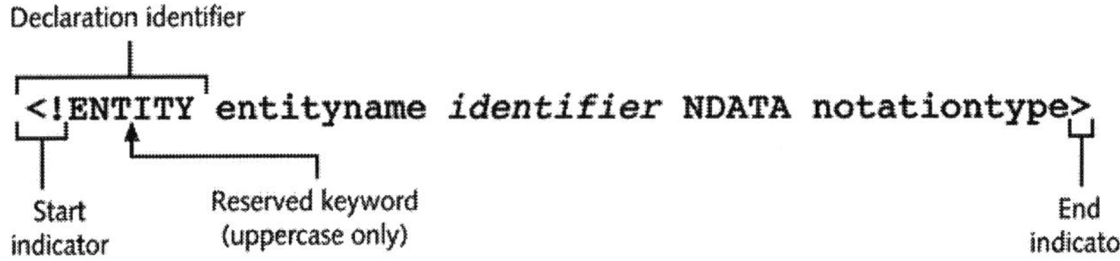

Exhibit 3-19: Unparsed entity declaration syntax

The following scenario includes some video MPEG footage from an association awards dinner. In the example, a notation type named `MPEG` is declared, by using its MIME type (video/MPEG) as its identifier. There is a declared empty element named `<VIDEO>` that has an attribute called "location." Location's value, `ASSOCIATION,` is the name of an entity. The unparsed entity `ASSOCIATION` references the video file, which, in turn is passed to the `VIDEO` element within the parent element `AWARDS` in the XML document proper.

```
<!DOCUMENT AWARDS [
<!ELEMENT AWARDS ANY>
<!ELEMENT VIDEO EMPTY>
<!ATTLIST VIDEO location ENTITY #REQUIRED>
<!NOTATION MPEG SYSTEM "video/mpeg">
<!ENTITY ASSOCIATION "videos/assoc_award.mpg" NDATA MPEG>
]>
<AWARDS>
<VIDEO location="ASSOCIATION"/>
</AWARDS>
```

Here, the processor interprets the empty `VIDEO` element and finds the entity named `ASSOCIATION` as the value of the `location` attribute. The processor then recognizes that the `ASSOCIATION` entity is to remain unparsed because of the `NDATA` keyword. So the processor passes the file `assoc_award.mpeg` to the application for processing. If the application was not built to process this data:

- An error might result.
- The user might be prompted by the application (presumably asking the user what they want done with the file).
- The application might ignore the file and continue.
- The application might "hang" (worst case scenario).

Do it!

B-4: Discussing entity and notation declarations

Exercises

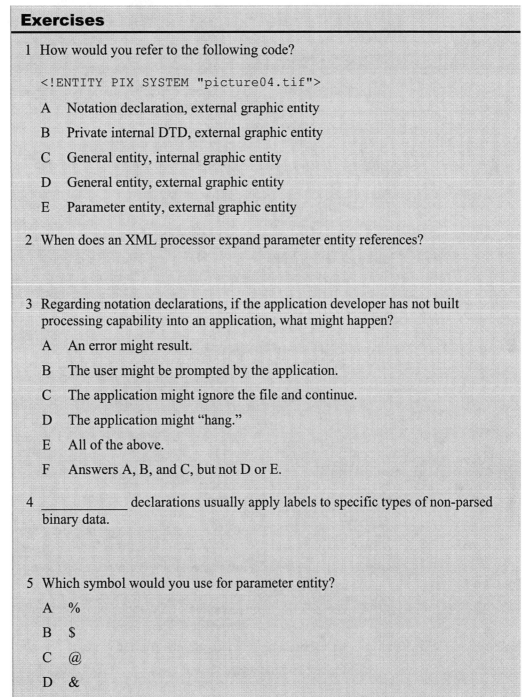

1 How would you refer to the following code?

```
<!ENTITY PIX SYSTEM "picture04.tif">
```

A Notation declaration, external graphic entity

B Private internal DTD, external graphic entity

C General entity, internal graphic entity

D General entity, external graphic entity

E Parameter entity, external graphic entity

2 When does an XML processor expand parameter entity references?

3 Regarding notation declarations, if the application developer has not built processing capability into an application, what might happen?

A An error might result.

B The user might be prompted by the application.

C The application might ignore the file and continue.

D The application might “hang.”

E All of the above.

F Answers A, B, and C, but not D or E.

4 ___________ declarations usually apply labels to specific types of non-parsed binary data.

5 Which symbol would you use for parameter entity?

A %

B $

C @

D &

DTDs and namespace declarations

Explanation

Exhibit 3-20 shows two versions of the contacts.xml document. In the top document, the `<CONTACTS>` element contains an `xmlns="http://www.TLSales.com/dtds/"` attribute. In the bottom document, the equivalent element is named `<ns:CONTACTS ...>` and contains an `xmlns:ns="http://www.TLSales.com/dtds/"` attribute. These attributes are called *namespace declarations*. The `xmlns` portion states this is an XML namespace declaration. Such declarations indicate to the XML parser that the elements in their respective documents conform to the specifications in the W3C's Namespaces in XML Recommendation. In the version of contacts.xml at the top of the following exhibit is called a default namespace declaration. The one in the lower document is called a *prefix namespace declaration* (note the prefix "ns").

```
<?xml version="1.0" encoding="UTF-8" standalone="no"?>
<?xml-stylesheet type="text/css" href="contacts.css" ?>
<!DOCTYPE contacts SYSTEM "contacts.dtd">
<!--edited with Notepad by Student Name-->
<CONTACTS xmlns= "http://www.TLSales.com/dtds/">
  <SALES>
       <NAME>Jim Sleek</NAME>
       <EMAIL>JSleek@TLSales.com</EMAIL>
       <PHONE>1 800 123-4567</PHONE>
       <HEAD/>
  </SALES>
  <CUSTSRV>
       <NAME>Nancy Nice</NAME>
       <EMAIL>NNice@TLSales.com</EMAIL>
       <PHONE>1 800 123-8900</PHONE>
       <HEAD/>
  </CUSTSRV>
</CONTACTS>
```

Default Namespace

```
<?xml version="1.0" encoding="UTF-8" standalone="no"?>
<?xml-stylesheet type="text/css" href="contacts.css" ?>
<!DOCTYPE contacts SYSTEM "contacts.dtd">
<!--edited with Notepad by Student Name-->
<ns:CONTACTS xmlns:ns="http://www.TLSales.com/dtds/">
  <ns:SALES>
       <ns:NAME>Jim Sleek</ns:NAME>
       <ns:EMAIL>JSleek@TLSales.com</ns:EMAIL>
       <ns:PHONE>1 800 123-4567</ns:PHONE>
       <ns:HEAD/>
  </ns:SALES>
  <ns:CUSTSRV>
       <ns:NAME>Nancy Nice</ns:NAME>
       <ns:EMAIL>NNice@TLSales.com</ns:EMAIL>
       <ns:PHONE>1 800 123-8900</ns:PHONE>
       <ns:HEAD/>
  </ns:CUSTSRV>
</ns:CONTACTS>
```

Prefix Namespace

Exhibit 3-20: Namespaces in DTDs

Namespace declarations overcome the need to creating unique names for datatypes with similar functions. They become necessary when you have to differentiate between similar names in the DTDs and the related documents (i.e., when you want to avoid "name collisions").

For example, in Exhibit 3-20, there is a `<NAME>` element nested within each of the `<SALES>` and `<CUSTSRV>` elements. However, if there were a need to use an element name like `<NAME>` elsewhere in contacts.xml to differentiate a department, division, or location, for example, you would have to use another unique name, like `<DEPT_NAME>`. By using namespace declarations, you can use `<NAME>` again, provided it has a unique prefix attached to it, for example, `<dpt:NAME>`.

Note: You can't use prefixes that begin with xml, XML, xMl, or any such combination. Such prefixes are reserved for use by XML and XML-related specifications.

Do not be confused by references to URLs in namespace declarations. A namespace is not really a physical device or location, but a logical device that only represents a collection of declarations for elements and components. Thus, that collection is represented by a unique name, which takes the form of a *Uniform Resource Identifier* (URI). The term URI is a generic term for all types of names and addresses for objects on the World Wide Web. The namespace name is actually a uniform resource locator (URL), which you might recognize as the address of a document or resource on the Web.

URLs are one form of URI. When a namespace with a URL is processed, browsers or other applications don't actually access the URLs. The URL simply adds uniqueness to the datatype names. The W3C Recommendation titled "Namespaces in XML" recommends the use of URLs as namespace names because URLs indicate domain names that are recognized as being functional across the Internet.

The scope of every namespace declaration is restricted to the element for which it is declared. In the Exhibit 3-20 examples, the namespace has been declared in the root `<CONTACTS>` element, so it is effective throughout the document. You can declare a namespace for child elements, but in that case, the namespace is valid only for the scope of that child element and its own subelements.

Default namespace declarations

In Exhibit 3-20, the declaration within the `<CONTACTS>` start tag in the top document is called a default namespace declaration. It indicates to the XML parser that, upon encountering an element with no prefix, the declarations for those elements would, by default, be found in the DTD document at the `http://www.TLSales.com` Web site. The namespace declaration is used as a logical device only, to establish uniqueness for the element name. The uniqueness is not that evident here, though. When the parser encounters an element name that has no apparent prefix, it recognizes the element as though it has `"http://www.TLSales.com/dtds/"` appended to the name (e.g., `<NAME>` is actually `<http://www.TLSales.com/dtds/:NAME>`), which imparts the desired uniqueness.

Prefix namespace declarations

In the lower example of Exhibit 3-20, the `<ns:CONTACTS>` element contains the declaration `xmlns:ns=http://www.TLSales.com/dtds/` in its start tag. That declaration is called a *prefix namespace declaration*, and it indicates that the parser will encounter at least one element with the `ns:` prefix attached to the element's name. It also tells the parser that the respective element, attribute, entity, and other declarations for those elements can be found at `http://www.TLSales.com` in the Web site's dtds directory.

The parser will never actually access the TLSales Web site, so there is no need to install a DTD document there. In fact, there is no compulsion even to create a `www.TLSales.com` Web site. The namespace declaration is simply used as a logical device to establish uniqueness for those elements whose names begin with the prefix "ns:".When the parser encounters an element with the prefix "ns:" it will recognize that element as though it had the entire Web site URL appended to its name as a prefix—that is, `<ns:NAME>` would be treated as though it was named `<http://www.TLSales.com/dtds/:NAME>`.

In effect, the declaration has told the parser that all the elements whose names begin with `ns:` belong to the same `ns:` "club." Those elements are uniquely different from any other elements, even if those elements have the same base name. The fact they have different prefixes makes them different from one another.

As you can see, with prefix namespace declarations, the uniqueness of element names is more obvious than it was with default namespace declarations.

Declaring namespaces in the DTD

Namespace declarations are applications of attributes. They must be declared in the respective DTDs. Because default namespace declarations and prefix namespace declarations differ, their declarations in DTDs also differ.

If you are going to use more than one namespace declaration in a document, then you have to declare all the `xmlns` attributes in your DTD.

Declaring default namespaces

Creating the appropriate declarations for the default namespace attribute is straightforward. From Exhibit 3-20, you can see that the <CONTACTS> element contains two child elements: <SALES> and <CUSTSRV>. Within the contacts.dtd file, the declaration for the <CONTACTS> element nust be:

```
<!ELEMENT CONTACTS (SALES, CUSTSRV)* >
```

A literal translation of that declaration is: "There is an element named <CONTACTS> that contains zero or more occurrences of elements named <SALES> and/or <CUSTSRV>."

After the element declaration is in place, you have to create a declaration for the attribute in <CONTACTS>. For example:

```
<!ATTLIST ns:CONTACTS xmlns:ns CDATA #FIXED
"http://www.TLSales.com/dtds/" >
```

The literal translation of this is: "Within the scope of the element named <CONTACTS>, a default namespace attribute named "`xmlns`" is in effect. The value for that attribute contains parseable character data. The value is fixed (i.e., it does not vary), and the value is `http://www.TLSales.com/dtds/`. For <CONTACTS> and its child elements, treat their names as if the value for the default namespace was appended as a prefix to their names."

When the XML parser recognizes the `xmlns` attribute, it starts the proper subroutines to deal with it. If you're going to use more than one namespace declaration then you need to insert all of the appropriate declarations into your DTD. You need to keep track of which prefixes go with which element names, and ensure that they don't cause name collisions within the DTD.

Declaring prefix namespace attributes

Creating the appropriate declarations to set up for the prefix namespace attribute is more complex than the default namespace declaration. This time, from the lower example in Exhibit 3-20, you can see that the `<ns:CONTACTS>` element contains two child elements: `<ns:SALES>` and `<ns:CUSTSRV>`. Within the contacts.dtd file, you might find that the declaration for the `<ns:CONTACTS>` element is still:

```
<!ELEMENT CONTACTS (SALES, CUSTSRV)* >
```

The literal translation is the same as before: "There is an element named `<CONTACTS>` that contains zero or more occurrences of elements named `<SALES>` and/or `<CUSTSRV>`." Now that this element declaration is in place, you need to create a slightly different declaration for the attribute to be found within the start tag for `<ns:CONTACTS>`, as follows:

```
<!ATTLIST CONTACTS xmlns CDATA #FIXED
"http://www.TLSales.com/dtds/" >
```

The literal translation of this is: "Within the scope of the element named `<ns:CONTACTS>`, a prefix namespace attribute named "`xmlns:ns`" is in effect. The value for that attribute contains parseable character data. The value is fixed (i.e., it does not vary), and the value is `http://www.TLSales.com/dtds/`. The value for the namespace is represented by the prefix ns:. For `<CONTACTS>` and its child elements, if you encounter an element name with the prefix `ns:`, treat the names as if the value for the default namespace was appended as a prefix to the names."

If you are inserting more than one prefix namespace into a document, then you must also insert a separate attribute declaration to that effect into your DTD. So, if you wanted to add a separate namespace attribute to the `<SALES>` element, for example `<SALES xmlns:sales="http://www.TLSales.com/sales/" >`, then you would add the following code to your DTD:

```
<!ATTLIST sales:SALES xmlns:sales CDATA #FIXED
"http://www.TLSales.com/sales/">
```

The new namespace declaration is in effect for the full extent of the `<SALES>` element. The `xmlns:sales` namespace declaration eclipses the `xmlns:ns` namespace declaration. After the processor reaches the end of the `<SALES>` element (that is, after it encounters the `<CUSTSRV>` element), the `xmlns:ns` namespace declaration is in effect again.

Limitations of DTDs with respect to namespace declarations

Because the concept of DTDs predates the development of the W3C Namespaces in XML Recommendation, DTDs do not provide the same level of support for namespaces that XML schemas do. Schema specifications were developed at approximately the same time as the W3C namespace specifications, so they are more flexible and comprehensive.

Do it!

B-5: Discussing DTDs and namespace declarations

Exercises

1 Default namespace declarations cannot be used in conjunction with prefix namespace declarations. True or false?

2 The following attribute is called a ________ variable declaration.

```
xmlns="http://www.myCompany.com/dtds/"
```

3 If you are going to use more than one namespace declaration, then you have to insert all of the appropriate declarations into your DTD. True or false?

4 What kind of namespace declaration is the following?

```
xmlns:ns=http://www.cnn.com/dtds
```

A Default

B Prefix

C External

D Web

5 ________ is the correct declaration to prevent name collisions.

A Notation declaration

B Parameter declaration

C Attribute declaration

D Namespace declaration

6 Which of the following indicates that a default namespace might be in use? (Choose all that apply.)

A `<ns:NAME>`

B `xmlns="http://www.TLSales.com/dtds"`

C `<NAME>`

D `<!ATTLIST ns:SALES xmlns:ns CDATA #FIXED "http://www.TLSales.com/sales/">`

Topic C: Document analysis and testing

Explanation

During XML document development, especially during DTD or schema development, it is beneficial to go through the process of document analysis, and record the results. *Document analysis* is the process of determining the effectiveness of XML document development. The people best qualified to perform this type of analysis are the users and creators of the documents.

Guidelines for document analysis

Several document analysis sources are readily available on the Internet, in libraries, and from other sources. Analysis includes, but is not necessarily limited to:

- XML document and DTD testing for well-formedness and validity.
- Document layout analysis with respect to access, knowledge integration, and content extraction (for learning and for data/information extraction for subsequent processing).
- Structure (recognition, visualization, and representation) of all components. For example, documents, hypertext, and non-parsed components.
- Access to textual information embedded in Internet images.
- Document image processing for Internet/intranet transmission: data compression, sound/color analysis, etc.
- Authoring, editing, and presentation systems for complex multimedia documents.
- Workflow management; possible reformatting for multimodal mobile access.

You must test and check your documents and DTDs for conformance to the W3C XML Recommendation, appropriateness to their intended task(s), and compliance with guidelines obtained in consultation with your users or other clients. All results from document analysis and testing should then be kept in a hard-copy report for handy reference.

It's a good idea to test your XML DTDs and documents using at least two validating XML parsers on at least two different operating systems.

Here are some reminders regarding DTD design:

- DTDs should be designed to be flexible, reusable, and practical.
- XML DTDs must be designed to comply with the XML well-formedness and validity constraints.
- Subsequent DTD development should be based on your document analyses.
- XML DTDs themselves must be valid XML and must not use any of the additional features of SGML that are not permitted in XML.

Documentation

An XML application is not considered complete or stable until it is documented. You should provide complete and detailed documentation with every DTD suite (the XML documents, the relevant DTDs, and other referenced entities). You should design the documentation so that both XML novices and experts can use it. It should detail the syntax, proper use, and client-specific definition for each element in a DTD. You should also include additional relevant information about each element, such as probable audio/visual presentation, as comments. You should also produce documentation for all XML documents (including all their relevant DTDs) that interoperate with the subject XML document/DTD suite.

Do it!

C-1: Creating and validating an XML document

Here's how	Here's why
1 Choose **File**, **New...**	To create a new XML file.
In the list box, select **XML Document**	
Click **OK**	To open the New file dialog box.
2 Verify that **DTD** is selected	
Click **OK**	To open the XML Spy dialog box.
3 Click **Window...**	
In the Project files window, expand the **DTD/Schemas** branch	(If necessary.)
Select **company.dtd**	
Click **OK**	The fully resolved filename for company.dtd appears in the Choose a file list box.
Click **OK**	To accept it. An Enhanced Grid view of an XML document appears in the main window.
4 Choose **File**, **Save As...**	To open the Save As dialog box.
In the File name text box, enter **acme**	To specify the file name.
Click **Save**	To save the new XML document.

Step	Action	Here's why
5	Right-click the **XML Files** folder	To add the XML document to the XML Files item in the Project window.
	Choose **Add Files...**	To open the Open dialog box.
	Double-click **acme.xml**	The acme.xml document is added to the XML Files item in the Project window.
6	Choose **View**, **Text view**	To view the default XML document for acme.xml.

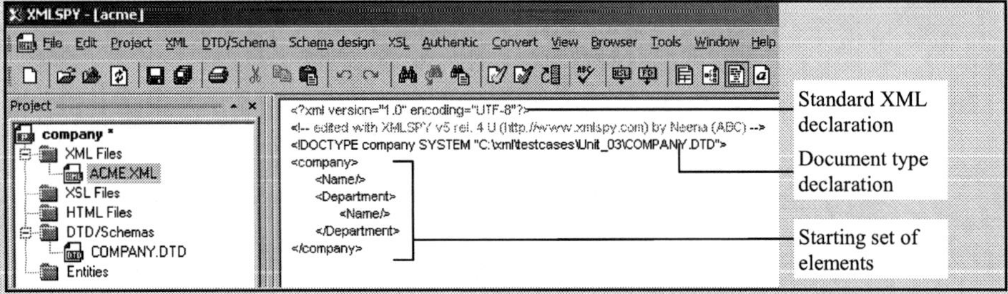

When you created the XML document, XML Spy created a default document similar to the one shown below. XML Spy has already added a number of elements to the default XML document.

The first line of the document contains the standard XML declaration with two attributes: the version and the document's language encoding. The third line is the Document Type Declaration, which provides information to the XML parser about the DTD. The first identifier following the word DOCTYPE is the root element, Company. The next identifier is SYSTEM, which denotes that the following URI references a DTD on the local system.

Step	Action	Here's why
7	Save your changes	
8	Under the Company element, replace `<Name/>` with **<Name>AcmeCo</Name>**	To add information to the XML document about company, department, and employees.
	Under the Department element, replace `<Name/>` with **<Name>IT</Name>**	

9 Under the DTD/Schemas folder in the Project window, double-click **company.dtd**	To review the company DTD. Your XML document now has a named company, and the company has a named department. Because a department can have zero (or more) employees, you should have a valid XML document.
Under XML Files in the Project window, double-click **acme.xml**	To return to the acme.xml document.
10 Choose **XML**, **Validate**	To validate the document. If the document is valid according to the company.dtd, a green check mark appears at the bottom of your main window.
If a red X appears, verify that the code reads as follows:	

```
<?xml version="1.0" encoding="UTF-8"?>
<!DOCTYPE Company SYSTEM
"C:\StudentData\<current_unit_folder>\Company.dtd">
<Company>
<Name>AcmeCo</Name>
<Department>
<Name>IT</Name>
</Department>
</Company>
```

Under the Name element inside the Department element, insert a new line and enter the following code:

```
<Employee EmpID="_001">
<FirstName>Erica</FirstName>
<LastName>Reynolds</LastName>
<PartTime/>
</Employee>
```

To add employees. This Employee has FirstName and LastName elements, and also has a PartTime element. The PartTime element is empty, but it has an attribute HourlyRate with a default value of "$9.75". A validating parser automatically includes this attribute in the element, but a non-validating parser, which does not use DTDs, will miss the default attribute value.

11 Choose **XML**, **Validate**

To validate the document. If you typed everything correctly, your document should be valid.

After the closing `</Employee>` tag, type:

To add another Employee element.

```
<Employee EmpID="_002">
<FirstName>David</FirstName>
<LastName>Campbell</LastName>
<FullTime Salary="$60,000" BenefitPkg="Tier2">
<StockOptionGrant TotalOptions="15,000" StrikePrice="$0.70">
</StockOptionGrant>
</FullTime>
</Employee>
```

12 Choose **XML**, **Validate**

Your document should appear as shown below.

```
<?xml version="1.0" encoding="UTF-8"?>
<!DOCTYPE Company SYSTEM
"C:\StudentData\<current_unit_folder>\Company.dtd">
<Company>
<Name>AcmeCo</Name>
<Department>
<Name>IT</Name>
<Employee EmpID="_001">
<FirstName>Erica</FirstName>
<LastName>Reynolds</LastName>
<PartTime/>
</Employee>
<Employee EmpID="_002">
<FirstName>David</FirstName>
<LastName>Campbell</LastName>
<FullTime Salary="$60,000" BenefitPkg="Tier2">
<StockOptionGrant TotalOptions="15,000" StrikePrice="$0.70">
</StockOptionGrant>
</FullTime>
</Employee>
</Department>
</Company>
```

Save your changes

13 Close XML Spy

Unit summary: Document type definitions (DTDs)

Topic A In this topic, you learned that **DTDs** and **schemas** facilitate XML **document modeling** by declaring a set of permissible elements, defining the content model for each element, and declaring the permitted attributes. You learned that a document might contain a stand-alone **internal DTD**; a reference to an **external DTD**; or a combination of an internal DTD plus a reference to another, external DTD. Finally, you learned how to **create a simple DTD** in XML Spy.

Topic B In this topic, you learned that a **content model** defines what an element might contain. There are several types of element content: **parsed character data**; **elements only**; **mixed content** (character data plus elements); **empty elements**; and **elements with no content restrictions.** Then, you learned about the operators used to define element content. Finally, you learned how to declare **elements**, **attributes**, **entities** and **notations** in a DTD, and you learned about **namespace declarations**.

Topic C In this topic, you learned how to undertake **document analysis** during and after the development of XML documents, DTDs, and schemas. You learned the **importance of recording the results** of your document analysis. You learned that XML documents are not considered complete or stable until they are documented. Finally, you **created and validated an XML document**.

Review questions

1 The __________ is a pattern that indicates what elements or data can be nested within other elements, the order in which the elements or data appear, how many are permitted, and whether they are desired or optional.

2 Which one of the following can also serve as an "or" operator?

A ,

B +

C *

D |

3 To specify that at least one of the child element(s) is desired, you would use a __________.

A plus sign

B comma

C vertical line

D question mark

4 Elements that contain other elements are said to have __________.

A element structure

B an element tag

C element content

D a complex element structure

5 What value would you use for `XML:space` to indicate that white space is significant and maintained?

A "keep"

B "true"

C "preserve"

D "valid"

6 The combination of the start indicator (<!) and the uppercase keyword is called the __________.

7 The coding immediately following the `PUBLIC` keyword is called the __________.

8 __________ specify the names of elements and the nature of their content.

9 __________ permit you to specify additional information for your elements.

10 The __________ specifies a name for the entity and defines what the entity represents (a string of text or an external file, for example).

11 __________ were developed to overcome the need to create unique names for data types with similar functions.

12 The __________ of every namespace declaration is restricted to the element for which it is declared.

13 __________ is the process of determining the effectiveness of XML document development.

14 DTDs declare all of the components that an XML language or document is permitted to contain, as well as the structural relationships among those components. True or false?

15 In a document type definition, the prolog is desired. True or false?

16 XML content cannot be processed without a DTD. True or false?

17 Generally, white space is considered significant in __________ content, and is insignificant in element content.

18 Which keyword would you use to indicate that the DTD can be found locally on the server?

Independent practice activity

Create a DTD called product.dtd and an XML document called product.xml file, based on the following specifications.

1 Create an external DTD file called product.dtd.

2 Create a root element called `<CATALOG>`.

3 Create an element called `<ITEM>` that has the sibling elements `<PRODUCT_DESC>`, `<IMAGE>` and `<PRICE>`.

4 Implement the ability to create many `<ITEM>`s in the document.

5 `<PRODUCT_DESC>` is a mandatory element containing text that can contain any character data.

6 `<IMAGE>` is an element containing text that contains the name of a graphics file.

7 `<PRICE>` is an element containing text and must be able to contain a dollar sign ('$').

8 `<PRICE_CURR>` is an attribute that implements a choice of either CDN or US dollars, with US as the default, if nothing is selected.

9 Save your work in the current unit folder. Save all your files and close.

10 After you have created the product.dtd file, use the DTD/Schema menu to generate a sample XML document with sample data.

Unit 4

Schema

Unit time: 120 minutes

Complete this unit, and you'll know how to:

A Identify the limitations of DTDs

B Describe schema and its components.

C Create and modify schema.

Topic A: XML Schema

Explanation

While DTDs provide a mechanism for modeling XML languages and documents, they have their limitations, which were well known when the first edition of the Extensible Markup Language (XML) 1.0 (First Edition) specification was accepted as a recommendation by the World Wide Web Consortium (W3C). Several XML-related modeling languages, most notably XML Schema, were developed to overcome these limitations.

Disadvantages of DTDs

Although DTDs are currently the most widely used tool in defining document types, there are few disadvantages to using DTDs with XML:

- DTDs have their own syntax, which differs from XML. This means that a DTD can't be processed with a standard XML parser. It would be better, and it would make learning easier, if one tool could process XML documents and their document models.
- DTDs have limited ability to describe the data in elements and attributes. For example, you can't indicate when character data should be numbers, date format, or currency.
- DTDs have limited support for namespaces, so they can't define or restrict the content of elements based on context sensitivity.

As an example of the last point, you can use a DTD to specify that an element named "company" must have a name element, an address element, and a phone element associated with it. However, a contact element for the company element also needs a name and a phone number, but unfortunately must have different elements defined for these items, like `contact_name` or `contact_phone`. Thus, in a DTD, you only get to specify the structure of the name or phone element once. DTDs are not hierarchical and therefore require you to specify new names for similar elements in different contexts of the same document.

To overcome these shortcomings, modeling languages were developed with hierarchical schemas that specify validation criteria. Here's a list of the most common languages:

- XML Schema
- Document Content Description (DCD)
- Regular Language description for XML (RELAX)
- Resource Description Framework (RDF) Schema
- BizTalk
- Schema for Object-oriented XML (SOX)
- Tree Regular Expressions for XML (TREX)
- Schema for Object-oriented XML (Schematron)
- Document Definition Markup Language (DDML)

Do it!

A-1: Discussing disadvantages of using DTDs

Exercises

1 DTDs are not hierarchical. True or false?

2 TREX, SOX, and DDML are examples of __________ languages.

3 You can process DTDs using any standard XML parser. True or false?

4 In a DTD, you can't indicate when character data should contain numbers, dates, or currency. True or false?

5 DTDs have limited support for namespaces. True or false?

The W3C XML Schema recommendations

Explanation

The W3C formed the XML Schema Working Group, which published an XML Schema Requirements document. This document listed and discussed the goals of the XML Schema language. The group subsequently continued to work on the new XML Schema Definition Language (XSD), as part of the W3C's XML Activity.

XSD development was facilitated by the experience that had been gained by using DTDs and previous schema languages. The Working Group intended for XSD to become the most flexible and powerful type of schema available. On May 2, 2001, the W3C's XML Schema Part 1: Structures, and XML Schema Part 2: Datatypes, were accepted as W3C Recommendations.

Note: You can find Part 1 of the Schema Recommendation at www.w3.org/TR/xmlschema-1/ and Part 2 at www.w3.org/TR/xmlschema-2/.

Many professionals predict that schemas will one day replace DTDs. However, DTDs still have a few advantages over schemas:

- **Tool support.** All SGML-related tools and many XML-related tools can already process DTDs.
- **Deployment.** A large number of document types are already defined using DTDs (for example, HTML, XHTML, DocBook, etc.).
- **Expertise and practical application.** Development in these two areas has grown since DTDs were introduced with the SGML standard ISO 8879 in 1986.

The two-part XML Schema Recommendation is an application of XML and is a large, complex standard. It lets you specify almost any kind of XML relationship, but it requires a lot of learning and a significant amount of time to implement it properly. It is referred to as *XML Schema* (also called *XSchema*).

By facilitating the development of better data descriptions and the definition of shared markup vocabularies, XML Schema helps to overcome one of the main problems for XML in the world of e-commerce and business-to-business (B2B) communication: the fact that XML systems of one company or industry cannot communicate with XML documents created for another company or industry. With XML Schema, different organizations can still create specific schema information for their own use, but because they are starting from a common standard, they can also generate compatible information that is easier for other systems to understand and use.

Do it!

A-2: Exploring W3C XML Schema recommendations

Exercises

1 What are some advantages that DTDs still have over Schemas?

2 Schema provides a standard that allows businesses and industries to more easily create systems that can communicate. True or false?

3 Schemas are generally more powerful than DTDs for e-commerce and business-to-business transactions. True or false?

Topic B: Schema description and components

Explanation

Like a DTD, a schema is a model for describing the structure and content of data. It describes the arrangement of elements, attributes, and text in a document.

Schema description

Exhibit 4-1 depicts the relationships among SGML, XML, languages related to XML, and some fictitious documents, schemas, and DTDs related to XML. The DTD concept was developed for content modeling in SGML-related languages. Thus, DTDs are the schema mechanism for SGML.

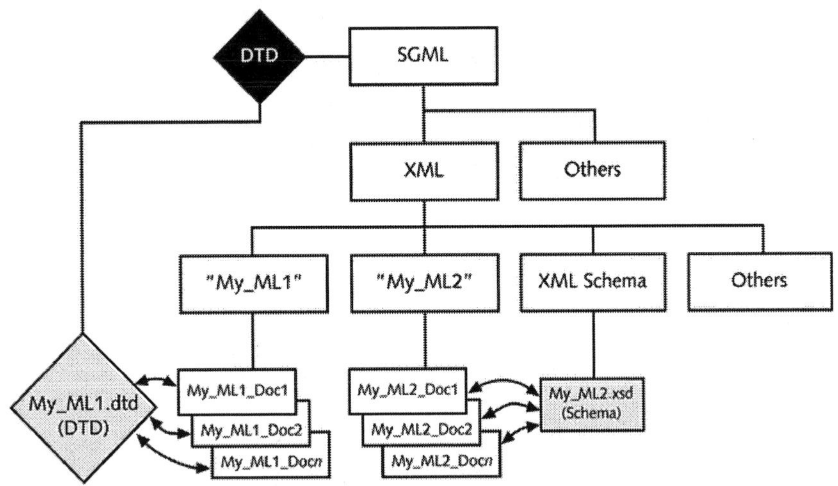

Exhibit 4-1: SGML, DTD, schema, and document relationships

One of the fictitious XML-related languages shown in Exhibit 3-20, called *My_ML1*, has several documents that are based on a content model document that, in turn, is based on SGML's DTD specifications. Thus, the content model document is called *My_ML1.dtd.*

XML Schema was developed as a content modeling language, an application of XML, and not as an application of SGML. Therefore, XML Schema pertains only to XML and XML-related languages and, thus, schemas pertain to XML-related languages and documents. The second fictitious XML-related language, *My_ML2*, has a content model descended from XML Schema. Thus, its content model document is called a schema.

Schema is a term borrowed from database technology. It describes the structure of data in relational tables. In the context of XML, a *schema* describes a model for an entire class of documents. The model describes the possible arrangement of elements, attributes, and text in a schema-valid document. In schemas, models are described in terms of constraints. A *constraint* defines what can appear in a given language or document.

There are two kinds of constraints: content model constraints and datatype constraints. *Content model constraints* define the elements that can appear in your document. They also describe the pattern of appearance, the number and type of components, and whether they are required or optional. The schema establishes the vocabulary and the grammar by using content model constraints. *Datatype constraints* describe the units of data that the schema considers valid.

The purpose of any document model, including schemas, is to provide a means to validate a document at machine speed. Any well-formed document that conforms to a schema's constraints is considered valid. In a large-scale environment, where vast amounts of information are being received from many and varied sources and sent to many and varied destinations, the ability to check document validity at high speed is critical. The faster you catch errors and transact business, the more efficient and profitable your business will be.

Although schemas and DTDs perform similar document modeling functions, their lexicons are different. Individual schemas define a class of XML documents, and XML documents that conform to a particular schema are called *instance documents*. This terminology is used where schemas are referenced. Note that instances and schemas might not exist as documents, although they might exist as byte streams, fields in database records, or as collections of XML "Information Items."

Do it!

B-1: Exploring schema description

Exercises

1 In schemas, models are described in terms of ___________.

A datatypes

B attributes

C elements

D constraints

2 XML documents that conform to a particular schema are called ___________.

A datatype constraints

B class

C instance documents

D content model documents

3 Which one of the following is a type of constraint?

A grammar

B class

C vocabulary

D content type

Schema components

Explanation

Exhibit 4-2 shows a simple external XML DTD ready to be converted to an XML schema.

```
<?xml version="1.0" encoding="UTF-8"?>
<!ELEMENT CONTACTS (DEPT+, NAME, EMAIL, PHONE)>
<!ELEMENT DEPT (#PCDATA)>
<!ELEMENT NAME (#PCDATA)>
<!ELEMENT EMAIL (#PCDATA)>
<!ELEMENT PHONE (#PCDATA)>
<!ATTLIST DEPT
        dept_name (Sales | Custsrv | Emplrel | President ) #REQUIRED
>
```

Exhibit 4-2: A simple DTD: contactsbydept.dtd

From the DTD, you can see that its respective XML documents each have a root element named `<CONTACTS>`, and this element contains four child elements named `<DEPT>`, `<NAME>`, `<EMAIL>`, and `<PHONE>`. There is at least one such listing, because there is a plus sign following the word `<DEPT>`. Every time a `<DEPT>` element occurs, it is followed by one `<NAME>`, `<EMAIL>`, and `<PHONE>` element. The content of all the `<DEPT>`, `<EMAIL>`, `<NAME>`, and `<PHONE>` elements is specified to be parsed character data. Each `<DEPT>` element has an attribute called `dept_name` and the value of the attribute is chosen from the enumerated list `Sales`, `Custsrv`, `Emplrel`, and `President`.

You can use XML Spy to convert a DTD to a schema. Exhibit 3-1 shows a schema based on the DTD in Exhibit 3-20. Note the file extension .xsd, which indicates that the file is a schema. The file extension is a holdover from the first days of XML Schema development, when the project was called XML Schema Definition Language (XSD).

```
<?xml version="1.0" encoding="UTF-8"?>
<!-- edited with XML Spy v5 rel. 4 U (http://www.xmlspy.com) by Student Name -->
<!--V3C Schema generated by XML Spy v5 rel. 4 U (http://www.xmlspy.com)-->
<xs:schema xmlns:xs="http://www.w3.org/2001/XML Schema" elementFormDefault="qualified">
    <xs:element name="CONTACTS">
        <xs:complexType>
            <xs:sequence>
                <xs:element name="DEPT" type="DEPTType" maxOccurs="unbounded"/>
                <xs:element ref="NAME"/>
                <xs:element ref="EMAIL"/>
                <xs:element ref="PHONE"/>
            </xs:sequence>
        </xs:complexType>
    </xs:element>
    <xs:complexType name="DEPTType">
        <xs:simpleContent>
            <xs:restriction base="xs:string">
                <xs:attribute name="dept_name" use="required">
                    <xs:simpleType>
                        <xs:restriction base="xs:NMTOKEN">
                            <xs:enumeration value="Sales"/>
                            <xs:enumeration value="Custsrv"/>
                            <xs:enumeration value="Emplrel"/>
                            <xs:enumeration value="President"/>
                        </xs:restriction>
                    </xs:simpleType>
                </xs:attribute>
            </xs:restriction>
        </xs:simpleContent>
    </xs:complexType>
    <xs:element name="EMAIL" type="xs:string"/>
    <xs:element name="NAME" type="xs:string"/>
    <xs:element name="PHONE" type="xs:string"/>
</xs:schema>
```

Exhibit 4-3: Corresponding XML schema: contactsbydept.xsd

The prolog

The first three lines of the schema are its prolog. The first line is the familiar XML declaration (also called the header). Like every XML document, the schema begins with this declaration, which states that the document is written in XML. Nothing should precede this header. The tag is essentially `<?xml …?>`, the XML version number is 1.0, and the document's language encoding specification is UTF-8. The next two lines are comment lines. In this example, the comments indicate the creator or editor of this schema (the generic "Student Name"), and what application was originally used to create it ("XML Spy v5.0").

The schema element

The fourth line in Exhibit 3-2, `<xs:schema>` is the start tag for the *schema element.* This element is the first element of the schema and is equivalent to the root element of an XML document—it's the parent element of all the other elements in the schema. The other elements are referred to as *subelements*. In this case, the `<xs:schema>` start tag also includes two attribute specifications, the namespaces, and the qualified or unqualified local elements.

Namespaces in schemas

In the `<xs:schema>` start tag, the `xmlns:xs` attribute is called the *namespace declaration*. Each namespace indicates to the XML processor that the definitions and treatments of elements and other datatypes in the schema are adopted from the W3C's Namespace Recommendation, as indicated by its value, the URL `http://www.w3.org/2001/XMLSchema`. When the processor encounters datatypes preceded by the prefix `xs:` (which represents the URL), it is told that the meaning of these datatypes is identical to the definition found for them in the W3C Schema recommendation. Thus, the datatypes have standard definitions and need no further definition before they are processed.

Each namespace represents a collection of element types and other datatype names and is identified by a unique name. That unique name takes the form of a Uniform Resource Identifier (URI), the most common of which are URLs. Although URLs are readily identified as Web addresses, here they are not actually used as addresses for anything. They are used to specify the names used in the schema. In the W3C Recommendation titled "Namespaces in XML," the W3C recommends the use of URLs as namespace names because URLs indicate domain names that are known to work throughout the Internet. Thus, they make names unique and are not rejected by the processor or the application.

The namespace declaration informs the processor about the URI and also provides an abbreviation for the URI. The abbreviation is used thereafter instead of the full URI or URL. For example, in the declaration:

```
xmlns:xs=http://www.w3.org/2001/XMLSchema:
```

- The `xmlns` portion states "this is a namespace declaration."
- The `xs` portion is the abbreviation that is used to relate the respective elements and other datatypes to the namespace.
- The `http://www.w3.org/2001/XMLSchema` portion is the unique URL.

After the namespace is defined, the element or other datatype name becomes a unique hybrid name, consisting of a prefix (which is the abbreviation for the URL portion of the namespace), then a colon, and then the local portion (the characters to the right of the colon). The local portion is generally the most meaningful to the context of the element or datatype.

Here's an example of such a hybrid name:

```
<xs:sequence>
```

In this example, the local part of the unique name is "sequence," and the URL part is the prefix `xs`, which according to the declaration in the schema element tag, actually stands for `http://www.w3.org/2001/XMLSchema`. A typical schema in an e-commerce environment actually uses elements and types from multiple schemas, each with its own different namespace.

All namespaces shown in Exhibit 3-3 have employed prefixes in their declarations, such as:

```
<xs:schema xmlns:xs="http://www.w3.org/2001/XMLSchema" />
```

But namespaces do not have to be declared explicitly with prefixes, as shown in the following example:

```
<schema xmlns="http://www.w3.org/2001/XMLSchema" />
```

Subsequently, when the parser encounters an element or attribute name with no prefix in the schema, then the URL mentioned in the declaration is presumed to be the namespace to which the element or attribute is associated. A variation of the default namespace is the following: a default namespace can be undeclared if an empty string is used for its value in the declaration. In the following example, no namespace is associated with the element or attribute name:

```
<schema xmlns="" />
```

In the schema validation process, the processor checks an instance document to see if it conforms to one or more schemas. The target namespace provides a method to do the checking. In the schema(s), the element and attribute declarations and type definitions are checked against corresponding elements and attributes in the instance documents.

The targetNamespace attribute

In the schema, you must first declare a target namespace by specifying a URL as a value for the `targetNamespace` attribute, and specify that both locally defined elements and locally defined attributes are unqualified. (You can specify the qualification of local elements and attributes globally by a pair of attributes—`elementFormDefault` and `attributeFormDefault`—on the schema element, or separately for each local declaration using the `form` attribute.) The `targetNamespace` attribute is normally placed within the schema element, although this is not a universal rule or practice. It can be placed within any element declaration. Its syntax is as follows:

```
targetNamespace="http://www.tlsales.com/Sch01"
```

Then, the instance document(s) should also declare a namespace, using the same URL as the target namespace in the schema declaration. You should place the declaration in the root element (generally) and use the following syntax:

```
xmlns:xxx="http://www.tlsales.com/Sch01"
```

You can use any prefix in the declaration. The prefix used should be appropriate to the document. The letters `xxx` in the syntax are one example of a prefix. The XML processor examines the instance document, reads the URI/URL in the namespace declaration, and looks for a schema with the identical URI/URL specified for the `targetNamespace` attribute of the schema element. Exhibit 3-4 shows the validation process.

This is why they're called *target namespaces*. They facilitate validation of conforming instance documents.

In the Exhibit 3-5 schema, there is neither a target namespace specification, nor a default namespace specification. This might indicate that this schema document is a *support namespace*, which also called a *chameleon namespace*. The author has probably decided to use a homogeneous namespace design, wherein several schema documents have been created, but all the schemas share one common umbrella namespace. The namespace attribute/declaration appears in the main schema document, but the support schema documents do not have their own namespace declarations. In the main schema, there is probably a statement like:

```
<xs:include schemaLocation="contactsbydept.xsd"/>
```

or

```
<xs:import namespace="http://www.tlsales.com"
  schemaLocation="contactsbydept.xsd"/>
```

When the parser encounters either of these elements with their respective attribute/value pairs, it accesses the document (in this case, contactsbydept.xsd) and treats it like a support schema. The supporting schema then adopts the namespace declared in the main schema document, in a manner similar to a chameleon taking on the colors of its surroundings. A "no target, no default" schema document like this is also said to be observing a *chameleon namespace* design. Homogeneous/chameleon namespaces can provide great flexibility in design, but they can also get you into trouble if you are not diligent with element types.

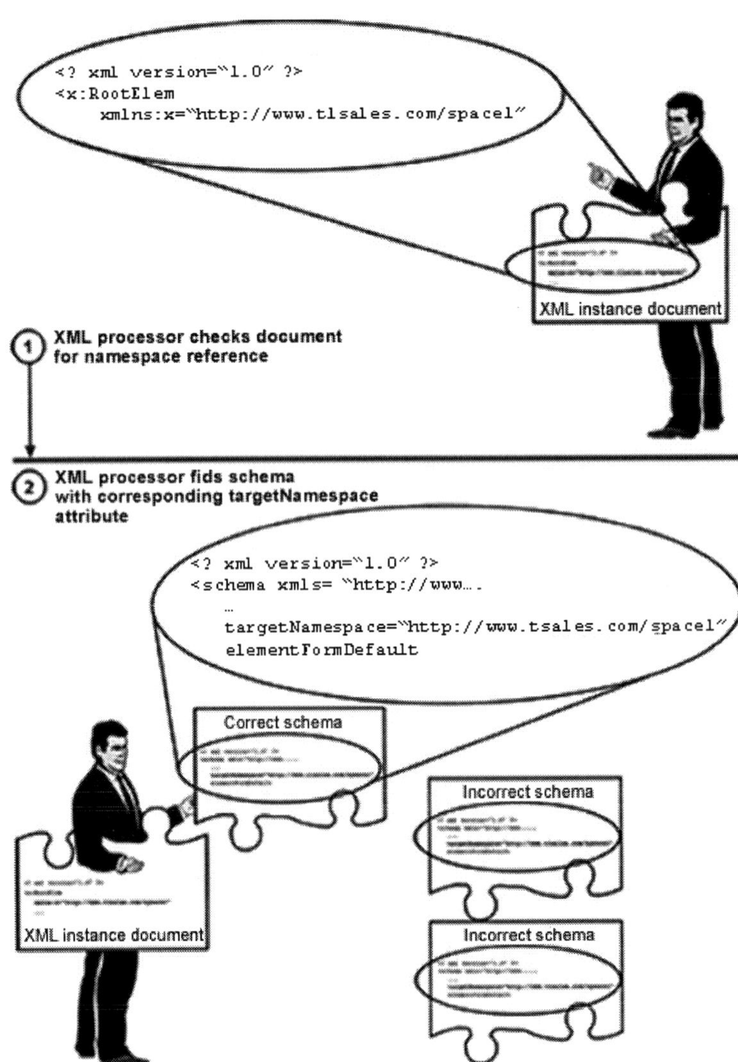

Exhibit 4-4: XML schema document validation

Qualified and unqualified locals

Local elements are elements in a schema that are declared in subelements of the schema element, but not in the scope of the schema element itself. Elements that are declared in the `<schema>` element are called *globally declared elements*. The schema element in Exhibit 3-20 includes an attribute named `elementFormDefault`, which has the value `qualified`.

During the schema design phase, the designer has to decide whether or not the name of the origin namespace of each local element should be displayed (or exposed) in the element's tag in the instance documents. The exposing of the origin namespace of those locally declared elements is called *qualifying* them. The designer incorporates the attribute `elementFormDefault` as a sort of binary on/off switch to illustrate their choice. If the value of the `elementFormDefault` attribute is `qualified`, the identity of the namespaces is shown in the tags of the local elements in the instance documents. The bold code in Exhibit 3-7 demonstrates this.

Schema (qualified)

```
<? xml version="1.0"  ?>
<schema xmls="http://www....
    ...
    targetNamespace="http://www.tlsales.com/space1"
    elementFormDefault="qualified">
         <element name="A" type ="string" />
         <element name="First" type ="FirstType" />
          <complexType name="FirstType" />
                     <element name="Second" type="SecondType" />
                     <element name="Third" type="ThirdType" />
                     <element ref="A" minOccurs="0" />
                     <element name="B" type="string" />
         </complexType>
         <complexType name="SecondType" />
                    <element name="C" type="string" />
                    <element name="D" type="boolean" />
         </complexType>
          <complexType name="ThirdType" />
                    <element name="E" type="string" />
                    <element name="F" type="boolean" />
           </complexType>
                       .
                       .
```

Instance Document

```
<? xml version="1.0"  ?>
<spl:First xmlns:spl="http://www.tlsales.com/space1"  />
         <spl:Second>
                  <spl:C> True or False: Are you OK? </spl:C>
                  <spl:D> True </spl:D>
         </spl:Second>
         <spl:Third>
                   <spl:E> True or False: Is this easy to understand? </spl:E>
                   <spl:F> True <apl:F>
          </spl:Third>
          <spl:A> This is a global comment </spl:A>
          <spl:B> This is a local comment </spl:B>
```

Exhibit 4-5: Qualified locals

Because the elements named `<A>` and `<First>` are declared within the `<schema>` element, but not within subelements of the schema, they are termed *global elements*. The elements named `<Second>, <Third>, <C>, <D>, <E>`, and `<F>` are *local elements*. In the schema, the first bolded term, `qualified`, indicates that this schema wants its conforming instance documents to expose the identity of the namespaces pertaining to all local elements declared in the schema (that is the `<Second>, <Third>, <C>, <D>, <E>`, and `<F>` elements).

The identity of the namespaces pertaining to the global elements `<First>` and `<A>` also have to be exposed. In the conforming instance document, the prefix `spl:` precedes all the element tags, because `spl:` represents the target namespace referred to in both the schema and the instance document.

On the other hand, if the value of the elementFormDefault attribute is unqualified, the identity of the namespaces pertaining to the schema's global elements is exposed, but not the namespaces pertaining to the schema's local elements. Exhibit 3-9 demonstrates this. Compare the instance documents of Exhibit 3-2 and Exhibit 3-10. In Exhibit 3-10, the tags for the <Second> and <Third> elements, as well as the tags for the elements named <C>, <D>, <E>, and <F>, do not contain the spl: prefix this time. Only the <First> element and the <A> element still retain that prefix. In other words, when you specify elementFormDefault="unqualified" in the schema document, the tags for those elements that have been locally declared in the schema contain their respective element names when they appear in the respective instance documents, but do not show any namespace reference.

Schema (unqualified)

```
<? xml version="1.0"  ?>
<schema xmls="http://www....
    ...
    targetNamespace="http://www.tlsales.com/space1"
    elementFormDefault="unqualified">
         <element name="A" type ="string" />
         <element name="First" type ="FirstType" />
          <complexType name="FirstType" />
                    <element name="Second" type="SecondType" />
                    <element name="Third" type="ThirdType" />
                    <element ref="A" minOccurs="0" />
                    <element name="B" type="string" />
         </complexType>
         <complexType name="SecondType" />
                   <element name="C" type="string" />
                   <element name="D" type="boolean" />
         </complexType>
          <complexType name="ThirdType" />
                   <element name="E" type="string" />
                   <element name="F" type="boolean" />
           </complexType>
             .
             .
```

Instance Document

```
<? xml version="1.0"  ?>
<spl:First xmlns:spl="http://www.tlsales.com/space1"
     <Second>
            <C> True or False: Are you OK? <C>
            <D> True <D>
      <Second:>
      <Third>
       <E> True or False: Is this easy to understand? <E>
       <F> True <F>
       </Third>
       <spl:A> This is a globally declared comment </spl:A>
       <B> This a locally declared comment <B>
</spl:First>
      .
      .
```

Exhibit 4-6: Unqualified locals

Do it!

B-2: Exploring the schema element and namespaces

Exercises

1 The schema element is equivalent to which element in an XML document?

2 When the XML processor encounters the following code in the schema element, what is it being told?

```
xmlns:xs="http://www.w3.org/2001/XMLSchema"
```

3 Which of the following indicates a default namespace?

A `xmlns:xs="http://www.w3.org/2001/XMLSchema"`

B `xmlns="http://www.w3.org/2001/XMLSchema"`

C `defaultNamespace="http://www.tlsales.com/Sch01"`

D all of the above

E none of the above

4 What has to happen in order for an XML instance document to be validated against a schema?

A A `targetNamespace` attribute is normally declared within the schema's schema element, and the instance document(s) also declares a namespace, using the URL `ww.w3.org/2001/XMLSchema` in its root element tag.

B All namespace declarations must mention `www.w3.org/2001/XMLSchema`.

C A `defaultNamespace` is normally declared within the schema element, and the instance document(s) also declares a namespace, using the same URL as the schema's default namespace, in its root element tag.

D A `targetNamespace` is declared within the schema's schema element, and the instance document(s) also declares a namespace, using the same URL as the schema's target namespace, in its root element tag.

E Both the schema and the instance document must have target and default namespaces and neither should mention `www.w3.org/2001/XMLSchema`.

5 What kind of design does a schema have when it has no target namespace declaration and no default namespace declaration?

6 When you see element tags that look like `<spl:name>` and `</spl:name>` in an instance document, then you know that "the locals are qualified." True or false?

Element types and compositors

Explanation

Exhibit 3-11 highlights the next element declaration following the schema element, the `<CONTACTS>` element. The `<CONTACTS>` declaration spans lines 5 through 7. The `xs:complexType` element tag on line 6 declares that `<CONTACTS>` is a *complex type* element—an element that contains attributes and/or subelements.

```
5. <xs:element name="CONTACTS">
6.       <xs:complexType>
7.             <xs:sequence>
```

Exhibit 4-7: Lines 5 through 7 of contactsbydept.xsd

The complex type is one variety of element type and is referred to as *data type* or *content type*. These types determine the appearance of elements and their content in the related XML instance documents. The other element type is the simple type. *Simple type* elements contain no attributes or subelements, just character data.

The `xs:sequence` element is specified on line 7 because the subelements within `<CONTACTS>` follow a specified sequence. The sequence element indicates that the elements contained within it must appear in an XML document in the same order as they appear in the sequence element. The sequence element is one type of compositor called the *sequence compositor*. *Compositors* are specialized XML Schema components that define groups of elements and attributes within the schema and, thus, within the related XML documents. There are three types of compositors:

- **Sequence compositors.** Indicate the sequence in which the elements must appear in an XML document.
- **Choice compositors.** Indicate that only one element can appear in the XML document at that point and that the element must be chosen from among the several choices which appear in the choice element.
- **All compositors.** Indicate that one or more of the elements within the all element can appear in the XML document in any order, as an unordered set of elements.

Do it!

B-3: Exploring element types and compositors

Exercises

1 Which of the following are types of compositors? (Choose all that apply.)

A choice

B cardinal

C simple

D qualified/non-qualified

E all

F sequence

2 A sequence compositor indicates the number of times an element might occur in instance documents. True or false?

3 How many types of compositors are there?

A 1

B 2

C 3

D 4

4 Which compositor indicates that one or more of the elements can appear in the XML document in any order, as an unordered set of elements?

A all

B class

C choice

D sequence

Attributes and cardinality

Explanation

Exhibit 4-8 shows the four subelements of <CONTACTS> element, declared in order.

```
8. <xs:element name="DEPT" type="DEPTType" maxOccurs="unbounded"/>
9. <xs:element ref="NAME"/>
10. <xs:element ref="EMAIL"/>
11. <xs:element ref="PHONE"/>
```

Exhibit 4-8: Lines 8 through 11 of contactsbydept.xsd

The first subelement within <CONTACTS> is <DEPT>. Unlike the other subelements, it contains character data and an attribute named dept_name, the value of which is selected from among several choices by the instance document author. The subelements <NAME>, <EMAIL>, and <PHONE>, do not have attributes; they contain character data only.

Within the declaration of the subelement <DEPT> there is type attribute with the value DEPTType. This attribute indicates that another complexType has been created, has been named DEPTType, and can be found later in the schema. XML Spy creates the complexType automatically when it processes the ATTLIST declaration in lines 7 and 8 of the DTD and sees that every <DEPT> element would have a desired attribute called dept_name. The name DEPTType follows a common (but not mandatory) XML convention: combining the element name DEPT with the word type. Otherwise, the name could be anything that a schema author chooses.

In the DTD corresponding to the schema, the plus sign (+) next to DEPT indicates its *cardinality*, that is, the number of times the <DEPT> element might occur in instance documents. The plus sign indicates that a <DEPT> element must occur at least once, but that there is no limit to the number of times it might occur. As the DTD is converted to a schema, XML Spy substitutes equivalent schema-related attributes to indicate that cardinality: *minOccurs* (the minimum number of occurrences) and *maxOccurs* (the maximum number of occurrences). The program also provides the specifications for these properties. However, while there appears to be a specification for maxOccurs, minOccurs has not been specified, because it doesn't need to be. The plus sign in the DTD indicated "at least once" and the default value of minOccurs is one.

The default value for maxOccurs is also one, but because the <DEPT> element might occur more than once, that default cannot prevail. So you use the maxOccurs attribute to specify a maximum occurrence value. Specifications for maxOccurs can be any positive integer, or the word "unbounded," which would indicate that there is no limit to the number of times <DEPT> might occur. Unbounded is selected because the schema dictates that <DEPT> can occur once or as many times as the document author might want.

The other elements (<NAME>, <EMAIL>, and <PHONE>) only occur once for each time a <DEPT> element appears. You could specify values for minOccurs and maxOccurs, but it's not necessary to do so for <NAME>, <EMAIL>, and <PHONE>.

Line 3 of the DTD indicates that content in the <DEPT> element is made up of parsed character data. At first glance, the <DEPT> element declaration in the schema doesn't seem to address that requirement. However, the declaration of the complexType element named DEPTType does. At this point, the declaration of the <DEPT> element is complete. Its declaration takes only one line because there are no subelements within <DEPT>.

Do it!

B-4: Exploring attributes and cardinality

Exercises

1 The plus sign (+) next to the DEPT element in the DTD is equivalent to what in the schema?

A minOccurs default; maxOccurs default

B minOccurs unbounded; maxOccurs unbounded

C minOccurs default; maxOccurs unbounded

D minOccurs 1; maxOccurs default

E none of the above

2 The number of times an element might occur in instance documents is called _________.

3 What maxOccurs value indicates that there is no limit to the number of times an element might occur?

A "Infinity"

B "unbounded"

C "1000"

D "no_limit"

Subelements: simple types and schema structures

Explanation

Declarations for the three remaining subelements under `<CONTACTS>` (`<NAME>`, `<EMAIL>`, and `<PHONE>`) follow the `<DEPT>` element declaration. Lines 4, 5, and 6 of the DTD indicate that these elements contain parsed character data only, with no subelements and no attributes. Thus, they are simple elements types. There are two kinds of simple types: those that are defined in the W3C Schema Recommendation (XML Schema), and those that are defined by the schema designer according to specific needs.

The following table lists several simple element types that are already defined in XML Schema.

Simple type	Definition
Binary	Contains binary values (e.g., 1001, 11101).
Boolean	Contains values such as True or False, 1 or 0.
Date	Contains a date in YYYY-MM-DD format.
Decimal	Contains a decimal value, positive or negative.
ENTITY, ENTITIES	Contains an ENTITY or ENTITIES attribute type, as described in the W3C XML Recommendation.
ID	Contains an ID attribute type, as described in the W3C XML Recommendation.
Int, integer	Contains an integer.
Language	Contains a language identifier (e.g., en-US, de, fr).
Qname	Contains an XML qualified name (i.e., contains a namespace reference plus a local name, separated by a colon).
String	Contains a string of text characters.
Time	Contains a time reference (e.g., 08:13:47.639).
AnyURI	Contains a Uniform Resource Identifier reference; the value can be absolute or relative.

You can approach simple element type declarations in one of two ways: the “Russian doll” (also called the nesting doll) approach, where a full element declaration is inserted every time the element is needed, as shown in Exhibit 3-12, or a flat catalog approach, by using global element references.

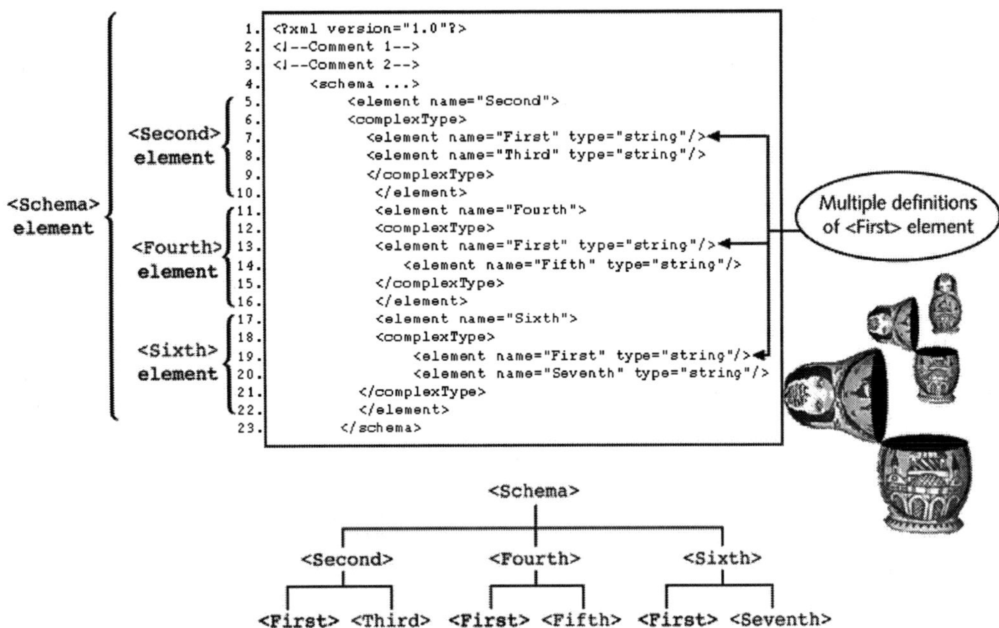

Exhibit 4-9: Simple nesting doll/Russian doll schema structure

In the generic schema in Exhibit 3-12, the element named `<First>` appears within three subelements (`<Second>, <Fourth>, and <Sixth>`) and is fully declared within each one. In each case, the declarations are identical, because the element name is the same. This is an example of the Russian doll approach. The elements are cloaked one within another. The tree diagram at the bottom of the exhibit illustrates the hierarchical structure of this simple schema.

There are disadvantages to this approach. The XML processor will use more resources to process this schema. Also, if you want to make changes to the First element, then you must make changes in three locations, within each of the subelements that contain the First element. This will take more time and introduces the risk that the changes are not made uniformly across the three locations.

Exhibit 3-13 shows a different approach, commonly called a “flat catalog” approach that employs global references and is intended to create a flatter schema structure. Note that the `ref=First` declaration, within the declarations of the `<Second>, <Fourth>, and <Sixth>` elements, points to the `<First>` element, which now is declared within the schema element. The `ref=First` reference indicates that the processor must look for the declaration of the `<First>` element within the schema element, and then look for a `<First>` element within the `<Second>, <Fourth>`, and `<Sixth>` elements in a conforming XML document.

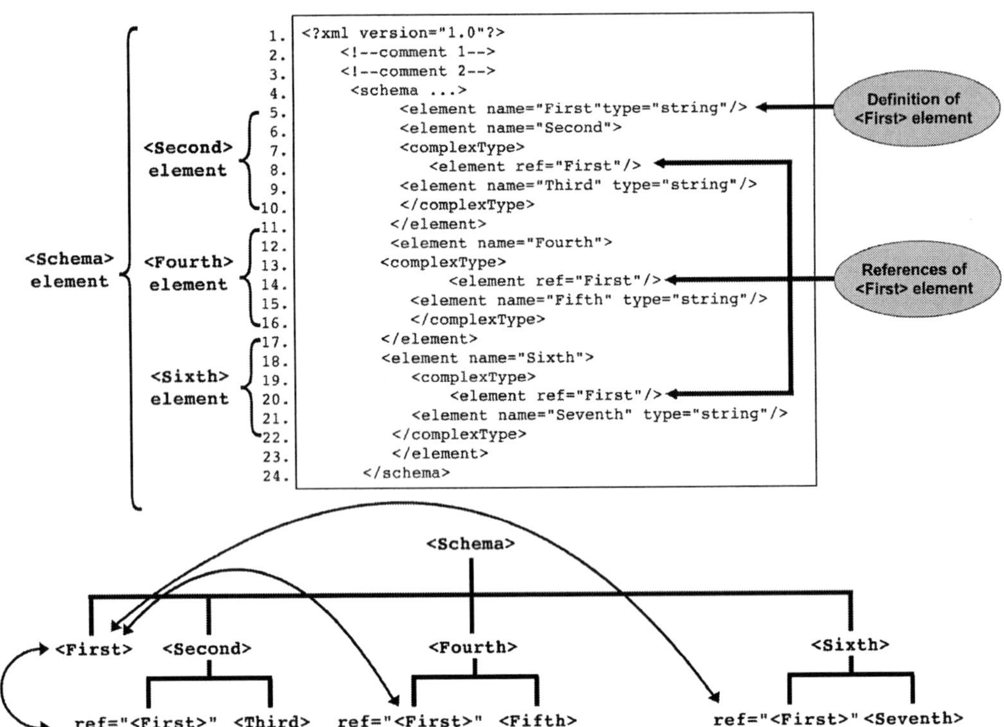

Exhibit 4-10: Simple flat catalog schema structure

With this approach, the <First> element is fully declared only once and in a specific location: within the schema element itself, and not within any of the subelements beneath the schema element. In any subelements that would contain the <First> element, the more simple and compact syntax is used to refer to the <First> element. During processing, the XML parser refers back to the <First> element declaration in the schema element.

This reference is termed a *global reference* (some designers also call it an *archetype*) because the element being referred to is declared within the schema element and not within any subelements below the schema element. This way, all the subelements below the schema element can refer to <First> without error.

If <First> were declared within one of the subelements beneath the schema element (for example, within <Sixth>), then <First> could not be referenced from elements stemming from <Second> or <Fourth>, which are <Sixth>'s siblings. It could only be seen from those elements stemming from <Sixth>.

The schema document language is called a *scoped language* because of this principle, where each element declaration is visible only within the element where it's defined, and all its descendants.

Advantages to the flat catalog approach include:

- A programmer can group all the common simpleType elements together in one location, immediately within the `<schema>` element.
- The schema's hierarchy is inherently flatter.
- Programmer and processor resources are saved.
- If a change has to be made to one of the common elements, you only need to make it in one location. This reduces the risk of nonuniform changes to elements, because references inherit the changes automatically.

By default, XML Spy uses the flat catalog approach. The simple types named `<EMAIL>`, `<NAME>`, and `<PHONE>` are fully declared within the schema element (at the bottom near the end tag, which is another XML convention). Then, in the `<CONTACTS>` complex element, there are "refs" to the respective simple types.

Note: The "ref" elements could also contain other context-specific attributes pertinent to the simple types (for example, indications of cardinality) that would not be specified in the global declarations.

Global references found in the various subelements of a flat catalog approach can only point to simple types, not complex types. If `<First>` had been a complex type, then the flat catalog approach could not be used. After the single-line element reference declarations (lines line 8 through 11) are completed, then the sequence (line 12), complexType (line 13), and element (line 14) end tags terminate the `<CONTACTS>` element declaration. These lines have been reproduced in Exhibit 3-15.

```
12.        </xs:sequence>
13.     </xs:complexType>
14.  </xs:element>
```

Exhibit 4-11: Lines 12 through 14 of contactsbydept.xsd

Do it!

B-5: Exploring simple types and schema structures

Exercises

1 If you are looking at a schema document, and you see an element such as `ref="address"`, what should you realize?

2 Choose the simple type that contains a time reference.

A Time

B Date

C AnyURI

D Qname

3 The simple type that contains a language identifier is __________.

4 What do the Russian doll and flat catalog refer to? How do they differ from one another?

5 String and Time are examples of __________.

6 Which one of the following is not a simple type?

A String

B Decimal

C ID

D Unbounded

7 __________ is the approach where a full element declaration is inserted every time the element is needed.

8 When the element being referred to is declared within the schema element and not within any subelements below the schema element, it is called a __________.

A local reference

B global reference

C unbounded reference

D generic reference

Complex type declaration

Explanation

In the `<DEPT>` element declaration, the designer inserted `type="DEPTType"` to indicate to the XML processor that `<DEPT>` is a complex element type and that another complex type declaration, named `DEPTType`, will follow. That declaration covers from lines 15 through 30, as shown in Exhibit 3-16.

```
15.  <xs:complexType name="DEPTType">
16.          <xs:simpleContent>
17.                  <xs:restriction base="xs:string">
18.                          <xs:attribute name="dept_name" use="required">
19.                                  <xs:simpleType>
20.                                          <xs:restriction base="xs:NMTOKEN">
21.                                                  <xs:enumeration value="Sales"/>
22.                                                  <xs:enumeration value="Custsrv"/>
23.                                                  <xs:enumeration value="Emplrel"/>
24.                                                  <xs:enumeration value="President"/>
25.                                          </xs:restriction>
26.                                  </xs:simpleType>
27.                          </xs:attribute>
28.                  </xs:restricion>
29.          </xs:SimpleContent>
30.  </xs:complexType>
```

Exhibit 4-12: Lines 15 through 30 of contactsbydept.xsd

Line 15 is a typical complex type element declaration. It specifies `DEPTType` as the value for the `name` attribute. The declaration looks identical to the one for `<CONTACTS>`, but at line 16, the `DEPTType` declaration deviates from the `<CONTACTS>` declaration. The `xs:simpleContent` element name indicates to the XML processor that the complex type named `DEPTType` is a simple content element, which contains character data only and no subelements. Simple content elements might also contain attributes but at line 16, the processor cannot yet determine whether `DEPTType` has attributes.

At this point, it might be helpful to consider the `complexType` declaration, from line 15 to line 30, as a container of elements, attributes, and other parameters that are useful for defining the complex type `<DEPT>` element. Line 17 gives further direction to the XML processor. It tells the processor that a restriction is applied to the element. Adding `base="xs:string"` indicates that the data is string data, and that the string data is restricted. In subsequent lines, the text strings are restricted to Sales, Custsrv, Emplrel, or President.

You have already encountered the principle of XML inheritance, which comes in two forms: restriction and extension. *Extension* is used to append additional elements to the content model of the base type. You use *Restriction* to restrict the content model of the base type. A simple restriction might be the consideration of only positive integers after the base model has been defined as integers.

The dept_name attribute: use and facets

Line 18 is an attribute declaration element, and it informs the processor that an attribute is used to express the restriction to the complex type named `DEPTType` (the restriction in line 17). The attribute's name is `dept_name`. Because the name does not have an `xs:` prefix, it is not defined in the XML Schema Recommendation. Therefore, a definition must be provided. Also, according to the `use="required"` attribute in the `<xs:attribute>` element, a value for the `dept_name` attribute must be provided in any conforming XML document. Otherwise, the document is not valid. The `use` attribute has three possible values:

- **Required.** The attribute is required.
- **Optional.** The attribute is optional.
- **Fixed.** The value of the attribute is fixed. Another attribute named value must also appear. The value specified for the value attribute determines the value of the use=fixed attribute.

Line 19 indicates that the attribute is a simple type. In fact, all attributes must be simple types. Line 20 tells the processor that there is a restriction placed on the value of the attribute. The `base` attribute type will be `NMTOKEN` (name token). An `NMTOKEN` attribute must consist of a single word or string with no white space in it, but there are no other constraints on the word. `NMTOKEN` attributes also meet the `base="xs:string"` parameter in line 17.

Lines 21 through 24 present the choices for the value of the `dept_name` attribute. Here, one type of facet—the enumeration—is used to define the values from which you can choose a department name. Each line provides one choice. From the `xs:enumeration` tag, you can see that this term is defined in the XML Schema Recommendation. Thus, you must take the attribute's value from the names explicitly listed here, the simple types listed within the `dept_name` attribute declaration element. You can choose only one.

To clarify, it is indicated in line 8 that only one department name can be chosen at a time. After you select the department name (or abbreviation), you must insert its `<NAME>, <EMAIL>`, and `<PHONE>` elements, and their respective information. However, after you insert the `<PHONE>` information for the first department, you can create another `<DEPT>` element to begin the cycle anew.

There is no limit on the department contacts you can enter, because maxOccurs is “unbounded” in line 8. Note how each department name or abbreviation also meets the restrictions listed on lines 17 and 20.

Now that you have declared the DEPTType complex type, the dept_name attribute, and its respective department name abbreviations in the schema, you can insert the end tags for attribute restriction (line 25), simpleType (line 26), DEPTType attribute (line 27), DEPTType restriction (line 28), simple element content (line 29), and DEPTType complexType (line 30) to terminate the DEPTType complexType element declaration.

Globally referenced simple types (archetypes)

Lines 31 to 33, as shown in Exhibit 3-20, list the full declarations of the simple type elements referenced in lines 9 through 11.

```
31.    <xs:element name="EMAIL" type="xs:string"/>
32.    <xs:element name="NAME" type--"xs:string"/>
33.    <xs:element name="PHONE" type="xs:string"/>
```

Exhibit 4-13: Lines 31 through 33 of contactsbydept.xsd

These are simple types because they do not have attributes or subelements. The prefix `xs:` in `type="xs:string"` indicates that string is a simple type already defined in the XML Schema Recommendation. References to these types are called *global references* or *archetypes* because the elements are declared within the schema element and not within any subelements below the schema element. You can refer to them from every subelement in the schema.

Do it!

B-6: Discussing the complex type declaration

Exercises

1 What are the two forms of XML inheritance? Which would you use to create a subset from a content model of your base type?

2 The content element that contains character data only and no subelements is _________.

A complex content element

B restrictive content element

C extension content element

D simple content element

3 Which form of XML inheritance restricts the content model of the base type?

A Restriction

B Extension

C Simple

D Global

4 The `xs:` prefix in the following indicates that string is a ________ type.

```
type="xs:String"
```

Mixed and empty content elements

Explanation

Like DTDs, schemas also support mixed content elements: those elements that contain subelements as well as character data at the same level. However, where DTDs cannot exert control over the order of child elements or the number of times they appear, schemas can, because they have a more complete syntax.

Here's an example of a portion of a schema that contains a mixed content element. It's a model for a request to the executive assistant of each department to provide contact information. Because the element contains other elements as well as text, the element is a complex type. Note the use of the `content="mixed"` attribute, which is included in the complexType element.

```
<xs:element name="contact_req" >
<xs:complexType content="mixed" >
<xs:element name="dept_exec_asst" type= "xs:string" />
<xs:element name="time_lmt_days" >
<xs:simpleType base="xs:integer" >
<xs:maxInclusive value="5" />
</xs:simpleType>
</xs:element>
</xs:complexType>
</xs:element>
```

A conforming XML document (such as the actual request letter) might contain this code:

```
<contact_req>
Dear <dept_exec_asst>Pat Green</dept_exec_asst>:
Please provide the name, e-mail address, and phone number of
the designated department contact by <time_lmt_days>
5</time_lmt_days>working days from the date of this memo.
Thanks in advance for your cooperation.
Dale Burgess, President
</contact_req>
```

Schemas also allow you to declare empty content elements. They are declared by using the `xsd:complexType` element type, but they deliberately omit the definition of a subelement within the complex type element. Here's an example of the declaration of the empty element `<HEAD>` that might ultimately be contained within the definition of the `<CONTACTS>` element:

```
<xs:element name="HEAD">
<xs:complexType>
</xsd:complexType>
</xsd:element>
```

Facets: defining data more precisely

The sample schema in this unit uses inheritance (restrictions or extensions) to more precisely define the values of attributes. It also illustrated how enumeration, one type of facet, could be used to more precisely define the values from which one can choose a department name to begin the description of a departmental contact. Facets provide a more precise definition for data contained within a simple type element or attribute. Their syntax is usually simple:

```
<facetname value="facetvalue"/>
```

For example, say you need to create a simple type subelement called `DiscountCode` under a customer element and you need the value of `DiscountCode` to be an integer with a value less than 999. Here's what that simple type element might look like:

```
<xs:element name="DiscountCode">
<xs:simpleType>
<xs:restriction base="xs:integer">
<xs:minInclusive value="1"/>
<xs:maxInclusive value="999"/>
</xs:restriction>
</xs:simpleType>
</xs:element>
```

Note that the `minInclusive` and `maxInclusive` facets provide the lower and upper boundaries, respectively, of the range of integers for the `DiscountCode` value. These facets (minInclusive, maxInclusive, and enumeration) are popular and valuable. Another popular facet , "pattern", is commonly used for the designation of Universal Product Codes (UPCs), International Standard Book Numbers (ISBNs), and other inventory-control numbers.

Whatever numbering system is adopted by an organization, the number pattern can be specified in XML document models. Here's the schema coding for a fixed-length UPC code commonly used by food merchandisers:

```
<!--UPC Bar Code for identifying products -->
<xsd:simpleType name="UPCcode">
<xsd:restriction base="xsd:string">
<xsd:pattern value="\d{1}-\d{5}-\d{5}-\{1}"/>
</xsd:restriction>
</xsd:simpleType>
```

Schema coding for an ISBN might look like this:

```
<!-- International Standard Book Number (ISBN) -->
<xsd:simpleType name="ISBN">
<xsd:restriction base="xsd:string">
<xsd:pattern value="\d{1}-\d{5}-\d{3}-\d{1}"/>
</xsd:restriction>
</xsd:simpleType>
```

The following table describes some other facets:

Name	Description
length	Specifies the length of a value. Limited to the value 2147483647. Items larger than this limit are not validated correctly.
minLength	Specifies the minimum length of a value, e.g., length of abbreviation for language, state, province, or country. Limited to the value 2147483647. Items larger than this limit are not validated correctly.
maxLength	Specifies the maximum length of a value, e.g., length of a delivery address. Limited to the value 2147483647. Items larger than this limit are not validated correctly.
maxExclusive	Defines a maximum exclusive upper bound of a datatype value. For example, "less than 10" would desire a maxExclusive value of 10 or a maxInclusive of 9.
minExclusive	Defines the exclusive lower bound of a datatype value. For example, "at least two" would desire a minExclusive value of two.
duration	Specifies a time period. The value designates a Gregorian year, month, day, hour, minute, and second. The number of seconds can include decimal digits. An optional preceding minus sign (-) can indicate a negative duration. If the sign is omitted, a positive duration is presumed. Example: to indicate a duration of two years, three months, six days, five hours, and 16 minutes, state P2Y3M6DT5H16M. Minus six hours looks like: -P6H.
totalDigits	Defines the maximum number of digits in the value of a given datatype. Derived from "decimal." The value of totalDigits must be a positive integer.
fractionDigits	Specifies the maximum number of digits in the fractional part of a value of a given datatype. Also derived from "decimal." The value of fractionDigits must be a nonnegative integer.
whiteSpace	Specifies what to do with white space in a datatype. Value must be preserve, replace, or collapse. If the datatype is specified as a string, the value of whiteSpace is usually specified as preserve.

Not all facets apply to all datatypes, and it's important to be careful when specifying facets with simple datatypes. Consult the W3C XML Schema Recommendation to check which facets go with which simple datatypes.

Do it!

B-7: Discussing facets

Exercises

1 What popular facet is used for the designation of UPCs, ISBNs, and other inventory-control numbers?

2 If you are using a base of integers and you want to designate a value of "less than 10" you could use a maxExclusive value of 10 or a maxInclusive of ___________.

3 minInclusive, maxInclusive, and enumeration are examples of ___________.

4 The following is an example of a ___________.

```
<xsd:pattern value="\d{1}-\d{5}-\d{5}-\{1}"/>
```

A facet

B structure

C sequence

D chameleon

Topic C: Creating a schema

Explanation

You can use XML Spy to create a schema from scratch. You can also use it to convert an existing DTD to a schema.

DTD to Schema conversion

You'll design *schema.xsd* for the contacts list. To do so, you'll use a quick method to create a small schema from existing DTD and XML files. This activity also illustrates that DTDs and schemas can be similar in how they work, even if they are coded differently. The schema does most of the tasks that a DTD does, but offers more control.

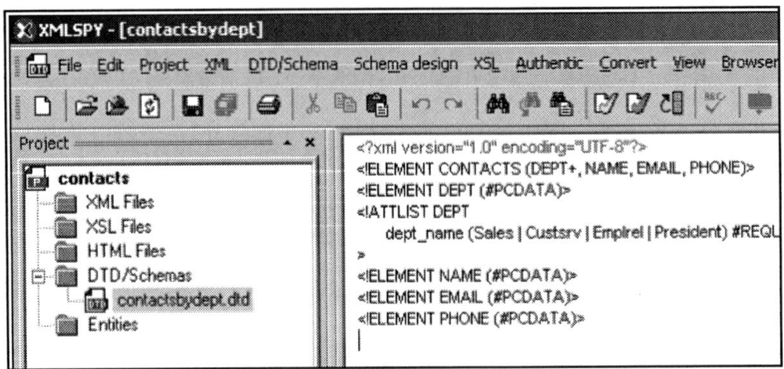

Exhibit 4-14: Contactsbydept.dtd in text view

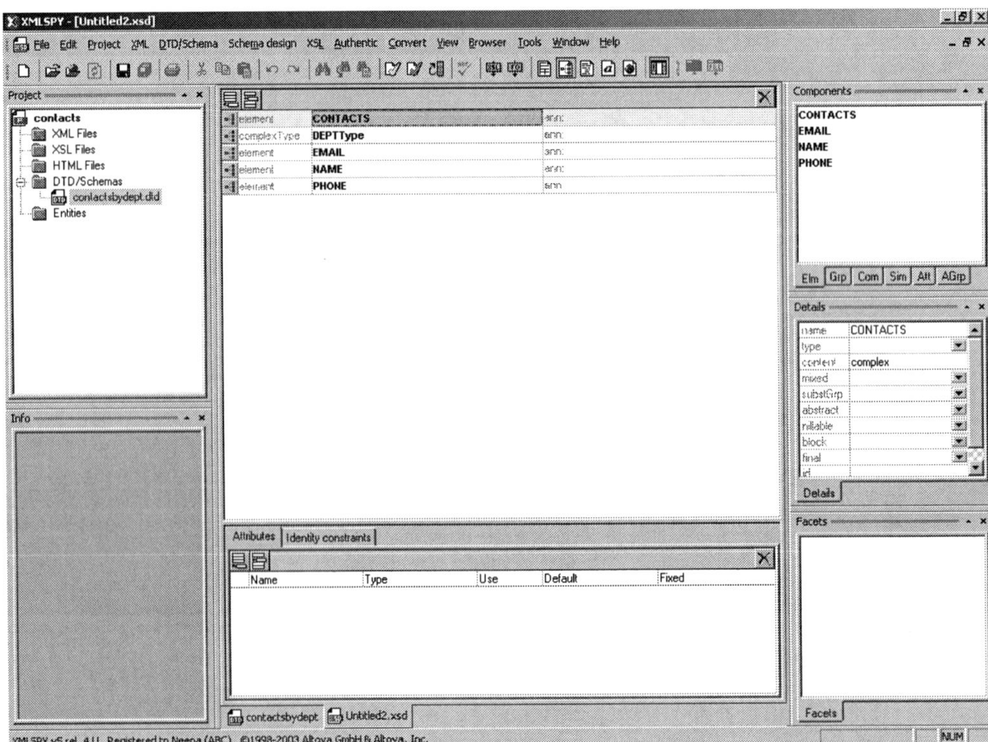

Exhibit 4-15: Contactsbydept.xsd

Do it!

C-1: Converting a DTD to Schema

Here's how	Here's why
1 Launch XML Spy	
2 Choose **Project**, **Open Project...**	
Click the **Look in** list arrow	
Navigate to the current unit folder	
Select **contacts**	
Click **Open**	
3 In the Project pane, double-click **DTD/Schemas**	
Double-click **contactsbydept.dtd**	
Choose **View**, **Text view**	To view the code, as shown in Exhibit 3-16.
4 Choose **DTD/Schema**	
Click **Convert DTD/Schema...**	To open the Convert DTD/Schema dialog box.
5 Select the **W3C Schema**, **Complex types**, and **Make global definition** option buttons	
Click **OK**	To convert the DTD to a schema. (As shown in Exhibit 3-17.)
Save the file as **contactsbydept.xsd**	In the current unit folder.

6 Click the **CONTACTS** element icon

element	CONTACTS
complexType	DEPTType
element	EMAIL
element	NAME
element	PHONE

To expand the Schema Design view of the element, and examine and compare the schema.

Observe the Details area in the right pane

The contacts element has been converted to a complex element because it contains other elements.

In the middle pane, click the **NAME** element

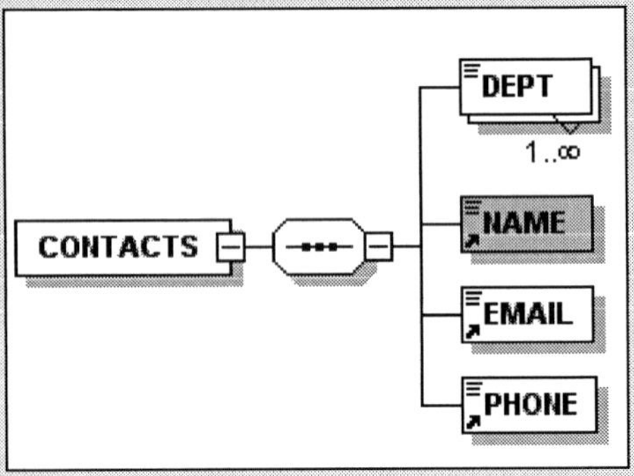

Observe the Details area in the right pane

Note that it has been converted to a simple element because it's a leaf and does not contain any other elements or attributes.

7 Save your changes

8 Click the **DEPT** element

Observe the Details area in the right pane

In the original DTD shown in Exhibit 3-18, the DEPT element was coded as DEPT+. Also note that the `DEPT` element has `!ATTLIST` defined as `dept_name` with a finite list of values.

9 Switch to Text view

To view the contactsbydept.xsd code.

Creating schema from scratch

Explanation

Next, you'll create an XML schema from scratch as a document model for a customer list, and use it to validate the elements and the data within the elements in an XML document. Then, you'll create a valid XML file that conforms to the new schema. Although you have conversion tools to convert DTDs to schemas, the results might not be what you want or need. Plan carefully to make sure that a schema file will be extensible and reusable.

Do it!

C-2: Creating XML schema from scratch

Here's how	Here's why
1 In the XML Spy Project pane, click **DTD/Schemas**	
Choose **File**, **New...**	To create a new schema.
Click **xsd W3CXML Schema**	
Click **OK**	To open an empty schema.
Double-click the highlighted field and replace the default root element text with **TLSales**	This is Schema Design view. TLSales is shown as a global component in the top pane, with attributes in the lower pane. The upper-right pane, called the *helper pane* or *Component Navigator*, displays TLSales in the Elm tab.
2 Choose **File**, **Save As...**	To save the new schema.
In the File name box, enter **customer.xsd**	
Click **Save**	
3 Choose **Schema design**, **Schema settings**	(To open the Schema Settings dialog box.) You will define a specific namespace and create a generic document model.
Select **Target namespace**	
In the Target namespace text box, enter **http://tlsales.com/namespace**	
Click **OK**	

4 Click the **TLSales** element component icon

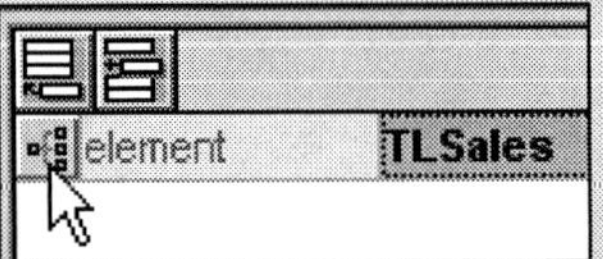

To add elements to the schema. A single blue box with the TLSales element appears.

Select the text under the box

Type **TLSales customer schema**

5 Right-click the **TLSales** element

Choose **Add Child**, **Sequence**

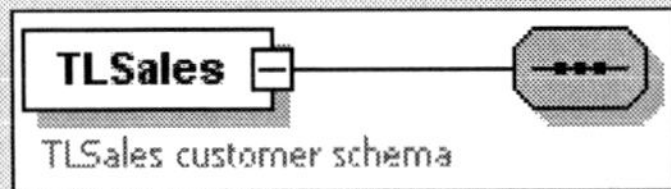

An octagon with a line and three dots appears. This is called the *Sequence compositor*.

6 Right-click the **Sequence compositor**

Choose **Add Child**, **Element**

Type **Address**

To specify the name of the element (as shown below).

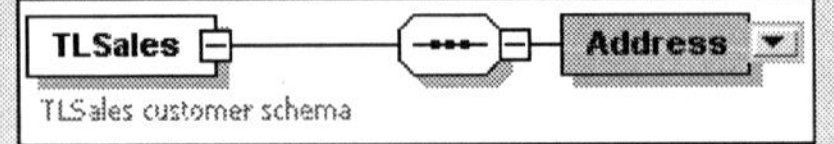

7 Right-click the **Sequence compositor**

Choose **Add Child**, **Element**

Type **Customer**

To specify the name of the element. You can use the current configuration for one Customer with an Address only. You'll change this configuration to have as many customers as necessary.

Press ENTER

8 Right-click the **Customer** element

From the shortcut menu, choose **Unbounded**

A small infinity symbol appears under the Customer element, as shown below, indicating a one-to-many relationship.

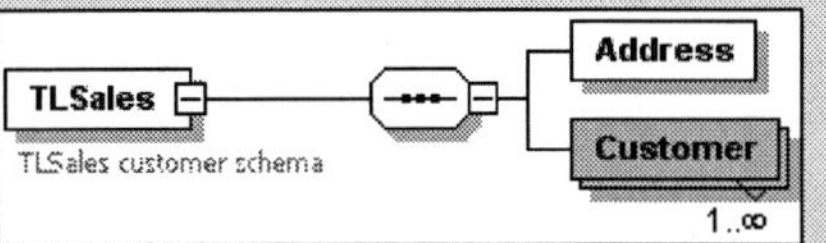

9 Right-click the **Address** element

You will add subelements to the Address element to store the XML data.

Choose **Add Child**, **Sequence**

Right-click the new **Sequence compositor**

Choose **Add Child**, **Element**

Type **Name**

You'll need to restrict the Name element to occur only once and to contain only text data. To do this, make sure the Name element is selected.

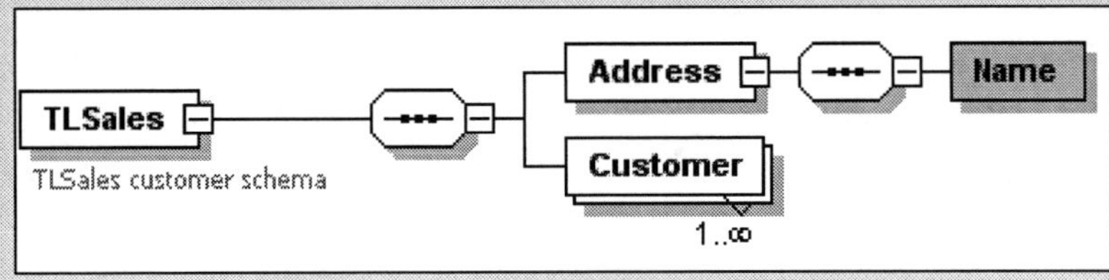

10 In the Details pane, select **xs:string** from the **type** list

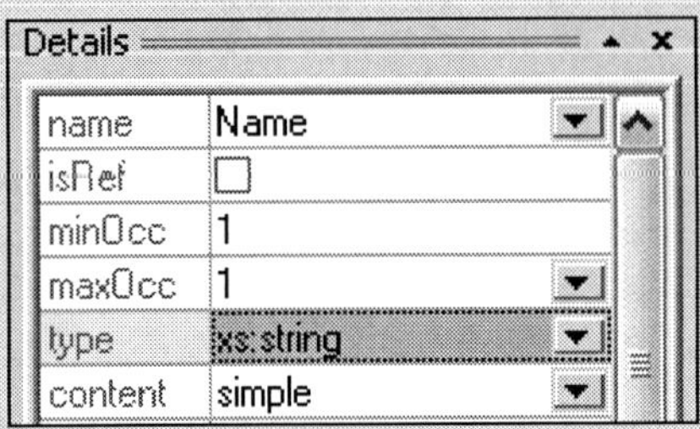

Note that the minOcc and maxOcc fields both default to a value of 1, which is desired. The Name element icon should now have three small lines in the top-left corner, denoting string text.

Click the **NAME** element

Hold down the CTRL key and drag to the right until a small plus sign appears, and then release

As shown below.

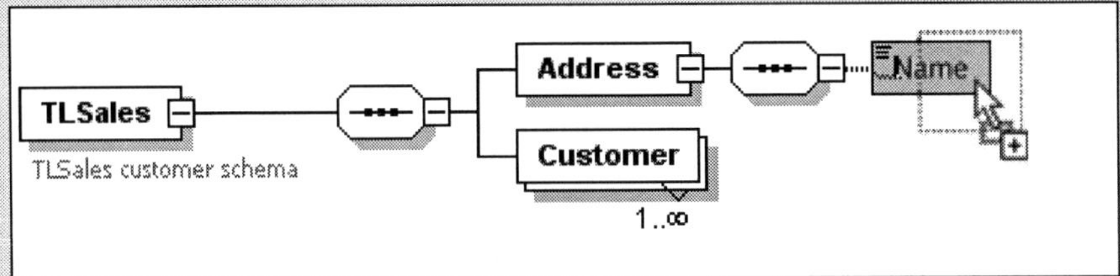

11 Double-click the second **Name** element twice

To select the text.

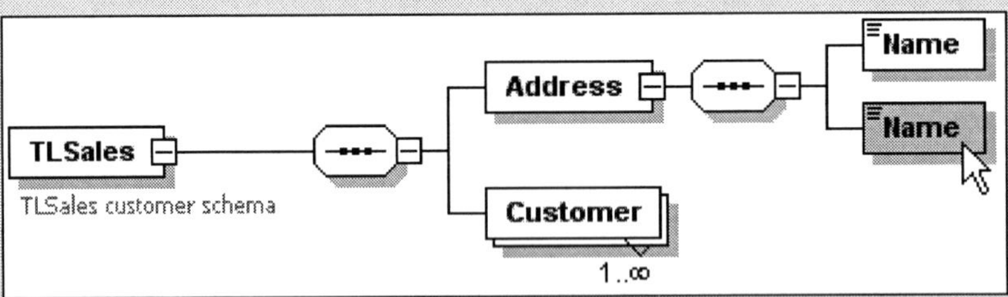

Change the element name to **Street**

12 Add one more element, named **City**

13 Choose **Schema design** — To configure the schema view to edit specific settings.

Click **View config** — A Schema display configuration dialog box appears.

Click the **Append** icon

Click the list arrow, and then select **type**

Click **OK** — The content model displays the type under each element.

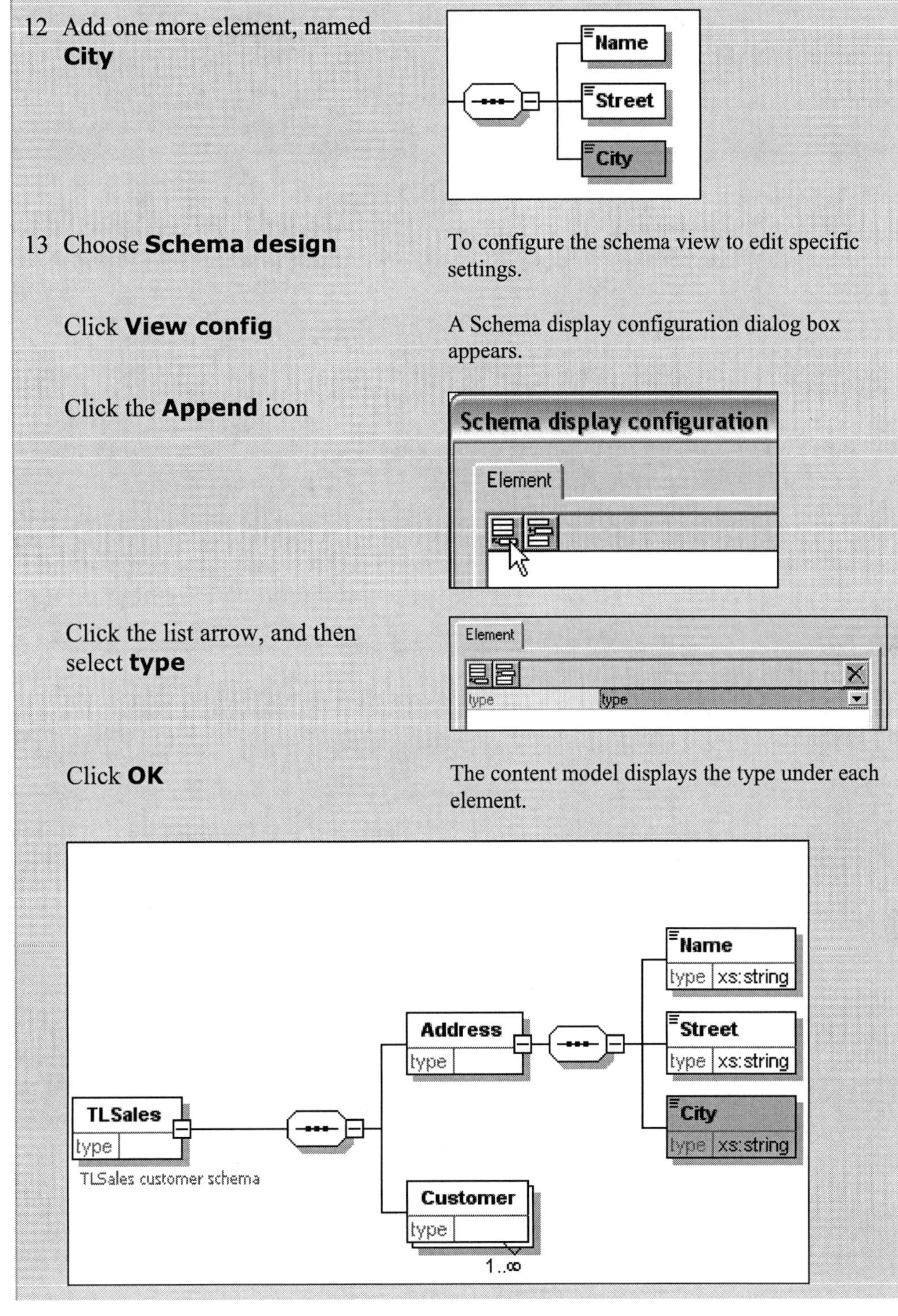

14	Create the following subelements to the Customer element: **First**, **Last**, **Phone**, **Fax**, **Email**, and **DiscountCode**	These will be simple types, meaning simple content models.
	Right-click the **Fax** element	
	From the shortcut menu, choose **Optional**	To set the Fax element as optional. It now appears with a dotted outline.
15	Click the **DiscountCode** element	You will change the requirements for the DiscountCode element so that it is an integer and limited to a value less than 999.
	In the details pane, click **type**	
	Select **xs:integer**	
	Click the **maxIncl** field of the Facets tab	
	Enter **999** as the maximum value allowed	
	Press ENTER	
16	Save your changes to the file and the project	

Global components in a schema

Explanation

You can add global components in a schema. You'll create a global AddressType component, which will create a template to handle the difference between United States (US) and Canadian address formats.

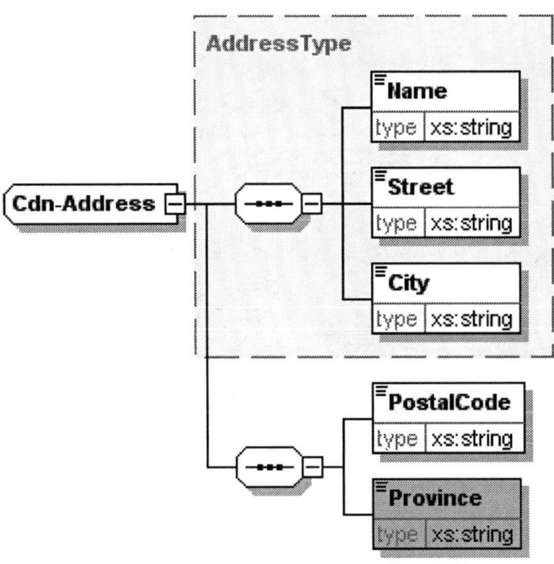

Exhibit 4-16: Province has the same requirements as PostalCode

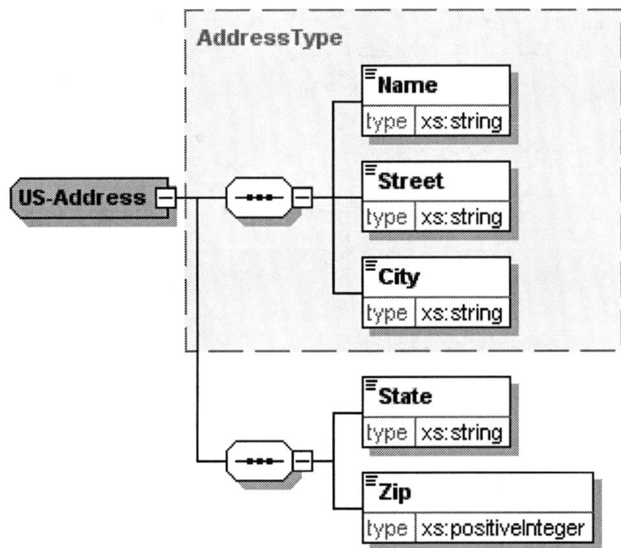

Exhibit 4-17: The US-Address model

Do it!

C-3: Adding global components in a schema

Here's how	Here's why
1 Right-click the **Address** element	
Choose **Make Global, Complex type**	The element appears in a yellow box, indicating that it's now a global component.
Click the **Display all Globals** icon	To display two global components, the TLSales and AddressType elements.
2 Click the **Com(plex)** tab of the Component Navigator	To verify that AddressType is also visible.
3 Double-click **AddressType**	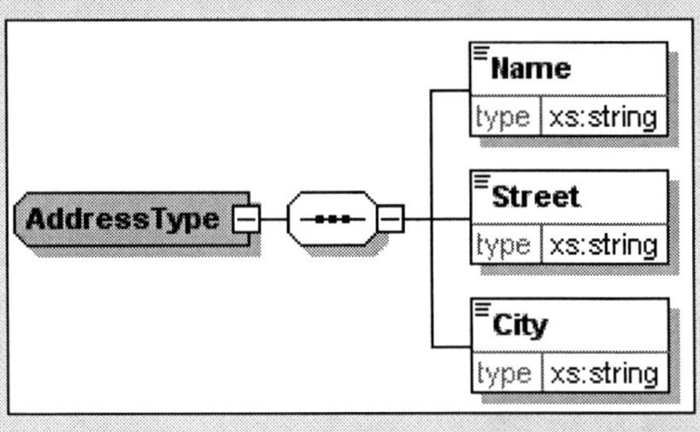 To view the new content model

4 Click the **Display all Globals** icon	You will create the different Address formats.
5 Click the **Append** icon	
Choose **ComplexType**	
In the text box, enter **Cdn-Address**	
Press ENTER	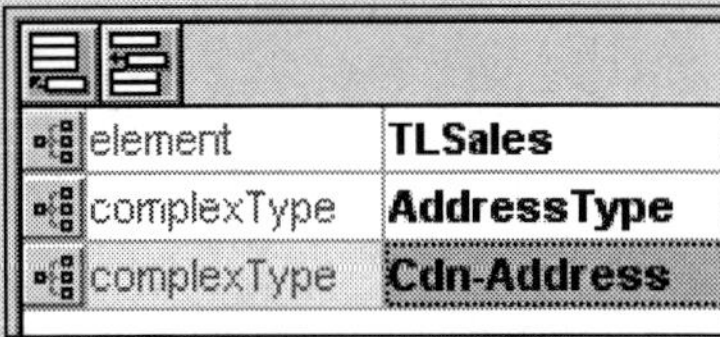
6 Click the **Cdn-Address** component icon	To view the new content model.
In the Details pane, click the **base** item	
Select **AddressType**	To view a copy of the AddressType content model in a yellow box. This is the generic part of the Address to which you can now add the requirements for a Canadian postal code.
7 Right-click the **Cdn-Address** element	
From the shortcut menu, choose **Add Child**, **Sequence**	To add another Sequence compositor. The new compositor appears outside of the generic global AddressType content model box.
8 Right-click the new Sequence compositor	
Choose **Add Child**, **Element**	
Type **PostalCode**	To specify the element name.
Press TAB	

9 From the type list box, select **xs:string**	PostalCode type xs:string 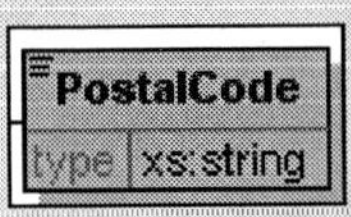
Create a second element named **Province** with the same requirements as PostalCode	As shown in Exhibit 3-19.
10 Create the second Address model for the US requirement	
Type **US-Address** as the name for the new global complex type	Use State instead of Province. The Zip code should be a xs:positiveinteger. The final model should look like Exhibit 3-20.
11 Save the file and the project	

Unit summary: Schema

Topic A

In this topic, you learned some of the **limitations of DTDs**. You learned that the W3C's XML Schema Working Group developed the "XML Schema Part 1: Structures" and "XML Schema Part 2: Datatypes" recommendations, which are called **"XML Schema"** or "**XSchema**."

Topic B

In this topic, you learned that document models are described in terms of **constraints**. You also learned that Schemas provide more **XML namespace support** than DTDs. You learned that **element types** determine the appearance of elements and their content in instance documents, and that **compositors** define groups of elements and attributes within the schema. You also learned that **XML inheritance** comes in two forms: **restriction** and **extension**, and that schemas provide the ability to declare **empty content elements** and **mixed content elements**. Finally, you learned how to define your data more precisely by using **facets**.

Topic C

In this topic, you **created schemas**. You learned how to **convert an existing DTD to a schema**. You also created a schema from scratch, and you learned how to **add global components** to your schema.

Review questions

1. A _________ defines what can appear in a given language or document.

2. _________ provide a more precise definition for data contained within a simple type element or attribute.

3. Target namespaces in the schema facilitate validation of conforming instance documents. True or false?

4. Choice compositors indicate that only one element can appear in the XML document, and that the element must be chosen from several choices. True or false?

5. Elements that are declared in subelements of the schema element, but not in the scope of the schema element itself, are called _________.

6. The approach that employs global references and is intended to create a flatter schema structure is called a _________.

7. The schema document language is called a _________ because each element declaration is visible only within the element where it is defined, and all its descendants.

8 What is the default schema structure used by XML Spy?

9 Which value of the "use" attribute do you choose if the attribute is optional?

Independent practice activity

1 You have been asked to validate a customer schema file called customer.xsd to see if it creates a valid XML file called customer.xml. Part of this process is to document everything for the users.

   a Create the customer.xsd and customer.xml files.

   b Validate the XML file.

   c Record the steps so that another user can successfully perform the same task.

2 Using the customer.xsd file that you have, create another schema file called Cdn-customer.xsd, like the one shown in Exhibit 3-20, to facilitate a corporate expansion. Make the sequence compositor unbounded.

   a Change the TLSales child element sequence to Customer, then Address.

   b Change the Address element type to Cdn-Address.

   c Finally, test the Cdn-customer.xsd file by creating a valid Cdn-customer.xml file.

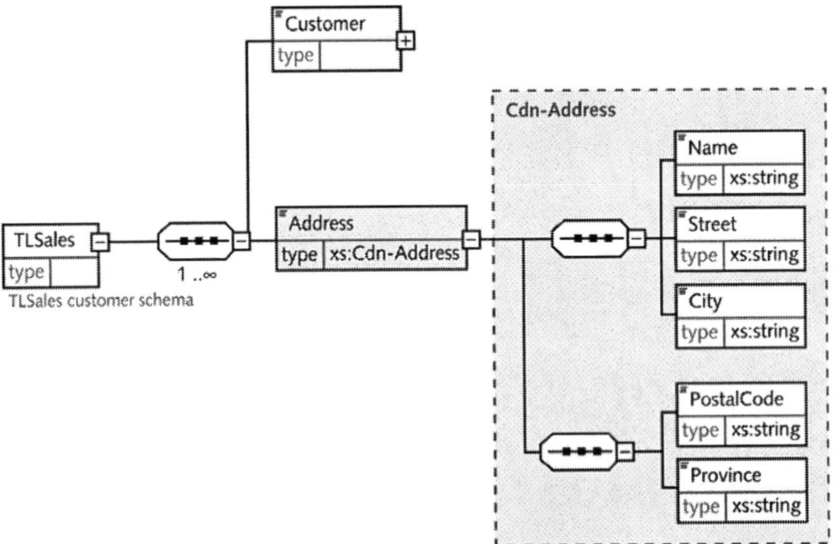

Exhibit 4-18: Model of Cdn-customer.xsd

Unit 5

Cascading Style Sheets (CSS)

Unit time: 40 minutes

Complete this unit, and you'll know how to:

A Identify the benefits and limitations of styling XML documents with CSS, and link an XML document to a style sheet.

B Apply simple CSS styles to an XML document.

Topic A: CSS and XML

Explanation

On its own, XML cannot control a document's visual design. You need to use a style sheet to tell a browser how each element should be displayed. There are two standard style languages for XML; CSS (Cascading Style Sheets) and XSL (Extensible Stylesheet Language). CSS is the standard style language for HTML documents, but you can also use it to style XML documents for viewing in a browser.

Applying CSS to XML

XML is most commonly used as a descriptive framework for data, and is not often used to present information in Web browsers. However, when you intend to display your XML documents over the Web, you can use CSS to enhance their visual presentation. By default, when Internet Explorer 5 displays an XML document, it only displays the document's tree structure.

By linking your XML document(s) to a CSS style sheet, you can control any visual design aspect of the document, including colors, layout, fonts and font sizes, borders, margins, and other styles. By linking your XML document(s) to an external style sheets, you can control the presentation of any number of documents from a single location.

Limitations of using CSS to style XML documents

While CSS allows you to specify fonts, colors, margins and layout specifications, it can't manipulate XML data, change the order of elements, or make computations. When you need that functionality, you need to use XSL. Therefore, CSS is only useful when you have transformed XML into an XML document that's intended for display over the Web, or when you have transformed XML to an HTML document. In other words, CSS is only useful with XML with the linear structure of the XML document is the intended display sequence.

XSL is a more powerful style language for XML, because it allows you to transform an XML document into other types of documents, including PDFs and standard HTML Web pages.

Do it!

A-1: Discussing CSS and XML

Questions and answers

1 Name some advantages to using CSS to style XML documents.

2 Name some disadvantages to using CSS to style XML documents.

Linking XML documents to a style sheet

Explanation

To link an XML document to an external style sheet, you need to insert the following processing instruction into the prolog of the XML document:

```
<?xml-stylesheet type="text/css" href="stylesheetname.css"?>
```

The first part of the processing instruction—`?xml-stylesheet`—informs the parser that the XML document must access an external style sheet. The media type specification `type="text/css"` follows next. Whenever an XML document uses an external style sheet, this specification must appear. It tells the parser what media type to specify in the HTTP data headers when the external style sheet is retrieved. Text/css means that the primary media type (also called the general media type) is text, while the media subtype (also called the specific format) is css.

Note: For further information regarding the text/css media type, refer to the Request for Comments RFC2318 on the Internet Society's Web site at www.ietf.org/rfc/rfc2318.txt.

The last part of the instruction `href="stylesheetname.css"` specifies the path and filename of the style sheet file. In this example, the parser looks for the style sheet file in the same directory as the XML document because the instruction does not include a path to the style sheet's filename. If it is not located in the same directory, you must include a path to its directory, as shown in the following example:

```
href="styles/mystyles.css"
```

Exhibit 4-1 shows another example of a CSS processing instruction. In contacts.xml, the third line specifies a style sheet file in the theme directory.

```
<?xml version="1.0" encoding="UTF-8" ?>
<!DOCTYPE CONTACTS SYSTEM "contacts.dtd" >
<?xml:stylesheet type="text/css"
href="http://localhost/username/theme/tlsales.css" ?>
<CONTACTS>
     <SALES>
          <NAME>Jim Sleek</NAME>
          <EMAIL>JSleek@TLSales.com</EMAIL>
          <PHONE>1 800 123-4567</PHONE>
     </SALES>
     <SALES>
          <NAME>Anna Gold</NAME>
          <EMAIL>AGold@TLSales.com</EMAIL>
          <PHONE>1 800 123-4567</PHONE>
          <HEAD />
     </SALES>
     <COURSES>
      Want to check out
      <LINK xml:type="simple" href="http://www.w3c.org"
       onClick="location.href='http://www.w3c.org' ">W3C</LINK>?
     </COURSES>
</CONTACTS>
```

tlsales.css is located in the *theme* directory.

Exhibit 5-1: contacts.xml refers to CSS file in the theme directory

When you open an XML document in Internet Explorer, the browser displays the document's tree structure. When you link the document to a style sheet, the browser displays the raw data, instead of the elements in the document tree. You can then add style rules to the style sheet to control how each element in the document is displayed.

Do it!

A-2: Linking an XML document to a style sheet

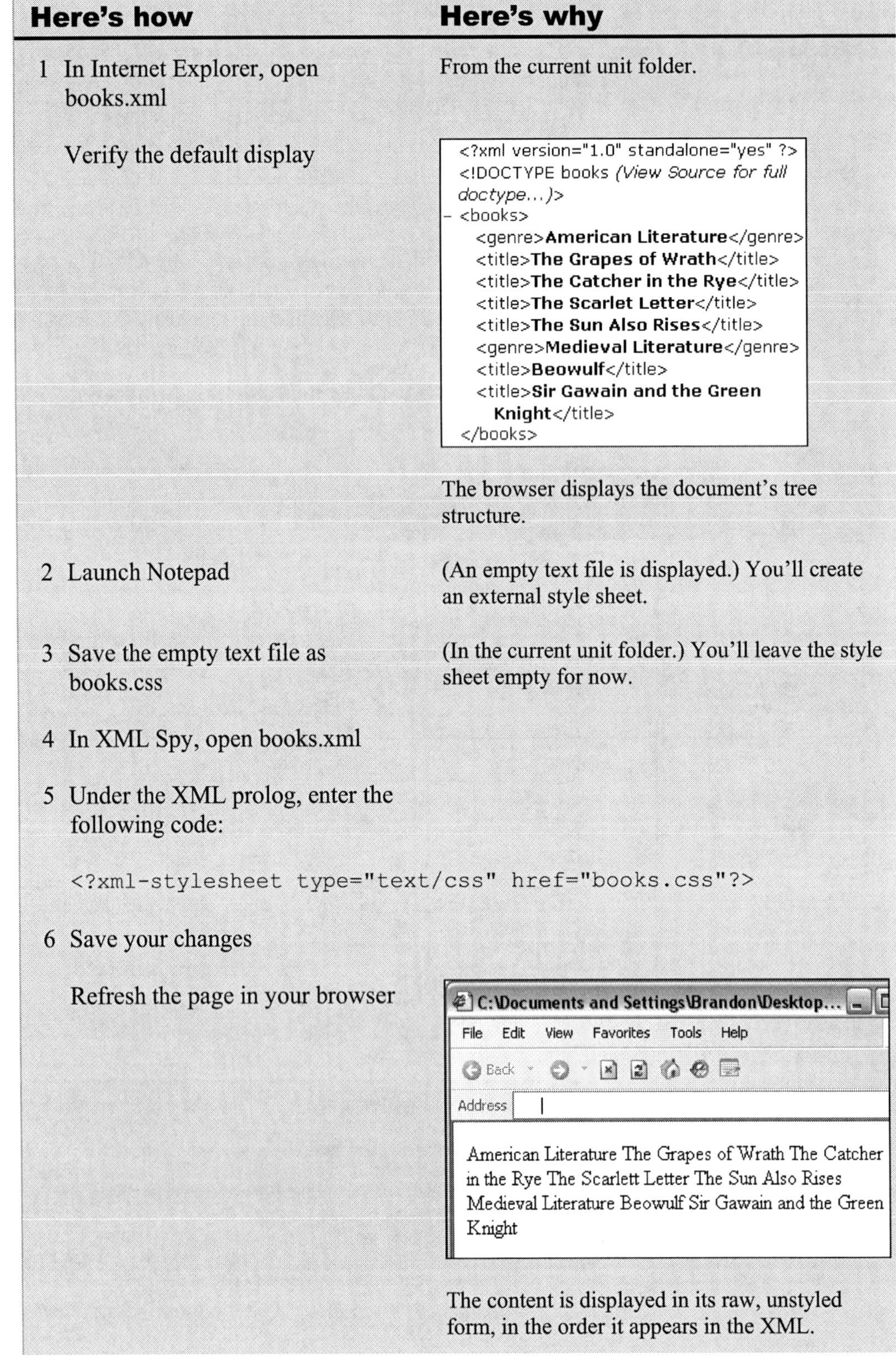

Here's how	Here's why
1 In Internet Explorer, open books.xml	From the current unit folder.
Verify the default display	<?xml version="1.0" standalone="yes" ?> <!DOCTYPE books *(View Source for full doctype...)*> - <books> <genre>**American Literature**</genre> <title>**The Grapes of Wrath**</title> <title>**The Catcher in the Rye**</title> <title>**The Scarlet Letter**</title> <title>**The Sun Also Rises**</title> <genre>**Medieval Literature**</genre> <title>**Beowulf**</title> <title>**Sir Gawain and the Green Knight**</title> </books> The browser displays the document's tree structure.
2 Launch Notepad	(An empty text file is displayed.) You'll create an external style sheet.
3 Save the empty text file as books.css	(In the current unit folder.) You'll leave the style sheet empty for now.
4 In XML Spy, open books.xml	
5 Under the XML prolog, enter the following code: `<?xml-stylesheet type="text/css" href="books.css"?>`	
6 Save your changes	
Refresh the page in your browser	C:\Documents and Settings\Brandon\Desktop... File Edit View Favorites Tools Help Back Address American Literature The Grapes of Wrath The Catcher in the Rye The Scarlett Letter The Sun Also Rises Medieval Literature Beowulf Sir Gawain and the Green Knight The content is displayed in its raw, unstyled form, in the order it appears in the XML.

Topic B: CSS styles

Explanation

A CSS style sheet is just a text file containing CSS rules. No XML or HTML tags are allowed in an external style sheet. There are several CSS properties you can use to apply styles to XML (and HTML) documents. In this topic, you'll write some basic CSS styles to modify the presentation of a simple XML document.

CSS rules and syntax

Unlike HTML, which is made up of pre-defined elements that all have default formatting when viewed in a browser, XML elements are the arbitrary creation of the XML author, and therefore have no meaning to a browser. That's why you need to use a style sheet if you intend to display your XML documents in a browser.

Using the XML document example in Exhibit 5-2, the tlsales.css style sheet might look something like Exhibit 5-3.

```
<?xml version="1.0" encoding="UTF-8" ?>
<!DOCTYPE CONTACTS SYSTEM "contacts.dtd" >
<?xml:stylesheet type="text/css"
href="http://localhost/username/theme/tlsales.css" ?>
<CONTACTS>
      <SALES>
          <NAME>Jim Sleek</NAME>
          <EMAIL>JSleek@TLSales.com</EMAIL>
          <PHONE>1 800 123-4567</PHONE>
      </SALES>
      <SALES>
          <NAME>Anna Gold</NAME>
          <EMAIL>AGold@TLSales.com</EMAIL>
          <PHONE>1 800 123-4567</PHONE>
          <HEAD />
      </SALES>
      <COURSES>
        Want to check out
        <LINK xml:type="simple" href="http://www.w3c.org"
         onClick="location.href='http://www.w3c.org' ">W3C</LINK>?
      </COURSES>
</CONTACTS>
```

Exhibit 5-2: The contacts.xml file, linked to tlsales.css

```
/* Sample Cascading Style Sheet File */

CONTACTS {font-family: Arial, Helvetica, sans-serif; font-size: 12pt}

SALES {display: block; color: rgb(000,000,128); text-align: center}
NAME {display: block; font-weight: bold; text-align: center}
EMAIL, PHONE {display: block; margin: 0.5cm; text-align: center}
LINK {display: inline; color: #0000FF; text-decoration: underline; cursor: hand}
```

Comment line

Five CSS style rules

Exhibit 5-3: The tlsales.css style sheet, which contains 5 style rules

Exhibit 4-7 shows how the contacts.xml document might look in Internet Explorer now that it's linked to tlsales.css.

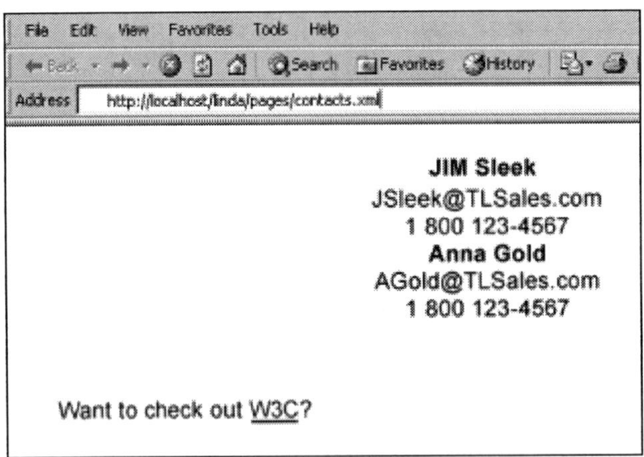

Exhibit 5-4: contacts.xml in Internet Explorer

The tlsales.css style sheet contains a comment line at the beginning, which is followed by five CSS style rules. The comment line is optional, but you can use them to indicate the author name and the date and time the style sheet was last modified.

There's no limit to the number of style rules you can have in a style sheet. CSS rules must follow a consistent syntax:

```
selector { property: value; property: value; }
```

The *selector* is the element you want to style. For example, if you want to style an element named `<Author>`, then you would use `Author` as your selector. After the selector comes the declaration. The *declaration* contains the CSS properties and their values. All CSS properties must be separated from their value with a colon. If you need more than one property for in a rule, you can separate the `property: value` pairs with a semicolon.

For example, here's a style rule that makes all `<Author>` elements navy blue and underlined:

```
Author { color: navy; text-decoration: underline; }
```

With XML, CSS selectors are case-sensitive. For example, if you have an element named `lastName`, your selector must be typed as `lastName`.

Combining selectors

If you want two or more elements to share the same styles, you don't have to write two copies of the same style rule. You can simply combine two selectors in a rule by separating them with a comma, like this:

```
Author, Co-author { color: navy; text-decoration: underline; }
```

Inheritance

Most CSS styles inherit from parent to child elements. In other words, if you apply a style to a parent element, its child elements will also pick up the styles. For example, say your XML document contains the following code:

```
<contact>
<firstName>John</firstName>
<lastName>Smith</lastName>
<phone>555-6228</phone>
</contact>
```

In your style sheet, you can create a rule for the contact element, and all its styles will inherit to its child elements, `firstName`, `lastName`, and `phone`. If you want an element to override an inherited style, you need to specify a style explicitly for that element.

Do it!

B-1: Discussing CSS rules

Questions and answers
1 How many major components does a style rule have, and what are they called?
2 The concept whereby a style specified for a parent element is passed to a child element, unless a specific rule is created for that child, is called __________.
3 The __________ portion of a rule lists the element or elements to which the style will apply.

Displaying inline and block elements

Explanation

In HTML, an element can either be a block or inline element. A block element creates its own line break, like a paragraph or heading. An inline element does not create a line break, and is typically intended to mark up a word or phrase within a block element. HTML elements are already defined as either inline or block elements by default; however, XML elements have no default formatting. When you create a style sheet to format an XML document, you need to use the `display` property to specify if you want an element to be a block or inline element. If you want an element to display as a block element, you would write:

```
elementName { display: block; }
```

If you want an element to display as an inline element, you would write:

```
elementName { display: inline; }
```

Fonts and colors

To customize an element's font face, font size, and color, you use the `font-family`, `font-size`, and `color` property, respectively. The following table lists each property's possible values and provides an example.

Property	Values
`font-family`	Any valid font family name, such as *Verdana*, *Arial*, *Helvetica*, *Times New Roman*, *Courier New*, or the generic family names *serif*, *sans-serif*, and *monospaced*. For example, if you want an element named `Price` to display in the font Verdana, you would write: `Price { font-family: Verdana; }`
`font-size`	Any positive integer, followed immediately by a unit of measurement. Valid units of measurement include points (pt), pixels (px), percentages (%), and ems (em). For example, if you want an element named `Price` to display at 22 pixels, you would write: `Price { font-size: 22px; }`

`color`	Any valid color name, hexadecimal value, or RGB notational value. Hexadecimal values are the most common method because there is consistent support for them across multiple browsers. For example, to make an element named Price display with navy blue text, you could write:
	
	`Price { color: navy; }`
	
	You could also use one of many possible hexadecimal values to achieve the same or similar color:
	
	`Price { color:  #000066; }`

Note: To view a complete list of all CSS properties and their values, go to:

```
http://www.w3.org/TR/REC-CSS2/propidx.html
```

Do it!

B-2: Creating CSS styles

Here's how	Here's why
1 Switch to books.css	(In Notepad). You'll add rules to the style sheet.
2 Enter the following code: `genre {font-size: 24px; display: block; }` Save your changes Refresh books.xml in your browser	 File Edit View Favorites Tools Help Back Address American Literature The Grapes of Wrath The Catcher in the Rye The Scarlet Letter The Sun Also Rises Medieval Literature Beowulf Sir Gawain and the Green Knight The two genre elements now display on their own line, in accordance with the display: block property, and the text is larger than the default font size. The book titles are all on one line because no display property is applied to them.
3 Switch to books.css	
4 On a new line, enter the following code: `title { color: navy; display: block; }`	
5 Save your changes and refresh books.xml in your browser	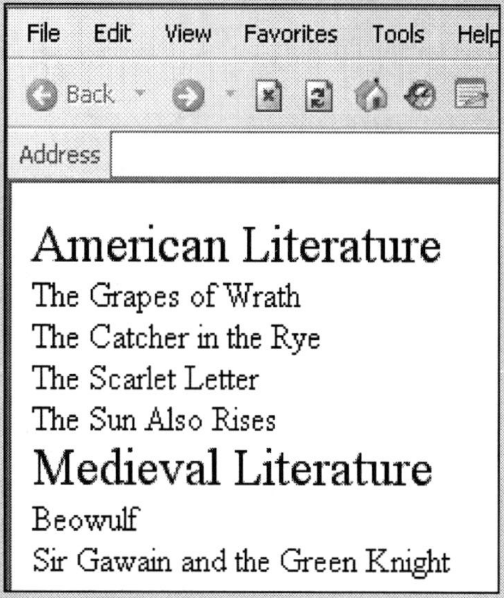 File Edit View Favorites Tools Help Back Address American Literature The Grapes of Wrath The Catcher in the Rye The Scarlet Letter The Sun Also Rises Medieval Literature Beowulf Sir Gawain and the Green Knight Each book title displays on its own line, in accordance with the display: block property, and the title text is navy.

6 Switch to books.css

7 On a new line, enter the following code:

```
books { font-family: sans-serif; }
```

8 Save your changes and refresh books.xml in your browser

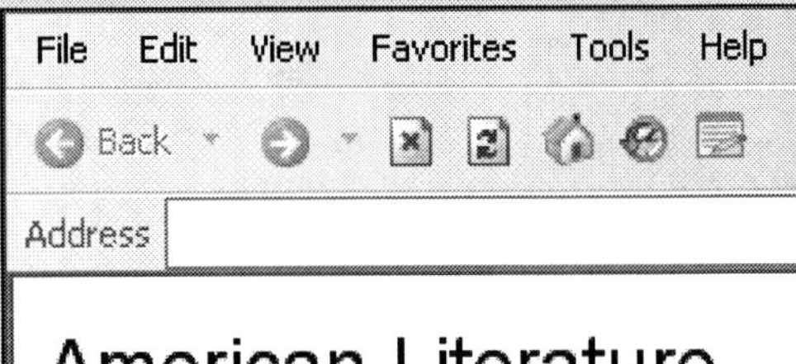

The style was applied to the books element, which is the parent of the genre and title elements. Therefore, the rule of inheritance applies, and both elements appear in a sans-serif font.

Classes

Explanation

CSS *classes* allow you to create and name your own styles and apply them to a single instance of an element, or share a style among different elements. Using the books.xml file as an example, say you want to make only one of the `<title>` elements red to indicate that it's out of print. You can't use `title` as a selector because the style will apply to all titles. To target one or more, but not all, instances of an element, you can use a class selector. A class selector begins with a period, and is followed immediately by your desired class name. For example:

```
.outOfPrint { color: red; }
```

To use this class style in an element, you need to use the class attribute using your class name as its value. For example:

```
<title class="outOfPrint">The Pond Thing</title>
```

To ensure that the books.xml file is valid, you must declare the `class` attribute in the appropriate DTD or schema. The books.xml file has an embedded DTD, so you would need to insert the following declaration:

```
<!ATTLIST outOfPrint class CDATA #IMPLIED>
```

This declaration states that the `<title>` element, and only the `<title>` element, accepts the `outOfPrint` attribute, whose value is character data.

Do it!

B-3: Applying a class style and updating the DTD

Here's how	Here's why
1 Switch to books.css	In Notepad.
On a new line, enter the following rule: `.saleItem { color: red }`	
2 Save your changes and close the style sheet	
3 Switch to books.xml	In XML Spy.
4 In the title element for The Scarlet Letter, insert the following code: `class="saleItem"`	
5 Under the last element declaration, add the following attribute declaration: `<!ATTLIST title class CDATA #IMPLIED>`	
6 Click [button]	(The green check mark button.) To validate the file.
Save your changes	

7 Refresh books.xml in your browser

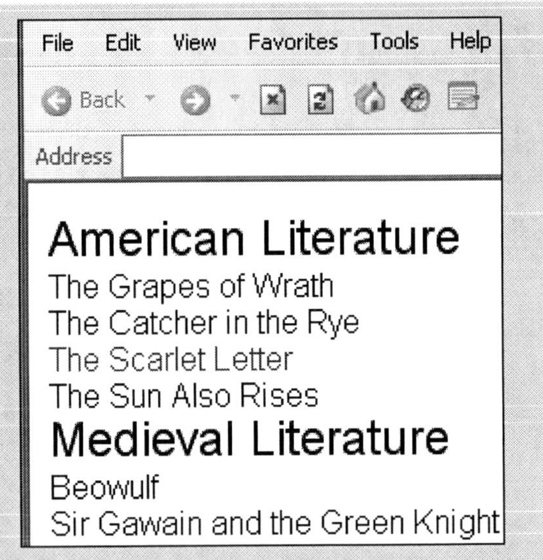

The Scarlet Letter is red, while the other titles are unaffected by the class style.

8 Close XML Spy

9 Close your browser

Unit summary: Cascading Style Sheets (CSS)

Topic A

In this unit, you learned the **advantages** and **limitations** of using **CSS** to style XML documents. You also learned how to **create an external style sheet** and **link an XML document** to it.

Topic B

In this unit, you learned the **syntax of CSS rules**, and you learned some fundamental **CSS properties**. You also learned about the principle of **inheritance**, and how to set an element as a **block** or **inline** element. Finally, you learned how to apply a **class style**, and how to include the **class attribute** in the attribute declaration list of a DTD.

Review questions

1 Why are there no default inline/block display values for XML elements as there are for HTML elements?

2 An element named `family` contains two PCDATA elements, `parent` and `child`. In a style sheet, you write the following code:

```
family { color: maroon; }
```

Which of the following will be true?

A The style will have no effect because the `family` element does not contain data of its own.

B All child elements of `family` will be maroon.

C Only the `parent` element will be maroon.

D Only the `child` element will be maroon.

3 If you want to use the `class` attribute in an XML document, you must make sure that the corresponding DTD contains an attribute declaration for the `class` attribute, or your XML document will not be valid. True or false?

A True

B False

Independent practice activity

Create a new class of your choice and apply it to two titles. Insert a new attribute declaration in the DTD to account for your new class. Validate the XML document, save your changes, and verify the results in your browser.

Unit 6

XML transformations

Unit time: 120 minutes

Complete this unit, and you'll know how to:

A Identify the need to transform XML data, and common transformation methods.

B Transform an XML document to HTML, apply conditional statements, and change XML grammar by using XSLT.

Topic A: Transforming XML documents

Explanation

Transforming the data in XML documents prepares that data for further processing. There are two phases to the transformation process. The first phase is a *structural transformation*, in which the data is converted from the structure of the incoming XML document to the structure of the desired output. The second phase is a *formatting transformation*, in which the new structure is changed to the desired format (e.g., HTML, PDF, etc.). Exhibit 6-1 shows the basic transformation process. We'll focus primarily on the transformation of XML documents by using the Extensible Stylesheet Language Transformation (XSLT) language, which is one aspect of the Extensible Stylesheet Language (XSL) trio—XSL, XSLT, and XPath.

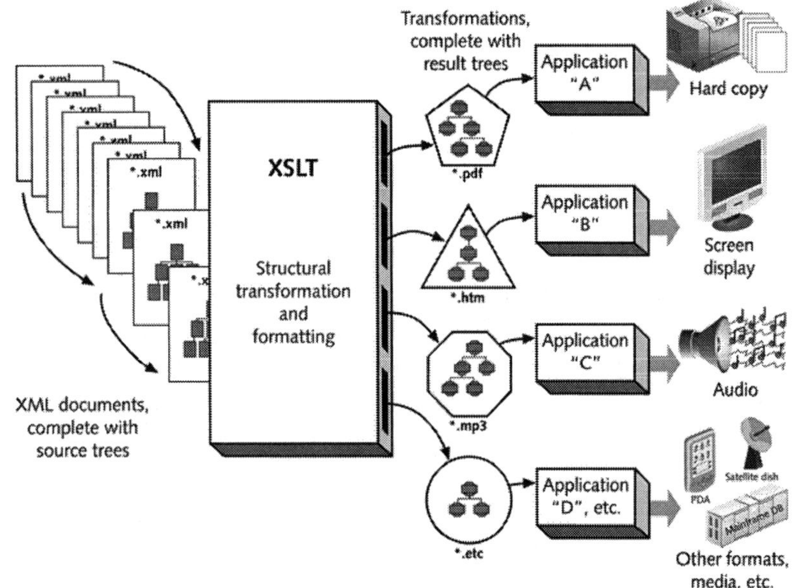

Exhibit 6-1: The XSLT transformation process

Why transform XML?

Even in its raw form, XML is reasonably easy to read and write. However, it is very rarely used in its raw or original form. XML data can take the form of a Web page, a print document, or an audio, image, or video file. To transfer XML data between applications on the same or different systems, the data has to be transformed from the data model used by one application to the model used in another.

For example, an invoice can be presented on a screen or printed page, but it can also be used as a form in an accounting or tax preparation application. Sports statistics, displayed on TV sets and browsers everywhere, are also summarized, indexed, and aggregated in databases. You transform XML data so that it can serve several different purposes.

Converting XML to HTML for display on the Web is one of the most commonly used transformations. After you transform the XML data into HTML format, you can display it on any browser.

Do it!

A-1: Discussing XML transformations

Exercises

1 What is the primary reason for performing XML transformations?

2 What is the first phase in the transformation process of an XML document?

A Formatting transformation

B Logical transformation

C Structural transformation

D Conceptual transformation

3 In a structural transformation, the data is converted from the structure of the incoming XML document to the structure of the desired output. True or false?

4 XML provides a standard way to interchange what type of data?

A Converted data

B Graphical data

C Unstructured data

D Structured data

Transforming data by using XSL, XPath and XSLT

Explanation

Originally, XSL's developers envisioned that XSL would be developed into a platform- and media-independent formatting language composed of two parts: a formatting language and a transformation language. The formatting language was to be a set of XML elements that would describe the various parts of page media, such as tables, headers, and footnotes. These descriptive elements would be the "formatting objects." The transformation language was intended to convert an XML document into a result tree, consisting of the XSL formatting objects. Thus, if the concept envisioned by the original developers had come to pass, XSL transformations would have consisted of a two-stage process: a structural transformation followed by formatting. However, during its development, the original XSL concept actually evolved into the following three XML-related languages:

- **XSL:** The XML vocabulary for specifying formatting objectives and other semantics.
- **XSL transformation (XSLT):** The language for transforming XML documents.
- **XML path language (XPath):** An expression language used to access or refer to parts of an XML document. Other XML-related languages also enlist aspects of XPath.

The XSL Version 1.0 Recommendation was endorsed in October 2001. Focusing on paged media, XSL 1.0 makes it possible to transform XML documents into professional quality products through the use of complex document formatting based on formatting objects and other properties.

XSL is a language for expressing stylesheets. Just as Cascading Stylesheets (CSS) are used with HTML documents, an XSL stylesheet is a file that describes how to display an XML document. XSL is compatible with CSS, although it uses a different syntax. XSL also adds advanced styling features that define two sets of elements: formatting objects and attributes. An XSL engine takes an XML document and an XSL stylesheet to produce a rendering of the document.

Using XPath for data transformation

The XML Path Language (Xpath) allows you to address specific parts of an XML document. For example, literal translations of XPath statements might be "select all paragraphs belonging to the chapter element," "select the third list item," and so on.

By using XPath, you can specify the locations of document structures or data in an XML document, and then process the information by using XSLT. In practice, it can be difficult to determine where XSLT ends and where XPath begins. XPath considers documents to be composed of nodes in a tree-like structure. XSLT uses XPath extensively to match nodes in an XML source tree.

Transforming data with XSLT

You can use XSLT to transform an XML document into any other format (e.g. another XML document, HTML, PDF, plain text, etc). XSLT stylesheets are nothing like Cascading Stylesheets (CSS). CSS concentrates on how data is displayed on the Web. XSLT stylesheets actually change the structure and type of an XML document (for example, to automatically generate tables of contents, cross-references, indexes, etc.). XSLT stylesheets can also transform an XML document into another XML document that has an entirely different XML grammar.

XSLT is different from conventional programming languages because it is based on template rules that specify how XML documents should be processed. Although conventional programming languages are often sequential, template rules can be followed in any order because XSLT is a declarative language. XSLT, like XPath, sees documents as a series of nodes in a tree-like structure. The XSLT stylesheet declares what output should be produced when a pattern in the XML document is matched.

Do it!

A-2: Discussing XSL, XPath, and XSLT

Exercises

1 What is considered the most common application of transformation today?

2 Transformations are affiliated with source node trees, while XSLT stylesheets are affiliated with result node trees. True or false?

3 Which of the following is true of XSLT?

A XSLT can transform one XML document into another type of file.

B XSLT needs XPath to transform XML data into another type of file.

C XSLT and CSS have similar functionality.

D XSLT concentrates on how data is displayed.

4 XSLT and XPath both consider documents to be composed of ________ in a tree-like structure.

5 The XSL transformation language was intended to convert an XML document into what type of tree?

A Source tree

B Result tree

C HTML tree

D Query context tree

6 Which of the following is not true of XSL?

A XSL is a language for expressing stylesheets.

B XSL describes how to display an XML document of a given type.

C XSL shares functionality with CSS.

D XSL uses the same syntax as CSS.

7 Which of the following is not true of XPath?

A XPath is a language that addresses specific parts of an XML document.

B XPath is a W3C recommendation.

C XPath is used to find information in an XML document.

D XPath does not consider documents to consist of nodes in a tree-like structure.

Topic B: Data transformation

Explanation

In this topic, you'll examine a sample transformation to reinforce XSLT transformation concepts, syntax, and structure. This transformation involves extracting a portion of the TLSales contact list, currently stored as an XML document called contacts.xml, and displaying the extracted portion in HTML format. The transformation process is demonstrated in Exhibit 6-2. Briefly summarized, the process is as follows:

1. An XML parser, or processor, is given an XML data document.
2. From references within the XML document, the XML parser locates a DTD (or a schema, if the author has specified one) and an XSLT stylesheet.
3. The parser then validates the XML document and XSLT stylesheet (because both should be well-formed XML documents).
4. The parser gives control to the XSL parser. The XSL parser, by using the XSLT stylesheet as its guide, performs the specified transformation and generates the appropriate result tree document. The result tree document is, in turn, used as the source document for subsequent processing by the respective application.

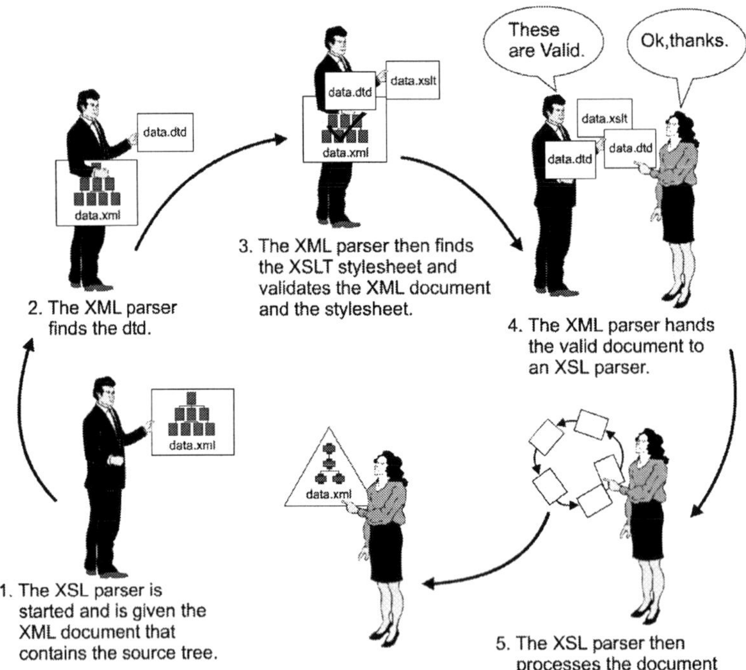

Exhibit 6-2: Basic XML/XSL parsing

Note: You can find several XSL processors at www.w3.org/Style/XSL/ or by reading "The XML Cover Pages—Extensible Stylesheet Language (XSL)" by Robin Cover at xml.coverpages.org/xsl.html. Some processors are stand-alone and some can be integrated with IDEs. The XML Spy IDE already contains an XSL parser.

The XML source document

Examine the source XML document in Exhibit 6-3. Note that the root element is named `<CONTACTS>` and that it contains nine child elements, eight identifying contacts in several TLSales departments. These include five contacts in Sales, one each in Customer Service and Employee Relations, and the President.

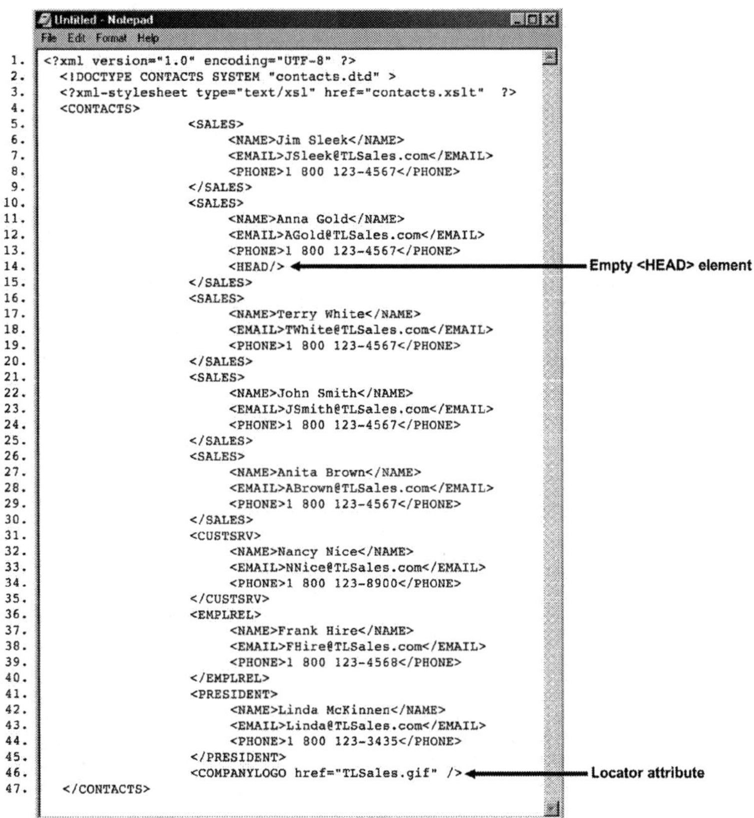

```
1.  <?xml version="1.0" encoding="UTF-8" ?>
2.    <!DOCTYPE CONTACTS SYSTEM "contacts.dtd" >
3.    <?xml-stylesheet type="text/xsl" href="contacts.xslt"  ?>
4.    <CONTACTS>
5.                  <SALES>
6.                       <NAME>Jim Sleek</NAME>
7.                       <EMAIL>JSleek@TLSales.com</EMAIL>
8.                       <PHONE>1 800 123-4567</PHONE>
9.                  </SALES>
10.                 <SALES>
11.                      <NAME>Anna Gold</NAME>
12.                      <EMAIL>AGold@TLSales.com</EMAIL>
13.                      <PHONE>1 800 123-4567</PHONE>
14.                      <HEAD/>
15.                 </SALES>
16.                 <SALES>
17.                      <NAME>Terry White</NAME>
18.                      <EMAIL>TWhite@TLSales.com</EMAIL>
19.                      <PHONE>1 800 123-4567</PHONE>
20.                 </SALES>
21.                 <SALES>
22.                      <NAME>John Smith</NAME>
23.                      <EMAIL>JSmith@TLSales.com</EMAIL>
24.                      <PHONE>1 800 123-4567</PHONE>
25.                 </SALES>
26.                 <SALES>
27.                      <NAME>Anita Brown</NAME>
28.                      <EMAIL>ABrown@TLSales.com</EMAIL>
29.                      <PHONE>1 800 123-4567</PHONE>
30.                 </SALES>
31.                 <CUSTSRV>
32.                      <NAME>Nancy Nice</NAME>
33.                      <EMAIL>NNice@TLSales.com</EMAIL>
34.                      <PHONE>1 800 123-8900</PHONE>
35.                 </CUSTSRV>
36.                 <EMPLREL>
37.                      <NAME>Frank Hire</NAME>
38.                      <EMAIL>FHire@TLSales.com</EMAIL>
39.                      <PHONE>1 800 123-4568</PHONE>
40.                 </EMPLREL>
41.                 <PRESIDENT>
42.                      <NAME>Linda McKinnen</NAME>
43.                      <EMAIL>Linda@TLSales.com</EMAIL>
44.                      <PHONE>1 800 123-3435</PHONE>
45.                 </PRESIDENT>
46.                 <COMPANYLOGO href="TLSales.gif" />
47.   </CONTACTS>
```


Exhibit 6-3: The contacts XML document

A *locator attribute* provides information to the processor regarding remote resources. In line 46, `href` is an ordinary locator attribute, because it refers to the location of the company logo image, a property of the `<COMPANYLOGO>` element.

The `<SALES>` element that identifies Anna Gold also contains the empty element `<HEAD>`, indicating that Anna is the head of the Sales Department. You could use this `<HEAD>` element for other types of processing, such as a search script that looks for and display department managers.

In the prolog portion of the contacts.xml document (at line 3), you'll find the document type declaration statement. The declaration tells the processor that the XML document is a `CONTACTS` type of document, and then points the processor to the external document type definition (DTD), which the processor must use to validate the XML document. Line 3 of the XML document is the processing instruction statement. The `type="text/xsl"` attribute tells the processor to apply an XSL stylesheet. (If the value was `"text/css"`, the processor would look for and apply a cascading stylesheet.) The `href="contacts.xslt"` attribute tells the processor where to look for the stylesheet file. In this case, the processor looks for the stylesheet in the same directory in which the XML document is located. If the stylesheet is at a different location, you include a directory path with the filename.

The attributes in the processing instructions are called *pseudo-attributes* because they do not describe element properties. They describe certain properties of the stylesheet mentioned in the declaration. The following tables lists six pseudo-attributes that can appear in such a declaration:

Pseudo-attribute	Explanation
alternate	"Yes" or "no." Default is "no."
charset	Optional; the character set pertaining to the stylesheet.
href	Required; indicates the location of the stylesheet; format is URI.
media	Optional; indicates the type of target media.
title	Optional; names the stylesheet.
type	Required; indicates the kind of stylesheet, e.g., "text/xsl" indicates XSL stylesheet.

Do it!

B-1: Exploring the XML source document

Exercises

1 Briefly describe a basic transformation process.

2 Which of the following is not a step of the XML parser process?

A The XML parser is given the XML document that contains the source tree.

B The XML parser finds the DTD.

C The XML parser finds the XSLT stylesheet and validates the XML document.

D The XML parser hands the invalid documents to an XSL parser.

3 Alternate, charset, href, title, and type are possible pseudo-attributes you might use in which of the following declarations?

A `<?xml-sort...?>`

B `<?xml-stylesheet...?>`

C `<?text-xsl...?>`

D `<?xsl-key...?>`

Interpreting the DTD

Explanation

Exhibit 6-4 shows the DTD used to build contacts.xml. In line 3, a plus sign appears next to the element name <SALES> within the element <CONTACTS>. The plus sign indicates that at least one <SALES> child element must appear within the <CONTACTS> element. On the same line, the question mark (?) next to <COMPANYLOGO> indicates that the appearance of a <COMPANYLOGO> element, which is declared empty in line 8, is optional within <CONTACTS>.

```
1.  <?xml version="1.0" encoding="UTF-8" ?>
2.  <!-- edited with XML Spy v5.0 4U (http://www.xmlspy.com) by Student Name -->
3.  <!ELEMENT CONTACTS (SALES+, CUSTSRV, EMPLREL, PRESIDENT, COMPANYLOGO?)>
4.  <!ELEMENT SALES (NAME, EMAIL, PHONE, HEAD?)>
5.  <!ELEMENT CUSTSRV (NAME, EMAIL, PHONE)>
6.  <!ELEMENT EMPLREL (NAME, EMAIL, PHONE)>
7.  <!ELEMENT PRESIDENT (NAME, EMAIL, PHONE)>
8.  <!ELEMENT COMPANYLOGO EMPTY>
9.  <!ELEMENT NAME (#PCDATA)>
10. <!ELEMENT EMAIL (#PCDATA)>
11. <!ELEMENT PHONE (#PCDATA)>
12. <!ELEMENT HEAD EMPTY>
```

Exhibit 6-4: The contacts DTD

On line 4, another question mark appears next to the element name <HEAD> within the <SALES> element. Again, it indicates that the element <HEAD>, which is declared empty in line 12, might or might not appear within a <SALES> element. The contacts.xml file indicated that an empty <HEAD> element appears in the <SALES> element specific to Anna Gold.

The source tree

Exhibit 6-5 shows the source tree structure defined within contacts.xml that was developed according to the contacts.dtd file and eventually validated against it. Note that the source tree is not just an element tree. It does not simply show the various elements in contacts.xml. The source tree also illustrates all the nodes types, including elements, attributes, and declarations. If contacts.xml contained any namespaces, then they would also appear in the source tree. After the complete transformation has taken place, you can compare the source tree with the result tree. Source trees are also valuable design tools for planning transformations.

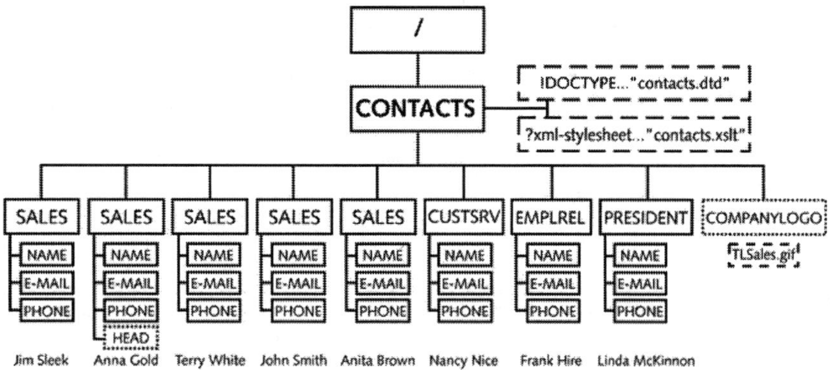

Exhibit 6-5: The contacts source tree

Note that the root node—represented by the box with the forward slash that signifies the entire document, including the prolog—is at the top of the source tree structure. Beneath it is the document node `CONTACTS` with its `DOCTYPE` definition and XML-stylesheet declaration. Beneath them, from left to right, are the child elements from contacts.xml. The order matches the order presented in contacts.xml. `COMPANYLOGO`, at the right side, is in a dotted-line box, which is a way to indicate that it's an empty element. Beneath `COMPANYLOGO` is the name of the GIF image for the company logo. The staff names were included at the bottom of the diagram to indicate that the order of the elements here corresponds to the order in the contacts.xml document.

Do it!

B-2: Discussing DTD and source tree structure

Exercises

1 Source trees are valuable design tools for ____________.

2 A source tree illustrates all types of nodes, including elements, attributes, and declarations. True or false?

3 During a basic transformation, the XML parser validates the XML document and its referenced XSLT stylesheet against ____________.

XSLT stylesheets

Explanation

Exhibit 6-6 shows an XSLT stylesheet named contacts_sort.xslt. The first line of the document is the *XML declaration* (also called *the header*). The XSLT stylesheet is a well-formed XML document and so must conform to XML document conventions. The first element tags follow immediately. Line 2 shows the stylesheet element. This tag tells the processor that the XML document is a stylesheet. This XSLT stylesheet, like all XSLT stylesheets, uses the `namespace xmlns:xsl="http://www.w3.org/1999/XSL/Transform"`.

Note: You could also use the `xsl:transform` tag instead of `xsl:stylesheet`, because it is considered a synonym for that term. The `xsl:transform` tag accepts the same attributes as `xsl:stylesheet`.

Conventional XSLT element tags begin with the prefix `xsl:` to tell the processor which version of XSLT to refer to and to show that the tag conforms to the W3C XSLT Recommendation. If a tag does not have an `xsl:` prefix, then the XSL parser passes the statement to the next processing phase. In this case, the next processing phase is the browser, which displays the HTML output. The `xsl:stylesheet` tag is followed by a version attribute, indicating the version of XSLT to which the stylesheet conforms.

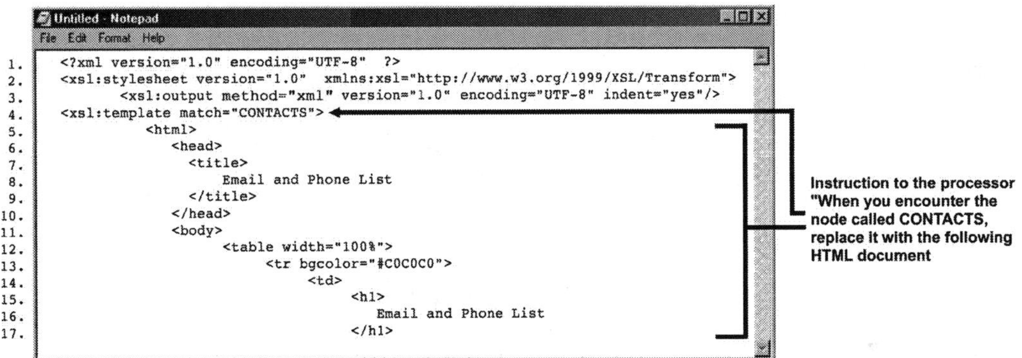

```
1.  <?xml version="1.0" encoding="UTF-8"  ?>
2.  <xsl:stylesheet version="1.0"  xmlns:xsl="http://www.w3.org/1999/XSL/Transform">
3.         <xsl:output method="xml" version="1.0" encoding="UTF-8" indent="yes"/>
4.  <xsl:template match="CONTACTS">
5.            <html>
6.               <head>
7.                 <title>
8.                     Email and Phone List
9.                 </title>
10.              </head>
11.              <body>
12.                    <table width="100%">
13.                         <tr bgcolor="#C0C0C0">
14.                              <td>
15.                                   <h1>
16.                                      Email and Phone List
17.                                   </h1>
```


Exhibit 6-6: The Sales contacts stylesheet

The `<xsl:stylesheet>` element usually forms the document element (i.e., the equivalent of the root element, but not to be confused with the concept of root nodes). However, an XSLT stylesheet might also be embedded in a non-XML resource or it might occur in an XML document other than as the document element. For more information about embedded stylesheets, refer to www.w3.org/TR/xslt under "Embedded Stylesheets" for further details.

The `<xsl:stylesheet>` element might contain several elements as direct children. Any element occurring as a child element of the document element `<xsl:stylesheet>` is referred to as a *top-level element.* Top-level elements are elements that provide additional specifications to the stylesheet. For details regarding the other elements, review the W3C XSLT Recommendation at www.w3.org/TR/xslt.

Element	Explanation
`xsl:include`	To include an additional XSLT stylesheet; has an `href` attribute whose value identifies and provides the location of the stylesheet.
`xsl:import`	To import a stylesheet; importing is the same as including except that the definitions and template rules in the importing stylesheet take precedence over those in the imported stylesheet.
`xsl:strip-space`	If an element name matches a name test in an `xsl:strip-space` element, then the element name is removed from the set of whitespace-preserving element names.
`xsl:preserve-space`	If an element name matches a specific name test in an `xsl:preserve-space` element, then the element name is added to the set of whitespace-preserving element names.
`xsl:output`	Allows stylesheet authors to specify how they want the result tree to be produced.
`xsl:key`	A stylesheet declares a set of keys for each document using this element; a key is a general identifier.
`xsl:decimal-format`	Declares a decimal-format, which controls the interpretation of a format pattern used by the format-number function. A name attribute specifies a particular format. If there is no name attribute, then the element declares the default decimal-format.
`xsl:namespace-alias`	Declares that one namespace URI is an alias for another namespace URI.
`xsl:attribute-set`	Defines a named set of attributes; a following name attribute specifies the name of the attribute set.
`xsl:variable`	With this element, you add an attribute called "name," and specify a parsed character data-related name as a value. That specified value becomes a variable name that you can combine with other specifications (for example, element names) to search for data or to create display specifications. For more details and examples, refer to www.w3.org/TR/xslt.
`xsl:param`	An element you can useto bind variables. The difference between xsl:param and xsl:variable is that the value specified on the xsl:param variable is only a default value for the binding. When its stylesheet is implemented, you can set other parameters. For more details and examples, refer to www.w3.org/TR/xslt.
`xsl:template`	Tells the processor how to transform a node for output.

With the exception of the `<xsl:import>` element or its alternate, `<xsl:include>`, which must come first when they are used, the top-level elements can occur in any order. Furthermore, the `<xsl:stylesheet>` element can contain elements that do not originate in the XSLT namespace, as long as the expanded names of such elements have non-null URIs (i.e., you cannot specify a namespace like `xmlns:abc=" "` and then attempt to use `abc:` as a prefix for an element name). They are otherwise acceptable, as long as they do not attempt to alter the behavior of XSLT elements and functions from that found in the W3C XSLT Recommendation.

An XSLT processor is free to ignore such top-level elements, and must ignore the top-level element without giving an error if it does not recognize the element's namespace URI. In line 3 of Exhibit 6-6, the stylesheet tells the processor what output to produce when a pattern in the XML document is matched.

The `<xsl:output>` element allows stylesheet authors to specify how they want the result tree to be displayed. It is only allowed as a top-level element. The `method` attribute of `<xsl:output>` identifies the method for displaying the result tree. The value must be a qualified name (that is, it must contain a prefix, a colon, and a local name portion). If you don't include a prefix, there are only three available options: `xml`, `html`, or `text`. The default is typically xml. If the value is a qualified name with a prefix, then the value is expanded into its expanded name, which should then specify the output method. In this instance, however, the result tree is specified to be a well-formed XML document.

There are ten possible attributes allowed within the `<xsl:output>` element, and they're all optional. They are:

Attribute	**Description**
`method`	The format for the output. Values include xml, html, text, and name.
`version`	The version of the output format version specified. The value is the version number.
`encoding`	The character set used for encoding. The value is the text specification (e.g., UTF=8, UTF=16, etc.)
`omit-xml-declaration`	Indicates that the XML declaration should be omitted in the output. Values are yes and no.
`standalone`	Indicates that the result should be a stand-alone document. Values are yes and no.
`doctype-public`	Indicates the public identifier to be used in the `<!doctype>` declaration in the output.
`doctype-system`	Specifies the system identifier to be used in the `<!doctype>` declaration in the output.

Attribute	Description
`cdata-section-elements`	Specifies a list of elements whose content will be output in CDATA sections.
`Indent`	Indicates that the output should be indented to indicate the hierarchical structure. Values are yes and no.
`media-type`	Specifies the media type of the output.

Of these ten attributes, four are specified in the top-level `<xsl:output>` element in line 3 of the contacts_xml.xslt example in Exhibit 6-6:

- method
- version
- encoding
- indent

The output method has been explicitly specified to be XML, although the specification could have been omitted and XML would still have been the default.

The `version` attribute specifies the version of the output method. In this case, XML version 1.0 is to be used for creating the result tree. If the XSLT processor does not support a specified version of XML, it should use a version of XML that it does support. The XML version specified in the stylesheet's XML declaration should correspond to the version of XML that the XSLT processor uses for outputting the result tree. The default value is version 1.0.

The `encoding` attribute specifies the preferred character encoding that the XSLT processor should use to output the result tree. The value should either be a character set registered with the Internet Assigned Numbers Authority (IANA) or should start with "x-". XSLT processors are required to respect values of UTF-8 and UTF-16. In fact, if no encoding attribute is specified, then the XSLT processor should use either of those two values. If another value is specified and the XSLT processor does not support it, then the processor might signal an error.

Occasionally, you might see a result tree containing a character that cannot be represented in the output encoding used by the XSLT processor. If that character occurs in a context where XML recognizes character references, then the character should be displayed as a character reference. Otherwise, the XSLT processor might signal an error.

The `indent` attribute specifies whether the XSLT processor might add additional white space when displaying the result tree; the value must be either yes or no. If the value is yes, then the XML output method might add white space to the result tree output to make the output more presentable. If the value is no, which is the default, there should be no additional white space.

Note: If your XML document contains mixed content (i.e., elements that contain both elements and text), then it is not advisable to specify the `indent="yes"`.

Do it!

B-3: Discussing XSLT stylesheets

Exercises

1 In an XSLT stylesheet, which element could be used instead of the `<xsl:stylesheet>` element?

2 In which of the following locations can you place the `<xsl:stylesheet>` element?

A In an element other than the document element

B In a non-XML resource

C In a document element

D All of the above

E A and C, but not B or D

3 An element occurring as a child element of `xsl:stylesheet` is called a __________.

4 When specifying a value for the encoding attribute of `<xsl:output>`, which of the following can you use?

A UTF-8

B ANSI 9964

C UTF-16

D Any character set registered with IANA

E Any character set starting with "x-"

F All of the above

5 If your source XML documents contain mixed content elements (i.e., elements which contain both elements and text), then what should you specify for the indent attribute of `<xsl:output>`?

6 Top-level elements include __________.

A xsl:css

B xsl:import

C xsl:version

D xsl:element

Query contexts and template rules

Explanation

XSLT and XPath consider documents to be composed of nodes in a tree-like structure. Before processing can begin, the relevant query context portion of the source tree—for example, the portion of the contacts.xml document that contains the information that is manipulated and copied to the output—must be selected with a combined XSLT/XPath expression. Another valuable thing to remember is that XSLT is different from conventional programming languages because XSLT is based on template rules that specify how XML documents should be processed. A template rule is specified with the `<xsl:template>` element.

Unless you specify a name attribute and its respective value, you must specify a match attribute. The value specified for the match attribute identifies the source node or nodes to which the new template rule applies. That value is an XPath expression. Meanwhile, the content listed between the `<xsl:template>` start tag and the `</xsl:template>` end tag is the template that appears in the output.

Line 4 of the contacts_xml.xslt file, which is reproduced in Exhibit 6-7, uses the top-level element `<xsl:template>` to begin the first (and only, in this case) template rule in the stylesheet, and to specify that the `<CONTACTS>` node is query context.

```
4. <xsl:template match="CONTACTS">
```

Exhibit 6-7: Line 4 of contacts_xml.xslt

Note that the XPath expression used to select the relevant portion of the XML document is `CONTACTS`. This specifies that the relevant query context of the contacts.xml document is the node called `<CONTACTS>`. Stated another way, `<xsl:template match="CONTACTS">` has set the context (also called matched the context) for subsequent queries. It is like saying to the processor, "When you encounter the node called `<CONTACTS>`, substitute the HTML document template defined between the `<xsl:template>` start tag and the `</xsl:template>` end tag." In this case, it is sufficient to select the document node `<CONTACTS>` because no changes are to be made above it, in the prolog. In addition, it simplifies the selection of child nodes later in the stylesheet.

This concept of the query context—that is, the context being processed by an XSL template at any given moment—is important both during the planning and design phases and later, during troubleshooting. If your XSL file doesn't create the output file you expect, understanding the processor's progress through its contexts can help you determine why it's malfunctioning and how to debug the problem.

Thus far we've discussed matching a specific node: the document element node named <CONTACTS>. If you need to match to another type of node, consult the following table to find the required syntax.

Note: The examples listed in this table pertain to the contacts.xml document.

Node	Syntax	Explanation
Document root	<xsl:template match="/">	Match the document's root node.
Element	<xsl:template match= "docnodename">	Match the document node.
	<xsl:template match= "docnodename/nodename">	Match a child to the document node.
	<xsl:template match= "docnodename//nodename">	Match the nodename grand-child(ren) of the document node.
	<xsl:template match= "docnodename/*/nodename">	Match all the nodename descendants of the document node.
Attribute	<xsl:value-of select= "@attributename">	Match the value of the specified attribute.
	<xsl:value-of select= "nodename/@*"	Match the value of all the attributes of the specified node.
Namespace	<xsl:template match= "documentnodename">	Match the document node and select the namespace value.
	<xsl:value-of select= "@xs:xmlns"/>	
Comment	<xsl:template match= "comment()">	Convert a comment from XML's <!--comment --> form to a form that another markup language can use.
Processing instruction	<xsl:template match= "/processing instruction()">	Match all the processing instructions in the document root.
	<xsl:template match= "/processing instruction(piname)">	Match a specific processing instruction piname in the document root.
Text	<xsl:template match= "text()">	Match all text.

As an alternative to including the template in the stylesheet, you can store the template in a file elsewhere and call it from the <xsl:template> tag. For example, a stylesheet could insert a template by using the following code:

```
<xsl:template name="templatename">
...</xsl:template>
```

HTML document templates

In Exhibit 6-8, lines 5 through 59 define the HTML document that's inserted as a template for the <CONTACTS> node during processing.

```
5.   <html>
6.       <head>
7.           <title>
8.                Email and Phone List
9.           </title>
10.      </head>
11.          <body>
12.              <table width="100%">
13.                  <tr bgcolor="#C0C0C0">
14.                      <td>
15.                          <h1>
16.                              Email and Phone List
17.                          </h1>
18.                      </td>
19.                      <td align="right">
20.                          <img alt="Logo">
21.                              <xsl:attribute name="src">
22.                                  <xsl:value-of select="COMPANYLOGO/@href" />
23.                              </xsl:attribute>
24.                          </img>
25.                      </td>
26.                  </tr>
27.              </table>
28.                <xsl:for-each select="SALES">
29.                    <xsl:sort select="NAME"/>
30.                        <h2>
31.                                <xsl:value-of select="NAME"/>
32.                        </h2>
33.                            <table width="70%">
34.                                <tr valign="top">
35.                                    <td width="40%">
36.                                        <table>
37.                                            <tr>
38.                                                <td>
39.                                                    <b><small>Phone:</small></b>
40.                                                </td>
41.                                                <td>
42.                                                    <xsl:value-of select="PHONE"/>
43.                                                </td>
44.                                            </tr>
45.                                            <tr>
46.                                                <td>
47.                                                    <b><small>Email:</small></b>
48.                                                </td>
49.                                                <td>
50.                                                    <xsl:value-of select="EMAIL"/>
51.                                                </td>
52.                                            </tr>
53.                                        </table>
54.                                    </td>
55.                                </tr>
56.                            </table>
57.                </xsl:for-each>
58.      </body>
59.  </html>
```

Exhibit 6-8: Lines 5 through 59 of contacts_xml.xslt

Lines 11 through 58 define the body of the template HTML document. If you're familiar with HTML coding, you can see that lines 12 through 27 define a single-row, two-column table. The table has a full width, and its first row has a silver background (`#C0C0C0` is the RGB hexadecimal color code for silver). Lines 21 through 23, reproduced in Exhibit 6-9, list some XSLT elements that specify the location of a logo image.

```
21. <xsl:attribute name="src">
22.     <xsl:value-of select="COMPANYLOGO/@href" />
23. </xsl:attribute>
```

Exhibit 6-9: Lines 21 through 23 of contacts_xml.xslt

This logo image will be inserted in the second cell of the table. Here is a literal translation of these three lines:

- An attribute exists in the HTML image tag. The attribute's name is `src`.
- The value of the new `src` attribute is the value extracted from the `href` locator found in `<COMPANYLOGO>` within the `<CONTACTS>` node (line 22).
- This is the end of the attribute definition (line 23).

The attribute expression implements the current template rule. At any point in the processing of an XSLT stylesheet, if another template rule is chosen by matching a pattern like "attribute," the template rule corresponding to "attribute" suspends the current `<xsl:template>` rule for the extent of the instantiation of "attribute." When the "attribute" template rule is finished, control passes back to the `<xsl:template>` rule. The term *instantiation* refers to the creation of a data structure with its own set of subroutines, which operate on specific data.

Do it!

B-4: Discussing query contexts and template rules

Exercises

1 What is a query context?

2 In the following expression, which components are mostly XSLT and which are mostly XPath?

```
<xsl:template match="CONTACTS">
```

3 What does the following coded instruction mean?

```
<xsl:value-of select="PHONE">
```

A The processor is being told that following instructions will affect the value of the <PHONE> node.

B The processor is being told to change the value of all nodes except <PHONE>.

C The processor is being told to change, and then print, the value of the node <PHONE>.

D The processor is being told to print the value of the node <PHONE>.

E None of the above.

4 The content listed between the `<xsl:template>` start tag and the `</xsl:template>` end tag is the template that appears in the output. True or false?

Repetitive loops and sorting

Explanation

Lines 28 through 57, reproduced in Exhibit 6-10, define the vital information that's harvested from contacts.xml: the names, e-mail addresses, and phone numbers of the Sales Department contacts.

```
28.     <xsl:for-each select="SALES">
29.       <xsl:sort select="NAME"/>
30.         <h2>
31.           <xsl:value-of select="NAME"/>
32.         </h2>
33.           <table width="70%">
34.             <tr valign="top">
35.               <td width="40%">
36.                 <table>
37.                   <tr>
38.                     <td>
39.                       <b><small>Phone:</small></b>
40.                     </td>
41.                     <td>
42.                       <xsl:value-of select="PHONE"/>
43.                     </td>
44.                   </tr>
45.                   <tr>
46.                     <td>
47.                       <b><small>Email:</small></b>
48.                     </td>
49.                     <td>
50.                       <xsl:value-of select="EMAIL"/>
51.                     </td>
52.                   </tr>
53.                 </table>
54.               </td>
55.             </tr>
56.           </table>
57.     </xsl:for-each>
```

Exhibit 6-10: Lines 28 through 57 of contacts_xml.xslt

The expression `<xsl:for-each select="SALES">` combines the XSLT element `<xsl:for-each>` with the XPath expression SALES. It tells the processor to "find all the SALES nodes in this, the CONTACTS node (as defined on line 4)." The "for-each" is a repetitive loop that processes all the subsequent instructions for each SALES node encountered. In other words, every SALES node is searched. The nodes are searched in document order (i.e., the order they appear in the document) unless a sort specification is provided. The for-each loop expression activates the current template rule again, for the extent of the instantiation of the for-each template rule. In any for-each loop, the context in which the processor is working changes to whatever SALES node it finds itself reading. On one pass, the context might be `"CONTACTS/SALES/NAME=Jim Sleek";` on the next, it might be `"CONTACTS/SALES/NAME=John Smith"`.

Line 29 provides the sort specification mentioned previously. The `<xsl:sort select="NAME"/>` tells the processor to search the SALES nodes in alphabetical order, according to the values found in the NAME node beneath each SALES node. `<xsl:sort>` can only appear as a child of `<for-each>` or `<apply-templates>`. There are other attributes available to `<xsl:sort>` besides the `select` attribute, including `lang`, `data-type`, `order`, and `case-order`. For more details, go to www.w3.org/TR/xslt#sorting.

Displaying the output

Lines 30 to 32 in Exhibit 6-11 tell the processor to take the value found in the respective node NAME (as they are read in alphabetical order) and output that value as a level-two heading. Lines 33 through 56 define another table. One of these tables is created each time another SALES node is read.

```
30.     <h2>
31.         <xsl:value-of select="NAME"/>
32.     </h2>
33.       <table width="70%">
34.         <tr valign="top">
35.           <td width="40%">
36.             <table>
37.               <tr>
38.                 <td>
39.                   <b><small>Phone:</small></b>
40.                 </td>
41.                 <td>
42.                   <xsl:value-of select="PHONE"/>
43.                 </td>
44.               </tr>
45.               <tr>
46.                 <td>
47.                   <b><small>Email:</small></b>
48.                 </td>
49.                 <td>
50.                   <xsl:value-of select="EMAIL"/>
51.                 </td>
52.               </tr>
53.             </table>
54.           </td>
55.         </tr>
56.       </table>
```

Exhibit 6-11: Lines 30 through 56 of contacts_xml.xslt

The end of the For-each loop

At line 57 of Exhibit 6-10, the processor reaches the end of the `<for-each>` loop. It returns to line 28 and repeats the SALES node investigation and subsequent table building until it encounters no new SALES nodes. Then, at last, the processor passes line 57 and is finished with the processing of contacts.xml.

Exhibit 6-12 displays the output of the XSL parser after that output file has been passed to a browser. Note that the Sales Department contacts are in alphabetical order, as prescribed in the XSLT stylesheet, and not as they appear in the original contacts.xml document.

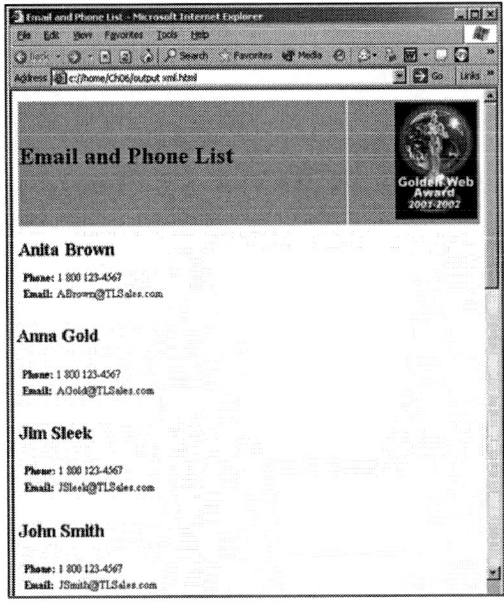

Exhibit 6-12: The HTML output

Do it!

B-5: Discussing repetitive loops and sorting

Exercises

1 For-each is a repetitive loop that processes all the subsequent instructions for its designated node. Each node is searched in ________ order unless another order is specified.

2 `<xsl:sort>` can only appear as a child of ________.

A <template>

B <for-each>

C <value-of>

D <apply-templates>

E <attribute>

3 The data in a source tree will always be the same as the data in the results tree. True or false?

Converting an XML document to HTML

Explanation

A common XML transformation is to convert an XML document to HTML for display in a browser. Another application of XSL transformation is to convert XML documents from one grammar to another. In the next activity, you'll use XSLT elements to display the content of the SALES element from the contacts.xml file, and add to an XSL transformation, and build another from scratch.

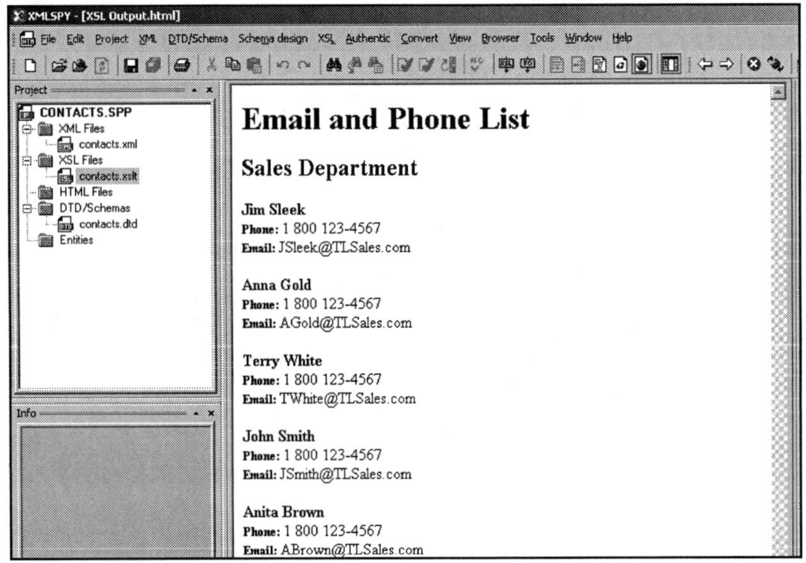

Exhibit 6-13: The data transformed to HTML

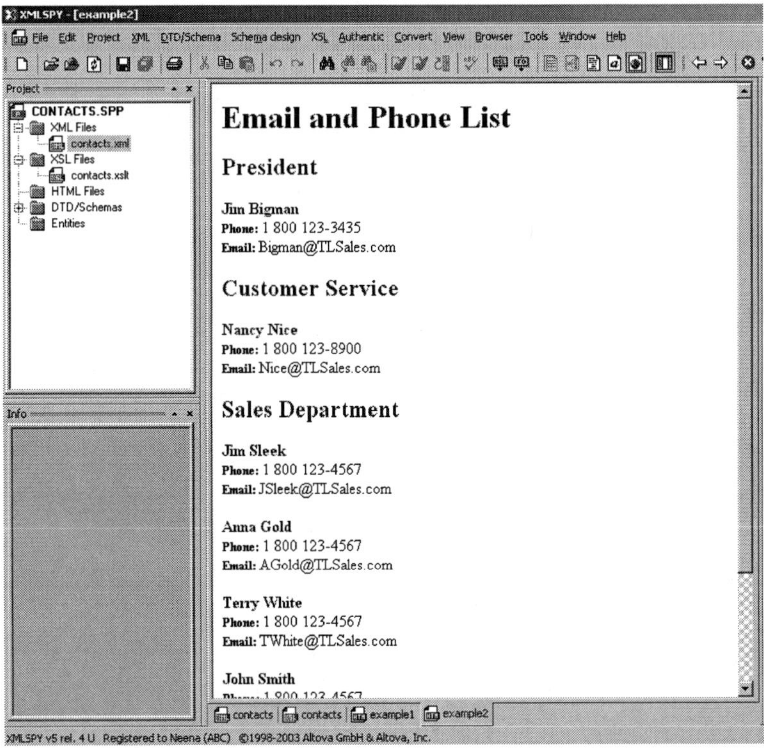

Exhibit 6-14: The HTML output after modifications

Do it!

B-6: Transforming an XML document to HTML using XSLT

Here's how	Here's why
1 Open XML Spy	
2 Choose **Project**, **Open Project...**	To open the Open dialog box.
Click the **Look in** list arrow	
Navigate to the current unit folder	
Select contacts.spp	
Click **Open**	
3 In the Project pane, double-click **XML Files**	
Double-click **contacts.xml**	To open the XML document and to review it.
Switch to Text view	To view the source code. The XML document contains a list of people and their contact information. Each person's name and contact information is contained within a SALES, CUSTSRV, or PRESIDENT element.
Locate the stylesheet declaration	The xml-stylesheet declaration identifies the stylesheet used with this document.
4 Click [validate button]	To validate the XML document. A green circle with a check appears in the lower-left corner of the XML Spy window.
In the Project pane, double-click **XSL Files**	
Double-click **contacts.xslt**	To open the XSL transformation file.
5 Observe the transformation file	Note that following the XML declaration, the transformation begins with the `xsl:stylesheet` root element, which specifies the XSL version and namespace prefix. The `xsl` namespace prefix is used as a convention, but you can use any other prefix. The next line is the `xsl:output` element, which specifies that this transformation will produce an HTML result tree.

6 In the HTML code, locate the `xsl:apply-templates` element that matches the CONTACTS element	When the transformation engine processes the source tree, this element will cause the `xsl:template` matching CONTACTS to process the element and then return to the line following `xsl:apply-templates`.
Locate the `xsl:for-each` element	This element will apply the transformation information for each instance of the SALES element within CONTACTS.
7 Click the **contacts.xml** tab	To display the XML document.
Choose **XSL**, **XSL Transformation**	To transform the file. The HTML output appears, as shown in Exhibit 6-13.
8 Switch to Text view	To review the HTML document generated by the transformation.
Examine the HTML code	Note how it compares with the XSL transformation and XML document information.
9 Choose **File**, **Save As...**	
Type **example1.html**	To specify the name of the file.
Click **Save**	To save the file in the current unit folder.

10	Click the **contacts.xslt** tab	To open the transformation file.
	Directly above the Sales Department heading, type: `<h2>President</h2>` `<xsl:for-each select="PRESIDENT">` `<b><xsl:value-of select="NAME"/></b>` ` ` `<b><small>Phone: </small></b>` `<xsl:value-of select="PHONE"/>` ` ` `<b><small>Email: </small></b>` `<xsl:value-of select="EMAIL"/>` ` ` `</xsl:for-each>` `<h2>Customer Service</h2>` `<xsl:for-each select="CUSTSRV">` `<b><xsl:value-of select="NAME"/></b>` ` ` `<b><small>Phone: </small></b>` `<xsl:value-of select="PHONE"/>` ` ` `<b><small>Email: </small></b>` `<xsl:value-of select="EMAIL"/>` ` ` `</xsl:for-each>`	
	Save your changes	
	If you receive a message about a missing schema, click **OK**	
11	Switch to contacts.xml	(In the project pane, double-click contacts.xml.) To display the XML document.
	Click [XSL]	To transform the file. The new HTML document appears. Note that the President and Customer Service Representative are now listed. The new HTML document should resemble Exhibit 6-14.
	Switch to Text view	To examine the HTML source code.
12	Choose **File**, **Save As...**	
	Save the file as **example2.html**	In the current unit folder.

Conditional statements and the mode attribute

Explanation

XSL provides two conditional processing statements: `xsl:if` and `xsl:choose`. The `xsl:choose` element is similar to a switch statement used in C++ or Java because it tests for a number of specific conditions, and provides a sink or default element if none of the conditions have been met. Unlike a switch statement, each `xsl:when` element can contain unrelated expressions. You'll use both condition elements to enhance the HTML output. You'll also create and initialize a variable that you'll use within the conditional statement.

A *mode* is an attribute of both the `xsl:template` or `xsl:apply-template` elements, and allows you to process the same section of the XML document more than once.

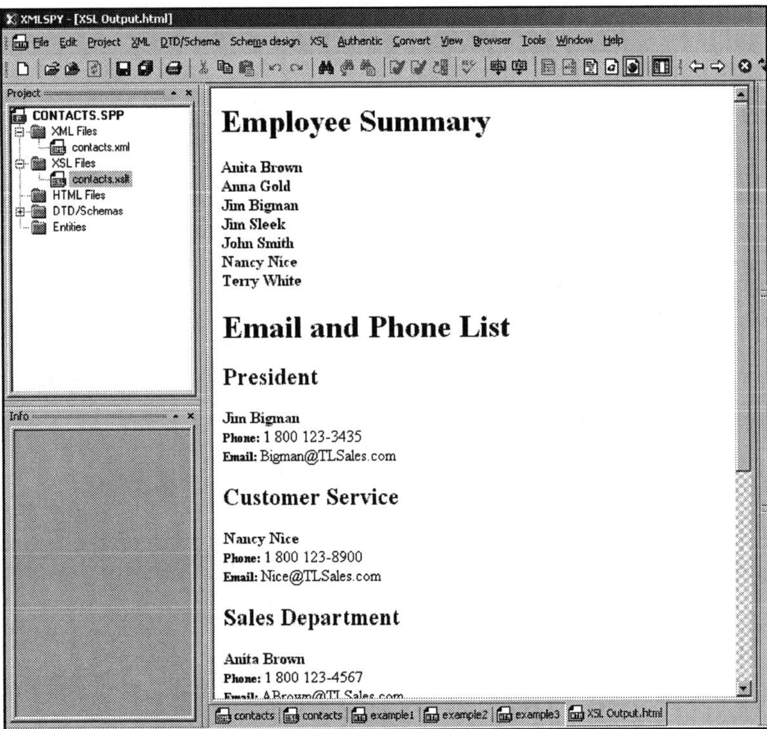

Exhibit 6-15: The HTML output after modifications

Do it!

B-7: Applying conditional statements and the mode attribute

Here's how	Here's why
1 Switch to **contacts.xslt**	The XSL transformation document appears.
2 Directly under the Sort By Name comment, type: `<xsl:sort select="NAME"/>` Save your changes	To sort the data by name.
3 Switch to contacts.xml	
Click [XSL button]	To transform the file. The new HTML document appears. Note that the names under the Sales Department are now sorted, beginning with Anita Brown.
4 Choose **File**, **Save As...**	
Save the file as **example3.html**	In the current unit folder.
5 Switch to contacts.xslt	To view the XSL transformation document.

In the `xsl:apply-templates` element matching `CONTACTS`, type the following code immediately after the `select="CONTACTS"` attribute:
`mode="main"`
The element should now appear as follows:
`<xsl:apply-templates select="CONTACTS" mode="main"/>`	

6 In the `xsl:template` matching `CONTACTS`, type the following code immediately after the `match="CONTACTS"` attribute:
`mode="main"`
The element should now appear as follows:
`<xsl:template match="CONTACTS" mode="main">`	

7 Immediately after the <body> tag, type:

```
<h1>Employee Summary</h1>
<xsl:apply-templates select="CONTACTS" mode="emplist"/>
```

Directly under the Employee List comment, type:

```
<xsl:template match="CONTACTS" mode="emplist">
<xsl:for-each select="*">
<xsl:sort select="NAME"/>
<b><xsl:value-of select="NAME"/></b>
<!--Dept Variables-->

<br/>
</xsl:for-each>
</xsl:template>
```

8 Switch to contacts.xml	To display the XML document.
Click [XSL button]	To transform the file. The new HTML document appears. Verify the new header and sorted list of employees. The new HTML document should look like Exhibit 6-15.
9 Switch to **contacts.xslt**	To edit the XSLT file.

Directly under the Dept Varibles comment, type:

```
<xsl:variable name="NodeName">
<xsl:value-of select="local-name()"/></xsl:variable>
<xsl:choose>
<xsl:when test=" $NodeName='PRESIDENT'">,
President</xsl:when>
<xsl:when test="$NodeName ='CUSTSRV'">, Customer
Service</xsl:when>
<xsl:when test="$NodeName ='SALES'">, Sales</xsl:when>
<xsl:otherwise>, Unknown</xsl:otherwise>
</xsl:choose>
```

This block of code first creates the variable, `NodeName`, which is initialized to the name of the context element by using the XPath function call `local-name()`. The condition compares the value within the `NodeName` variable with a set of possible element values.

10 Directly under the If Statement comment, type:	To add an `xml:if` element.
`<xsl:if test="HEAD">, <em>Head of Department</em></xsl:if>`	
11 Save your changes	
Switch to contacts.xml	To display the XML document.
Click [XSL button]	To view the revised HTML output in the main window. It now displays job titles for every employee in the Employee Summary and a department head identifier for Anna Gold.
12 Choose **File**, **Save As...**	
Save the file as **example4.html**	In the current unit folder.

Using XSLT as transformation language

Explanation

XSL is also used as transformation language (for converting the structure of a source XML document into a result tree consisting of XSL formatting objects). XSL transformation can convert XML documents from one grammar to another. You'll transform contacts.xml into a second XML file where every employee is an `EMPLOYEE` element, and the job type is stored as an attribute.

Do it!

B-8: Changing XML grammar with XSLT

Here's how	Here's why
1 Choose **File**, **New...**	To open a Create new document dialog box.
Click **xslt Extensible Stylesheet Language**	
Click **OK**	Note that XML Spy creates a shell stylesheet with a `xsl:stylesheet` element and a `xsl:output` element. The method attribute of the `xsl:output` element is set to "xml."
2 Choose **File**, **Save As...**	To save the XSL transformation.
Save the file as **contacts2.xslt**	In the current unit folder.
3 In the project pane, right-click **XSL Files**	
Choose **Add Files**	The Open dialog box appears.
Navigate to the current unit folder	If necessary.
4 Select **contacts2.xslt**	
Click **Open**	The contacts2.xslt file is displayed under the XSL Files branch in the project pane.

5 Immediately below the `xsl:output` element, type:
`<xsl:template match="/">`
`<CONTACTLIST>`
`<xsl:apply-templates select="CONTACTS"/>`
`</CONTACTLIST>`
`</xsl:template>`
	This is the `xsl:template` that matches the source tree's root element. It creates the result tree's root and then refers to the `xsl:template` matching `CONTACTS`.

6 Following the XSL code you just entered, type:

```
<xsl:template match="CONTACTS">
<xsl:for-each select="*">
<xsl:sort select="NAME"/>
<EMPLOYEE>
<xsl:attribute name="branch">main</xsl:attribute>
<NAME>
<xsl:value-of select="NAME"/>
</NAME>
<POSITION>
<xsl:value-of select="local-name()"/>
</POSITION>
<PHONENUM>
<xsl:value-of select="PHONE"/>
</PHONENUM>
<EMAIL>
<xsl:value-of select="EMAIL"/>
</EMAIL>
</EMPLOYEE>
</xsl:for-each>
</xsl:template>
```

The template iterates through the child elements of CONTACTS, sorting them by name and organizing them as EMPLOYEE elements. The `xsl:attribute` declares a branch attribute within EMPLOYEE and initializes the value to "main." The XPath function `local-name()` returns the local part of an element's name, without the namespace prefix.

7 Save your changes

8 Switch to contacts.xml

9 Modify the `xml-stylesheet` declaration to reference contacts2.xslt; the fourth line should appear as follows:

```
<?xml-stylesheet type="text/xsl" href="contacts2.xslt"?>
```

10 Click [XSL button] — To transform the file. A new XML document appears.

11 Switch to Text view — To view the source code.

12 Choose **File**, **Save As...**

Save file as **examples.html**

Close XML Spy

Unit summary: XML transformations

Topic A

In this topic, you learned about **XML data transformation** .You learned that XML data transformation is done in two phases: **structural transformation** and **structural formatting**. You learned how and why data is transformed. You also learned how **XSL**, **XPath**, and **XSLT** transform data.

Topic B

In this topic, you learned that the XML parser validates the XML document and its referenced XSLT stylesheet against a referenced DTD or schema. Then, the XSL parser uses the XSLT stylesheet as its guide, and performs the transformation. You learned about various **elements of XSL**, and you learned how to **transform an XML document to HTML** using XSLT. Finally, you learned how to use basic **conditional processing statements**, and you used XSLT to **change the grammar** of an XML file.

Review questions

1 The first phase of transformation is a ____________ transformation, in which the data is converted from the structure of the incoming XML document to the structure of the desired output.

2 The transformation language was intended to convert an XML document into a ____________, consisting of the XSL formatting objects.

3 ____________ is a language for finding the information in an XML document.

4 The ____________ is an element you can use to bind variables. It uses an attribute called *name*.

5 Before processing can begin, the relevant ____________ portion of the source tree must be selected with a combined XSLT/XPath expression.

6 The term ____________ refers to the creation of a data structure with its own set of subroutines, which operate on specific data.

7 The original XSL concept evolved into what three XML-related languages?

8 With ____________, the processor is told to apply an XSL type stylesheet to the document.

9 Which of the following is not a top-level element?

A xsl:include

B xsl:import

C xsl:param

D xsl:indent

10 Which of the following is not an xsl:output attribute?

A method

B version

C standalone

D variable

11 The syntax `<xsl:template match="/">` matches which of the following document's node?

A document's node

B root node

C a child to the document node

D the nodename grandchildren

12 ____________ specifies the preferred character encoding that the XSLT processor should use to output the result tree.

Independent practice activity

1 Create an XSLT stylesheet named bikes.xslt that transforms the bikes.xml document into the HTML page shown in Exhibit 6-16. Use any HTML or CSS formatting options that you want.

2 Use bikes.xml, bikes.dtd, and all the image files from the C:\StudentData\current unit folder.

3 You'll need to change the paths for some elements in the file to reference your C:\StudentData\current unit folder.

4 Test your results in Internet Explorer. If you view your results in XML Spy's Browser view, the images might not show up.

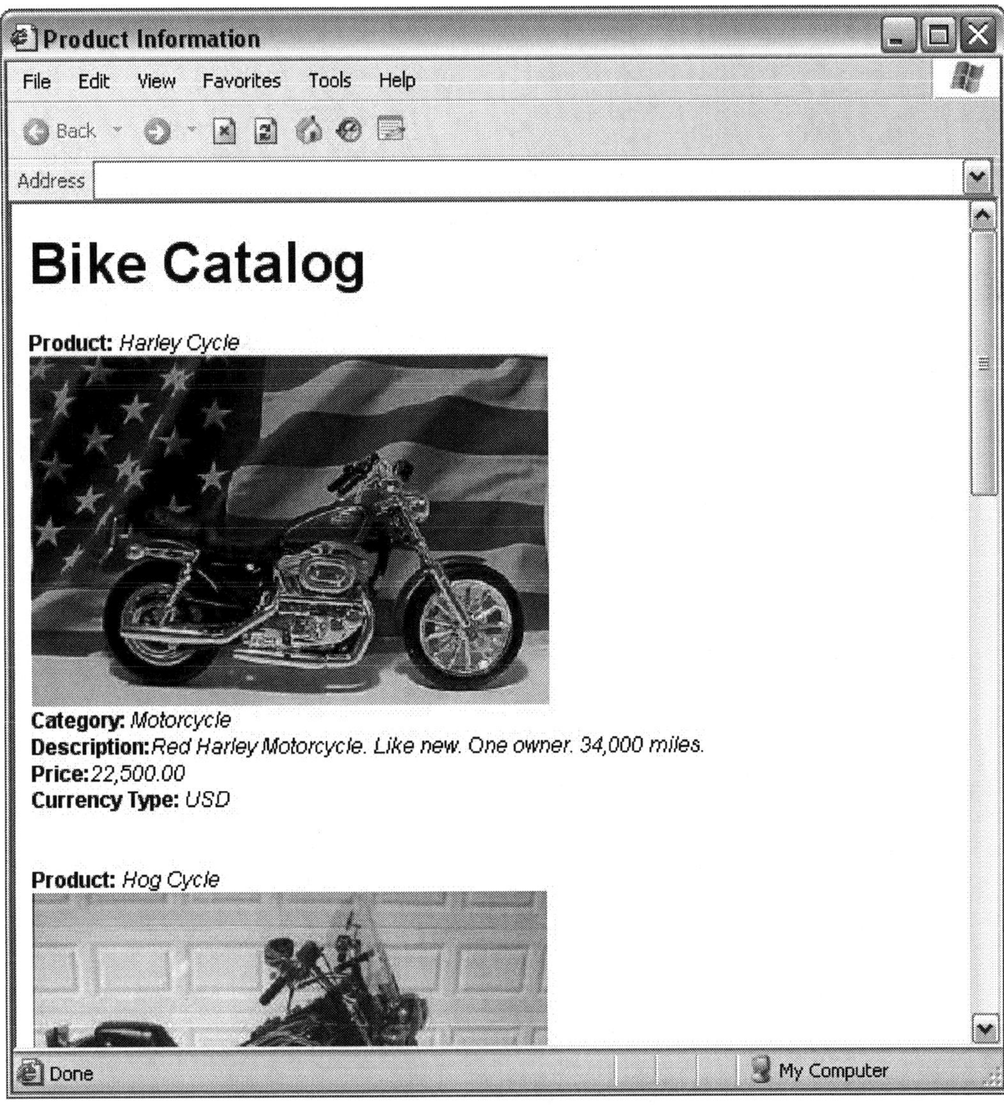

Exhibit 6-16: The transformed bikes.xml document, viewed in Internet Explorer

Unit 7
Linking in XML

Unit time: 120 minutes

Complete this unit, and you'll know how to:

A Identify the purpose and basic functionality of XLink.

B Identify restrictions and basic XLink syntax.

C Validate XLinks and create a simple XLink.

D Identify the purpose of Xpointer and its basic functionality and syntax.

Topic A: XML Linking Language

Explanation

By using *XML Linking Language* (commonly called XLink, but also called XML Linking and, occasionally, XLL), you can create links in XML documents. You can use it to create simple HTML-like unidirectional links (i.e., one source/one destination) or sophisticated links with several sources and destinations.

Introduction to XLink

The XML Linking Language 1.0 was published as a W3C Recommendation on June 27, 2001, so it has become the sanctioned W3C solution for linking in XML. XLink was created to overcome the limitations of HTML links by:

- Reconciling XML's functionally relevant element names with HTML's predefined and specific elements such as `<A>` (for "anchor") or `<IMG>` (for "image").
- Linking your document with multiple sources and destinations, when HTML identifies only one source and destination per link.
- Locating link definitions in separate locations (for example, link databases), so that the write permission for their corresponding documents does not have to be given to as many individuals.
- Using standard XML constructs (e.g., concepts, syntax, formats, etc.).
- Complying with XML's rules for well-formedness and validity.
- Indicating to the reader or developer something about the nature and behavior of the link (title, destination, traversal rules, etc.).
- Remaining compatible and complementary with HTML.
- Providing other XML-related functionality.

Types of XLinks

For XML and XLink, *links* are defined as explicit relationships between addressable units of information or services in XML documents (i.e., between resources or even portions of resources). The links might be of two types: hyperlinks (that is, links that are intended primarily to be viewed and used at the discretion of users), or links that are intended only for computer functioning, with automatic instructions for the system. While HTML can provide links that require user activation, XLinks are capable of providing both types of functionality.

XLinks are divided into two types according to their structure: simple and extended. Each can be configured for human activation or to provide instructions to the system.

Simple links

A *simple link* (also referred to as a *simple-type link*) is a link that associates exactly two participating resources, one local and one remote, with an arc traversing from the local resource to the remote resource. Therefore, a simple link is always an outbound link. The simple link is the category into which HTML links fall.

Exhibit 7-1 shows a simple link. It could, for example, represent the name of a TLSales course appearing as a link that, when clicked, leads to information about the course content and costs.

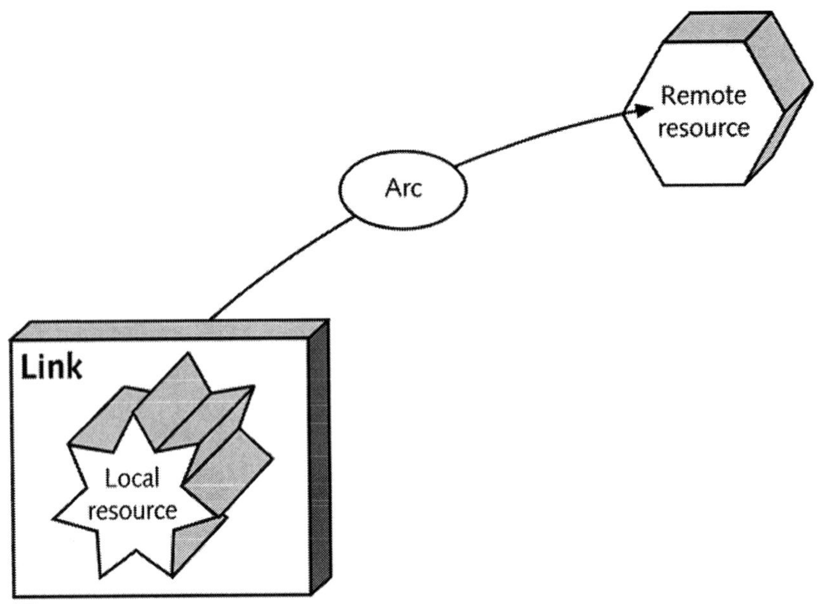

Exhibit 7-1: A generic simple-type link

Extended links

An *extended link* is a link that offers full XLink functionality, including inbound and third-party arcs (arcs between remote resources), as well as arcs that can simultaneously connect a local resource to several remote resources. As a result, the structure of an extended link can be fairly complex, and might include elements for pointing to remote resources, elements for containing local resources, elements for specifying arc traversal rules, and elements for specifying human-readable resource and arc titles. Exhibit 7-2 shows an example of an extended link.

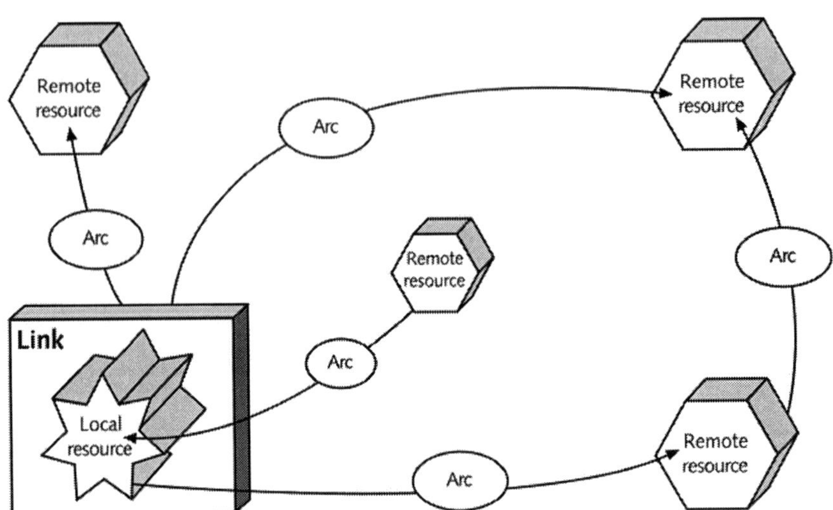

Exhibit 7-2: Extended-type link

It might be helpful to think of simple links as a subset of extended links. The purpose of a simple link is to provide a convenient shorthand version of an equivalent extended link. You could convert a simple link back into extended link format, but several structural changes would be required, because a properly constructed simple link is capable of combining all the basic functions of a combined extended-type element, a locator-type element, an arc-type element, and a resource-type element.

Exhibit 7-3 shows a comparison between the XML code of a simple link and an equivalent extended link. Note that the coding of the simple link could be made even shorter if, for example, default behavior for XLink attributes like `xlink:type` and `xlink:show` are declared within the affiliated DTD or schemas.

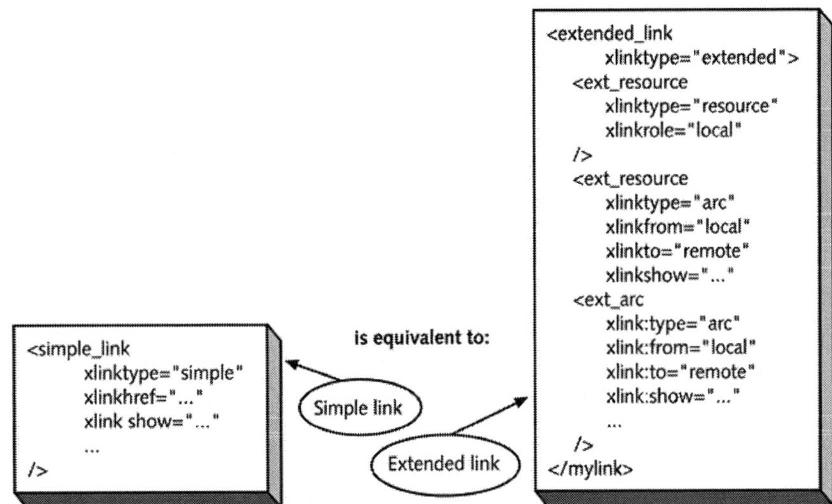

Exhibit 7-3: Comparison of XLink code: simple vs. extended link

Simple-type links are used as a shorthand form for otherwise extended links, and are appropriate only for certain simple situations, like the one shown in Exhibit 7-3. Extended links, while more complex, are still far more flexible and powerful.

Do it!

A-1: Exploring XLink basics

Exercises

1 Which of the following are true of simple links?

A It is the category into which HTML links would fall.

B It can either be an inbound or an outbound link.

C It associates exactly two participating resources, one local and one remote.

D It is named "simple" because its `href` attribute has the value "simple."

E Its arc goes to the local resource from the remote resource.

2 The purpose of a ___________ is to provide, when applicable, a convenient shorthand version of an equivalent extended link.

3 Which of the following is not true of XLink?

A It links your document with multiple sources and destinations.

B It locates link definitions in separate locations.

C It uses standard XML constructs (e.g. concepts, syntax format...).

D It identifies only one source and destination per link.

Resources

Explanation

Resources include files, images, documents, and programs. The following table lists several types of XLinks resources. Note that the definitions overlap and that the resources might also be portions of resources.

Resource type	Description
Starting resource	A resource from which a traversal is begun.
Ending resource	A destination resource for a traversal.
Local resource	An XML element that participates in a link by being a linking element or a child to a linking element.
Remote resource	A resource, or portion of a resource, that participates in a link, addressed with a Universal Resource Identifier (URI) reference; it might even be in the same XML document or inside the same linking element.

Traversing links

Traversal simply means to follow a link from where it starts to where it ends. The process of traversal always involves a pair of participating resources. All information about how to traverse a pair of resources, including the direction of traversal and any subsequent application behavior resulting from the link, is called an *arc*.

If two resources participate in a link, but there is only one source and one destination, then the link is *unidirectional*. However, if there are two arcs connecting the same pair of resources, but they switch places as starting and ending resources, then the link is *multidirectional*. A multidirectional link, as the W3C mentions in the XLink Recommendation, is not the same thing as "going back" (i.e., pressing the back button) after traversing a link.

The W3C defines an *outbound arc* as one that has a local starting resource and a remote ending resource (i.e., the link direction is away from the linking element). Conversely, if the ending resource is local but the starting resource is remote, then the arc is *inbound*. A variation of these concepts is the *third-party arc*, where neither the starting resource nor the ending resource is local.

Do it!

A-2: Discussing resources and link traversal

Exercises

1 A ___________ includes files, images, documents, and programs.

2 A ___________ resource is the resource from which traversal begins.

3 An ___________ resource is the destination resource for a traversal.

4 A ___________ resource participates in a link by being a linking element or being a child to a linking element.

5 ___________ are not XLink resources.

A Starting resources

B Remote resources

C Local resources

D Reverse resources

6 In an ___________ link, the direction is away from the linking element.

7 In a ___________ link, there are two resources: one source and one destination.

8 In an ___________ link, the ending resource is local, and the starting resource is remote.

9 What is an arc?

Topic B: Creating links with XLink

Explanation

In XML, as in HTML, resource links are represented by elements. According to XLink, the linking elements are found in the appropriate XML documents. Unlike HTML, however, which provides only the <A> and <IMG> elements for linking, you can give XLinks any name you want. What makes them behave as links are the attributes you assign to them. The W3C uses the term "assert" to describe this process. Paraphrasing the XLink Recommendation, "links are asserted by elements that have start tags containing the appropriate linking attributes."

XLink namespace and global attributes

To create linking elements, a declaration of the XLink namespace is required. However, the declaration must be within the linking element's start tag. Here's an example of such an XLink namespace declaration:

```
<elementname xmlns:xlink="http://www.w3.org/1999/xlink">
```

XLink elements (commonly called *XLinks*) are denoted by the linking attributes placed in their start tags. These attributes are called *global attributes*. Not only do they indicate which elements are linking elements, but they also allow you to specify other properties about the links and their resources, such as when to load the linked resources, and how they should appear after they load. First and foremost, XLinks always have an attribute named `type`. There are ten global XLink attributes. They are grouped according to their functions in the following table.

Attribute	Description
XLink definition/assertion attribute	
`type`	Indicates the XLink element type (simple, extended, locator, arc, resource, or title); a value for this attribute *must* be supplied, and must be one of the following: simple, extended, locator, arc, resource, title, or none.
Locator attribute: permits an XLink application to find a remote resource (or resource fragment)	
`href`	Can be used on simple-type elements; must be used on locator-type elements; value must be a URI reference or must result in a URI reference after a specific escaping procedure described in XLink 1.0.

Attribute	Description
Semantic attributes: describe the meaning of resources in the context of a link	
`role`	`Can be used on extended-type, simple-type, locator-type, and resource-type elements; value must be a URI reference, with some constraints as found in XLink 1.0. The URI reference identifies some resource that describes the intended property.`
`arcrole`	`Can be used on arc-type and simple-type elements; value must be a URI reference, with constraints as described in XLink 1.0. The URI reference identifies some resource that describes the intended property; if no value is supplied, no particular role value is inferred.`
`title`	Can be used on extended-type, locator-type, resource-type, arc-type, and simple-type elements; used to describe the meaning of a link or resource in a fashion readable by users. A value is optional (if one is supplied, it should contain a string that describes the resource); this information is highly dependent on the type of processing being done.
Behavior attributes: Signal behavior intentions for traversal to a link's remote ending resource(s)	
`show`	Can be used on the simple-type and arc-type elements; used to communicate the desired presentation of the ending resource on traversal from the starting resource; when used on arc-type elements, they signal behavior intentions for traversal to whatever ending resources are specified.
`actuate`	Can be used on the simple-type and arc-type elements; used to communicate the desired timing of traversal from the starting resource to the ending resource.
Traversal attributes	
`label`	Can be used on resource-type and locator-type elements; value must be an NCName (any name that begins with a letter or underscore and has no space or colon in it, because its author might add a namespace prefix to it).
`from`	Can be used on the arc-type element; value must be an NCName; if a value is supplied, it must correspond to the same value for some label attribute on a locator-type or resource-type element that appears as a direct child inside the same extended-type element as the arc-type element.
`to`	Can be used on the arc-type element; the value must be an NCName; as with "from," if a value is supplied, it must correspond to the same value for some label attribute on a locator-type or resource-type element that appears as a direct child inside the same extended-type element as the arc-type element.

When the `show` attribute is used, the values specified for it must be one of the following:

- `new` (For opening a new window.)
- `replace` (For replacing the existing window.)
- `embed` (For embedding the new resource inside the existing one.)
- `other` (For behavior of the application being unconstrained and the application looking for direction from other markup present in the link.)
- `none` (For behavior being unconstrained, but no other markup being present to help the application determine the appropriate behavior.)

The `actuate` attribute can have one of the following values:

- `onLoad` (Used when the application must traverse to the ending resource immediately on loading the starting resource; however, if a single resource contains multiple arcs that have behavior set to `show="replace"` and `actuate="onLoad"`, then application behavior is unconstrained.)
- `onRequest` (Used when the application must traverse from the starting resource to the ending resource only on a post-loading event. For example, when a user clicks on the starting resource, or software finishes a countdown.)
- `other` (Used when behavior is unconstrained and the application must look to other markup to determine the appropriate behavior.)
- `none` (Used when behavior is unconstrained by this specification, but no other markup is present to help the application determine the appropriate behavior.)

The `type` attribute must have one of these values: simple, extended, locator, arc, resource, title, or none. The following table explains these values:

Value	Description
`simple`	Provides syntax for a common outbound link (two participating resources); less functionality; no special internal structure; conceptually a subset of extended links, but with different syntax.
`extended`	Provides full functionality (e.g., inbound arcs, third-party arcs, links with multiple participating resources); can be fairly complex; can help an XLink application process other links).
`locator`	Addresses the remote resources participating in an extended link.
`arc`	Provides traversal rules among an extended link's participating resources.
`resource`	Supplies local resources that participate in an extended link.
`title`	Describes the meaning of an extended link or resource in readable terms; provides readable labels for the link.
`none`	Any XLink-related content or attributes have no XLink-specified relationship to its element. For example, "none" can help XLink applications avoid having to check for the presence of an `href`.

The specification of the `type` attribute designates the XLink element type as simple, extended, locator, arc, resource, title, or none. This designation complies with XLink convention, where a linking element containing a `type` attribute whose value is `V` is called a "`V-type element.`" For example, the following linking element, called `<payments>`, is referred to as a *locator-type element*:

```
<payments xlink:type="locator">
```

Accordingly, the element type dictates the XLink-imposed constraints that such a linking element must follow. The element type also influences the behavior of XLink applications when they encounter the linking element.

Do it!

B-1: Exploring XLink's namespace and global attributes

Exercises

1 To use your linking elements, the declaration of the XLink namespace is needed. Where must this declaration be inserted?

2 Which of the following syntax is a valid XLink namespace declaration?

A `<elementname xmlns:xlink="http://www.w3.org/1999/xlink">`

B `<attributename "http://www.w3.org/">`

C `<attributename xlink="http://www.w3.org/1999/xlink">`

D `<elementname xmlns: "http://www.w3.org/">`

3 __________ is not a value of the global attribute type.

A Simple

B Extended

C Arc

D Global

4 __________ is not an XLink global attribute.

A Type

B Href

C Role

D Local

5 __________ is a value of the `actuate` global attribute.

A New

B Onload

C Embed

D Replace

Restrictions on XLink types and attributes

Explanation

As you develop and define linking elements, two restrictions apply. First, given an element of a particular type, only certain attributes can be combined with them. Customarily, the simple-type element wants only an `href` locator attribute. The following table summarizes the hierarchy of declared attributes in a linking element. (This table applies only to extended-type elements.)

Parent element type	Accepted child attributes
`simple`	No applicable child attributes
`extended`	Locator, arc, resource, title
`located`	Title
`arc`	Title
`resource`	No applicable child attributes
`title`	No applicable child attributes

Secondly, given a particular declared element type, only some combinations of XLink attributes apply. Exhibit 7-4 indicates the restrictions to the combinations of global attributes and `type` attribute values that cooperate in the definition of a linking element. Each R indicates that one or more of the `type` attribute values are required before the linking element can function. Each O indicates which `type` attribute values are optional. A blank table entry indicates that the `type` attribute value cannot be used.

Global attribute name	**Type attribute values**					
	simple	extended	locator	arc	resource	title
type	R	R	R	R	R	R
href	O		O			
role	O	O	O		O	
arcrole	O			O		
title	O	O	O	O	O	
show	O			O		
actuate	O			O		
label			O		O	
from				O		
to				O		

Exhibit 7-4: Restrictions to the combinations of global attributes

Do it!

B-2: Discussing restrictions

Exercises

1 As linking elements are developed and defined, what two restrictions apply?

2 The simple-type element can have a child attribute. True or false?

A simple-type XLink

Explanation

The following is a brief example of the application of the previous two tables in a simple-type linking element named <contacts>:

```
<!-- contacts is a simple-type element that needs an href
attribute to point to a resource. -->

<contacts xmlns:xlink="http://www.w3.org/1999/xlink"
xlink:type="simple"
xlink:href="administration.xml"
xlink:show="new" />
```

Exhibit 7-5 shows this simple-type link.

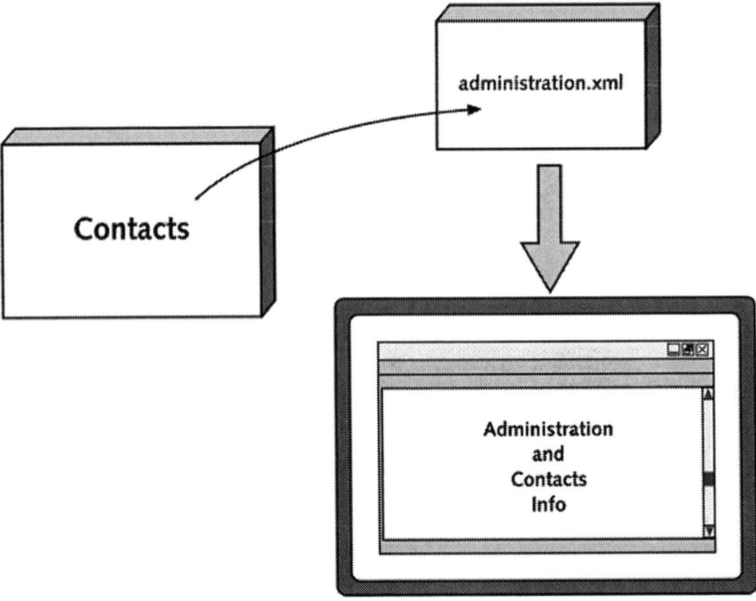

Exhibit 7-5: The simple-type contacts link

Note that the link element <contacts> declared the XLink namespace first, then its simple type. The element then specified the target resource, and used the optional `show` attribute to tell the application to open a new window to display the resource.

Extended-type XLinks

A common task for Human Resource professionals is to track the professional development of their fellow employees. Suppose you're one of TLSales' HR professionals, and you want to express in XML the relationship between TLSales' employees and their respective environments (that is, their work history prior to employment and their training at TLSales after they were hired). This includes making links from an employee to a description of their experience and also making links to descriptions of where they had previously worked. The data for each employee might be written like the way it has been written as follows:

```
<?xml version="1.0"?>
<HRInfo>
<surname>Sleek</surname>
<name>Jim</name>
<hired>Dec 1, 1895</hired>
<terminated></terminated>
<background>
<education>Columbia University, 1994</education>
<SSN>101010101010</SSN>
</background>
</HRInfo>
```

Brief descriptions of Mr. Sleek's work history might be included in separate files such as:

```
<?xml version="1.0"?>
<workhistory>
<company>Smith, Smith, Smith & Smith</company>
<state_city>NY NYC</state_city>
<timeframe begin="1994" end="1995"/>
<title>Floor Sales/Pitchman</title>
<duties>
<DutyList>Sales, demos, inventory</DutyList>
</duties>
</workhistory>
```

As you can see, fulfilling the requirement to create a file that relates employees to their respective experience and work history is a task beyond a simple strategy like adding links to HTML documents. There are many other factors to consider, including:

- One employee has probably had several kinds of experience (here, one link might connect one resource to many other resources).
- One employee has likely worked with several organizations.
- All links must be meaningful. Having one kind of work experience is likely not equivalent to having worked for a specific company, and this should be conveyed in the documents.

Now that there is a sufficient amount of information with which to build an extended-type link, the resources must be specified. However, the employee and environment documents are stored in separate documents outside of this XML document, so those documents are beyond HR's control. In that case, you use XLink's locator-type element type(s) to refer to them. The strategy is not to impose an element name, but to mark remote resources as locators by using XLink attributes.

```
<environment xmlns:xlink="http://www.w3.org/1999/xlink"
xlink:type="extended">

<!-- The resources involved in our link are the employee
     their experience and their work history -->

<employee xlink:type="locator" xlink:label="employee"
xlink:href="sleek.xml"/>
<experience xlink:type="locator" xlink:label="training"
xlink:href="inventory.xml"/>
<experience xlink:type="locator" xlink:label="training"
xlink:href="checkout.xml"/>
<experience xlink:type="locator" xlink:label="training"
xlink:href="orderdesk.xml"/>
<history xlink:type="locator" xlink:label="workhistory"
xlink:href="smithx5.xml"/>
<history xlink:type="locator" xlink:label="workhistory"
xlink:href="petersdriveinn.xml"/>
</environment>
```

To specify the relationships among these resources, you specify arcs between them (see the bold print):

```
<environment xmlns:xlink="http://www.w3.org/1999/xlink"
xlink:type="extended">
<!-- The resources involved in our link are the employee -->
<!-- their experience and their work history -->
<employee xlink:type="locator" xlink:label="employee"
xlink:href="sleek.xml"/>
<experience xlink:type="locator" xlink:label="training"
xlink:href="inventory.xml"/>
<experience xlink:type="locator" xlink:label="training"
xlink:href="checkout.xml"/>
<experience xlink:type="locator" xlink:label="training"
xlink:href="orderdesk.xml"/>
<history xlink:type="locator" xlink:label="workhistory"
xlink:href="smithx5.xml"/>
<history xlink:type="locator" xlink:label="workhistory"
xlink:href="petersdriveinn.xml"/>
<bind xlink:type="arc" xlink:from="employee"
xlink:to="training"/>
<bind xlink:type="arc" xlink:from="employee"
xlink:to="workhistory"/>
</environment>
```

As shown in this example, when using XLink, all you need is an XML document containing elements and attributes. In the same document, all the resources and relationships are clearly specified. Exhibit 7-6 shows this extended-type link.

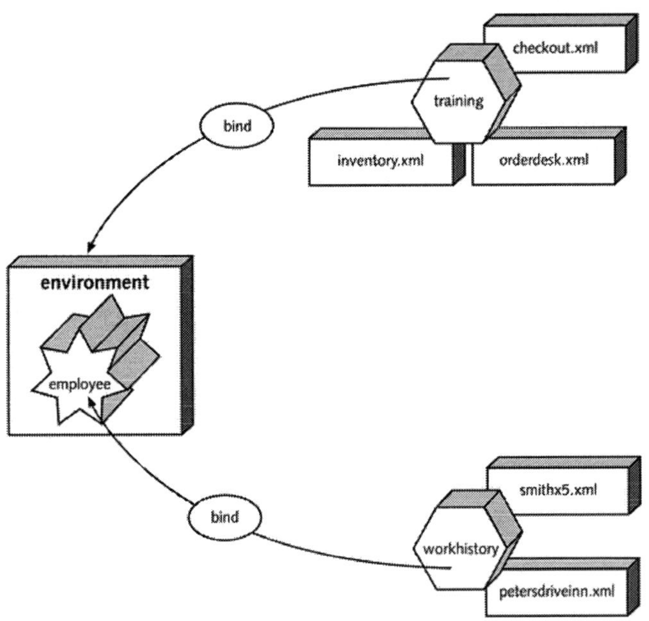

Exhibit 7-6: A simple extended-type link: an employee's environment

Do it!

B-3: Exploring an XML document containing an XLink

Here's how	Here's why
1 Open XML Spy	
2 Choose **Project**, **Open Project...**	The Open dialog box appears.
Click the **Look in** list arrow	
Navigate to the current unit folder	
Open **contacts.spp**	
3 In the project pane, expand XML Files	
Double-click **contacts.xml**	To open the XML document.
4 Switch to Text view	To view the XML code. Note that the xml-stylesheet declaration references the contacts.css stylesheet.
5 Choose **View**, **Browser view**	To view the formatted XML document.
6 Switch to Text view	The `CONTACTS` element has an XLink namespace declaration that's used for the global attributes set of XLink. Although the elements that need links are in a separate namespace, they become XLink elements by incorporating the `xlink:type` attribute.
7 In the Project pane, expand **XSL Files**	
Double click **contacts.css**	To open the stylesheet.
8 In the Project pane, expand **DTD/Schemas**	
Double-click **contacts.dtd**	To open the DTD in the main window. Note that the `WHATSNEW` element contains a child element called `SITE`. This element is meant to contain a link in the XML document.

Topic C: Validating XLinks

Explanation

For XLinks to function correctly and reliably, their respective elements and documents must be well-formed and valid. That means that the linking elements and attributes must be declared in the referenced DTDs and schemas. To illustrate how this is done with various elements and attributes, a number of examples follow.

Employee data with a resource-type linking element

This example focuses on simple employee information. It uses a local resource-type linking element. The employee is Mr. Sleek of the Sales Department. The `<employee>` element appears as follows:

```
<employee xlink:label="jsleek">
<name>Jim</name>
<surname>Sleek</surname>
</employee>
```

An entry in a DTD for the linking element `<employee>` might look like this:

```
<!ELEMENT employee (name,surname)>
<!ATTLIST employee
xlink:type (resource) #FIXED "resource"
xlink:title CDATA #IMPLIED
xlink:label NMTOKEN #IMPLIED
xlink:role CDATA #IMPLIED>
```

Note that the linking element has three other XLink-based attributes besides `xlink:type`. As mentioned before, `xlink:title` is a semantic attribute that gives a short description of the resource. The second attribute, `xlink:label`, is a traversal attribute that identifies the element later, when arcs are built. The third attribute, `xlink:role`, describes a property of the resource.

It's important to note that the subelements `<name>` and `<surname>` are of no significance to XLink. Therefore, in this example, you can presume that they are declared elsewhere in the DTD.

Remote data information with a locator-type linking element

Locator-type linking elements point to remote resources. For example, let's say that you're building a link to a remote resource pertaining to the Sales Department. The locator-type `<department>` linking element might appear as follows:

```
<department xlink:label="sales" xlink:href="sales.xml"/>
```

Here's the DTD code for the `<department>` locator-type element:

```
<!ELEMENT department EMPTY>
<!ATTLIST department
xlink:type (locator) #FIXED "locator"
xlink:title CDATA #IMPLIED
xlink:role CDATA #IMPLIED
xlink:label NMTOKEN #IMPLIED
xlink:href CDATA #REQUIRED>
```

Locator-type elements can have the same title, role, and label attributes as resource-type elements. However, they also need an `href` semantic attribute, which ultimately points to the remote resource.

Remote employee data by using inbound link arcs

An inbound link consists of an arc from an external resource (which is located with a locator-type element) towards an internal resource (specified with a resource-type element). Arc-type elements use additional child `to` and `from` attributes to designate the start and end points of the specified arc. Note the arc-type element `<empl_record>`.

```
<empl_record xlink:type="arc" xlink:from="jsleek"
xlink:to="sales"/>
```

In addition to the traversal attributes `to` and `from`, arcs might include the `show`, `title`, `actuate`, and `arcrole` attributes. The DTD would include the following code:

```
<!ELEMENT acted EMPTY>
<!ATTLIST acted
xlink:type (arc) #FIXED "arc"
xlink:title CDATA #IMPLIED
xlink:show (new|replace|embed|other|none) #IMPLIED
xlink:from NMTOKEN #IMPLIED
xlink:to NMTOKEN #IMPLIED>
```

Extended-type linking element

Combining all the examples results in the following arc from a local to a remote resource:

```
<!-- A local resource -->
<employee xlink:label="jsleek">
<name>Jim</name>
<surname>Sleek</surname>
</employee>

<!-- A remote resource -->
<department xlink:label="sales" xlink:href="sales.xml"/>

<!-- An arc that binds them -->
<empl_record xlink:type="arc" xlink:from="jsleek"
xlink:to="sales"/>
```

To encapsulate relationships, an overall container element is needed—that is, an extended-type linking element. Extended-type links can point to remote resources and local resources, and can also contain arcs and a title.

Exhibit 7-7, Exhibit 7-8, Exhibit 7-9, and Exhibit 7-10 depart from the existing discussion, to show the evolution of a simple, generic extended-type linking element named `<extLink>`. The first coding for the extended-type link (shown in Exhibit 7-7) consists of its start tag and end tag. The start tag contains the `xlink:type` attribute which specifies that the element is an extended-type link. The rectangle above the code box indicates the creation of the link.

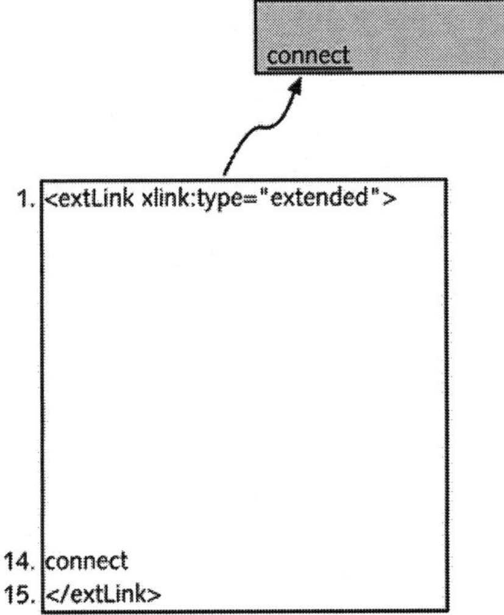

Exhibit 7-7: Phase 1: creating the XLink element

Exhibit 7-8 shows the references to the remote resources: balls of different sizes that represent two different HTML documents. Each document is specified to be of a locator type, meaning they are the remote resources of an extended link. Both get the label "hatchball," to indicate that only one arc is necessary to initiate contact with both remote sources.

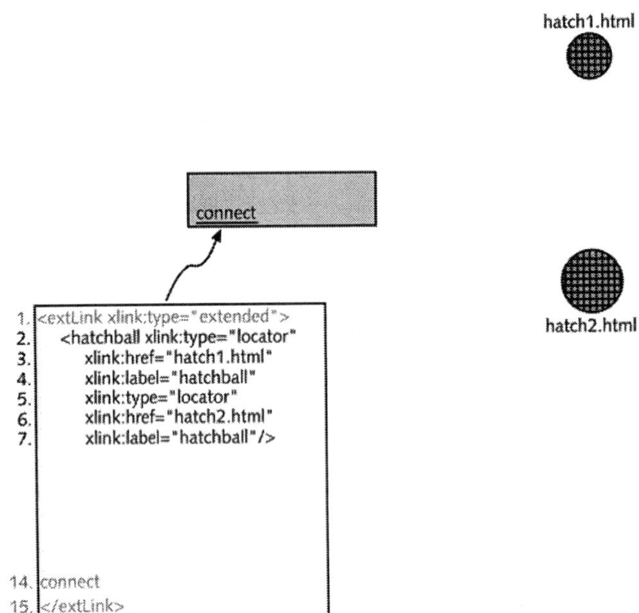

Exhibit 7-8: Phase 2: refer to remote resources

Exhibit 7-9 shows the creation of the local resource. Its element name is `<stripeball>`. The type is specified to be “resource,” indicating that it’s the local resource participating in the link. Its label, though, is “not-hatch,” to ensure there is no confusion with the remote hatchball resources.

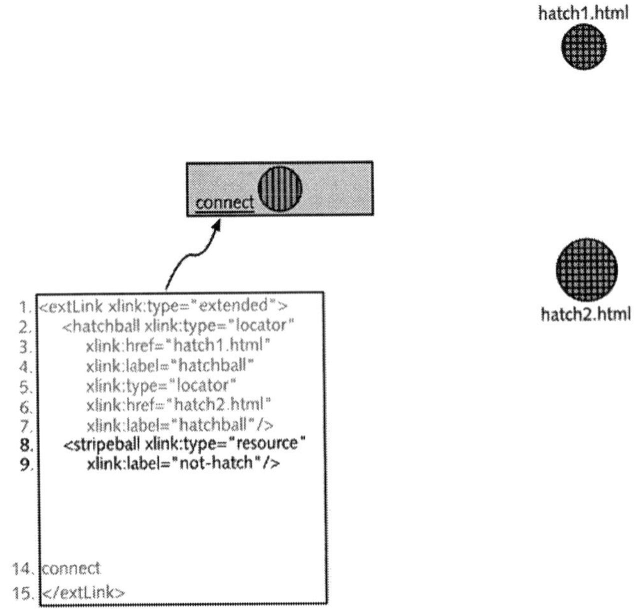

Exhibit 7-9: Phase 3: refer to local resources

Exhibit 7-10 shows the creation of an element named `<go>` that is specified by an arc. It has the arbitrary title "X" and is told that it arcs from the local resource, labeled "not-hatch," to all the remote resources that have been given the label "hatchball" The word "connect" acts as the visible presence for the `<extLink>` element; that is, it acts as the hyperlink.

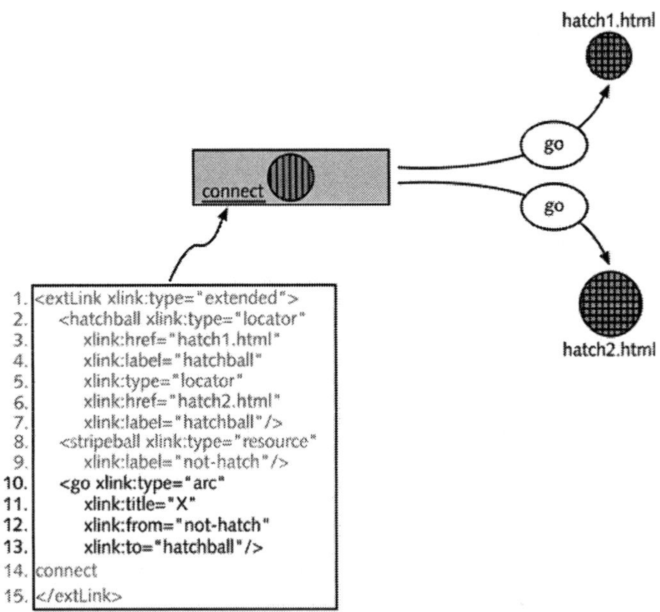

Exhibit 7-10: Phase 4: creating arcs

Think of extended-link elements as meaningful containers for resources and arcs. Returning to the TLSales example, note in the following DTD code how the extended-type element called `<staff>` contains the `<employee>`, `<department>`, and `<empl_record>` elements:

```
<!ELEMENT staff (employee,department,empl_record)*>
<!ATTLIST staff
xmlns:xlink CDATA #FIXED
http://www.w3.org/1999/xlink"
xlink:type (extended) #FIXED "extended"
xlink:title CDATA #IMPLIED>
```

Combining all the previous TLSales elements results in a complete and valid extended-type link, which should validate against the DTD code. From the quick illustration in Exhibit 7-7, Exhibit 7-8, Exhibit 7-9, and Exhibit 7-10, you should now recognize the components of the following extended link. Again, the one-to-many link is something that is not possible in HTML.

```
<staff xlink:title="TLSales Staff Information">
<employee xlink:label="jsleek">
<name>Jim</name>
<surname>Sleek</surname>
</employee>
<department xlink:label="HRInfo" xlink:title="Sales"
xlink:href="sales.xml"/>
<department xlink:label="HRInfo" xlink:title="Partners"
xlink:href="partners.xml"/>
<empl_record xlink:type="arc" xlink:from="jsleek"
xlink:to="HRInfo"/>
</staff>
```

Validating simple links

Conceptually, simple-type linking elements can be considered a subset of extended links. They can exist as a notation for linking elements where you don't need the power, flexibility, and resource overhead of an entire extended-type link. All the XLink-related aspects of a simple link are encapsulated in one element. XLink doesn't care about the subelements of a simple-type link, only about the linking element itself and its attributes.

To review, the valid XLink attributes for a simple-type link are `href`, `title`, `role`, `arcrole`, `show`, and `actuate`. The following is an example of DTD code for a typical simple-type link element:

```
<!ELEMENT director (#PCDATA)>
<!ATTLIST director
xmlns:xlink CDATA #FIXED
"http://www.w3.org/1999/xlink"
xlink:type (simple) #FIXED "simple"
xlink:href CDATA #IMPLIED
xlink:show (new) #FIXED "new"
xlink:actuate (onRequest) #FIXED "onRequest">
```

Here's the simple-type element link that corresponds to the DTD code above:

```
<president xlink:href="gwbushjr.xml">George W. Bush
Jr.</president>
```

Adding XLink

In the following activity, you will construct a simple XLink that is the XML equivalent to an HTML hyperlink because it provides access to an external Web page identified by a Uniform Resource Identifier (URI). At the time of this writing, Netscape is the only commercial browser that supports XLink functionality.

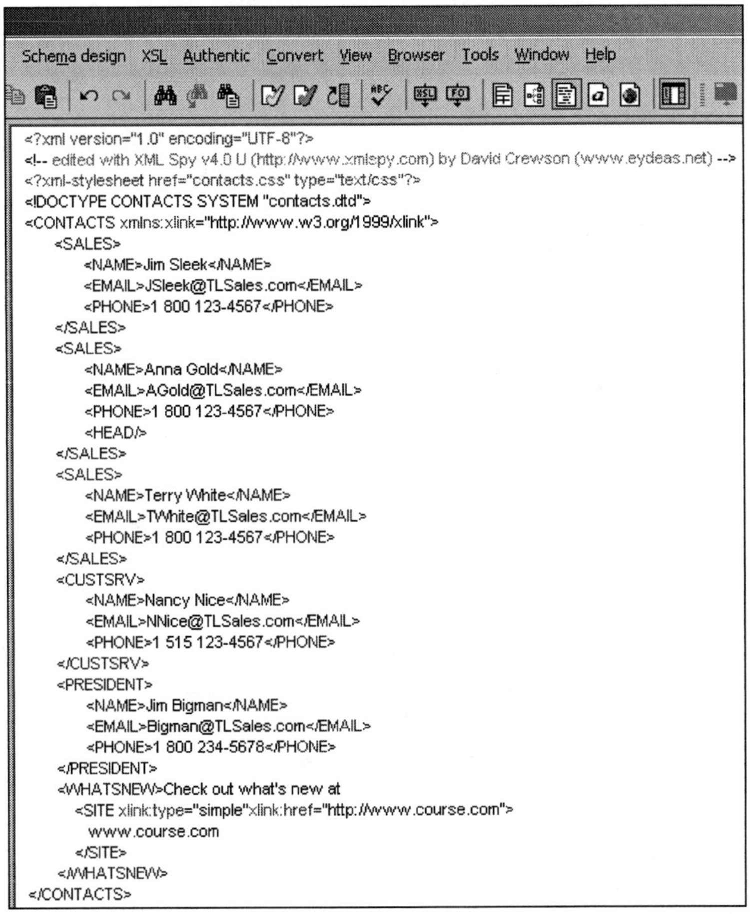

Schema design XSL Authentic Convert View Browser Tools Window Help

```
<?xml version="1.0" encoding="UTF-8"?>
<!-- edited with XML Spy v4.0 U (http://www.xmlspy.com) by David Crewson (www.eydeas.net) -->
<?xml-stylesheet href="contacts.css" type="text/css"?>
<!DOCTYPE CONTACTS SYSTEM "contacts.dtd">
<CONTACTS xmlns:xlink="http://www.w3.org/1999/xlink">
    <SALES>
        <NAME>Jim Sleek</NAME>
        <EMAIL>JSleek@TLSales.com</EMAIL>
        <PHONE>1 800 123-4567</PHONE>
    </SALES>
    <SALES>
        <NAME>Anna Gold</NAME>
        <EMAIL>AGold@TLSales.com</EMAIL>
        <PHONE>1 800 123-4567</PHONE>
        <HEAD/>
    </SALES>
    <SALES>
        <NAME>Terry White</NAME>
        <EMAIL>TWhite@TLSales.com</EMAIL>
        <PHONE>1 800 123-4567</PHONE>
    </SALES>
    <CUSTSRV>
        <NAME>Nancy Nice</NAME>
        <EMAIL>NNice@TLSales.com</EMAIL>
        <PHONE>1 515 123-4567</PHONE>
    </CUSTSRV>
    <PRESIDENT>
        <NAME>Jim Bigman</NAME>
        <EMAIL>Bigman@TLSales.com</EMAIL>
        <PHONE>1 800 234-5678</PHONE>
    </PRESIDENT>
    <WHATSNEW>Check out what's new at
      <SITE xlink:type="simple"xlink:href="http://www.course.com">
       www.course.com
      </SITE>
    </WHATSNEW>
</CONTACTS>
```

Exhibit 7-11: contacts.xml showing an XLink

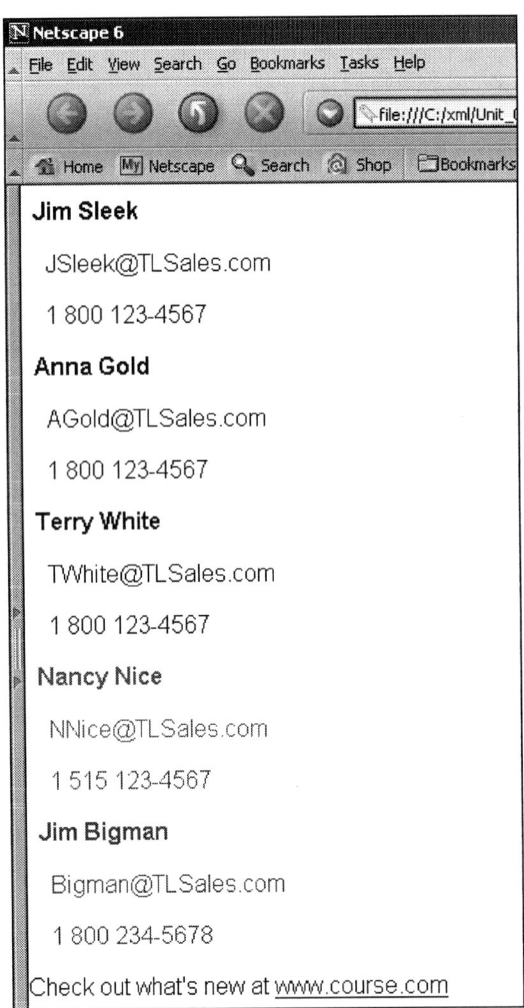

Exhibit 7-12: contacts.xml in Netscape

Do it!

C-1: Adding a link to an XML document

Here's how	Here's why
1 Switch to contacts.xml	You will add a link to this XML document.
2 Directly above the </CONTACTS> end tag, type:	

```
<WHATSNEW>Check out what's new at
  <SITE xlink:type="simple"
   xlink:href="http://www.course.com"> Course.com
  </SITE>
</WHATSNEW>
```

	Your document should now resemble Exhibit 7-11.
3 Save your changes	
4 In the XSL Files branch of the Project pane, double-click **contacts.css**	You will create a new rule in this stylesheet.
After the last rule in the file, type:	

```
SITE { color: navy; text-decoration: underline;
       cursor: hand }
```

	Data in a `SITE` element will display as navy blue underlined text that shows a hand pointer when users mouse over the text.
5 Save your changes	
6 Open contacts.xml in Netscape	The document should resemble Exhibit 7-12.
7 Click the **Course.com** link	To navigate to the external website.
Close Netscape	

Extended links

Explanation

At the time of writing, there are not many software programs that provide complete XLink functionality. In particular, most Web browsers do not yet support extended links.

Do it!

C-2: Examining an XML document with extended links

Here's how	Here's why
1 Add **sales.xml** to the project	In the Project pane, right-click XML Files. Choose Add Files, and select sales.xml.
2 Open **sales.xml**	
3 Switch to Text view	The XML document appears in raw form. In the `CONTACTS` element, the `xlink:type` attribute is set to extended. This indicates that the element contains child elements that participate in extended linking. The `ss` namespace creates unique labels to identify child elements of `CONTACTS` that participate in the extended links.
4 Locate the three resources that participate in the document's extended links—one internal and two external	The `NAME` element contains the internal resource declaration `xlink:type="resource"` that identifies the element as participating as an internal or inline resource. The `xlink:role` attribute defines a unique identifier to the resource that is used in the link definition. The `xlink:title` provides readable descriptions about the link.
Locate the `SALESREPORT` and `NEWORDER` elements	These elements represent external resources and are identified by the `xlink:type="locator"`. They participate in the link by referencing or locating the external resource defined by the `xlink:href` attribute.
5 Locate the three arcs in the document	CreateOrder and GetOrderSalesReport link the external resources in both directions. In HTML, you would have to modify both resources to create a two-way link, but with XLink, even though both resources exist in separate locations, they are linked without having to modify the resources themselves.
Locate the `xlink:from` and `xlink:to` attributes of the arc-type element	These attributes identify the source and destination resources. The `xlink:show` determines how the destination resource is displayed. In this case, the resource replaces the current resource in the browser window. The `xlink:actuate` attribute tells the browser to wait for the request before loading the resource.
6 Locate `GetSalespersonSalesReport`	It links the local `NAME` element with the `SALESREPORT` element located externally. Note that the `xlink:show` attribute is set to new. When the link is activated, the destination resource appears in a new browser window.

Topic D: XML Pointer (XPointer)

Explanation

In the words of the W3C, "(XPointer), which is based on the XML Path Language (XPath), is still under development. It supports addressing into the internal structures of XML documents. It allows for traversals of a document tree and choice of its internal parts based on various properties, such as element types, attribute values, character content, and relative position."

Discussing the XPointer language

The XML Pointer Language (XPointer) extends the ability of XPath to find subresources. XPath is a declarative language used for addressing and pattern matching. Being an extension of XPath means XPointer can reach more precise locations in a document without having to download more data than necessary or without needing to provide additional elements, attributes, or other components to the document. However, you can still add markup to documents and take advantage of the flexibility that it gives you. XPointer is used in conjunction with XLink to access resources more precisely.

To see how XPointer works with XLink, look at the example of the simple-type linking element named `<MEETING>` in Exhibit 7-13. Note that the XPointer features are placed in the linking element `<MEETING>` through the use of the locator attribute `xlink:href`.

```
<MEETING xmlns:xlink="http://www.w3.org/1999/xlink"
                        xlink:type="simple"
                        xlink:show="new"
xlink:href="http://www.TLSales.com/mtg_agenda.xml
              #xpointer(/child::*[position()=2])...etc />
agenda
</MEETING>
```

Exhibit 7-13: An XPointer working with XLink

XPointer expressions resemble XPath expressions in syntax and effect, but XPointer adds new features called extensions, XPointer references, and fragment identifiers, among others. These features allow XPointer to:

- Use URI references to address into the internal structure of XML documents
- Address points and ranges, in addition to the entire (XPath) nodes (Users can now select parts of documents by using their mouse.)
- Use string matching in searches

The major advantage provided by the XPointer extensions is the ability to refer more precisely to XML document subresources. This provides a level of precision that HTML, XLink and XPath could not reach. With XPointer, the user is even given the ability to click on more precise pieces of information, which can also save time and bandwidth, and provide documents with more precise and clearer information.

Addressing a document's internal structure with a URI

In the example shown in Exhibit 7-13, the value specified for the locator attribute `xlink:href` was a URI that allows the application to drill down to a subresource within the specified URL. The example shown in Exhibit 7-14 shows just the URI value portion, minus the "...etc.," of the locator attribute, so that you can see the URI's basic parts more clearly.

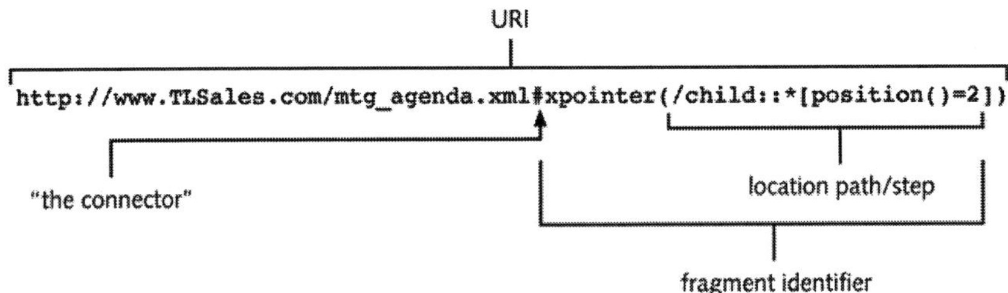

Exhibit 7-14: A generic XPointer URI

Note that the URI reference begins with a Web site address (`http://www.TLSales.com`), followed by the name of the specific XML document to be searched (mtg_agenda.xml) at that site. The XPointer-specific information follows that, and is connected to the Web site URI and XML document portions by a hash symbol (`#`), also called a pound sign or number sign.

There are two types of such connectors; each instructs the parser to initiate link behavior in a specific manner. The hash connector initiates link behavior similar to HTML; the entire linked resource is downloaded, and the focus is then shifted to the identified fragment.

The other connector is the vertical bar character (`|`), also called a pipe. When the pipe is used, subsequent behavior is left to whatever is written in the application, which might or might not download the entire resource, depending on its author's needs. Downloading of the entire resource can be prevented, and discrete subresources can be retrieved and served back to the requestor in the application. This way, bandwidth can be conserved and other connection costs can also be optimized.

The fragment identifier begins immediately after the connector and is composed of the keyword `xpointer` combined with the location (also called the locationpath) or even the location steps (in the Exhibit 7-14 example, the location path is equal to just one location step).

Note: At various points, the XPointer reference might be called one of several names: fragment identifier, XPointer reference, XPointer, reference, location, link target, and others. No matter which term is used, they all refer to the same concept. They are listed here because this concept has many name variations, depending on the organization, industry, and author.

Exhibit 7-15 represents a Web page that includes the link named "agenda." As the mouse pointer is placed over "agenda," the entire URI—the URL plus the hash connector and the fragment identifier—appears in the status bar at the bottom of the window (in Exhibit 7-15, "etc." again substitutes for the fragment identifier in the identifier). When clicked, this link initiates the display of whatever content is found at the referenced location.

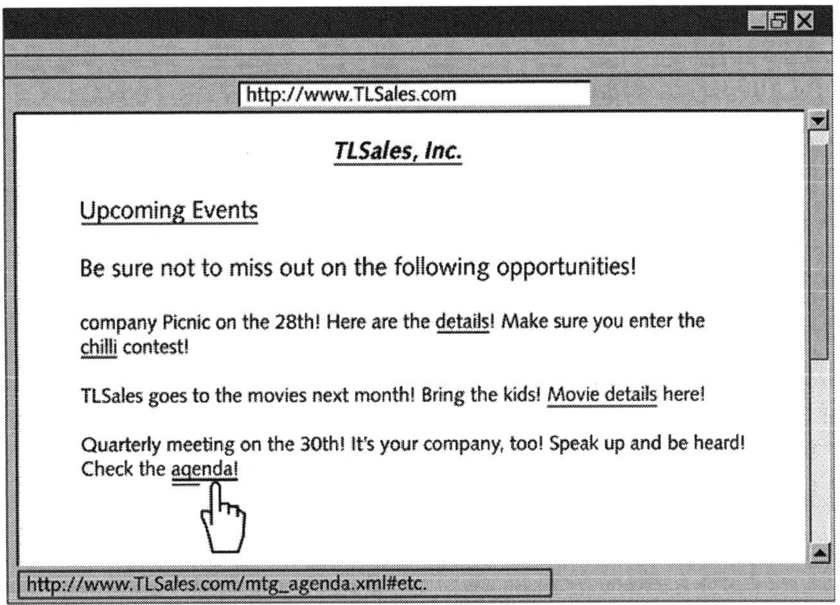

Exhibit 7-15: XPointer construct on a generic Web page

Do it!

D-1: Discussing XPointer

Exercises

1 What three features make XPointer an "extension" to XPath?

2 The major advantage provided by the new XPointer extensions is the ability to refer more precisely to XML document subresources, introducing a level of precision that HTML, XLink, and XPath can't reach. True or false?

3 Which of the following is not true about the fragment identifier?

A It begins immediately after the connector.

B It is composed of the keyword xpointer combined with the location.

C It refers to the same concept of XPointer reference.

D It begins before the connector.

Fragment identifier components

Explanation

XPointer fragment identifiers are composed of the xPointer keyword followed by the basic addressing component, the location (i.e., a description of a subresource location). XPointer location descriptions can represent precise locations in XML documents, especially when they are used in tandem combinations.

The location is composed of a location path, which in turn is made up of one or more location steps. If there is more than one location step in the location path, the location steps are separated by a forward slash (/) character.

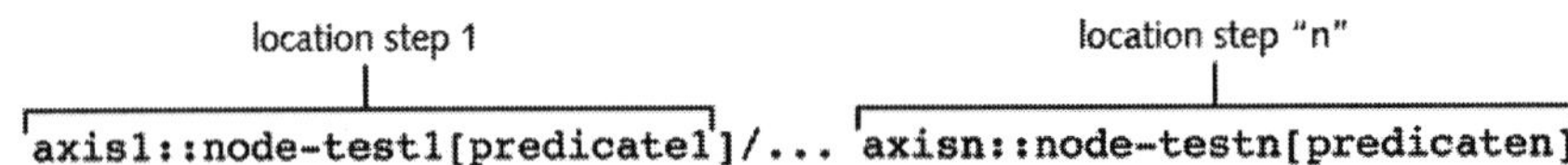

Exhibit 7-16: Generic location path

The location steps contain components like (XPath) nodes, axes, node tests, and zero or more predicates, as well as the (XPointer) points and ranges. Exhibit 7-17 shows individual location step.

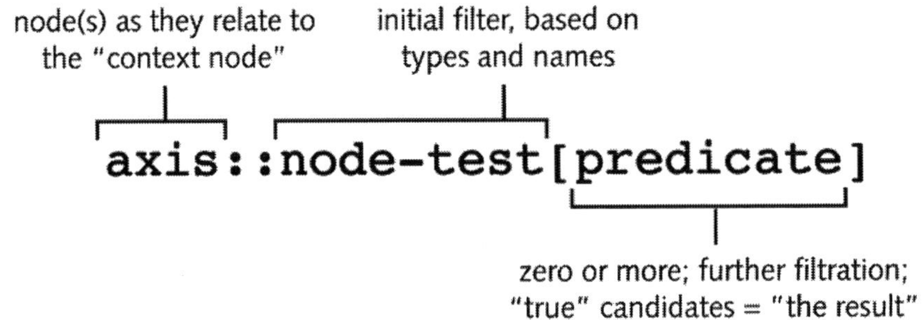

Exhibit 7-17: Generic location step

The steps are evaluated left to right, starting with the context defined in the location step at the far left. Whatever result is finally distilled from the step at the far right must have also survived the far-left step. In other words, whatever results there are to the location step must have answered "yes/true" to the conditions imposed by it.

If a location path is prefixed with a forward slash (/), then the screening must have begun with the document's root node as the initial context. (Recall that each XPath context consists of the context node(s), integer-value positions and sizes, and variable bindings, function libraries, and namespace declarations.)

The formal grammar for XPointer and other XML-related languages is Extended Backus-Naur Form (EBNF) notation, an example of which is shown in Exhibit 7-17, and which is described in W3C XML Recommendation 1.0 and other references. EBNF has been around since 1960 and is commonly used to describe programming grammar and syntax. However, rarely does a variation of EBNF actually play a role as it does in the description of location steps in XPointer extensions. In EBNF parlance, the ": :" means "the expression on the left is defined by the expression on the right."

The TLSales management team XML document (mgt_team.xml) is shown in Exhibit 7-18. In the expression `child::MGT[position()=3]`, child is an axis name, MGT is a node test, and `[position ()=3]` is the predicate. Here, the parser is told to check the child elements of the context node, and select the data from the third element named `<MGT>`.

```
<?xml version="1.0" encoding="UTF-8" standalone="yes"?>
<?xml-sylesheet type="text/css" href="contacts.css"?>
<!---edited with Notepad by Student Name -->
<MGT_TEAM>
	<MGT id="sales.mgr">
		<LASTNAME>Gold</LASTNAME>
		<FIRSTNAME>Anna</FIRSTNAME>
	</MGT>
	<MGT id="custsrv.mgr">
		<LASTNAME>Smith</LASTNAME>
		<FIRSTNAME>Dale</FIRSTNAME>
	</MGT>
	<MGT id="mktg.mgr">
		<LASTNAME>Jones</LASTNAME>
		<FIRSTNAME>Chris</FIRSTNAME>
	</MGT>
	<MGT id="admin.mgr">
		<LASTNAME>Wong</LASTNAME>
		<FIRSTNAME>Kelly</FIRSTNAME>
	</MGT>
	<MGT id="exec.mgr">
		<LASTNAME>McKinnon</LASTNAME>
		<FIRSTNAME>Linda</FIRSTNAME>
	</MGT>
</MGT_TEAM>
```

Exhibit 7-18: mgt_team.xml

Here's another example based on mgt_team.xml:

```
/descendant::MGT/child::LASTNAME
```

In this example, the parser is instructed to examine all the descendant elements of the context node, and select data from all the `<LASTNAME>` elements that have an `<MGT>` element as a parent. You can see that, from the nature of this example, the parser will look more precisely for the specified data.

Do it!

D-2: Discussing fragment identifier components

Exercises

1 What is the difference between a fragment identifier and a location path? What is the difference between a location path and a location step?

2 Which of the following is not true about location?

A It is a description of a subresource.

B It is composed of a location path.

C It follows the XPointer keyword.

D It is not part of the XPointer fragment identifiers.

3 ____________ is/are not a component of the location steps.

A Zero or more predicates

B Result

C Axis

D Node test

4 If there is more than one location step in the location path, then the location steps are separated by ____________.

A /

B #

C ?

D <

XPointer axes

Explanation

The axis, shown in Exhibit 7-17, might represent one or more XPath-style nodes, within which the subresource is found. These axes become more familiar with practice and by examining the options available to you. Axes provide "look at" instructions to the parser. The parser is told what its position is when it commences its search and in which direction to search. XPointers use the same axes as XPaths. The following table lists the available axes:

Axis	Instruction to parser
`child`	Look at the children of the context node.
`descendant`	Look at all descendants (i.e., the children, children's children, etc.) of the context node.
`parent`	Look at the parent node of the context node (if you're at the root, this is "empty").
`ancestor`	Look at all ancestor nodes from the parent back to the root (that includes the parent of the context node, the parent's parent, and so forth, back to and including the root node).
`following-sibling`	Look at the sibling nodes to the right; that is, look at the following siblings of the context node. (Remember, a sibling is a node on the same level as the context node.)
`preceding-sibling`	Look at the sibling nodes to the left; that is, look at all the preceding siblings of the context node.
`following`	Look at all the nodes in the document that follow the context node, excluding descendants and excluding attribute nodes and namespace nodes.
`preceding`	Look at all preceding nodes in the document, excluding any ancestors and excluding attribute nodes and namespace nodes.
`attribute`	Look at the attributes of the context node.
`namespace`	Look at the namespace declarations in the context node.
`self`	Look at the context node itself.
`descendent or self`	Look at the union of the context node and its descendants.
`ancestor or self`	Look at the union of the context node and its ancestors.

XPointer node tests

The node test is a preliminary filtering test (based on element names or a type of processing instruction). Although XPointers use the same axes as XPaths, XPointers use some node tests that XPaths do not. The following table lists the node tests you can use with XPointers, and what they match to:

Node tests	Matches
`*`	Any element
`node( )`	Any node
`test( )`	A text node
`comment( )`	A comment node
`processing-instruction( )`	A processing instruction node
`point( )`	A point in a resource
`range( )`	A range in a resource

Note: To extend XPath to include points and ranges, the XPointer specification created the concept of a "location," which can be an XPath node, a point, or a range. However, node tests are still called node tests, not location tests, even though they function correctly with the new points and ranges.

XPointer predicates

The predicate is the final filter, the one that focuses most on context size and position, the results of which are considered to have indicated a boolean-like "yes/true" response to its conditions. XPointers support the same types of predicate expressions as XPaths. The following are the types of expressions you can use in XPointer predicates:

- **Node sets.** A location path can be used as an expression.
- **Booleans.** True/False determinations; "or" and "and" expressions can be used.
- **Numbers.** Represent floating-point numbers; include a special "Not-a-Number" (NaN) value, positive and negative infinity, and positive and negative zero; the +, (must be preceded by white space), div and mod operators are permitted.
- **Strings.** A sequence of zero or more Unicode characters.
- **Result tree fragments.** Parts of XML documents that are not complete nodes or sets of nodes; created by document () functions, etc.

Do it!

D-3: Discussing XPointer axes and node tests

Exercises

1 The ____________ axis looks at all nodes that follow the context.

2 The ____________ axis looks at the sibling nodes to the left.

3 Which of the following does not refer to an XPointer reference?

A Fragment identifier

B Link target

C Location

D XPointer

E All of the above

F None of the above

4 Which of the following is true about the "child" axis name of XPointer available axes?

A It looks at the children of the context node.

B It looks at the attributes of the context itself.

C It looks at the context node itself.

D It looks at the namespace declaration in the context node.

5 ____________ is not one of the node tests you can use with XPointers.

A `parent( )`

B `node( )`

C `text( )`

D `point( )`

XPointer location set functions

Explanation

The following table lists several kinds of XPointer functions that return specific location sets:

Functions	Explanation/Description
`id()`	Returns all the elements whose ID attribute values match the one specified.
`here()`	Returns a location set with one location: the current location.
`origin()`	Same as here( ), except that this function works with out-of-line links.
`root()`	Returns a location set with one location: the root node.

You can use the `id()` function to return locations with ID attribute values that are a match to the location part of the extension. The `here()` function refers to the current element, not just the current node; it is useful because XPointers are usually stored in text nodes or attribute values. The `origin()` function is much like the `here()` function, but you use it with out-of-line links, which are not covered in this text due to time constraints. The `root()` function works like the / character—it refers to the root node, corresponding to the beginning of the prolog.

Pointing to IDs: the id() function

The simplest example of an XPointer refers to an ID attribute in the element(s) to which you want to point. For example, a TLSales management team list might use the `<MGT>` element to define different management IDs.

In Exhibit 7-18, if you intend to point specifically to Kelly Wong, for example, the fragment identifier of your XPointer might be expressed as `#id(admin.mgr)`. The full URI would be `http://www.TLSales.com/mgt_team.xml#id(admin.mgr).`

Counting elements: the position() function

The `position()` function acts as a counter for the various elements that the parser might encounter in the early processing stages. The expression `child::MGT[position()=3]` instructs the parser to look among the child elements to the context node, and fetch the data from the third `<MGT>` element found there.

Do it!

D-4: Discussing XPointer location set functions

Exercises

1 __________ is a function of XPointer functions that does not return specific location sets.

A `id()`

B `root()`

C `here()`

D `point()`

2 Which of the following is true about the `root()` function of XPointer functions?

A It returns a location set with one location: the root node.

B This function is used with out-of-line links.

C It returns the current location.

D It returns all the elements whose id attribute values match the one specified.

3 Which of the following is true about the `id()` function of XPointer functions that return specific location sets?

A It returns a location set with one location, the current location.

B It returns all the elements whose id attribute value match the one specified.

C This function is used with out-of-line links.

D It returns a location set with one location: the root node.

XPointer examples

Explanation

The following table lists several XPointer reference examples. They all refer to the agenda for the mtg_agenda.xml document depicted in Exhibit 7-19.

Example	Explanation/description
`*`	All the element children of the context node.
`.`	The context node itself.
`**`	The parent of the context node.
`@*`	All the attributes of the context node.
`@ID`	The ID attributes of the context node.
`text()`	All text node children of the context node.
`ITEM`	The <ITEM> element children of the context node.
`//ITEM`	All the <ITEM> descendants of the document root.
`ITEM[4]`	The fourth <ITEM> child of the context node.
`ITEM[first()]`	The first <ITEM> child of the context node.
`*/TIME_REQ`	All the <TIME_REQ> grandchildren of the context node.
`ITEM[TIME_REQ]`	The <ITEM> child of the context node that have <TIME_REQ> children.
`//AGENDA/ITEM[4]/ SUMMARY`	The <SUMMARY> element of the fourth <ITEM> element of the <AGENDA> element.

```
<?xml version="1.0" encoding="UTF-8" standalone="yes"?>
<?xml-sylesheet type="text/css" href="contacts.css"?>
<!---edited with Notepad by Student Name -->
<AGENDA>
       <ITEM id="1Q_REVS">
              <SPONSOR>Gold</SPONSOR>
              <TIME_REQ units="hours">1.0</TIME_REQ>
              <SUMMARY>
                     <COMMENT>Improved over 4Q</COMMENT>
       </SUMMARY>
       </ITEM>
       <ITEM id="COMPLAINTS">
              <SPONSOR>Smith</SPONSOR>
              <TIME_REQ units="hours">0.5</TIME_REQ>
              <SUMMARY>
                     <$REQD amount="$Cdn">0</$REQD>
              </SUMMARY>
       </ITEM>
       <ITEM id= "ADV_PLAN">
              <SPONSOR>Jones</SPONSOR>
              <TIME_REQ units="hours">1.0</TIME_REQ>
              <SUMMARY>
                     <COMMENT>Reduce ratio; more WWW</COMMENT>
                     <$REQD amount="$Cdn">2.5 million</$REQD>
              </SUMMARY>
       </ITEM>
       <ITEM id="Q_A'>
              <SPONSOR>Manocha</SPONSOR>
              <TIME_REQ units="hours">0.5</TIME_REQ>
              <SUMMARY>
                     <COMMENT>Improved</COMMENT>
                     <$REQD amount="$Cdn">0</$REQD>
              </SUMMARY>
       </ITEM>
       <ITEM id=""REORG">
              <SPONSOR>McKinnon</SPONSOR>
              <TIME_REQ units="hours">0.5</TIME_REQ>
              <SUMMARY>
                     <COMMENT>On schedule/under budget</COMMENT>
              </SUMMARY>
       </ITEM>
  </AGENDA>
```

Exhibit 7-19: Meeting agenda (XML document)

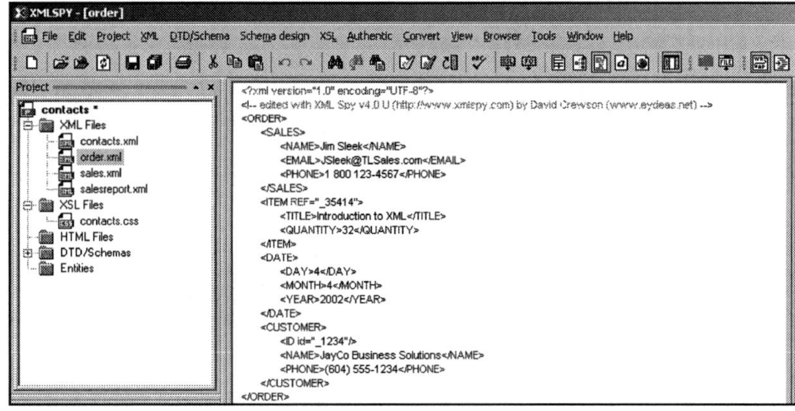

Exhibit 7-20: Order.xml

Do it!

D-5: Examining XPointer expressions

Here's how	Here's why
1 In the Project pane, right-click **XML Files**	To review XPointer expressions.
Choose **Add Files...**	
2 Press and hold the CTRL key	
Select **order.xml** and **salesreport.xml**	
Click **Open**	To add order.xml and salesreport.xml to the project.
3 Double-click **order.xml**	To open the XML document.
Switch to Text view	The order document is shown in Exhibit 7-20.
4 Observe the relationship between the `NAME` element and the root element (`/ORDER/SALES/NAME`)	
5 Open **salesreport.xml**	
6 Switch to Text view	In the `SALESREPORT` element, note how the value for `TITLE` is obtained. `TITLE` contains an `xlink:href` attribute that identifies a URI called order.xml. Using an XPointer expression that finds the value of the TITLE element where its parent element, ITEM, has an ID type attribute with a value of _35414 further refines the reference location.

7 Review the structure of the order.xml document:

```
<ORDER>
-- elements removed --
<ITEM REF="_35414">
<TITLE>Introduction to XML</TITLE>
<QUANTITY>32</QUANTITY>
</ITEM>
-- elements removed -
<ORDER>
```

"//" tells the parser to search all `ITEM` elements, and the `id()` function selects the `ITEM` with the appropriate value.

8 Locate the `SALESPERSON` locator type.

This XPointer expression is part of an external resource that participates in the GetSalesPerson link. The `xlink:href` attribute refers to the `NAME` element in the order.xml file. The GetSalesPerson arc-type handles this link as it would any other resource. When the link is selected, a new browser window appears with the `NAME` fragment of the external resource as the active document. Because the XPointer is contained in a locator-type resource element, the actual reference is completely transparent to the arc-element.

XPointer points

Explanation

With XPath, you can locate data only at the node level. In XSL transformations, XPath was adequate because you are working with XML nodes. However, such an approach is not adequate for all purposes, especially for referencing subresources with XLink. For example, a user working with an XML document might find it useful to click a particular point, or even select a range, to access additional or alternate XML content. Such information might not start and end on node boundaries, and thus might contain parts of various trees and subtrees.

To obtain finer control over XML data, you can work with points and ranges in XPointer. A *point* is a specific location in a document. A *range* is made up of all the XML content between two points, which can include parts of elements and text strings.

To support points and ranges, XPointer extended XPath's nodes into locations. Every location is an XPath node, point, or range. Therefore, XPath's node sets have become location sets in the XPointer specification.

To define an XPointer point, you use two items—a node and an index that can hold a zero or a positive integer. The node identifies the point's origin; the index indicates how far away the referenced point is from that origin.

There are two different types of points—node-points and character-points, so their index values should be expressed differently.

Node-points

Any origin node (also called the container node) might or might not have child nodes. If it does, then the point found in the node is called a *node-point*. The index of a node-point is measured in child nodes. Here, the index of a node-point must be equal to or less than the number of child nodes in the origin node. If you use an index of zero, the point is immediately before any child nodes. An index of zero indicates the point before any child nodes, and a nonzero index *n* indicates the point immediately after the nth child node. For example, an index of 2 means a point is located immediately after the second child node.

Character-points

If the origin node can contain only text but no child nodes, then the index is measured in characters. As a result, these are called *character-points.*

The index of a character-point must be a positive integer or zero, and less than or equal to the length of the text string in the node. An index of zero indicates that the point is immediately before the first character. If the index is 4, then the point is immediately after the fourth character. Character-points cannot be preceded or followed by siblings or children. XPointer collapses all consecutive white space into a single white space. Also, there is no placement of points inside start and end tags, processing instructions, comment, or any markup. The characters referred to are strictly within the data.

Creating character-points and node-points

To create a point, use the `start-point()` function:

```
xpointer(location path/node test/start-point()
[position()=position-number])
```

An example of character and node point is shown in Exhibit 7-19. If you want to place a reference character-point just before the "t" in Smith, in the second ITEM element (the one that addresses COMPLAINTS), then you would write:

```
xpointer(/AGENDA/ITEM[2]/SPONSOR/text()/start-point()
[position()=3])
```

If you want to place a reference node-point just before the `TIME_REQ` node in the third item `(ADV_PLAN)`, you would write:

```
xpointer(/AGENDA/ITEM[3]/node()/start-point() [position()=1])
```

The long form references to these examples are, respectively:

```
http://www.TLSales.com/mtg_agenda.xml#xpointer(/AGENDA/ITEM[2]
/SPONSOR/text()/start-point()[position()=3])
```

and

```
http://www.TLSales.com/mtg_agenda.xml#xpointer(/AGENDA/ITEM[3]
/node()/start-point()[position()=1])
```

XPointer ranges

A *range* is the XML structure between two points: a start point and an end point. However, both have to be in the same document and the start point cannot occur after the end point. If the start point and the end point coincide at the same location, then the range is *collapsed.*

Furthermore, a range does not have to be completely contained within one subtree of a document. It can extend from one subtree to another. All you need is a valid start point and a valid end point, and they both must be in the same document.

To create a range, use the following syntax:

```
xpointer(location path/node test/start-point()
[position()=position-number] to (location path/node
test/start-point() [position()=position-number])
```

As another example, if you want to find the quick summary statement regarding Quality Assurance (Q_A) at TLSales, you would write:

```
xpointer(/AGENDA/ITEM[4]/SUMMARY/COMMENT/text()/start-
point()[position()=0] to
/AGENDA/ITEM[4]/SUMMARY/COMMENT/text()/start-
point()[position()=8])
```

XPointer abbreviations

XPointer adds some abbreviated forms of reference to facilitate the common practices of referencing elements by location or ID. Examples of such abbreviations follow:

Say you want to locate Ms. Gold's comment regarding first quarter revenues mtg_agenda.xml. The comment looks like this:

```
<COMMENT>Improved over 4Q</COMMENT>
```

The original code for this is:

```
http://www.TLSales.com/mtg_agenda.xml#xpointer(/child::*[posit
ion()=1]/child::*[position()=3]/ child::*[position()=1]/
```

The abbreviated code would be:

```
http://www.TLSales.com/mtg_agenda.xml#1/3/1
```

You can use words as location steps, not just numbers. But the words must correspond to ID values of elements. In the mtg_agenda.xml document, the fifth `ITEM` element has an `id=REORG`. You might want to read its (child) `SPONSOR` element (which shows "McKinnon"). The original code for this would be:

```
http://www.TLSales.com/ mtg_agenda.xml#xpointer(/child::*
[id("REORG")]/child::*[position()=1]
```

Use the element's ID value as a location step, and you'll get this:

```
http://www.TLSales.com/mtg_agenda.xml#REORG/
```

The last example uses an `id()` function. To do this, you must make sure the ID attributes are declared in a DTD or schema. However, not all XML documents have DTDs or schemas, so XPointer provides the capability to specify alternative patterns with multiple XPointers. Here's how one of these "crossfires" might look:

```
http://www.TLSales.com/mtg_agenda.xml#xpointer(id("REORG"))
xpointer(//*[id="REORG"])/1
```

If the first XPointer fails, the second XPointer should take over. It locates any element that has an attribute named "id" with the specified value.

Selecting an implementation

Many XML developers, programmers, or authors express concerns about the fact that the IT industry has fallen behind the W3C on XLinking and XPointing, and that implementations, especially browsers, are slow to adopt the concepts and practices mentioned in the respective Recommendations. The following lists were gleaned from several sources (including the W3C). The list might not be comprehensive and there is no guarantee or warranty regarding the performance of any of these applications.

The following is a list of XPointer implementations:

- Fujitsu XLink Processor, developed by Fujitsu Laboratories Ltd. This is an implementation of XLink and XPointer.
- Libxml is the Gnome XML library's beta implementation of XPointer. The full syntax is supported, but the test suite does not yet cover all aspects.
- 4Xpointer is an XPointer Processor written in Python by Fourthought, Inc.

The following is a list of XLink implementations:

- Mozilla M17 Browser (Mozilla) is an open source browser with restricted XLink support.
- Link (Justin Ludwig) is a small, XLink-aware XML browser.
- Reusable XLink XSLT transformations are XSLT templates that permit the transformation of extended links to HTML and JavaScript representations.
- XMLhack and XLink news are the latest XLink news and software releases.
- X2X (empolis UK Ltd.) is an XML XLink engine that permits linking between documents and information resources without needing to change the resources that are being linked.
- Xlinkit.com is a lightweight application that provides rule-based XLink generation and checks the consistency of distributed documents and Web content.
- Amaya, the W3C editor/browser, now supports simple XLinks.
- XLink2HTML is a set of XSLT stylesheets for the creation of HTML representations of XLink elements.
- XTooX is a free XLink processor that turns extended-type, out-of-line links into inline links. Available under the GNU Lesser General Public License.

Do it!

D-6: Examining XPointer point and range

Here's how	Here's why
1 Locate the BUYER element in salesreport.xml	Note that the xlink:href attribute indexes the second element within order.xml URI.
2 Assume that the referenced code appears in order.xml as: <CUSTOMER> <ID id="_1234"/> <NAME>JayCo Business Solutions</Name> <PHONE>(604) 555-1234</PHONE> </CUSTOMER>	
	The point defined in CUSTOMER refers to the value in the NAME element. If CUSTOMER contained CDATA instead of elements, then the point would refer to the location immediately following the second character.
3 Locate the DATE element in salesreport.xml	This element is similar in functionality to the CUSTOMER element except that the xlink:href identifies a range.
	The /ORDER/DATE/DAY portion of the expression references the DAY element and is defined as the start point of the range. The range-to() function defines the end point. The range of elements inserted into the salesreport document consists of the DAY, MONTH, and YEAR elements from the order document.
4 Switch to order.xml Locate the DATE element <DATE> <DAY>4</DAY> <MONTH>4</MONTH> <YEAR>2002</YEAR> </DATE>	
	To relate it to the range expression given in salesreport.xml. The date portion of order.xml is shown here.
5 Close XML Spy	

Unit summary: Linking in XML

Topic A

In this topic, you learned about **XLink**. You learned there are two types of XLinks: **simple links** and **extended links**. You also learned about link traversal and how to use **resources**.

Topic B

In this topic, you learned how to **identify restrictions** and basic **XLink syntax**. You also learned about XLink's **global attributes**. Then, you set up and reviewed an XML document containing an XLink.

Topic C

In this topic, you learned how to validate XLinks and create a simple XLink. You reviewed examples of a **resource-type linking** element, a **locator-type linking** element, **inbound link arcs**, and an **extended-type linking** element.

Topic D

In this topic, you learned about the **XPointer language**. You learned about **XPointer axes**, **node tests**, **predicates**, and **location set functions**. You also learned about XPointer **points** and **ranges**.

Review questions

1 _______________ offer full XLink functionality, including inbound and third-party arcs, as well as arcs that can simultaneously connect a local resource to several remote resources.

2 After a `type` attribute is specified, that specification designates the XLink _______________ as simple, extended, locator, arc, resource, title, or none.

3 The _______________ parent element type permits locator, arc, resource, and title child attributes in linking elements.

4 XPointer fragment identifiers are composed of the xpointer keyword, followed by the basic addressing component, the _______________.

5 The _______________ might represent one or more XPath-style nodes, within which the sub-resource is found.

6 The _______________ is a preliminary filtering test.

7 The index of a node-point is measured in _______________.

A character points

B child characters

C characters

D child nodes

Unit 8
XML APIs

Unit time: 90 minutes

Complete this unit, and you'll know how to:

A Describe XML APIs and the difference between object-based interfaces and event-based interfaces.

B Work with DOM objects.

C Identify the advantages and disadvantages of DOM and SAX, and when to use one over the other.

Topic A: Introduction to XML APIs

Explanation

XML data must be read by a program to perform an action. To access XML data, you use XML Application Programming Interfaces (APIs). XML APIs define the way you can access and manipulate an XML document through an application. The Document Object Model (DOM) and Simple API for XML (SAX) are two APIs that provide a standard programming interface and can be used in a wide variety of environments and applications.

XML parsers and interfaces

A typical XML program consists of two components: a parser and an application. A *parser* is a software component that reads an XML document and makes its data available for further processing. It exposes the structures and tags within an XML document, making it easy to process XML documents. The communication between the parser and the application is facilitated by an interface. The two basic types of interfaces facilitating this communication are

- Object-based interfaces
- Event-based interfaces

Object-based interfaces

When you use an object-based interface, the parser explicitly creates a tree of objects that contains all the elements present in the XML document. It provides a document-centric view of your XML data. The Document Object Model (DOM) is an object-based interface, and it's an official W3C standard.

Exhibit 8-1 shows an XML document named contacts.xml. The element `<CONTACTS>` forms the root element. It has two child elements named `<SALES>`. The `<SALES>` element, further, has three child elements, `<NAME>`, `<EMAIL>`, and `<PHONE>`; and two attributes, `id` and `region`.

```
<CONTACTS>
        <SALES id="a1" region="NY">
                <NAME>Jim Sleek</NAME>
                <EMAIL>JSleek@TLSales.com</EMAIL>
                <PHONE>1 800 123-4567</PHONE>
        </SALES>
        <SALES id="a2" region="MD">
                <NAME>Anna Gold</NAME>
                <EMAIL>AGold@TLSales.com</EMAIL>
                <PHONE>1 800 123-4567</PHONE>
        </SALES>
</CONTACTS>
```

Exhibit 8-1: contacts.xml

Exhibit 8-2 illustrates how an object-based parser would process this XML document. The object-based parser reads this XML document and builds a tree of objects in memory that matches the elements in the document. Exhibit 8-2 shows the tree that's built in the memory. The parser recognizes `<CONTACTS>` as the top-level element and creates a corresponding object to represent it. The parser then creates an object for the next element, `<SALES>`, and attaches this object to the `<CONTACTS>` object. This process continues until the entire document is read and the object tree is complete. Note that all the components—elements, attributes, and the attribute values—form the tree. Because it maintains the entire data structure in memory, an object-based parser tends to consume a lot of memory.

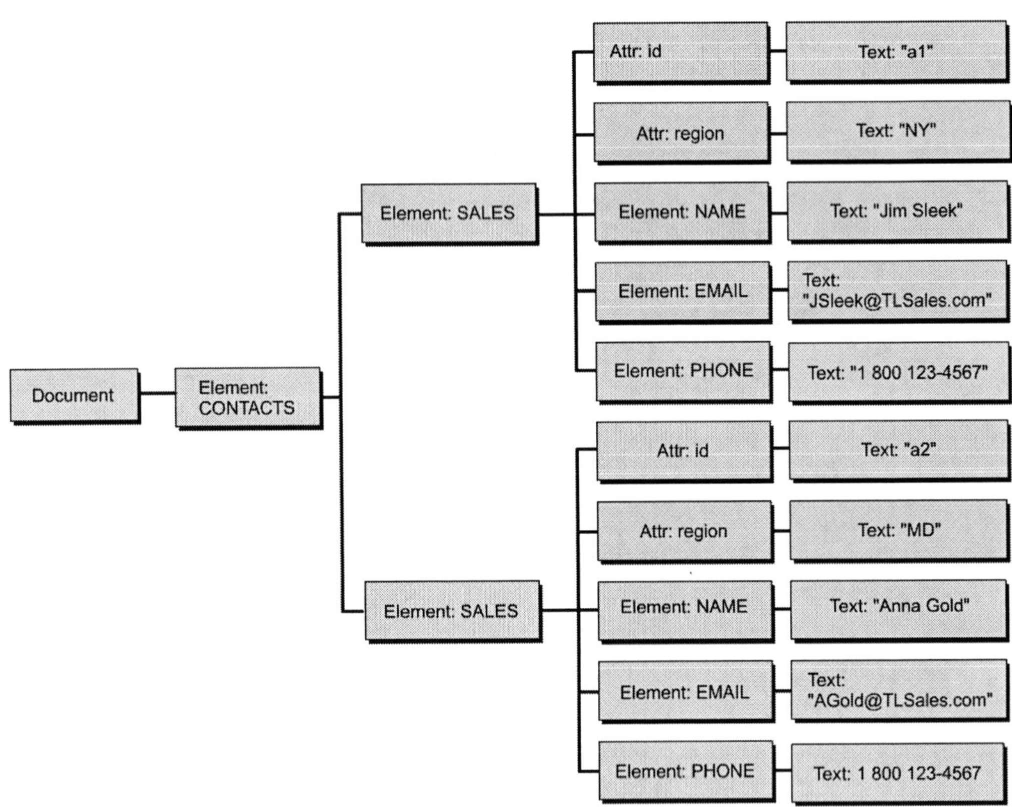

Exhibit 8-2: DOM representation of contacts.xml

Event-based interfaces

When you use an event-based interface, the parser reads the XML document and generates events as it finds opening and closing tags, entities, processing instructions, text, etc. The application listens to these events as they are generated, and determines the tree and the response to each event. Thus, an event-based parser provides a serial-access mechanism to access an XML document. Simple API for XML (SAX) is an industry standard event-based interface for XML parsing.

Event-based parsers use less memory and consume less resources because there is no need to build a large tree in memory as you are scanning for a particular element, attribute, and/or content sequence in an XML document.

Do it!

A-1: Exploring XML parsers and interfaces

Questions and answers
1 A typical XML program consists of two components: __________ and ________.
2 ____________ is an event-based application programming interface.
3 Event-based parsers provide a document-centric view of XML. True or false?
4 When you use a ____________, the parser explicitly creates a tree of objects that contains all the elements present in the XML document.
5 Of the two, _______________ use less memory.

The Document Object Model (DOM)

Explanation

The DOM was developed by the World Wide Web Consortium (W3C) to support both HTML and XML documents. It defines the interfaces for different objects comprising the DOM, but does not provide specifics of implementation.

- **DOM Level 1.** Concentrates on HTML and XML document models. It contains functionality for document navigation and manipulation. DOM Level 1 was released as a W3C Recommendation in October 1998.
- **DOM Level 2.** Adds a style sheet object model to DOM Level 1, and defines functionality for manipulating the style information attached to a document. It also defines an event model and provides support for XML namespaces.
- **DOM Level 3.** Specifies content models (DTD and Schemas) and document validation. It also specifies document loading and saving, document views, document formatting, and key events.

All DOM implementations need to, at least, provide the functionalities described in DOM Level 1 recommendation.

With the XML DOM, you can create an XML document, navigate its structure, and add, modify, or delete its elements. It is designed for use with any programming language and any operating system.

To use the XML data in your application, you first need to load the document into memory by using an XML parser. After the document is loaded, you retrieve and manipulate its information by accessing the DOM.

The document tree

As an object-based interface, DOM provides access to the information stored in your XML document in the form of a hierarchical object model. It defines classes of objects to represent every element in an XML document. Exhibit 8-3 shows the hierarchy of the DOM objects. When DOM processes an XML document, it breaks down the XML document into individual components such as elements, attributes, comments, etc. It then creates a tree-view of the XML document. It considers every component in the document as a node.

A *node* represents an object, which has methods and properties. You can access the information in your XML document by interacting with the tree of nodes using these methods and properties. Each node in the document tree can have any number of child nodes. These child nodes represent the branches of the tree. All nodes, except for the root node, have a parent node. The tree is an exact map of the tree of elements in the XML document.

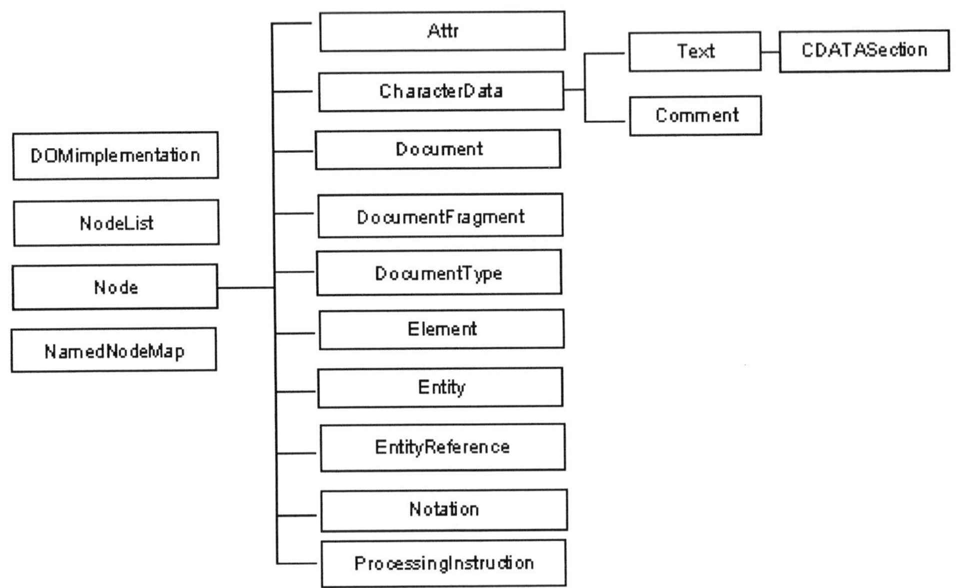

Exhibit 8-3: The DOM hierarchy

You can access the individual elements in the node tree by using the methods and properties of the objects defined in the DOM hierarchy. For example, if you want to enumerate each individual node of an XML document, you can access the `childNodes` property of the `documentElement` (which forms the root element of the document) with a for/each loop.

Advantages of the DOM

Because the DOM creates and holds an object tree of the entire XML document in memory, it helps you to randomly access and navigate the document. You don't have to handle the data in the order it arrives. For example, you can easily add or delete an element in the XML document by using DOM. Thus, it makes document manipulation a simple task. Because the DOM tree exactly maps to the XML document, it ensures conformity to well-formedness and grammar.

Disadvantages of the DOM

When you are working with very large XML documents, DOM might not be the best option to use because the overhead associated with loading and keeping the entire document tree in memory can become excessive.

Simple API for XML (SAX)

SAX is an alternative API for processing an XML document. It was developed by the members of XML-DEV mailing list. It was originally developed as an API for the Java language. Currently, languages such as Perl and Python have extended support to SAX. The MSXML parser exposes it as a COM object so that it can be accessed by VB and other scripting languages. Unlike DOM, SAX is not endorsed by an official standards body but is widely used and is considered a de facto standard.

SAX uses an event-based approach to access and manipulate XML documents. With SAX, as the parser reads through the XML document, it notifies your application of a stream of parsing events. *Events* tell the application that something has occurred to which it might want to react. These events are then captured and processed by *event handlers* that listen to the event and act in response to them. The events are related to the elements in the XML document being read. The events are fired when:

- The parser encounters opening element tags.
- The parser encounters closing element tags.
- The parser encounters CDATA and PCDATA sections.
- The parser encounters processing instructions, entities, and comments.
- The parser encounters parsing errors.

The following example shows a simple block of XML. It lists the department and details of a contact.

```
<?xml version="1.0"?>
<CONTACTS>
<SALES id="a1" region="NY">
<NAME>Jim Sleek</NAME>
<EMAIL>Jsleek@TLSales.com</EMAIL>
<PHONE>1 800 123-4567</PHONE>
</SALES>
</CONTACTS>
```

The SAX parser reads the XML declaration and generates a corresponding event for it. When the parser encounters the first opening tag, `<CONTACTS>`, it generates the second event. The third event is generated when the parser encounters the next tag in sequence: the opening `<SALES>` tag. Next, the parser sees the opening `<NAME>` tag and generates its fourth event. The parser then encounters the content of that element: Jim Sleek. It generates an event by passing this content as a parameter to the application. The next event is the closing of that element. In the same manner, events are generated for the EMAIL and PHONE elements. Finally, events are generated for the remaining closing tags, and all the application has left to do is provide methods that are called when these events are fired.

Advantages of SAX

SAX is a better option when you're working with large XML documents because SAX does not create a document tree in memory and therefore consumes fewer resources. This also makes SAX more efficient.

With SAX, your application can start processing the document even before the parser has finished reading the XML document. The application does not have to wait for the entire document to be read by the parser, as is the case with DOM.

If you want to extract only a small part of information from an XML document, it would be inefficient to read all the data into memory. In such instances, SAX is a preferred approach to access the information fast and efficiently.

Disadvantages of SAX

Because the document is not in memory, you cannot navigate through the document as you can with a DOM tree. Therefore, your application must explicitly buffer all those events, which it might want to use at a later stage.

Current browsers don't support SAX. At present, there isn't any mainstream browser that has a built-in SAX-compliant parser.

Do it!

A-2: Exploring SAX and DOM

Questions and answers

1 By using DOM, you can create an XML document, navigate its structure, and add, modify, or delete its elements. True or false?

2 DOM gives you access to the information stored in your XML document as a _____________ object model.

3 The events generated by SAX are captured and processed by ___________ that listen to the event and act in response to them.

4 By using ____________, your application can start processing the document even before the parser has finished reading the XML document.

Topic B: DOM interfaces and objects

Explanation

The DOM Core interface defines a set of objects and interfaces to access and manipulate document objects. In this topic, you'll learn about the DOM objects, their properties and methods, and how to use these methods and properties to modify an XML document.

The Node object

Node object forms the core object in DOM. Most of the DOM objects are derived from the Node object. The Node object represents a node in the document tree. A node can be any type of node present in the document tree, such as an element node, a text node, and an attribute node.

To help you traverse through the document tree, the Node object defines several properties. The following table lists these properties and their description:

Property	Description
`attributes`	Returns a list of attributes for the current node.
`childNodes`	Returns a list of all the children for the current node.
`firstChild`	Returns the node's first child.
`lastChild`	Returns the node's last child.
`nextSibling`	Returns the next sibling node.
`nodeName`	Returns the name of the node, depending on its type.
`nodeType`	Returns the type of node as a numeric value.
`nodeValue`	Returns, or sets, the value of the node.
`ownerDocument`	Returns the root node of the document.
`parentNode`	Returns the parent node for the current node.
`previousSibling`	Returns the previous sibling node.

The node object also provides methods to add, remove, and replace nodes. The following table provides a list of methods for all node types and their description:

Method	Description
`appendChild()`	Appends a node as a child of the current node.
`hasChildNodes()`	Returns true if this node has any child nodes.
`cloneNode()`	Returns an exact clone of this node. If the Boolean value is set to true, the cloned node contains all the child nodes as well.
`insertBefore()`	Inserts a new node before the existing node.
`removeChild()`	Removes the specified node.
`replaceChild()`	Replaces one node with another node.

```
<?xml version="1.0"?>

<SALES id="a1" region="NY">
   <NAME>Jim Sleek</NAME>
   <EMAIL>Jsleek@TLSales.com</EMAIL>
   <PHONE>1 800 123-4567</PHONE>
</SALES>
```

Exhibit 8-4: sales.xml

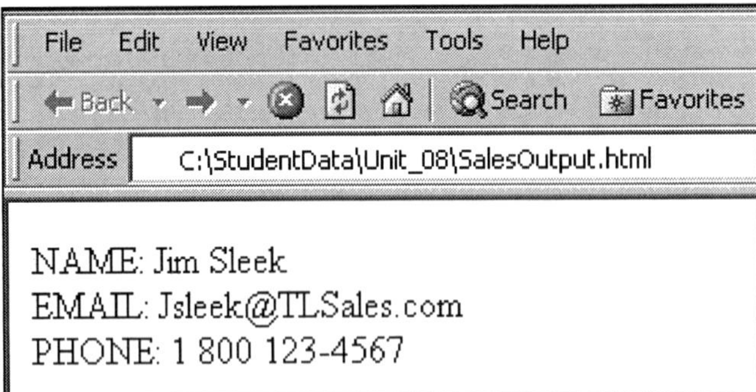

Exhibit 8-5: SalesOutput.html in browser

Do it!

B-1: Applying the nodeName and nodeValue properties

Here's how	Here's why
1 Open Notepad	You'll write a small script in an HTML document to see how the `nodeName` and `nodeValue` properties work.
2 Choose **File**, **Save As...**	
3 In the File name text box, enter sales **SalesOutput.html**	To specify the file name.
4 Click **Save**	
5 Type the following code:	

```
<html>
<body>
<script type="text/vbscript">
```

The first two lines specify the opening tags for the html and body elements. The third line is the opening script tag with the `type` attribute set to "vbscript", specifying the scripting language we'll use.

6 Type the following code:

```
set xmlDoc=CreateObject("Microsoft.XMLDOM")
xmlDoc.async="false"
xmlDoc.load("sales.xml")
```

`CreateObject("Microsoft.XMLDOM")` creates an instance of XML DOM object by using the `CreateObject` method. By setting the `async` property to false, the next line of code forces all operations on the XML document to occur synchronously. By using the `load()` method, the last line loads the XML document, sales.xml, in memory (as shown in Exhibit 8-4).

7 On the next line, type:

```
for each x in xmlDoc.documentElement.childNodes
  document.write(x.nodeName & ": ")
  document.write(x.childNodes(0).nodeValue & "<br />")
next
```

To add a for-loop control to enumerate all the child nodes of the current node, SALES. It iterates through all the child nodes of the SALES element, and extracts the name and values of these nodes by using the `nodeName` and `nodeValue` properties.

8 Type the following code: To close the tags.

```
</script>
</body>
</html>
```

9 Save your changes and open SalesOutput.html in Internet Explorer

Make sure you save the file in the current unit folder.

Examine the output

As shown in Exhibit 8-5. The output shows the name of the child nodes of the SALES element and their respective values.

The Document object

Explanation

Document is the topmost element in a DOM node tree. All nodes in a node tree are child nodes of the document element. The document element is needed in all XML documents. Document is a descendant of Node object, and inherits its properties from the Node object. It adds three new properties to it:

- `documentElement` (Returns the root element of the document.)
- `doctype` (Returns the DTD or Schema for the document.)
- `implementation` (Returns the implementation object for the XML document.)

The Element object

The element object is a descendant of the Node object. It represents all element nodes in the document. In addition to the properties inherited from Node object, Element defines a property called `tagName`, which returns or sets the name of the node.

The following table describes some of the methods of the Element object:

Method	Description
`getAttribute()`	Returns the value of the specified attribute.
`getElementsByTagName()`	Returns the specified node, and all its child nodes, as a nodeList.
`normalize()`	Puts the text nodes for the current element, and its child nodes, into one text node; returns nothing.
`removeAttribute()`	Removes the specified attribute's value. If the attribute has a default value, this value is inserted.
`removeAttributeNode()`	Removes the specified attribute node. If the attribute node has a default value, this attribute is inserted.
`setAttribute()`	Adds a new attribute.
`setAttributeNode()`	Adds a new attribute node.

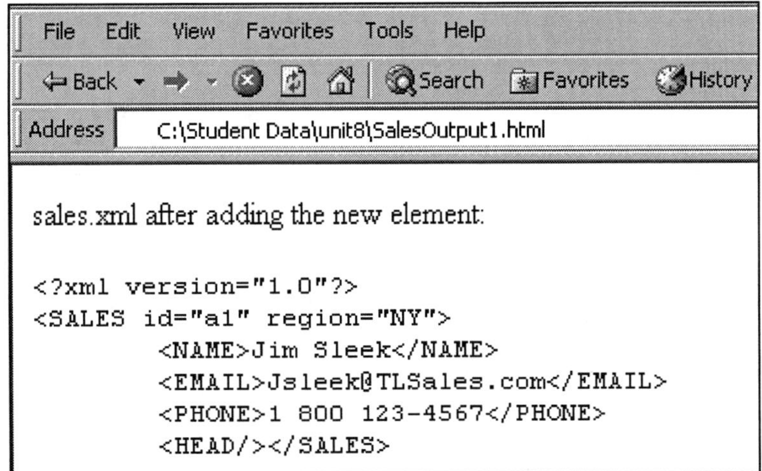

Exhibit 8-6: SalesOutput1.html

Do it!

B-2: Adding an element node to an XML document

Here's how	Here's why
1 In Notepad, Choose **File, New**	You'll add a new element by using DOM methods and properties.
2 Save the empty file as **SalesOutput2.html**	
3 Type the following code:	

```
<html>
<body>
<script type="text/vbscript">
set xmlDoc=CreateObject("Microsoft.XMLDOM")
xmlDoc.async="false"
xmlDoc.load("sales.xml")

set newElement=xmldoc.createElement("HEAD")
xmldoc.documentElement.appendChild(newElement)

document.write("sales.xml after adding the new element:")
document.write("<xmp>" & xmlDoc.xml & "</xmp>")

</script>
</body>
</html>
```

Here's how	Here's why
	To create a new element called HEAD by using the `createElement()` method and appending this element as a child of the SALES element by using the `appendChild()` method.
4 Save your changes	
5 Open SalesOutput2.html in Internet Explorer	
Examine the output	The output shows the new element, HEAD, appended as a child element of the SALES element, as shown in Exhibit 8-6.

The Attr object

Explanation

The Attr object returns an attribute of an element object as an attribute node. The Attr object has the same properties and methods as nodes in general. The properties of the Attr object are:

- `name` — Sets or returns the name of the attribute.
- `specified` — Returns true or false, indicating if the node's value is set in the document or not.
- `value` — Sets or returns the value of the attribute.

The Attr object is also inherited from the Node object and therefore inherits its properties and methods.

The Text object

The Text object represents the text of an element or an attribute. It also inherits various properties from the Node object, as it is a descendant of the latter. It defines a method called `splitText()`, which splits the text at the specified character number and returns the rest of the text.

The CDATASection object

The CDATASection object represents the CDATASection nodes in an XML document. It is used to escape the text that would otherwise be considered as XML markup. The text of a CDATASection is stored in a Text node. It might contain characters that need to be escaped outside of a CDATA section.

A CDATASection object does not have its own methods and properties. It inherits its properties and methods from Text and Node objects.

The Comment object

The Comment object represents the comment nodes in an XML document. It represents all the characters that appear between `<!--` and `-->`. The comment nodes do not have any node name but they have node value. The content of the comment is its node value.

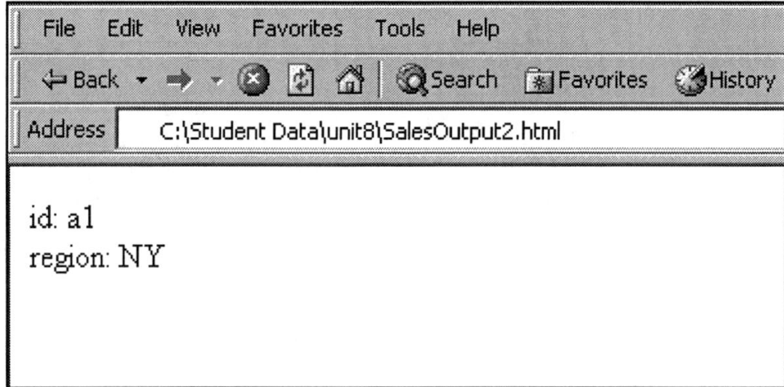

Exhibit 8-7: SalesOutput2.html showing the two attributes and their values

Do it!

B-3: Extracting an attribute's name and value

Here's how	Here's why
1 In Notepad, create a new file and save it as **SalesOutput3.html**	You'll learn how to use the `name` and `value` properties of the `Attr` object.
2 Type the following code:	

```
<html>
<body>
<script type="text/vbscript">

set xmlDoc=CreateObject("Microsoft.XMLDOM")
xmlDoc.async="false"
xmlDoc.load("sales.xml")

for each x in xmlDoc.documentElement.attributes
  document.write(x.name & ": ")
  document.write(x.value & "<br/>")
next

</script>
</body>
</html>
```

Here's how	Here's why
	To extract the name and values of the SALES element from sales.xml by using the `name` and `value` properties.
3 Save your changes	
4 Open SalesOutput2.html in Internet Explorer	
Examine the output	The output shows the two attributes of the SALES element, `id` and `region`, with their respective values, as shown in Exhibit 8-7.

Topic C: SAX versus DOM

Explanation

Both SAX and DOM are complementary to each other and are best for different situations. Choosing one over the other should depend on each unique situation.

When to use SAX

SAX follows an event-based approach to process an XML document. It offers an excellent alternative to DOM in the following situations:

- When you're working with large XML documents
- When you need to retrieve a small subset of information
- When you need to create your own document structure
- When you need to abort parsing

Working with large XML documents

As the SAX parser does not need to create the document tree in memory, it uses significantly less memory to process an XML document than the DOM. With SAX, memory consumption does not increase with the size of the file. For example, a 100 kilobyte (KB) document can occupy up to 1 megabyte (MB) of memory by using DOM; the same document would occupy significantly less memory when using SAX.

Retrieving a small subset of information

In some cases, you might not want to read the entire content of an XML document to achieve the desired output. For example, if you want to extract data of only those persons in the contacts list who belong to the sales department, it would be unnecessary to load the data of all other departments in the contacts list. With SAX, your application can scan the data for contacts related only to the sales department, and then create a slimmed-down document structure. Scanning only a small percentage of the document results in a significant savings of system resources and increased efficiency.

Creating your own document structure

If you want to create a data structure by using only high-level objects, such as sales, name, and e-mail, and then combine the data from this XML document with another XML document, you can use SAX. Rather than build a DOM structure with low-level elements like attributes and processing instructions first and then destroy them, you can build the document structure more efficiently and quickly by using SAX.

Abort parsing

With SAX, you can abort processing at any time. Thus, you can use it to create applications that retrieve specific data. For example, you can create an application that searches for a name in a sales element. When the application finds the name, it returns the value, and then stops processing.

When to use DOM

Some of the scenarios where it might be better to use DOM to process your XML documents include:

- When you need to randomly access the document data
- When you need to perform an XSLT transformation
- When you need to create or modify an XML document
- When you need complex XPath filtering

Random access of document data

If you want to access information randomly across an XML document, it is better to use the DOM to create a tree structure for the data in memory. When you use SAX, the document is not kept in memory. Therefore, you must handle data in the order in which it is processed. SAX can be difficult to use when the document contains many internal cross-references, such as ID and IDREF attributes. The DOM stores the document in memory; therefore, you can access its parts without reading the entire document.

Performing XSLT transformations

The DOM is a better option when you need to perform XSLT transformations. For example, to create multiple views of the same data, you must transform it by using one of two style sheets. For this transformation to take place, you must also create two instances of the DOM. One stores the XML source; the other stores the transformed content.

Creating or modifying an XML document

You can use the DOM to create or modify a document in memory, as well as read a document from an XML source document. SAX is designed for reading, not writing, XML documents. The DOM is the better choice for modifying an XML document and saving the changed document to memory.

Complex XPath filtering

If you have to perform complex XML Path Language (XPath) filtering and retain complex data structures that hold context information, you must use DOM. Because DOM creates a document tree, it retains the context information automatically. If you use SAX in such a scenario, you must retain the context information yourself.

Do it!

C-1: Discussing SAX and DOM

Questions and answers

1 If an XML document is very large, it is an efficient approach to use SAX. True or false?

2 Describe typical scenarios where it is preferred to use SAX over DOM.

3 You cannot create or modify an XML document in memory when using DOM. True or false?

4 Describe typical scenarios where DOM is a preferred approach over SAX.

5 For your own personal or work-related project, which API will you use, and why?

Unit summary: XML APIs

Topic A

In this topic, you learned about **XML APIs**. You learned the difference between **object-based interfaces** and **event-based interfaces**. You learned that an object-based interface creates a **document tree** in memory while an event-based interface **generates events**. Then, you learned about two of the most common XML APIs: **DOM** and **SAX**.

Topic B

In this topic, you learned about different **DOM objects** and their **methods** and **properties**. You learned **how to add an element to an existing XML document** by using DOM. You also learned **how to extract attribute names and values**.

Topic C

In this topic, you learned that DOM and SAX each have specific **advantages and limitations**. You learned some **typical scenarios** where it's preferable to use the DOM over SAX, and vice-versa.

Review questions

1 _____ is an object-based application programming interface.

2 DOM creates a ______ in memory that is an exact map of the tree of elements in the XML document.

3 SAX is an object-based application programming interface. True or false?

4 The ____ property of the Node object returns the following sibling of the current node.

5 The ____ method of the Node object appends a node as a child of the current node.

6 The ____ property returns the root element of the document.

7 The element object is a descendant of Node. True or false?

8 A ____ object does not have its own methods and properties.

9 If you want to access information randomly across an XML document, which approach is typically preferable?

10 If you want to retrieve a small subset of information from an XML document, which approach is typically preferable?

Unit 9

XML data binding basics

Unit time: 90 minutes

Complete this unit, and you'll know how to:

A Use data binding and data consumer elements.

B Integrate XML data and use data binding and table repetition agents.

C Work with data source objects and navigate recordsets.

Topic A: Data binding fundamentals

Explanation

Data binding involves mapping, synchronizing, and moving data from a data source, usually on a remote server, to an end user's local system where the user can manipulate the data. After a remote server transmits data, the user can perform some minor data manipulations on their own local system. The remote server does not have to perform all the data manipulations nor repeatedly transmit variations of the same data.

Data binding

Data consumers are elements in a Web page that are designated to receive and render data. Data binding involves manipulating the data on the local system, for example, searching, sorting, and filtering. When you bind data in this way, the remote server doesn't have to manipulate the data and then retransmit the results; you can perform data manipulations locally.

Exhibit 9-1 shows a simplified database architecture diagram. The cylinder in the upper-left corner of Exhibit 9-1 represents the data source, and the terminal screen in the lower-right corner represents the data presentation.

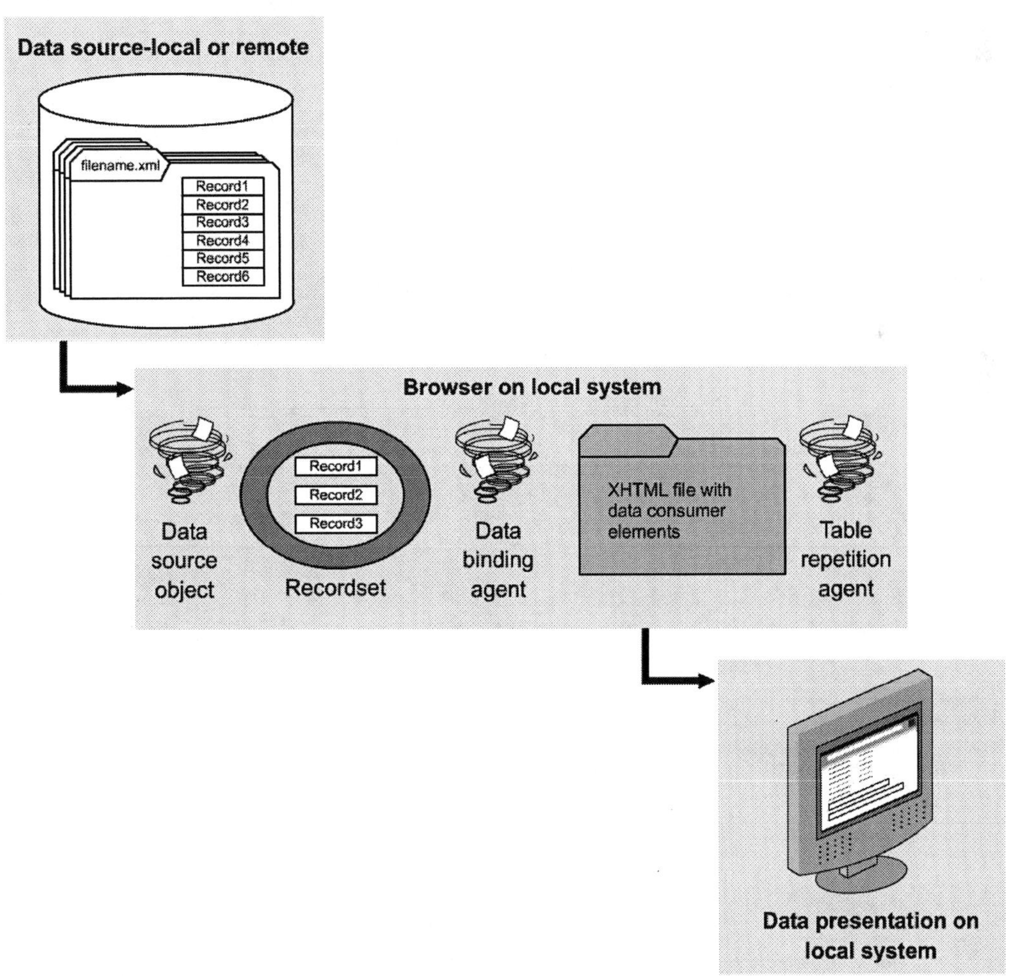

Exhibit 9-1: Database architecture diagram

The data source provides the data, and the appropriate applications retrieve and synchronize the data and present it on the terminal screen. If the data changes, the applications are written so they can alter their presentation to reflect those changes.

Data binding reduces traffic on the network and reduces the work required of the Web server (especially for minor data manipulation), while using the resources on the local client system more efficiently. Binding data also separates the task of maintaining data from the tasks of developing and maintaining binding and presentation programs. Separating those tasks allows the database administrator and the Web page designer to work independently, which is especially beneficial on large projects. You can bind XML elements and attributes that represent data components to presentation models by using Java, C++, JavaScript, and HTML, for example.

Do it!

A-1: Discussing data binding fundamentals

Questions and answers

1 Which of the following is not true of data binding?

A Data binding involves mapping and synchronizing data in a data source to a data consumer.

B Data binding involves moving data from a data source to a local system and then manipulating the data.

C In data binding, the data source provides the data, and the appropriate applications retrieve and synchronize the data and present it on the terminal screen.

D Data binding increases traffic on a network.

2 Data binding involves moving data from a __________ to a local system, and then manipulating the data.

A data source

B user

C group of elements

D stylesheet

3 Data binding __________ the Web server.

A increases the work of

B combines the task of maintaining data with the task of developing and maintaining biding and presentation programs on

C reduces the work of

D formats the data on

Data consumers

Explanation

While you're designing your Web site, you identify the information and data that you want to present to end users. After you acquire or develop that data, you create the documents that appear as Web pages.

Data consumers—also called *bindable elements* or *data consumer elements*—are elements in an HTML or an XHTML document that are predefined to receive and render data. (XHTML is a strict form of HTML that's designed as an application of XML.) You can then use these elements to display the results of data queries.

The following is a list of elements that can function as data consumers:

- `<a>`
- `<applet>`
- `<button>`
- `<div>`
- `<frame>`
- `<img>`
- `<input>`
- `<label>`
- `<iframe>`
- `<legend>`
- `<object>`
- `<param>`
- `<select>`
- `<span>`
- `<table>`
- `<textarea>`

Exhibit 9-2 shows an HTML file that could be used in a data-binding scenario. In this figure, `<table>` and `<div>` are shown in bold text, and are set as data consumers.

Note: Besides using HTML elements, you can also bind data by using Java applets and ActiveX controls.

Data consumer elements can bind two types of data: single-valued or tabular. *Single-valued data consumer elements*, such as the `<span>` element, bind with a single value from the records found in the data source. For example, you'll learn how to use `<span>` to select the price for an item or to select a part name. On the other hand, with *tabular data consumer elements*, such as the `<table>` element, you can insert more than one value—in fact, you can insert a complete structured set of records—from the data source. For example, you'll learn how to use `<table>` to select a part name and number from an external data file. Inserting more than one value at one time is called *set binding*.

```
<html>
  <!--Filename - parts2.html -->
  <head>
     <title>Parts List</title>
  </head>
  <body>
      <xml id="PList"  src="partslist.xml"  />
      <p> </p>
      <h1>TLSales</h1>
      <h2>Parts List</h2>
      <p>
          <table cellspacing="1" cellpadding="1" width="75%" border="1" datasrc="#PList">
            <tbody>
             <tr bgcolor="purple">
                 <td>Name:</td>
                 <td>
                    <div dataFld="name" />
                 </td>
               </tr>
               <tr>
                 <td>Part Number:</td>
                 <td>
                    <div dataFld="partNo" />
                 </td>
               </tr>
               <tr>
                 <td>In stock:</td>
                 <td>
                    <div dataFld="stock" />
                    </td>
               </tr>
               <tr>
                 <td>Price:</td>
                 <td>
                    <div dataFld="price" />
                 </td>
               </tr>
            </tbody>
          </table>
       </p>
    </body>
 </html>
```

Exhibit 9-2: Data consumer elements

Do it!

A-2: Discussing data consumers

Exercises

1 The `<table>` element is known as a typical __________.

A data consumer

B data supplier

C data source consumer

D repetition agent

2 __________ are elements in an HTML document that are predefined to receive and render data.

A Data consumers

B Valued data

C Set binding data

D Grouping data

3 __________ data consumer elements, such as the `<span>` element, bind with a single value from the records found in a data source.

4 With __________ data consumer elements, you can insert more than one value.

5 Inserting more than one value at a time is called __________.

A converting

B combining

C set binding

D inserting

6 Describe an example of a data binding application you might want to create.

Extended attributes

Explanation

Using data consumer elements to insert data is only one step toward displaying XML data on a Web page. You must also include instructions that tell the browser where to find the data and exactly what data to display.

In Exhibit 9-2, `<table>` and `<div>` are bindable elements. The `<table>` element includes a `datasrc` attribute and each `<div>` element contains a `datafld` attribute. These are examples of HTML's *extended attributes*. The `datasrc` attribute indicates the name of the data source to search and the `datafld` attribute indicates what record(s) to retrieve from the data source. You can use many kinds of data sources, including Oracle, IBM DB2, and other formats.

Without `datasrc` and `datafld` attributes, the browser or other application won't know where to find the data, or what data to retrieve. You generally find the `datasrc` and `datafld` attributes in close proximity to one another in a Web document. Occasionally, you find them in the same element start tag, as indicated earlier in the `<span>` element example.

To bind a single-valued element to data, use both the `datasrc` and `datafld` attributes, as shown in the following example:

```
Price: <span datasrc="#PList" datafld="Price"> </span>
```

This code tells the browser, "Immediately after displaying the text string `Price:`, insert the value obtained from the Price field that's in the data source named PList. Insert the value on the same line as `Price:`." (The `<span>` element is an inline element, so it doesn't create a line break.)

Note that the `datasrc` attribute includes a hash mark (#) just before the data source name. The hash mark is mandatory and indicates that the value is the name of a data source. The `datafld` attribute names the field in the data source that is queried.

Do it!

A-3: Discussing extended attributes

Exercises

1 To display XML elements by using a `<table>` element and specify the name of a data source, you must precede the name of the data source with a __________.

2 Without `datasrc` and `datafld`, the browser or other application won't know where to find the data, or what data to retrieve. True or false?

The <div> and <span> elements

Explanation

In the world of data binding, the <div> and <span> elements are called *grouping elements*. They provide a way to keep elements together and add structure to XML-related documents. The <div> element defines logical divisions in your Web page. The <div> tag is a block-level element, so it creates a line break.

Other than the line break it creates, the <div> tag does not have any default formatting, unlike many HTML elements. To add formatting to it, such as alignment and colors, you can use CSS. In Exhibit 9-3, the <div> contains the name of a bicycle part. The name will appear on its own line.

```
<html>
  <!--Filename – parts1.html -->
  <head>
    <title>Parts List</title>
  </head>
  <body>
    <xml id="PList" src="partslist.xml" />
    <p> </p>
    <h1>TLSales</h1>
    <h2>Parts List</h2>
    <p>Part Name</p>
    <p>
      <div datasrc="#PList" datafld="name" />
    </p>
...etc.
```

Exhibit 9-3: The <div> element

The following is a list of <div> attributes that you're most likely to use with XML data binding:

- `datasrc` — Specifies the location of the data source.
- `datafld` — Specifies the data to look for within the data source.
- `id` — A unique identifier for the element.

You can also use the <span> element as a data consumer. Like the <div> tag, <span> does not have any default formatting. It's an inline element, which means it will not create a line break. You can add formatting to the <span> element with CSS.

You can use <span> when you want to change the style of inline text. For example, if you use a Level 2 Heading (<h2>) that reads "`Sale Ends January 15!`" and you want only the words "`January 15`" to be red, you can use <span> as follows:

```
<h2>Sale Ends <span style="color: red">January 15</span>!
</h2>
```

The sale date text is still defined as part of the heading, but it will display in red because of the inline style in the <span> tag.

Exhibit 9-4 shows another way you can use the <span> element.

```
<html>
  <!--Filename – parts1.html -->
  <head>
    <title>Parts List</title>
  </head>
  <body>
    <xml id="PList"  src="partslist.xml"  />
    <p> </p>
    <h1>TLSales</h1>
    <h2>Parts List</h2>
    <p>
      Part Name: <span datasrc="#PList" datafld="name" ></span>
    </p>
...etc.
```

Exhibit 9-4: The <span> element

As in the <div> example in Exhibit 9-3, you can use <span> as a data consumer. Here, it tells the browser to search for the name of a bicycle part.

Note: The <span> element cannot contain block-level elements, such as <p>, <div>, or <h1>.

Do it!

A-4: Exploring <div> and <span>

Questions and answers

1 The `<div>` element is a __________ element, which means it creates a line break.

A data consumer

B grouping tag

C block-level (or block)

D binding

2 The __________ attribute is used to uniquely identify an element.

A `datasrc`

B `datafld`

C `id`

D `name`

3 The __________ attribute is used to search a field in a data source.

A `getFieldValue`

B `source`

C `field`

D `datafld`

4 The `datasrc` attribute specifies __________.

A style information

B a specific record in a data source

C a control name

D the name and location of the data source

The <table> element

Explanation

The data retrieved from a data source is often best displayed in a table. With the `<table>` element, you can insert entire sets of records at one time for data set binding.

To achieve data set binding, you include the `datasrc="value"` attribute in the `<table>` tag. Each child element in the table can inherit the value of the `datasrc` attribute, but must specify its own `datafld="value"` attribute to display specific records.

For example, in Exhibit 9-5, the `<table>` specifies that its data comes from a data source named PList, which was defined in the `<xml>` element as the partslist.xml document. The `<td>` element, a child element of `<table>`, includes `<div>` to display the data in the name field of the PList data source.

```
<html>
    <!--Filename - parts2.html -->
    <head>
       <title>Parts List</title>
    </head>
    <body>
      <xml id="PList"  src="partslist.xml"  />
      <p> </p>
      <h1>TLSales</h1>
      <h2>Parts List</h2>
      <p>
        <table cellspacing="1" cellpadding="1" width="75%" border="1" datasrc="#PList">
            <tbody>
               <tr bgcolor="purple">
                    <td>Name:</td>
                    <td>
                       <div dataFld="name" />
                    </td>
               </tr>
               <tr>
                    <td>Part Number:</td>
  ...etc.
```

Exhibit 9-5: A table that displays specific data from a data source

If you want a child element within the parent table to obtain its data from a different source, the child element can have its own `datasrc` and `datafld` specifications. For example, if the `<div>` element in Exhibit 9-5 were to get its information from another data source, such as `#PList2`, the corresponding portion of code would look like this:

```
<p>
<table cellspacing="1" cellpadding="1" width="75%" border="1"
datasrc="#PList">
<tbody>
<tr bgcolor="purple">
<td>Name:</td>
<td>
<div datasrc="#PList2" datafld="name"/>
etc.
```

Do it!

A-5: Using the <table> element for data set binding

Exercises

1 To achieve a data set binding, you include the __________ attribute in the start tag of the `<table>` element.

A `datasrc="value"`

B `datafld="value"`

C `src="value"`

D `fld="value"`

2 Each child element in `<table>` can inherit the value of the __________ attribute, but must specify its own __________ attribute to display data values.

3 The following code, on its own, will successfully display the data source data in a browser. True or false?

```
<table>
 <tr>
  <td>First Name:</td>
  <td><div datafld="Fname"/></td>
 </tr>
</table>
```

Topic B: Integrating XML data sources

Explanation

To display updated data on a Web page, your browser must access a data source. The data source can be a simple ASCII delimited text file, another XML file, or a more complex relational database table. For simple Web sites, the data might even be stored within the same HTML file that displays the rest of the Web page. For larger Web sites, however, the data is typically stored externally, and when users issue requests through their browsers, the data is accessed and transmitted across a network. When XML documents are used for data storage, the data is stored in elements called `data islands`.

If data is included in the same HTML document as the rest of the Web page, it's known as an *internal data island.* If the XML data are included in a separate document, they are called *external data islands.* The following sections explain how Internet Explorer integrates internal and external XML data islands.

Internal data islands

Exhibit 9-6 shows an HTML document named parts1.html that contains an internal data island, a parts list defined by a set of XML tags.

```
<html>
    <!-- Filename - parts1.html -->
    <head>
       <title>Parts List</title>
    </head>
    <body>
      <xml id="PList">
          <partslist>
               <part>
                    <name>Seat</name>
                    <partNo>1234</partNo>
                    <stock>12</stock>
                    <Price>$59.99</Price>
               </part>
          </partslist>
          </xml>
          <p> </p>
          <h1>TLSales</h1>
          <h2>Parts List</h2>
          <p>
             <table cellspacing="1" cellpadding="1" width="75%" border="1" datasrc="#PList">
                  <tbody>
                     <tr bgcolor="purple">
                          <td>Name:</td>
                          <td>
                               <div dataFld="name" />
                          </td>
                     </tr>
                     <tr>
                          <td>Part Number:</td>

        ...etc.
```

Exhibit 9-6: HTML file containing internal XML data island

The data island is internal because it's contained in the same HTML file that presents the rest of the Web page. The data is called an island because it consists of XML elements in an HTML document structure.

The `id` attribute in the `<xml>` element defines the XML data island. The `id` value specifies the name of the data source. When you use an internal data island, do not include a `src="value"` attribute in the `<xml>` element because that indicates that an external data island must be accessed.

In summary, you include an `<xml>` element to embed XML data in an HTML document. Within the `<xml>` element is an XML document. In this example, `<partslist>` is the root element in the XML document shown in Exhibit 9-6. Nested within it is the actual data, enclosed in XML data elements.

When an `<xml>` element is wrapped around the other XML data elements, as it is in parts1.html, the structure is called inline because the `<xml>` child elements fall between the `<xml>` element's start tag and end tag.

The `<xml>` element is often called unofficial HTML element because it is not part of any official HTML standard. It's a Microsoft extension to HTML, included in the HTML Document Object Model, a standard Application Programming Interface (API) for HTML, and is supported by Internet Explorer 5 and later. Browsers that do not support data binding safely ignore the `<xml>` element and its contents.

Note: Internal data islands are appropriate for small amounts of data. If you want to access larger amounts of data, use external data islands.

```
<td><table border="1" style="border-collapse: collapse; width: 95%" datasrc="#inventory" datafld="inventory.part">
<thead>
<tr>
<th>Name</th>
<th>Part Number</th>
<th>In Stock</th>
<th>Price</th>
</tr>
</thead>
<tbody><tr>
<td><div datafld="name" /></td>
<td><div datafld="partnum" /></td>
<td><div datafld="stock" /></td>
<td><div datafld="price" /></td>
</tr></tbody>
</table></td>
```

Exhibit 9-7: inventory.html showing a data set

Do it!

B-1: Creating an internal data island

Here's how	Here's why
1 Open XML Spy	You will create an internal data island.
2 Choose **File**, **New...**	
Select **HTML Document**	
Click **OK**	A new HTML document appears.
3 Save the file as **inventory.html**	
4 Replace the text in the `<title>` element with the following:	(If necessary, switch to Text view first.)
Inventory Summary	
5 Replace the default paragraph with the following:	
<h1>Inventory</h1>	
6 On the next line, type:	To insert an internal data island.

```
<xml id="inventory">
<store>
<location>Whistler, BC</location>
<inventory>
<part>
<name>Seat</name>
<partnum>1234</partnum>
<stock>12</stock>
<price>$59.99</price>
</part>
<part>
<name>Handle Bars</name>
<partnum>2345</partnum>
<stock>5</stock>
<price>$34.99</price>
</part>
</inventory>
</store>
</xml>
```

7 Save your changes	

8 After the closing </xml> tag, type:	To insert a tabular consumer data element.

```
<table width="400" border="1" datasrc="#inventory">
<tr>
<td style="color:white; background-color:black;
font-weight:bold">
Store: <span datafld="location"/>
</td>
</tr>
</table>
```

	The start tag for the table element has a datasrc attribute with the same value as the XML element's id, prefixed with a number sign. The datasrc attribute references the data island you inserted.
9 Switch to Browser view	Note that the content of the <location> element appears in the browser window.
10 Switch to Text view	
11 Directly above the closing </table> tag, type:	

```
<tr>
<td>
<table width="100%" datasrc="#inventory"
datafld="inventory">
<tr>
<td>
<table border="1" datasrc="#inventory"
datafld="inventory.part">
</table>
</td>
</tr>
</table>
</td>
</tr>
```

12 Within the innermost table element, type the following:

As shown in Exhibit 9-7.

```
<thead>
<tr>
<th>Name</th>
<th>Part Number</th>
<th>In Stock</th>
<th>Price</th>
</tr>
</thead>
<tbody>
<tr>
<td><div datafld="name" /></td>
<td><div datafld="partnum" /></td>
<td><div datafld="stock" /></td>
<td><div datafld="price" /></td>
</tr>
</tbody>
```

Note that some of the table cells contain `<div>` elements with `datafld` attributes. These attributes reference the elements within the XML data island.

13 Save your changes

Switch to Browser view

All of the data from the two part elements are displayed within the table.

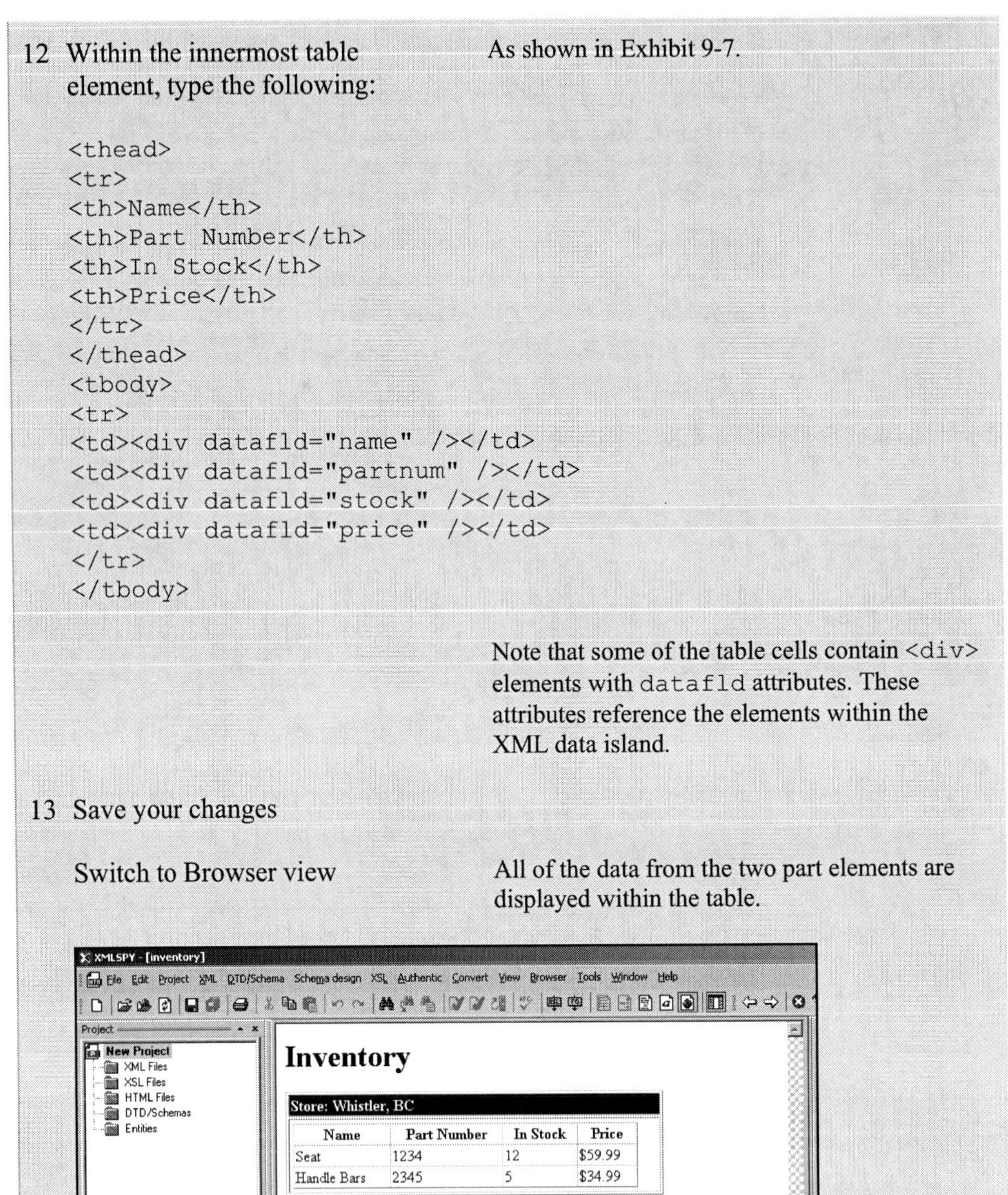

External data islands

Explanation

To use an external data island, you store XML data in an XML file that's separate from the HTML document. Then you add the `src` attribute to the `<xml>` element tag in the HTML document. The value of the `src` attribute is the filename and location of the XML file containing the data. The separate XML file becomes your external data island.

Exhibit 9-8 shows an HTML file named parts2.html that references an external data island located in an XML file named partslist.xml. The parts2.html file is almost identical to parts1.html, the file that contains the internal data island, except for the following differences:

- In parts2.html, the `<xml>` element is a declared empty element.
- The `<xml>` element contains an additional attribute, `src="partslist.xml"`, which references the external data island.

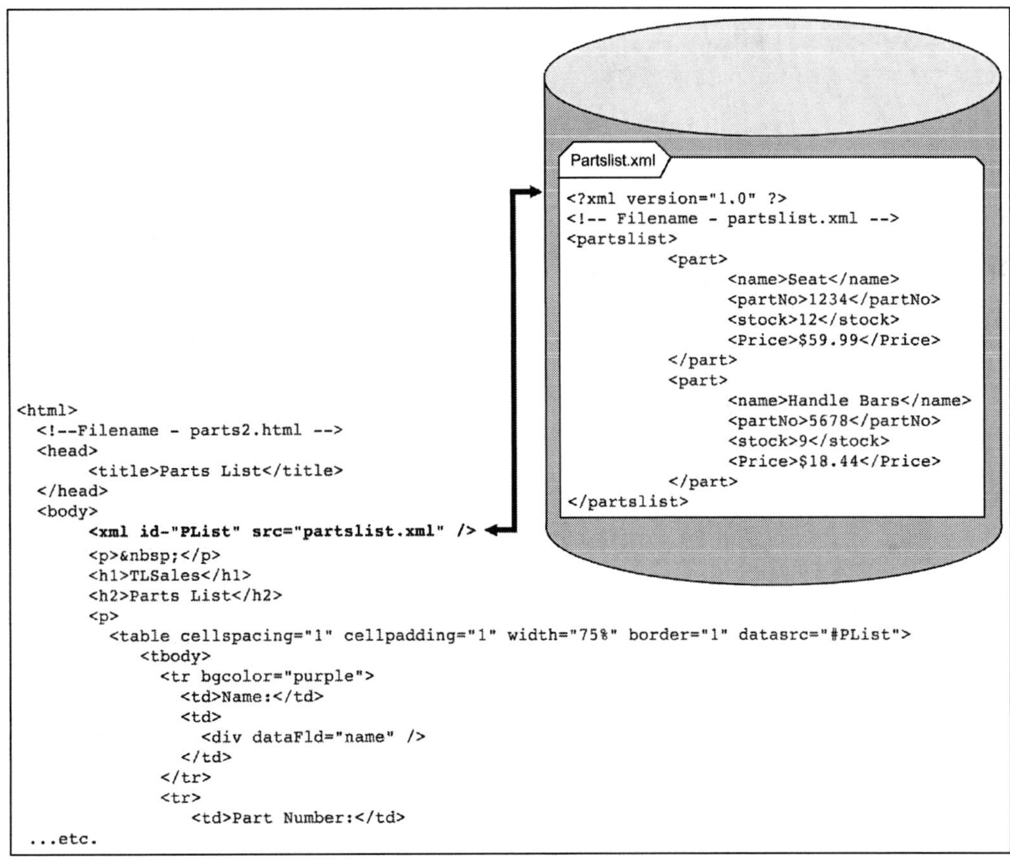


```
<?xml version="1.0" ?>
<!-- Filename - partslist.xml -->
<partslist>
        <part>
                <name>Seat</name>
                <partNo>1234</partNo>
                <stock>12</stock>
                <Price>$59.99</Price>
        </part>
        <part>
                <name>Handle Bars</name>
                <partNo>5678</partNo>
                <stock>9</stock>
                <Price>$18.44</Price>
        </part>
</partslist>
```

```
<html>
  <!--Filename - parts2.html -->
  <head>
       <title>Parts List</title>
  </head>
  <body>
       <xml id-"PList" src="partslist.xml" />
       <p> </p>
       <h1>TLSales</h1>
       <h2>Parts List</h2>
       <p>
         <table cellspacing="1" cellpadding="1" width="75%" border="1" datasrc="#PList">
            <tbody>
              <tr bgcolor="purple">
                <td>Name:</td>
                <td>
                  <div dataFld="name" />
                </td>
              </tr>
              <tr>
                 <td>Part Number:</td>
  ...etc.
```

Exhibit 9-8: HTML file referencing external XML data island

When you use an external data island, the browser looks for an `<xml>` element with the `id` value set to the name of the data source, in this case, PList. Then it interprets the `src="partslist.xml"` attribute, which indicates that the data is in an external source called partslist.xml.

External data islands are recommended because they allow you to separate data from its presenting document. The data is kept in one XML file, and the data consumers are kept in a separate HTML file. Using this strategy and file structure, Web page designers and database administrators can work on separate tasks, and maintaining the data is a much easier task.

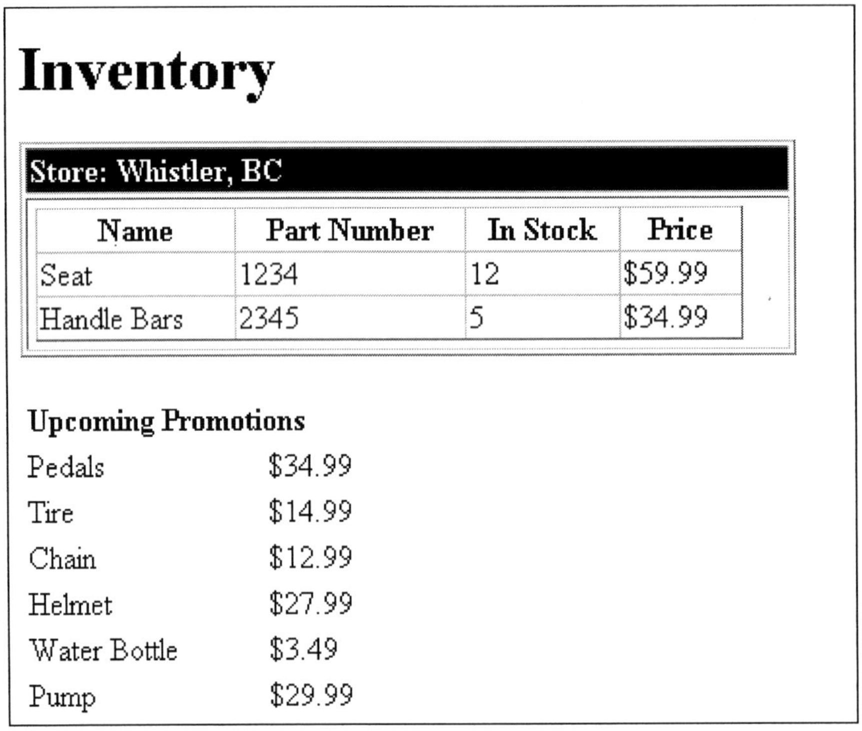

Inventory

Store: Whistler, BC

Name	Part Number	In Stock	Price
Seat	1234	12	$59.99
Handle Bars	2345	5	$34.99

Upcoming Promotions

Pedals	$34.99
Tire	$14.99
Chain	$12.99
Helmet	$27.99
Water Bottle	$3.49
Pump	$29.99

Exhibit 9-9: Browser view of inventory.html

Do it!

B-2: Creating an external data island

Here's how	Here's why
1 Switch to Text view	
2 Directly above the existing `<xml>` element, type: `<xml id="specials" src="specials.xml" />`	In the same way that the HTML document references data source information from the internal data island, the document can reference information from an external XML file.
3 After the outermost closing `</table>` tag, type: (see code below)	
4 Switch to Browser view	To see the updated document (as in Exhibit 9-9).
Compare the displayed data with the data in the external XML file	
5 Save your changes and close the document	

Code for step 3:

```
<br/>
<table width="200" datasrc="#specials">
<thead>
<tr>
<th colspan="2" align="left">
Upcoming Promotions
</th>
</tr>
</thead>
<tbody>
<tr>
<td><div datafld="item"/></td>
<td><div datafld="price"/></td>
</tr>
</tbody>
</table>
```

6 With a/an __________, XML data is stored in an XML file that's separate from the HTML document.

A internal data island

B external data island

C data field

D data key

7 If the XML data elements are inside the HTML page itself, they are called __________ data islands.

Pairing data sources and data fields

Explanation

Exhibit 9-10 shows how to use the `datasrc` attribute in both internal and external data islands.

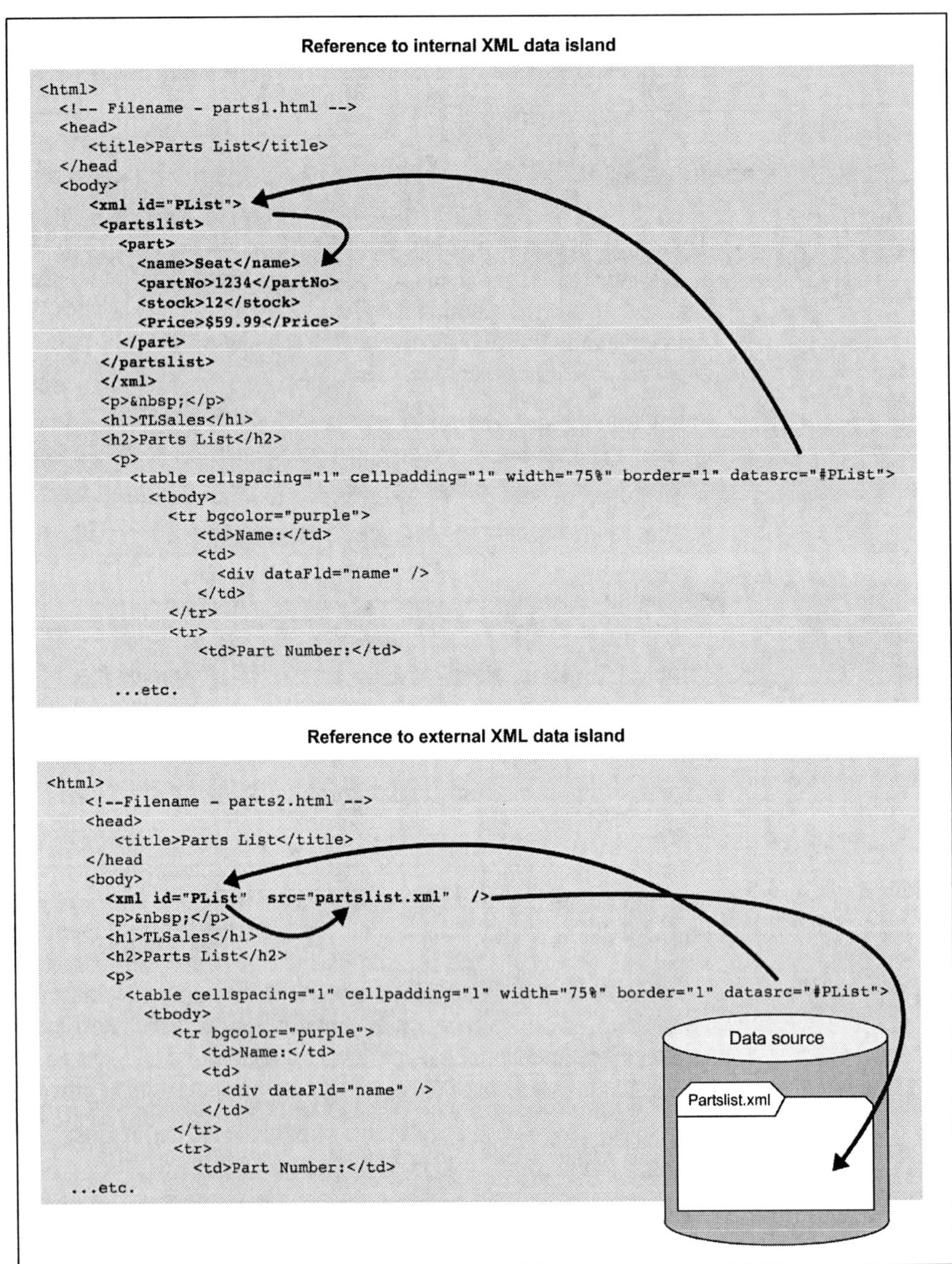

Reference to internal XML data island

```
<html>
  <!-- Filename - parts1.html -->
  <head>
     <title>Parts List</title>
  </head
  <body>
     <xml id="PList">
      <partslist>
        <part>
          <name>Seat</name>
          <partNo>1234</partNo>
          <stock>12</stock>
          <Price>$59.99</Price>
        </part>
      </partslist>
      </xml>
      <p> </p>
      <h1>TLSales</h1>
      <h2>Parts List</h2>
       <p>
         <table cellspacing="1" cellpadding="1" width="75%" border="1" datasrc="#PList">
           <tbody>
             <tr bgcolor="purple">
                <td>Name:</td>
                <td>
                  <div dataFld="name" />
                </td>
             </tr>
             <tr>
                <td>Part Number:</td>
       ...etc.
```

Reference to external XML data island

```
<html>
    <!--Filename - parts2.html -->
    <head>
       <title>Parts List</title>
    </head
    <body>
      <xml id="PList"  src="partslist.xml"  />
      <p> </p>
      <h1>TLSales</h1>
      <h2>Parts List</h2>
      <p>
        <table cellspacing="1" cellpadding="1" width="75%" border="1" datasrc="#PList">
          <tbody>
             <tr bgcolor="purple">
                <td>Name:</td>
                <td>
                  <div dataFld="name" />
                </td>
             </tr>
             <tr>
               <td>Part Number:</td>
  ...etc.
```


Exhibit 9-10: The datasrc attribute

In both cases, the `datasrc` attribute affiliates the XML data island with the `<table>` element in the HTML document. The `datasrc` attribute points to the `<xml>` element with the `id` attribute identical to the value of the `datasrc` attribute. That `<xml>` element then points to the XML data island, whether internal or external to the HTML document. Remember that data binding involves three tasks: locating a data source, retrieving the data, and then displaying the data. You use the `datasrc` attribute to perform the first task of identifying the data source.

When the browser loads a Web page that references a data source, it scours the HTML for data consumers, such as `<table>`, `<td>`, `<div>`, and `<span>`. To retrieve and display the appropriate data from the data source, the browser looks for a `datafld="value"` attribute in the start tags of these data consumers. The `datafld="value"` attribute is also known as the *`data field key`*. The value of the datafld attribute is the name of the element in the data source that contains the data. In database terms, the value is the name of the field that contains the data. Adding the data field key completes the second step in the data-binding task: it binds the XML element data to a position within the HTML file.

In general, the `datafld` attribute assigns the content of a specific element to a bindable element. The browser then displays that content as specified in the HTML document.

Note: When you use XML namespaces, you must also declare them in the `datafld` binding. For example, if you name a targeted field `<v:customername>` instead of `<customername>`, the specified `datafld` value would be "`v:customername`", and not the unqualified `customername`.

Data binding and table repetition agents

A *`data binding agent`* utility establishes and maintains the synchronization of the data values to the HTML document. Appropriate dynamic link libraries in Internet Explorer implement the binding agent and a table repetition agent, and they operate as background processes.

When Internet Explorer loads a page, the binding agent searches it, looking for data consumer elements, and then determines which data source object (DSO) to use, based on the attribute values found in the start tags of certain elements. When the binding agent recognizes all data consumers and DSOs, it synchronizes the data that flows between them. For example, when the DSO obtains more data from its data source, the binding agent is the process that actually transmits the new data to the consumers. Conversely, when an end user updates a databound element on a Web page, the binding agent should notify the DSO and a display-to-data source process should be initiated.

The binding agent can also send scriptable signals and messages to alert a developer to changes in the data.

As the Web page receives data from the data source, the `table repetition agent` in the browser works with the `<table>` data consumer elements to expand the table rows. This means you do not need to recode the table to create cells when the Web page receives additional data. This dynamic table behavior is demonstrated in Exhibit 9-11.

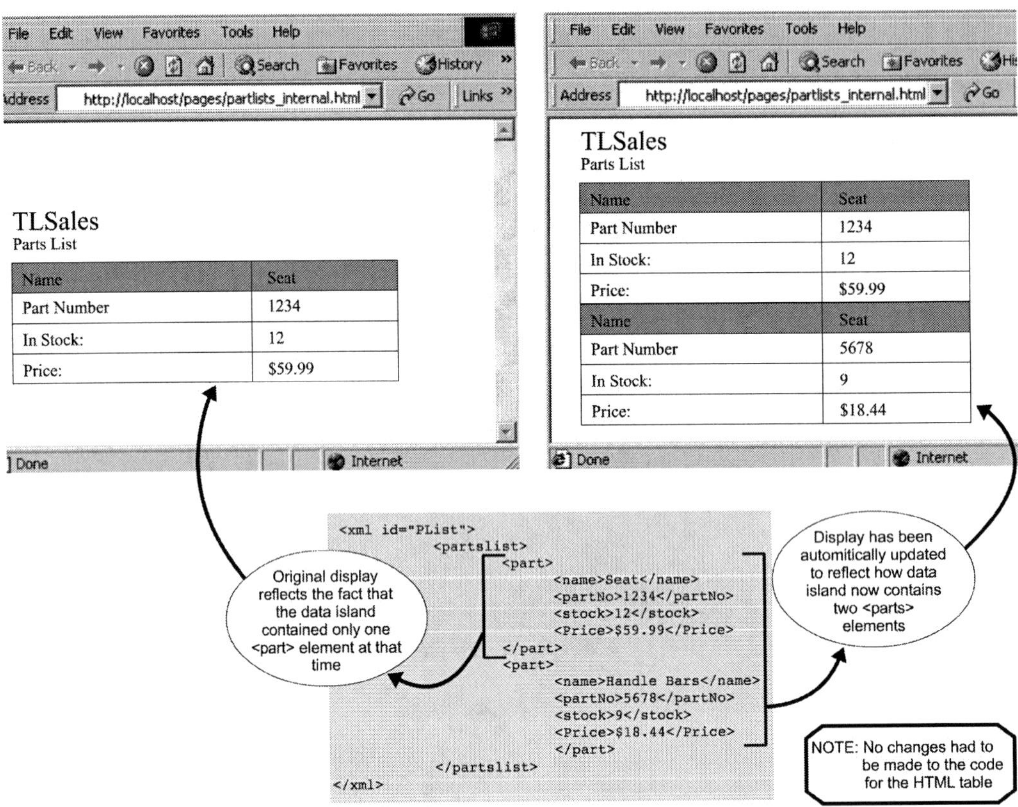

Exhibit 9-11: Dynamic table behavior

The parts list on the left indicates that, at the time the page is originally displayed, its XML data source contained only one XML `<part>` element with its respective child element data fields (the part number, number in stock, and price). The parts list on the right represents the same HTML page after the XML data file has been updated. It now contains two XML `<part>` elements—the seat and a set of handle bars. The table repetition agent in the browser expanded the HTML table to accommodate the new data. If you added a third XML `<part>` element to the XML data file, the table would again expand dynamically. Because the browser expands the table on the client system, you can optimize network bandwidth.

Do it!

B-3: Discussing data binding agents

Questions and answers

1 As a Web page receives data from the data source, the table repetition agent in the browser works with the data consumer elements to expand the table rows. True or false?

2 A ___________ utility establishes and maintains the synchronization of the data value to the HTML document.

A data binding agent

B set binding

C repetition agent

D table agent

3 Describe a Web site scenario wherein data binding would prove to be a powerful and efficient solution.

Topic C: Data source objects

Explanation

Internet Explorer (version 5 and later) uses data source objects to implement data binding. Developed along with Dynamic HTML (DHTML), Data Source Objects (DSOs) download data along with a Web page, and work with the data binding agent and table repetition agent, if necessary, to update data automatically. If the XML data changes, the page is automatically updated the next time the browser requests it. This is particularly useful when you want to display current information in forms, tables, fields, or other objects on your Web site. Internet Explorer contains several data source objects for use with various kinds of data, including:

- Tabular data control
- Remote data service
- Java Database Connectivity (JDBC) DataSource applet
- Custom data source object
- MSHTML data source object
- XML data source object

How the DSO returns data

Each DSO gathers data from different sources and has unique methods for manipulating the data. They access the respective data sources, query for specific data, and then provide the returned data to the consumer elements in the HTML file.

After you create and identify your data, you specify in the HTML file the DSO that provides the data. Each DSO requires a different element or attribute. For example, you could specify the JDBC DSO by including an `<applet>` element with appropriate attributes and child elements. To specify the RDS DSO, you include an `<object>` element with its respective attributes and child elements.

When you use an internal XML data island, you specify the XML DSO by using the `<xml>` element with the `id="value"` attribute. When you use an external data island, you add an `src="filename.xml"` attribute.

To understand how the DSO acts during data retrieval and conveyance, take a look at the XML data source file usedbikes.xml in Exhibit 9-12. The entire data source is contained within the `<import>` element. It contains three records, each defined within a `<row>` element. Each record contains five fields: the `<desc>`, `<color>`, `<mileage>`, `<aprice>`, and `<image>` elements. Each field contains data. To be a valid XML file, the data file must conform to a DTD or schema.

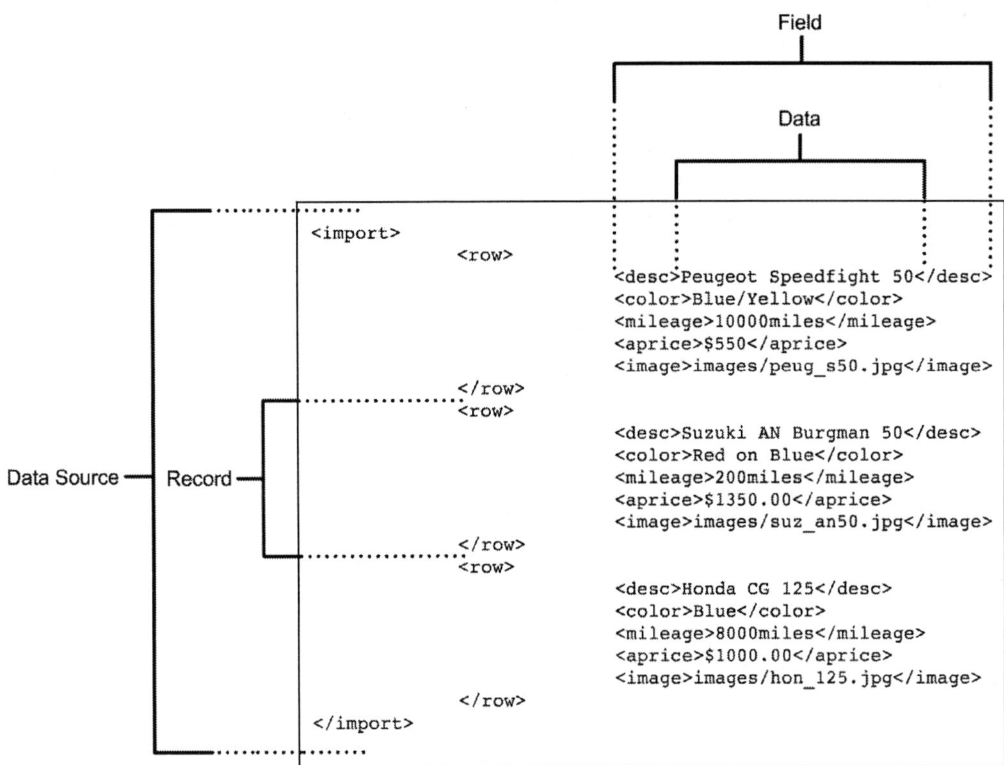
Field
Data
<import>
<row>
<desc>Peugeot Speedfight 50</desc>
<color>Blue/Yellow</color>
<mileage>10000miles</mileage>
<aprice>$550</aprice>
<image>images/peug_s50.jpg</image>
</row>
<row>
<desc>Suzuki AN Burgman 50</desc>
<color>Red on Blue</color>
<mileage>200miles</mileage>
<aprice>$1350.00</aprice>
<image>images/suz_an50.jpg</image>
</row>
<row>
<desc>Honda CG 125</desc>
<color>Blue</color>
<mileage>8000miles</mileage>
<aprice>$1000.00</aprice>
<image>images/hon_125.jpg</image>
</row>
</import>
Data Source
Record

Exhibit 9-12: Simple data source file–usedbikes.xml

Exhibit 9-13 shows the Web page named usedbikes.xml, the XML data source file usedbikes.xml from Exhibit 9-12, and the data the DSO retrieves from usedbikes.xml. This data, a subset of all the data in usedbikes.xml, is called a *`recordset`*. The `datafld` attributes in the HTML file instruct the DSO to query the data source for mileage and price information. Each time the DSO obtains the data from one mileage field and one price field, it constructs one record. In other words, a single record can be defined as one row of data. The records that the DSO builds are data objects. The data is conveyed to the system's RAM record by record, and the DSO combines them into a recordset that is passed to the binding agent and table repetition agent, if necessary.

The recordset contains records from the fields specified and bound by the `datafld` attributes in the HTML file. The recordset does not contain data from all five fields in the data source. The DSO recordset is a sub-recordset of the data source.

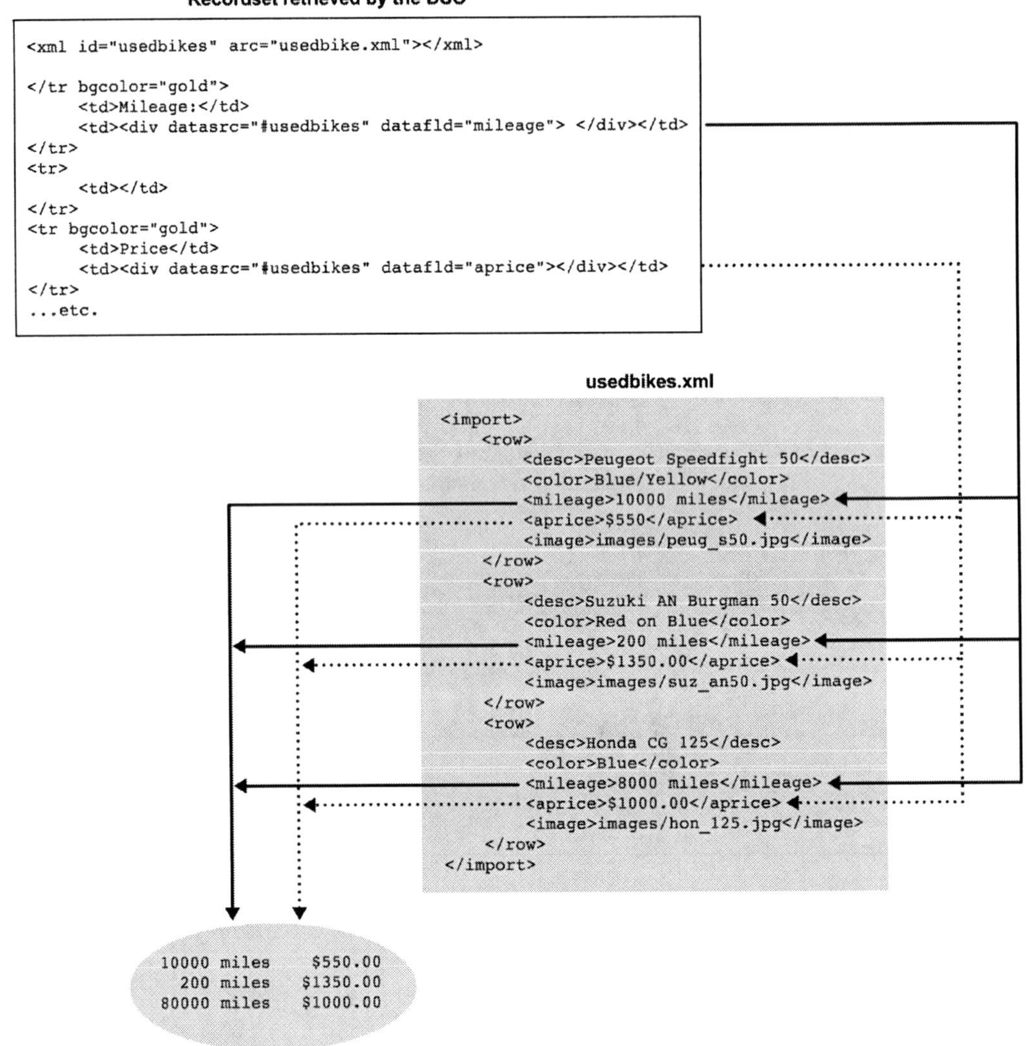
Recordset retrieved by the DSO
<xml id="usedbikes" arc="usedbike.xml"></xml>
</tr bgcolor="gold">
<td>Mileage:</td>
<td><div datasrc="#usedbikes" datafld="mileage"> </div></td>
</tr>
<tr>
<td></td>
</tr>
<tr bgcolor="gold">
<td>Price</td>
<td><div datasrc="#usedbikes" datafld="aprice"></div></td>
</tr>
...etc.
usedbikes.xml
<import>
<row>
<desc>Peugeot Speedfight 50</desc>
<color>Blue/Yellow</color>
<mileage>10000 miles</mileage>
<aprice>$550</aprice>
<image>images/peug_s50.jpg</image>
</row>
<row>
<desc>Suzuki AN Burgman 50</desc>
<color>Red on Blue</color>
<mileage>200 miles</mileage>
<aprice>$1350.00</aprice>
<image>images/suz_an50.jpg</image>
</row>
<row>
<desc>Honda CG 125</desc>
<color>Blue</color>
<mileage>8000 miles</mileage>
<aprice>$1000.00</aprice>
<image>images/hon_125.jpg</image>
</row>
</import>
10000 miles $550.00
200 miles $1350.00
80000 miles $1000.00
recordset

Exhibit 9-13: Data copied into recordset

Do it!

C-1: Discussing how DSO returns data

Questions and answers

1 The data source object acts as a data supplier to create and manage __________.

A recordsets

B tables

C documents

D records

2 Which statement best describes a DSO?

A An ActiveX control feature that updates automatically

B An ActiveX control feature that represents a live connection to the data source that updates automatically

C An ActiveX connection to a data file, XML file, or database

3 The `datafld` attributes in the HTML file instructs the __________ to query the data source for information.

A datasrc

B DSO

C DOS

D recordset

Data nesting and the two-level rule

Explanation

So far, the data source files we've worked with have been fairly flat. That is, the records, fields, and data have not been nested deeply, element within element. You can nest both `<table>` elements and XML data elements several layers beneath the root elements of their documents.

With data binding, if you nest the data any deeper than two levels from the root element, you must add a `datafld="value"` attribute to the consumer element start tag. As the value of that `datafld` attribute, you must also add a full path specification to the parent element of the data fields. Think of this as the two-level rule.

In Exhibit 9-14, the XML source file named custcredit.xml nests up to three levels below the `<customer>` root element. The corresponding HTML document also has three levels of nested tables. Some of the `datafld` attributes for the `<table>` elements need full path descriptions to allow the DSO to access the data. 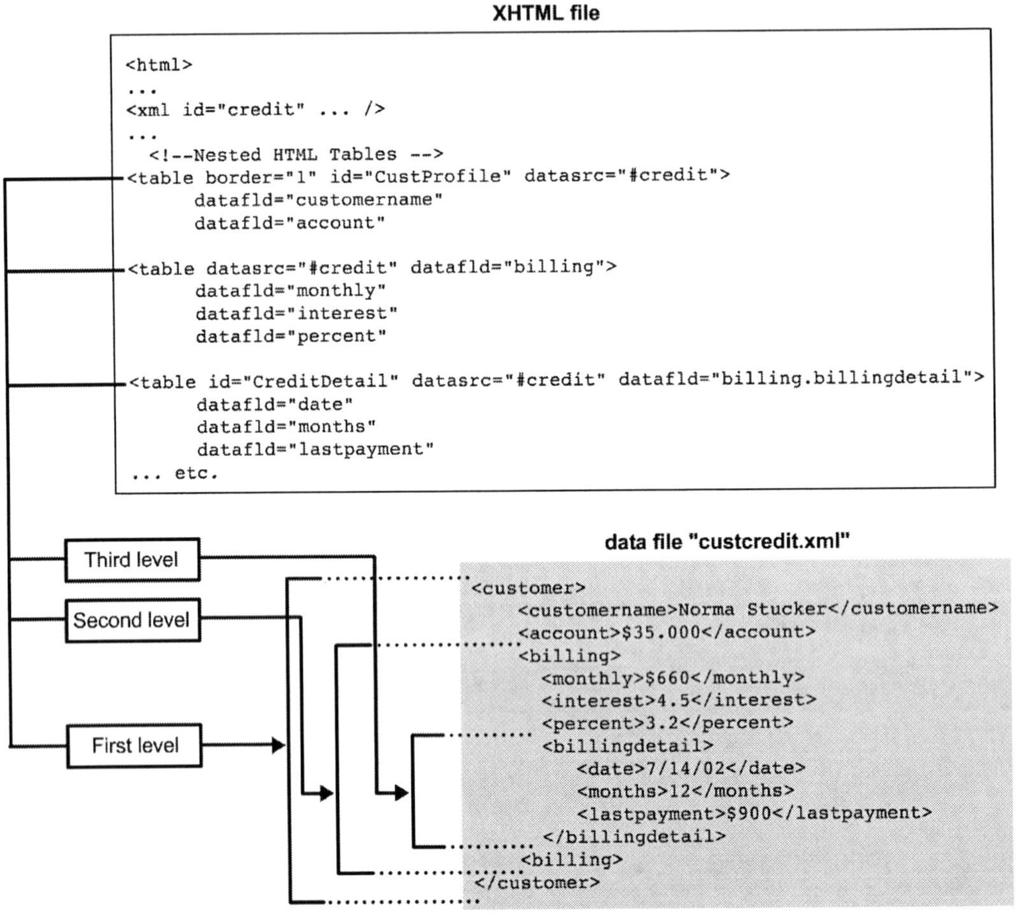

XHTML file

```
<html>
...
<xml id="credit" ... />
...
  <!--Nested HTML Tables -->
<table border="1" id="CustProfile" datasrc="#credit">
      datafld="customername"
      datafld="account"

<table datasrc="#credit" datafld="billing">
      datafld="monthly"
      datafld="interest"
      datafld="percent"

<table id="CreditDetail" datasrc="#credit" datafld="billing.billingdetail">
      datafld="date"
      datafld="months"
      datafld="lastpayment"
... etc.
```

Third level

Second level

First level

data file "custcredit.xml"

```
<customer>
    <customername>Norma Stucker</customername>
    <account>$35.000</account>
    <billing>
      <monthly>$660</monthly>
      <interest>4.5</interest>
      <percent>3.2</percent>
      <billingdetail>
         <date>7/14/02</date>
         <months>12</months>
         <lastpayment>$900</lastpayment>
      </billingdetail>
    <billing>
</customer>
```

Exhibit 9-14: The Two-Level Rule

The first level `<table>` element includes `datafld` attribute values that specify `customername` and `account`. This element does not need a path to bind the `datafld` attribute because the data in custcredit.xml falls within the two-level rule. The targeted fields in custcredit.xml and their data are listed immediately beneath the root `<customer>` element.

The second level <table> element includes `datafld` attribute values that specify `monthly`, `interest`, and `percent`. Again, according to the two-level rule, this element does not need a path because the targeted fields and data are nested only once. However, you can add a path to clarify where the data is stored. In Exhibit 9-14, a `datafld` attribute is set to "billing." This `billing` element is queried to return the actual data.

The third level <table> element includes `datafld` attribute values that specify `date`, `months`, and `lastpayment`. To bind this <table> element, the value of its `datafld` attribute must be a full path to the element being queried because the nesting of the `billingdetail` element exceeds the two-level rule. In Exhibit 9-14, `datafld='billing.billingdetail'` appears in the <table> element.

Note that this specification concatenates the names of the parent elements of the targeted fields—in other words, it combines them and uses a period as the delimiter. This is the standard syntax for a full path value that references more than one element.

Note: If you specify the full path of the `datafld` attribute within a <table> element, you don't need to specify the same path to the subsequent `datafld` values referenced within the same table (e.g., within the <td> tags). Those elements inherit the full path from their parent elements. However, if an element specifies a different data source and its targeted fields are nested more than two levels deep, they need their own full path specifications.

Do it!

C-2: Discussing data nesting and the two-level rule

Questions and answers

1 If you nest data any deeper than two levels from the root element, you must add a ____________ attribute to the consumer element start tag.

A `datasrc="value"`

B `key="value"`

C `datafld="value"`

D `src="value"`

2 In what situation(s) would a full `datafld` path be required?

A When an XML file is too long for data elements to display properly.

B When an XML element is nested more than two layers deep, including the root element.

C When the number of XML element's sibling elements exceeds three.

D When an XML element is nested more than two layers deep, excluding the root element.

Navigating recordsets

Explanation

Recordsets returned by the DSO are separate data objects, and can be navigated or manipulated by any element, function, or program that understands data binding.

This provides the following opportunities:

- The users of your Web page can process and manipulate records, resulting in a more flexible and informative presentation.
- There is no need to send requests back to a Web server for navigation and manipulation, which saves bandwidth.

One way to navigate recordsets is by using simple JavaScript techniques. For example, Exhibit 9-15 shows an HTML file called usedbikes.html that has been split into three sections. Part A shows JavaScript code contained within a `<script>` element. Part B defines an HTML table. Part C defines a set of HTML buttons that are used to execute the JavaScript functions defined in Part A.

```
<html>
<head>
<title>TLSales Data Binding Example</title>
    <!-- Filename -usedbikes.html-->
    <style>td {color: white} label {font-weight:bold}</style>
    <script language="JavaScript">
       function moveNext()
         {
          usedbikes.recordset.MoveNext();
          if(usedbikes.recordset.eof;
           {
            usedbikes.recordset.MoveFirst();
           }
         }
        function movePrevious()
        {
          usedbikes.recordset.MovePrevious();
          if(usedbikes.recordset.bof;
           {
            usedbikes.recordset.MoveLast();
           }
         }
     </script>
</head>
```

PART A

```
<body>
<xml id="usedbikes" src="usedbikelist.xml"></xml>
<table border="2" cellpadding="0" cellspacing="0">
   <tr bgcolor="silver">
      <td><img datasrc="#usedbikes"
datafld="Image"></td>
      <td valign="TOP">
          <table cellpadding="0" cellspacing="0"
BGCOLOR="#0B5F64" height="100%">
               <tr bgcolor="gold">
                 <td>Desc: </td><td nowrap><span
datasrc="#usedbikes" datafld="dusk"></td>
               </tr>
               <tr>
                  <td> </td>
               </tr>
               <tr bgcolor="gold">
                  <td>Colors: </td><td><div
datasrc="#usedbikes" datafld="color"></div></td>
               </tr>
               <tr>
                  <td> </td>
               </tr>
               <tr bgcolor="gold">
                  <td>Tel: </td><td><div
datasrc="#usedbikes" datafld="mileage"></div></td>
               </tr>
               <tr>
                  <td> </td>
               </tr>
               <tr bgcolor="gold">
                <td>Price:</td>
                <td><div datasrc="#usedbikes"
datafld="aprice"></div></td>
                </tr>
        </table>
     </td>
</tr>
```

PART B

```
<tr bgcolor="#0D4A6C0">
 <td>
 <input type="button" onClick="usedbikes.recordset.MoveFirst();
 value="<<" alt="Move First">
  <input type="button" onClick="movePrevious();"
 value="<<" alt="Back">
<input type="button" onClick="moveNext();"
 value="<<" alt="Next">
<input type="button" onClick="usedbikes.recordset.MoveLast();"
 value="<<" alt="Move Last">
</td>
<td>Dept:<span datasrc="#usedbikes" datafld="Dept"></span></td>
</tr>
</table></body></html>
```

PART C

Exhibit 9-15: HTML file with JavaScript–usedbikes.html

Exhibit 9-16 shows the XML file named usedbikes.xml, which is the external data island for the HTML file usedbikes.html shown in Exhibit 9-15. Both files illustrate how you can create and navigate a customized DSO recordset.

```
<import>
        <row>
                <desc>Peugeot Speedfight 50</desc>
                <color>Blue/Yellow</color>
                <mileage>10000miles</mileage>
                <aprice>$550</aprice>
                <image>images/peug_s50.jpg</image>
        </row>
        <row>
                <desc>Suzuki AN Burgman 50</desc>
                <color>Red on Blue</color>
                <mileage>200miles</mileage>
                <aprice>$1350.00</aprice>
                <image>images/suz_an50.jpg</image>
        </row>
        <row>
                <desc>Honda CG 125</desc>
                <color>Blue</color>
                <mileage>8000miles</mileage>
                <aprice>$1000.00</aprice>
                <image>images/hon_125.jpg</image>
        </row>
</import>
```

Exhibit 9-16: XML data source file

The browser queries the records in usedbikes.xml, then returns the information from all five fields in each record to create a recordset. Exhibit 9-17 shows that recordset. It also indicates the `BOF` (beginning of file) and `EOF` (end of file) positions. When navigating through a recordset, the JavaScript navigation functions always refer to these positions.

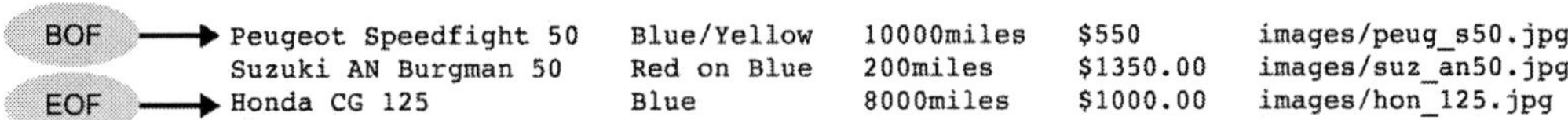

Exhibit 9-17: Navigating the recordset

The JavaScript function in usedbikes.html (in Exhibit 9-15) defines the following four functions: `moveNext`, `movePrevious`, `moveFirst`, and `moveLast`. These functions allow the user to navigate through the recordset. Users see a rendered HTML display similar to the one shown in Exhibit 9-18. The HTML code at the bottom of usedbikes.html defines the relationships between the functions and the buttons. When users click a button, the Web page runs the corresponding JavaScript function.

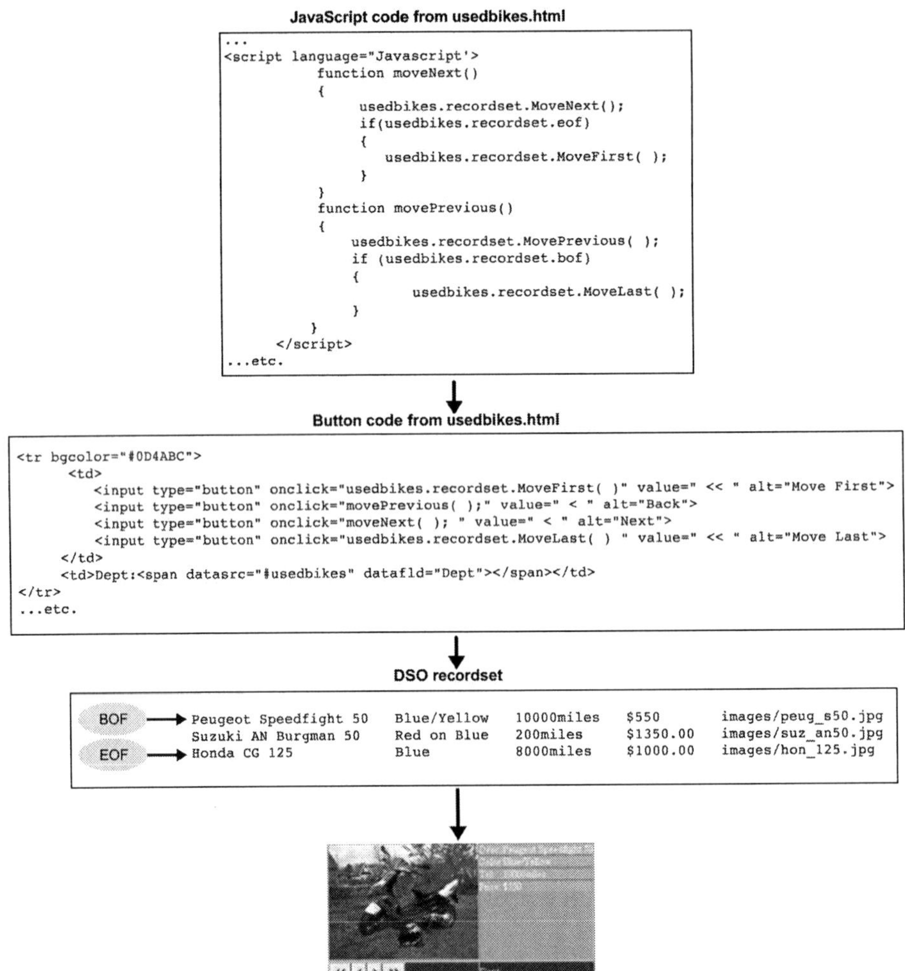

JavaScript code from usedbikes.html
...
<script language="Javascript'>
function moveNext()
{
usedbikes.recordset.MoveNext();
if(usedbikes.recordset.eof)
{
usedbikes.recordset.MoveFirst( );
}
}
function movePrevious()
{
usedbikes.recordset.MovePrevious( );
if (usedbikes.recordset.bof)
{
usedbikes.recordset.MoveLast( );
}
}
</script>
...etc.
Button code from usedbikes.html
<tr bgcolor="#0D4ABC">
<td>
<input type="button" onclick="usedbikes.recordset.MoveFirst( )" value=" << " alt="Move First">
<input type="button" onclick="movePrevious( );" value=" < " alt="Back">
<input type="button" onclick="moveNext( ); " value=" < " alt="Next">
<input type="button" onclick="usedbikes.recordset.MoveLast( ) " value=" << " alt="Move Last">
</td>
<td>Dept:<span datasrc="#usedbikes" datafld="Dept"></span></td>
</tr>
...etc.
DSO recordset
BOF
EOF
Peugeot Speedfight 50 Blue/Yellow 10000miles $550 images/peug_s50.jpg
Suzuki AN Burgman 50 Red on Blue 200miles $1350.00 images/suz_an50.jpg
Honda CG 125 Blue 8000miles $1000.00 images/hon_125.jpg

Exhibit 9-18: Evolution of on-screen navigation

The JavaScript and HTML code work together to allow an end user to navigate through the recordset. The process is as follows:

- When a user clicks the MoveFirst (<<) button, the `MoveFirst()` function points to the first record in the recordset, and the HTML code retrieves the information for that record—the Peugeot Speedfight 50—and displays it on the page.
- When a user clicks the Back (<) button, the `MovePrevious()` function points to the previous record unless it is already at the top (i.e., the BOF position). If it is at BOF, the `MoveLast()` function is executed and points to the last record in the recordset.
- When a user clicks the Next (>) button, the `MoveNext()` function points to the next record unless it is already at the bottom (i.e., the EOF position). If it is at EOF, the `MoveFirst()` function is executed and points to the first record in the recordset.
- When a user clicks the MoveLast button (>>) button, the `MoveLast()` function points to the last record in the recordset.

The dataPageSize attribute

After you bind data consumer elements such as a `<table>` element and its child elements to a data source, the Web page displays all the records obtained by the DSO from the data source. If the recordset is large, the dynamic table behavior might cause a page to grow beyond what is practical to display. In this case, you can include a `dataPageSize="value"` attribute in the start tag of the data consumer element to specify the maximum number of records that should be displayed at any one time. Use the following syntax:

```
<table border="1" id="CustProfile" datasrc="#credit"
dataPageSize="10">
```

To make the user move to the next and previous pages of records viewed in the table, you could code `nextPage()` and `previousPage()` methods in the HTML document, in a manner similar to the navigation code described earlier.

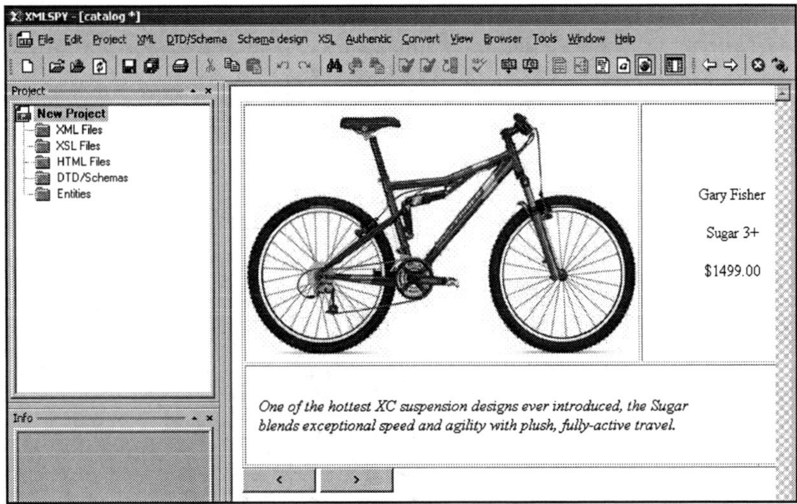

Exhibit 9-19: catalog.html rendered in XML Spy's browser view

Do it!

C-3: Creating navigation components

Here's how	Here's why
1 Choose **File**, **New...**	To open the Create new document dialog box.
Select **HTML Document**	
Click **OK**	
2 Save the file as **catalog.html**	In the current unit folder.
3 For the document title, enter **Catalog**	`<title>Catalog</title>`
4 Delete the default paragraph and replace it with:	

```
<input type="button" style="width:75;"
onclick="movePrevious();" value="<" alt="Previous Item">
<input type="button" style="width:75; "
onclick="moveNext();" value=">" alt="Next Item">
```

To add a set of Next and Previous buttons to allow users to navigate through the catalog. The HTML input element adds a button, and the `alt` attribute holds the text for the button. When the user clicks a button, the event handler declared in the `onClick` attribute is called.

5 Directly after the document title, type:	To add the JavaScript code for the Next and Previous buttons.

```
<script language="JavaScript">
function moveNext()
{
catalog.recordset.MoveNext();
if (catalog.recordset.eof)
catalog.recordset.MoveFirst();
}
function movePrevious()
{
catalog.recordset.MovePrevious();
if (catalog.recordset.bof)
catalog.recordset.MoveLast();
}
</script>
```

The functions simply operate upon a collection object containing the entire set of item elements from the catalog.xml data source. The `moveNext` function moves forward in the collection until the end is reached, and then cycles to the first element. The `movePrevious` function is similar, but moves in the opposite direction.

6 Save your changes	
7 After the closing </html> tag, type: `<xml id="catalog" src="catalog.xml" />`	To add the external data island.
8 Directly after the opening <body> tag, type:	This code creates a table that will be populated with data about three different bikes.

```
<table width="600" border="1">
 <tr>
  <td>
   <img width="400" height="250"
    datasrc="#catalog" datafld="image"/>
  </td>
  <td width="200" align="center">
   <div datasrc="#catalog" datafld="manufacturer">
   </div><br/>
   <div datasrc="#catalog" datafld="model">
   </div><br/>
   <div datasrc="#catalog" datafld="price">
   </div>
  </td>
 </tr>
 <tr>
  <td height="100" colspan="2">
   <div style="font-style:italic;"
        datasrc="#catalog" datafld="description">
   </div>
  </td>
 </tr>
</table>
```

9 Save your changes	Note that the table element does not have a `datasrc` attribute, but each <div> element refers to the catalog data source. Each <div> element binds to the current value for the data source element specified in the `datafld` attribute. When the user clicks on one of the navigation buttons, the event handler function changes the current record, and the data bound to the elements is updated.
Switch to Browser view	To view the rendered document as shown in Exhibit 9-19. Notice the buttons below the table.
Click each button a few times	To verify that the application is successful.
10 Close XML Spy	

Unit summary: XML data binding basics

Topic A In this topic, you learned about **data binding** and **data consumer elements**. You learned how to bind data by using two HTML data consumer element types (**single-valued** or **tabular**) and **extended attributes**. You also learned how to use the `<div>`, `<span>` and `<table>` elements for **data set binding**.

Topic B In this topic, you learned how to **integrate XML data sources with HTML documents**. You also learned to apply **internal** and **external data islands.** You also learned how to use tables as binding agents.

Topic C In this topic, you learned how to work with **data source objects**, and how data source objects return data. You learned about **data nesting** and the **two-level rule**. You also learned how to **create a simple navigation application**.

Review questions

1 If a recordset that's bound to a table is too long, what attribute can you use to reduce the amount of rows displayed inside the table?

A `recordsetReduce`

B `dataPageSize`

C `nextpage()`

D `previouspage()`

2 Which of the following are not tabular consumers?

A <span>

B <table>

C <input type=button>

D <div>

3 Which of the following is not true?

A Single-valued data consumer elements, such as the `<span>` element, bind with single values from the records found in the data source.

B As the Web page receives data from the data source, the table repetition agent in Internet Explorer works with the `<table>` data consumer elements to expand the table rows.

C `<span>` is a single-valued data consumer element.

D `<span>` is a tabular data consumer element.

4 Which of the following is true?

A In data binding, the data source provides the data, and the appropriate applications retrieve and synchronize the data and present it on the terminal screen—if the data changes, the applications won't be able to alter their presentation to reflect those changes.

B `<table>` is a single-valued data consumer element.

C Data binding causes traffic on the network and increases the work of the Web server.

D Data consumer elements can bind two types of data: single-valued or tabular.

5 Data binding also separates the task of __________ data from the tasks of developing and maintaining binding and presentation programs.

6 The `datafld="value"` attribute is also known as the __________.

Independent practice activity

Refer to the activities in this unit to create an HTML file that will serve as another internal data island that contains sales information for the products listed in inventory.html. Sales information can include product name, part number, stock number, price, and the name of the sales associate. Display the sales data in a series of tables. Then create an external data island that includes product information for a summer sale.

Appendix A
XML authoring tools

This appendix covers these additional topics:

A XML authoring tools, including simple text editors and graphical text editors.

B XML integrated development environments.

Topic A: XML editors

Explanation

Choosing your authoring tool will dictate the look, structure, and interoperability of your XML documents during the creation, modification, and conversion process. There are three basic categories of XML authoring tools: simple text editors, graphical text editors, and integrated development environments (IDEs). Several authoring applications are available within each category.

Simple text editors

Simple text editors have few features. For example, you can't change the look and feel of your text with these programs; you can use them to write ASCII (although not UNICODE) text. Nevertheless, these simple applications are all capable of producing XML documents because all XML tags and symbols use characters found on the standard keyboard. You can easily write XML in any text editor or word processor that can save to plain text format.

Although simple text editors are XML's most basic and economical creation and editing tools, they are limited in their display capabilities. They are simple and portable because of their small size, and found on virtually every platform as part of a basic operating system installation. Developers who prefer a simple, bare-bones approach to XML authoring will use a text editor such as:

- Microsoft Notepad
- Microsoft WordPad
- vi (found on virtually every UNIX-based platform)
- Emacs (originated on UNIX-based platforms—where it has become more and more popular—but also occasionally installed on Windows systems)
- Apple/Macintosh's SimpleText or SimpleText Pro

Exhibit A-1 shows what an XML file would look like if it had been created with Microsoft Notepad.

GNU Emacs, also called Emacs, is a more extensible and customizable text editor than vi, Notepad, or WordPad, and can also be used to create or modify XML documents. Emacs has long been the preferred UNIX-variant (it functions on virtually all UNIX variants) text editor by many. Emacs capabilities include:

- Online documentation
- Extensibility through its Emacs Lisp language
- Support for many languages and scripts
- Many extensions that add functionality, including a Web browser
- Variable width and variable height fonts
- Functionality on MS Windows NT, Windows 9X, Windows 2000, and Windows XP

Note: To obtain Emacs, visit the GNU Project Web site at:

`http://www.gnu.org/software/software.html`

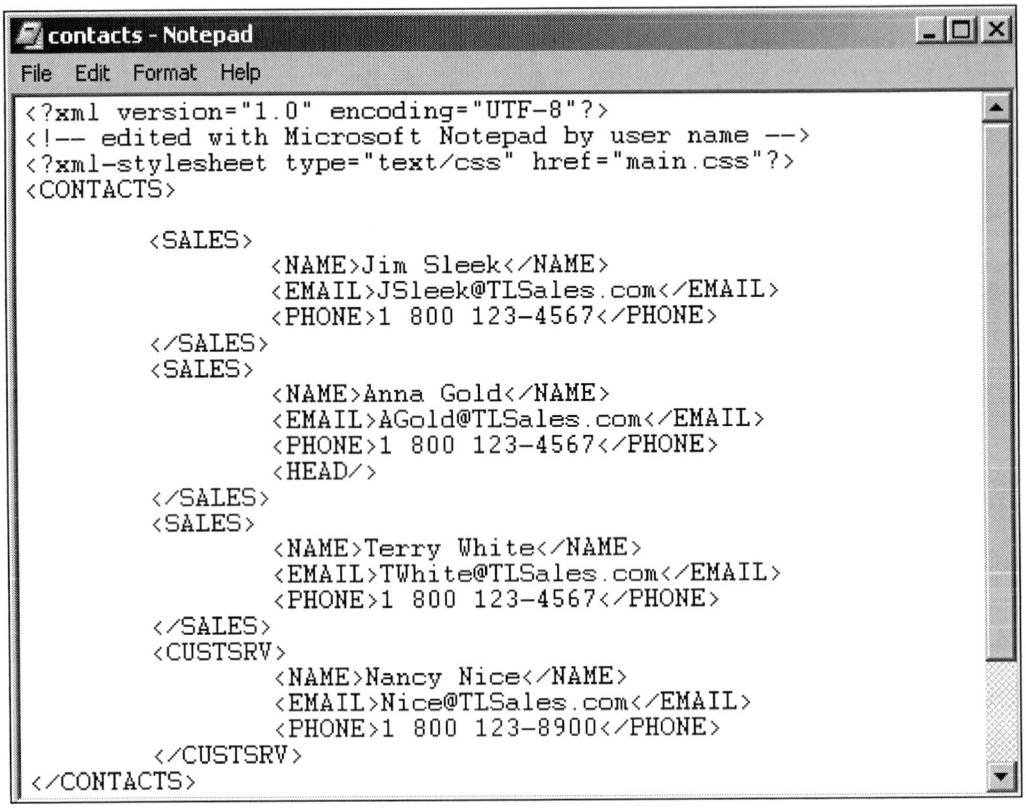

```
contacts - Notepad
File  Edit  Format  Help
<?xml version="1.0" encoding="UTF-8"?>
<!-- edited with Microsoft Notepad by user name -->
<?xml-stylesheet type="text/css" href="main.css"?>
<CONTACTS>

        <SALES>
                <NAME>Jim Sleek</NAME>
                <EMAIL>JSleek@TLSales.com</EMAIL>
                <PHONE>1 800 123-4567</PHONE>
        </SALES>
        <SALES>
                <NAME>Anna Gold</NAME>
                <EMAIL>AGold@TLSales.com</EMAIL>
                <PHONE>1 800 123-4567</PHONE>
                <HEAD/>
        </SALES>
        <SALES>
                <NAME>Terry White</NAME>
                <EMAIL>TWhite@TLSales.com</EMAIL>
                <PHONE>1 800 123-4567</PHONE>
        </SALES>
        <CUSTSRV>
                <NAME>Nancy Nice</NAME>
                <EMAIL>Nice@TLSales.com</EMAIL>
                <PHONE>1 800 123-8900</PHONE>
        </CUSTSRV>
</CONTACTS>
```

Exhibit A-1: contacts.xml viewed in Microsoft Notepad

Graphical text editors

Using simple text editors can slow development time. Some developers have difficulty getting a feel for their XML documents when they are confined to viewing only raw code, with no colors, highlights, and other features. As a result, many dedicated XML authoring tools are designed to look and function like word processors. Unlike simple text editors, graphical XML editors can:

- Represent the markup more clearly by color-coding tags.
- Hide the markup completely and apply a stylesheet immediately to give the various document parts their own emphasis or style.
- Provide Drag-and-drop features.
- Provide Click-and-drag highlighting.
- Provide special user-interface mechanisms for manipulating XML markup, such as attribute editors or drag-and-drop relocation of elements.
- Provide a menu of legal elements, which is a good tool for rigidly structured XML applications (e.g., filling out forms, entering data into a database).

By using a dedicated editor, developers can simply type the content or content references, choose fonts and colors, and save the document as they would save a Web page. This approach is called "what you see is what you get" or *WYSIWYG* (pronounced "whizzeewig").

A popular feature in higher-end XML authoring tools is automatic structure checking. By resisting any attempt to add an element that doesn't belong in a given context, the tool tries to prevent the author from making syntactic or structural mistakes while writing and editing.

While promoting good document structure and simultaneously preventing inadvertent mistakes, structure checking can also slow your progress when you experiment with the order of the document elements, most commonly during the initial drafting phase of a document.

The first graphical editors for structured markup languages were based on SGML, of which XML is a restricted form. However, because SGML was much bigger and more complex, those editors were often prohibitively expensive and difficult to maintain. XML's relative simplicity led to the development of simpler and more affordable editors.

Microsoft XML Notepad

XML Notepad is Microsoft's dedicated XML graphical text editor. Its interface consists of a two-pane display. On the left is the document's element structure; on the right are the corresponding element values. A typical presentation is shown in Exhibit A-2.

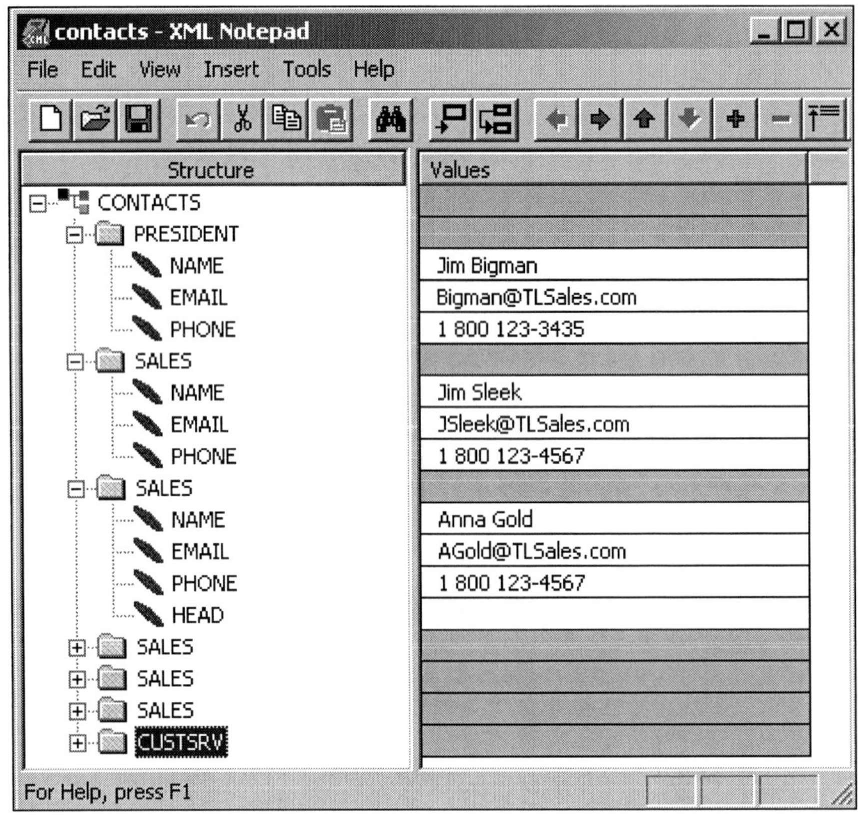

Exhibit A-2: contacts.xml created with Microsoft XML Notepad

Note: To download XML Notepad, go to the Microsoft Developer Network (MSDN) Web site: http://msdn.microsoft.com/library/default.asp?url=/library/enus/dnxml/html/xmlpaddownload.asp.

XAE

The XML Authoring Environment for Emacs (XAE) is add-on software you can use to create, transform, and display XML documents.

Note: You have to install Emacs and Java on your system prior to installing XAE. XAE can be obtained through the host Web site at http://xae.sunsite.dk/.

XML Pro

XML Pro is a product of Vervet Logic. XML Pro is a Sun Java-based XML modeling application that runs on any Java 2 virtual machine that has version 1.2 of the Java Runtime Environment (JRE 1.2, also called Java 2 or JDK 1.2) installed. XML Pro is integrated with the IBM XML 4J Parser and can be installed on Windows 95 or 98, Windows NT 4.0, Solaris UNIX, and Linux. XML Pro can function as a standalone editing application or it can be integrated with enterprise XML suites. For example, Vervet promotes the purchase of XML Pro in a bundle with Open Text's Near & Far Designer, a DTD creation and editing tool.

Note: You can download the latest trial version of XML Pro at www.vervet.com/demo.html.

A typical XML Pro display is shown in Exhibit A-3.

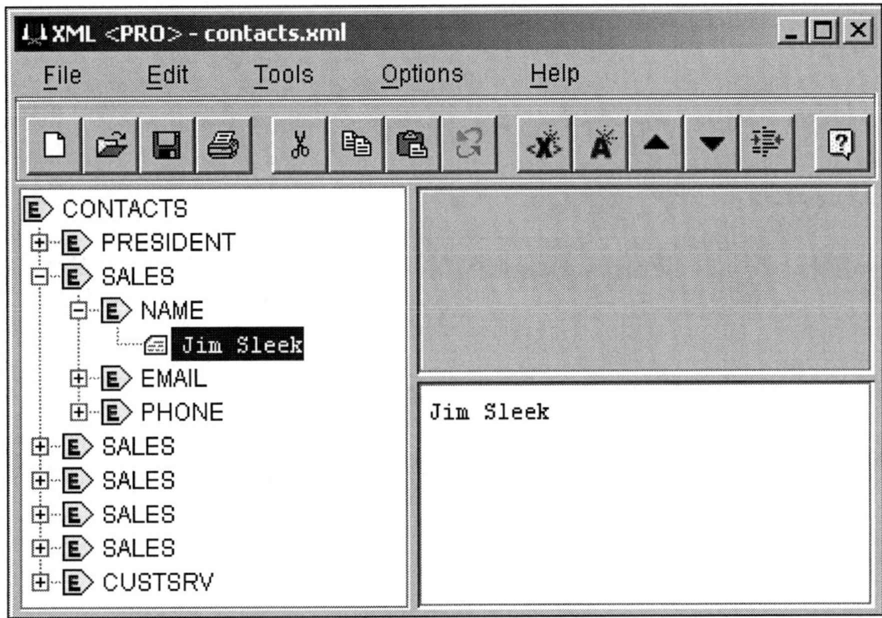

Exhibit A-3: contacts.xml created with XML Pro by Vervet Logic

Adobe FrameMaker + SGML

Adobe FrameMaker is high-end editing and composition tool for publishers. It originally came with its own markup language (MIF), but focused on SGML and XML as they became more prominent. Its extended package (Adobe FrameMaker +SGML) reads and writes SGML and XML documents. However, when modifying an existing XML document, the extended package must be able to find and interpret a DTD.

When integrated with HTML editors, FrameMaker can customize and fine-tune HTML and XML publishing. FrameMaker content can be published so that it fits seamlessly into a Web site's design.

Note: For more information regarding Adobe FrameMaker, go to the Adobe Web site at http://www.adobe.com/products/framemaker/main.html.

SoftQuad XMetaL

XMetaL's interface resembles a word processor and makes it easy for anyone to create XML content or convert documents from other formats, including Microsoft Word and Microsoft Excel. Some versions provide templates with replaceable text, custom dialog boxes, and drop-down menus. Currently available for Windows-based PCs only, XMetaL can be integrated with existing publishing and document management systems, and provides document revision controls.

Note: You can download a trial version of XMetaL from the SoftQuad Web site at http://www.softquad.com/top_frame.sq.

Conglomerate

With Conglomerate, you can create, revise, archive, search, convert, and publish information in several media (such as print and online), by using a single source document. It allows you to revise and merge documents while easily keeping track of changes. The system consists of a graphical front end for all user operations, and a server/database combination that performs storage, searching, revision control, transformation, and publishing. Conglomerate is free software, licensed under the GNU GPL, so it's based on open standards. Software is available at www.conglomerate.org.

Topic B: Integrated development environments

Explanation

Integrated development environments (IDEs) are a combination of text and code editors, compilers, debuggers, and GUI developers. IDEs provide a user-friendly framework for many modern programming languages (e.g., Microsoft's Visual Basic, or IBM's Visual Age for Java). You might already be familiar with some popular HTML IDEs, such as Macromedia's DreamWeaver or Microsoft's FrontPage.

XML IDEs

XML IDEs not only create and edit XML documents, they also handle all the major aspects of XML design, creation, and modification, such as:

- XML editing and validation
- XML DTD editing and validation (some IDEs include schema)
- Extensible Stylesheet Language (XSL) editing and transformation

Larger, sophisticated IDEs facilitate the building of large projects by development teams. One common feature is the provision of shared file repositories that use check-in and checkout systems, ensuring that no two developers can modify the same file simultaneously.

Some IDE tools might also provide *versioning*, which means that at certain points in the development cycle, the developer might decide to save the entire project in its state at that time. Thus, the developer creates a particular version of the project. Versioning helps developers return to that version of the project at some point in the future to either start upgrading from that point again, or simply to compare code with whatever version they are presently working on.

At certain strategic points in a project cycle, all of the project files are moved into a development or staging environment, where they are tested before they are deployed in a production environment. Exhibit A-4 depicts developers working independently on their respective files.

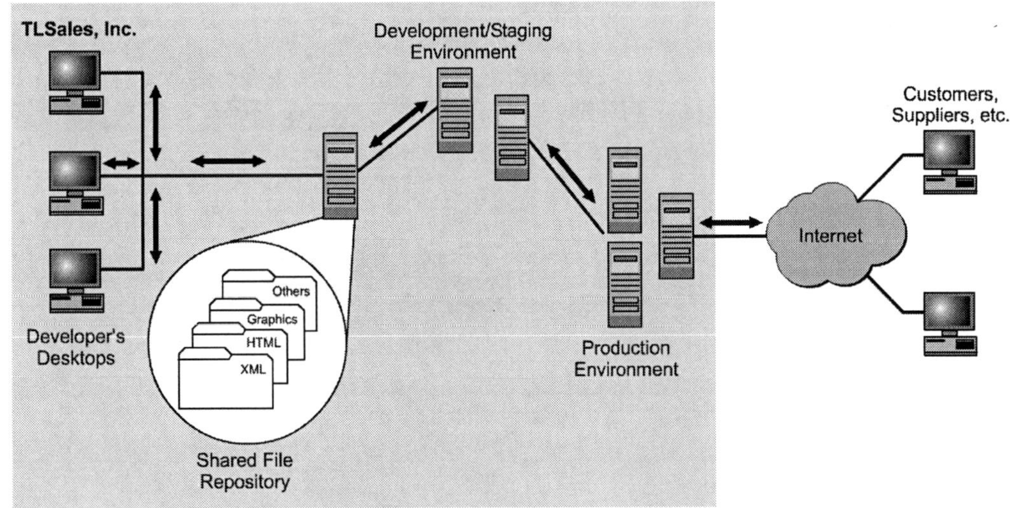

Exhibit A-4: An Integrated Development Environment

During this time, those files are created and/or edited, and testing is performed on each individual's desktop. The files they are working on are likely housed inside a common repository. This is achieved by setting up folder or file system shares over the network. Developers version their code, and a Web master moves their files into a development or staging environment for testing. The development or testing environment is modeled after the final production environment, but is usually smaller in scale. After the files are tested and all bugs are worked out of the code, the files are then promoted by the Web master into the production environment, where they are made available to the end user. Rarely are files moved directly from a developer's desktop into production.

Xeena

Xeena is a visual XML editor from the IBM Haifa Research Laboratory that runs on Win32 and UNIX platforms. Xeena is a Java application built on top of the Java Swing component set and XML parser (an application) for Java. Not a complete IDE, Xeena is "IDE-capable." It is different from the authoring tools that are in transition from text editor to IDE, which could be termed "editor-plus." Xeena is more like an "IDE-minus."

Xeena provides the ability to edit valid XML documents derived from any valid DTD. The Xeena editor takes a given DTD as input and then automatically builds a palette containing the elements defined in the DTD. Authors can create, edit, or expand any document derived from that DTD by using a visual tree-directed strategy. This needs a minimum learning curve because only valid constructs or elements are presented to authors, depending on the context they are working in (i.e., Xeena has a context-sensitive palette). It makes only the authorized element icons sensitive because Xeena is aware of the DTD grammar, which automatically insures that all generated documents are valid according to the given DTD. Xeena also supports XML schema. Other features include:

- Offers intuitive viewing and editing of XML documents in a tree view.
- An XML source viewer.
- Provides customization of the display.
- Offers an editor that is a multiple-document interface (MDI) application with full support to edit multiple XML documents and copy, cut, and paste from one document into another.

Xeena can be integrated with other document management applications, document versioning systems, and repositories. It can also be configured as a team-authoring tool, with checkout and check-in functionality. Exhibit A-5 shows how Xeena displays an XML file.

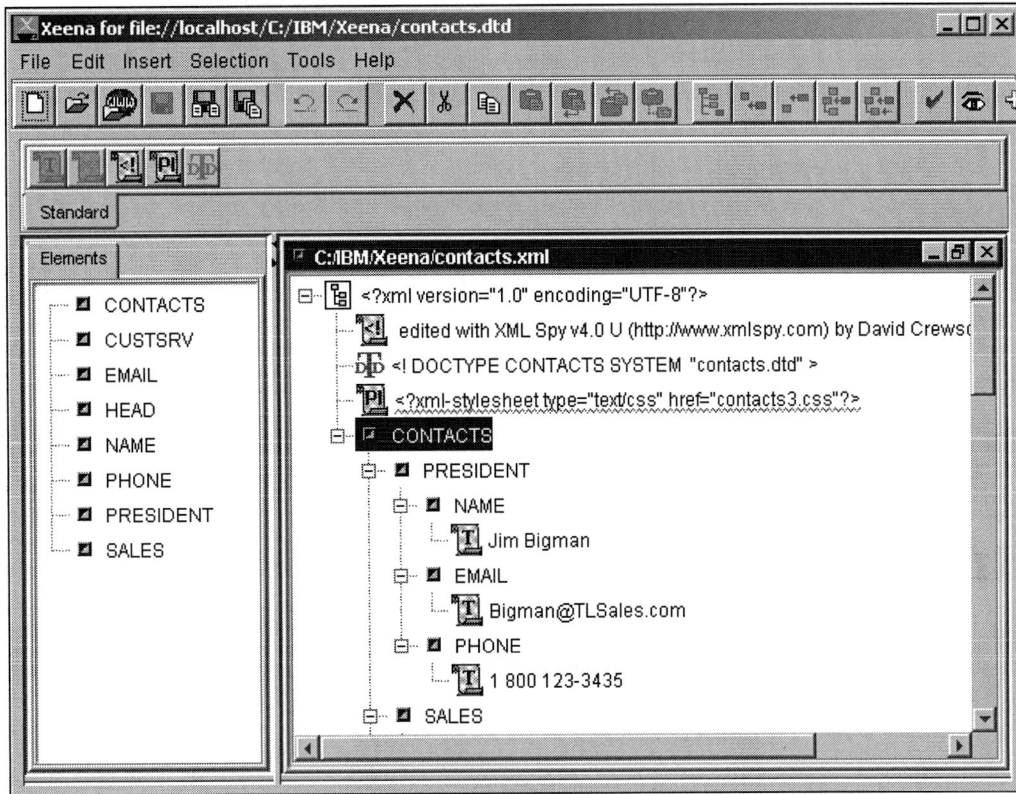

Exhibit A-5: contacts.xml created with IBM's Xeena

Note: For further information on Xeena, or to download a trial version, go to its Web site at http://www.alphaworks.ibm.com/tech/xeena.

XML Spy

Altova, Inc. focuses entirely on XML software products. They released their first version of XML Spy in February 1999. XML Spy is a 32-bit Windows application that supports all the major character-set encoding schemes, including Unicode. It can also import text files, Word documents, and data from Access, Oracle, and SQL server databases.

XML Spy also supports both DTDs and XML schema. Its editor provides five different document views: a grid view for structured editing, a database/table view that shows repeated elements, a text view of lower-level work, a graphical XML schema design view, and an integrated browser view. Exhibit A-6 shows an XML file as it would appear in XML Spy.

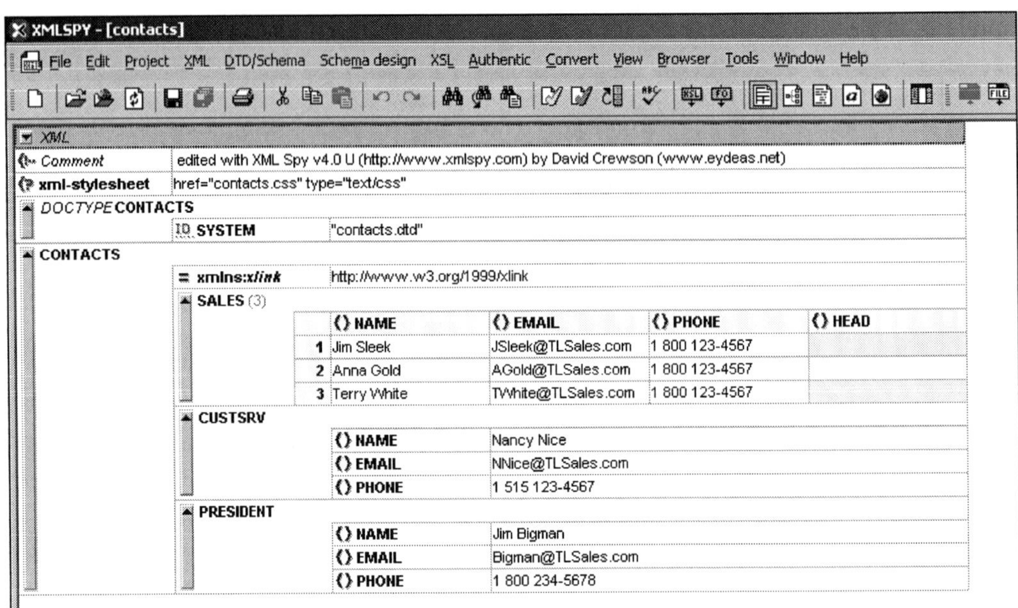

Exhibit A-6: contacts.xml created with Altova's XML Spy

Note: At Altova's Web site (http://www.xmlspy.com), you can download XML Spy's free, 30-day evaluation version.

Turbo XML

TIBCO Software's Turbo XML is an IDE that combines three additional XML applications: XML Authority, XML Instance, and XML Console. It is the first XML IDE to offer comprehensive support for the XML Schema Recommendation. You can investigate Turbo XML and other TIBCO XML software, as well as download a trial version of Turbo XML, at the TIBCO Web site, http://www.tibco.com/products/extensibility/solutions/turbo_xml.html. Exhibit A-7 shows an XML file, as it would appear in Turbo XML.

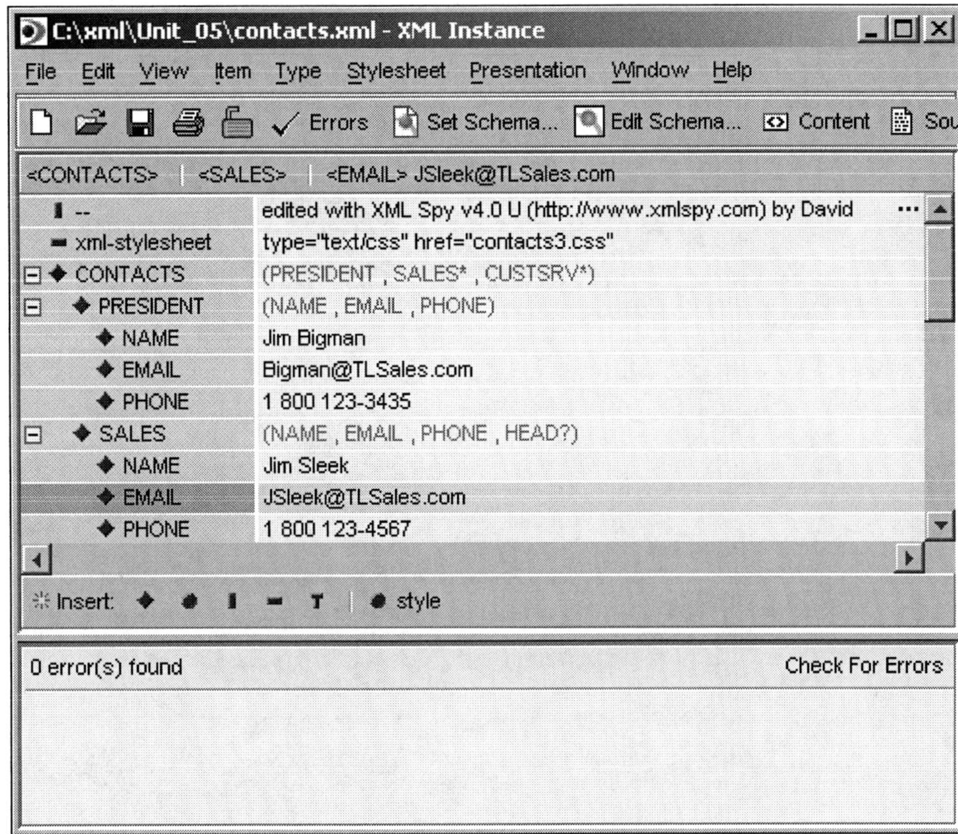

Exhibit A-7: contacts.xml created with TIBCO's Turbo XML

Komodo

A cross-platform, multilanguage IDE developed on Mozilla, Komodo supports all of the features that you expect in an IDE, including: an editor with several syntax features (including background syntax checking); an integrated debugger; a "file watcher" for monitoring log files; a project manager for organizing multiple files into projects; a sample project to demonstrate functionality; customizable preferences; online help, and more. It can be found at http://aspn.activestate.com.

Arbortext Epic editor

Arbortext has been around a long time in the world of electronic publishing. Its product, Epic Editor (preceded by a product called Adept), designed for creating XML and SGML content, can be used by teams of authors in several locations; it can be used with large amounts of material, and can be used to create multiple output formats (e.g., the World Wide Web, CD-ROM, print, and wireless).

You can create text and tables, place graphics, and configure links with the Epic Editor. Epic Editor is used to author Web content and many types of business and technical documents. It has over two dozen key features. You can visit Arbortext's Web site at www.arbortext.com for further information regarding Arbortext Epic Editor.

Appendix B
Introduction to XHTML

This appendix covers these additional topics:

A Evolution and advantages of XHTML.

B XHTML variants and DTDs.

C XHTML utilities provided by the W3C.

Topic A: Understanding XHTML

Explanation

The *Extensible Hypertext Markup Language* (XHTML) is an application of XML. XHTML consists of all the predefined components in HTML version 4.01 combined with XML standards and syntax, including the provision for introducing unique components. Thus, XHTML closely resembles HTML 4.01, but is a stricter and cleaner version of it. Unlike XML, XHTML is designed to eventually replace HTML as the primary tool for designing Web sites. XML is defined as a markup language and a metalanguage, designed to describe data. HTML, by contrast, was originally designed to display data. In XML-related documents, the content has to be marked up and structured correctly with appropriate elements. Proper markup and structure results in well-formed documents. Well-formed documents that conform to their respective DTDs or schemas are considered valid documents. It follows, then, that if every XHTML document is a complete XML document that also conforms to the XML Recommendation, then it must be compatible with all general-purpose XML tools and processors. XHTML is the first step toward a modular and extensible XML-based Web.

Advantages of XHTML

There are several advantages to using XHTML instead of HTML or to converting HTML documents to XHTML:

- XHTML is extensible.
- XHTML is portable.
- XHTML is modular.
- XHTML is backward and future compatible.

XHTML is extensible

With XHTML, you can introduce unique organization- or industry-related elements or additional attributes. Adding new logical components in such a manner increases functionality. To introduce them is as simple as declaring a namespace, defining the components in another DTD or schema, and adding or modifying a stylesheet.

XHTML is modular

XHTML is already fairly modular. XML has approved several module-related W3C Recommendations, and appropriate DTDs and schemas are being developed. As the development of XHTML modularity continues, XHTML languages and documents, and their descendants, integrate existing XHTML core modules with unique industry or organizational modules. This modular approach facilitates the development of documents and languages to serve almost any Internet or intranet purpose, and contributes to future portability to meet the needs of alternate computing devices.

XHTML is portable

The W3C's XHTML family is, and continues to be, designed so that applications on alternate platforms can communicate and exchange XHTML-based data. Eventually, it will be possible to develop XHTML-conforming languages and content that any XHTML-conforming user agent uses, and vice versa. When new devices are developed, they are more quickly and comfortably adopted into the family of Web-related communications.

XHTML is backward and future compatible

Properly constructed XHTML documents are compatible with most HTML browsers in use today. XHTML documents are also compatible with existing and future XML-related browsers and applications.

Topic B: XHTML variants and DTDs

Explanation

The W3C Recommendation released on January 26, 2000, describes XHTML 1.0 as its own family of document types (also called *variants*), which are successors to those defined earlier by HTML 4. The variants are called Strict, Transitional, and Frameset. Each variant has its own DTD that declares a logical structure for using XHTML in a particular manner. The XHTML 1.0 Recommendation also defines the respective Strict, Transitional, and Frameset DTDs. Each DTD consists of at least four kinds of declarations: element declarations, attribute list declarations, entity declarations, and notation declarations. As the DTD declares a set of allowed elements, it specifies the vocabulary of the document or language. The DTD also defines the grammar of the language by specifying the content model for each element. The content model is the pattern that indicates what elements or data can go inside another element, in what order they appear, how many of each can appear, and whether they are required or optional. The DTD declares a set of allowed attributes for each element and each attribute declaration defines the name, datatype, default values (if any), and behavior (e.g., if it is wanted or optional) of the attribute(s). Finally, the DTD provides other mechanisms (entity declarations and notation declarations) to make managing the model easier.

XHTML variants

Each XHTML developer must determine which variant to use and must specify the name of an XHTML variant. You do this by inserting the appropriate specification in the DOCTYPE declaration at the beginning of the XHTML document. After the parser reads that declaration statement, it knows which variant is being used and validates the document against the specified DTD. Here's an example of such a statement:

```
<!DOCTYPE html PUBLIC "-//W3C//DTD XHTML 1.0 Strict//EN"
"http://www.w3.org/TR/xhtml1/DTD/xhtml1-strict.dtd">
```

This statement tells the parser that the DTD is to use the strict variant, and that the DTD is found within the directory structure at the public W3C Web site. The W3C maintains and updates all the DTDs and other informational resources at this Web site.

The XHTML 1.0 Strict variant

There are three variants of XHTML 1.0. The Strict variant is used when you want really clean structural markup, free of tags and attributes associated with formatting. The Strict variant and its associated DTD are used with W3C's Cascading Style Sheet language (CSS) to generate the desired fonts, colors, and layout effects. Again the DOCTYPE declaration statement for the Strict variant is as follows:

```
<!DOCTYPE html PUBLIC "-//W3C//DTD XHTML 1.0 Strict//EN"
"http://www.w3.org/TR/xhtml1/DTD/xhtml1-strict.dtd">
```

The Strict DTD contains elements, attributes, and other components that have not been deprecated or that do not appear in framesets. Exhibit B-1 shows how the DOCTYPE definition statement appears in a simplified, generic, Strict variant-related XHTML document. In this exhibit, the DOCTYPE definition has been placed in bold text for emphasis.

```
<?xml version="1.0"?>
<--The following document declaration defines the document type and specifies the DTD-->
<!DOCTYPE html PUBLIC "-//W3C//DTD XHTML 1.0 Strict//EN"
      "http://www.w3.org.TR.xhtml1-strict.dtd">
<--The rest of this example document resembles HTML-->
<html xmlns="http://www.w3.org/1999/xhtml">
     <head>
         <title> Welcome to TLSales, Inc.!</title>
     </head>
     <body>
             <p> We Hope You Like Our Merchandise!</p>
     </body>
</html>
```

Exhibit B-1: XHTML document declaring a Strict DTD variant

The XHTML 1.0 Transitional variant

Those who are writing Web pages for the general public commonly use the Transitional variant. Although developers can take advantage of XHTML features such as style sheets, they might also want to make small adjustments to their markup so that those who visit their Web sites with older browsers—ones that can't understand style sheets—can still see the text and formatting. Thus, the DTD and documents use the body element with attributes such as bgcolor, text, and link.

The `DOCTYPE` declaration statement for the Transitional variant is as follows:

```
<!DOCTYPE html PUBLIC "-//W3C//DTD XHTML 1.0 Transitional
//EN" "http://www.w3.org/TR/xhtml1/DTD/xhtml1-
transitional.dtd">
```

The Transitional DTD includes everything in the Strict DTD, plus deprecated elements and attributes. Exhibit B-2 shows how the proper `DOCTYPE` definition statement appears in a typical, generic Transitional variant-related XHTML document.

```
<?xml version="1.0"?>
<--The following document declaration defines the document type and specifies the DTD-->
<!DOCTYPE html PUBLIC "-//W3C//DTD XHTML 1.0 Transitional/EN"
      "http:///www.w3.org.TR.xhtml1-transitional.dtd" >
<--The rest of this example document resembles HTML-->
<html xmlns="http://www.w3.org/1999/xhtml">
     <head>
         <title> Welcome to TLSales, Inc.!</title>
     </head>
     <body>
             <p> We Hope You Like Our Merchandise!</p>
     </body>
</html>
```

Exhibit B-2: XHTML document declaring a Transitional DTD variant

The XHTML 1.0 Frameset variant

Use the Frameset variant when you want to partition the browser window using frames. The Frameset DTD includes everything in the Transitional DTD, plus frames. Here's the Frameset DOCTYPE declaration statement:

```
<!DOCTYPE html PUBLIC "-//W3C//DTD XHTML 1.0 Frameset//EN"
"http://www.w3.org/TR/xhtml1/DTD/xhtml1-frameset.dtd">
```

This DTD is almost identical to the Transitional DTD. The only difference is that, in Frameset XHTML documents, the content portion of the html element is not called the body element; it is instead called the frameset element. The proper `DOCTYPE` definition statement appears in Exhibit B-3.

```
<?xml version="1.0"?>
<--The following document declaration defines the document type and specifies the DTD-->
<!DOCTYPE html PUBLIC "-//W3C//DTD XHTML 1.0 Frameset//EN"
"http:///www.w3.org.TR.xhtml1-frameset.dtd" >
<--The rest of this example document resembles HTML-->
<html xmlns="http://www.w3.org/1999/xhtml">
     <head>
         <title> Welcome to TLSales, Inc.!</title>
     </head>
     <body>
             <p> We Hope You Like Our Merchandise!</p>
     </body>
</html>
```

Exhibit B-3: XHTML document declaring a Frameset DTD variant

If copies of the most frequently accessed DTDs are installed on your local system or network, you also have to change the system identifier (SYSTEM, plus a URI has to be included) in the DOCTYPE definition statement. By using a local copy of the DTD, you can speed up the load time of your documents. It's up to you to keep track of any changes to the respective DTDs and standards.

Converting Web sites to XHTML

It is not recommended that you convert a Web site from HTML to XHTML manually, especially when several utilities are available to help you. However, if you decide to convert manually, you should become familiar with XHTML's XML-related syntax rules.

To manually convert a Web site from HTML to XHTML, follow these guidelines:

1. Create a prolog for every applicable document: the most important addition is the DOCTYPE declaration. If this is to be a Web site conversion—likely requiring some backward compatibility with older browser versions—the transitional DOCTYPE declaration is recommended. Although the browsers themselves won't process the statement, it is used when your XHTML files are validated.
2. Change tag and attribute names to lowercase: XHTML is case sensitive and only accepts lowercase HTML tags and attribute names. You can use a fix-up utility to insert lowercase tags and attribute names.
3. Insert quotation marks around all attribute values: this is a time-consuming job, so it helps to use an XHTML utility like HTML TIDY.
4. All empty element tags must have a terminating slash (/). To ensure compatibility with multiple browsers, you need to insert a space before the slash. For example:

   ```
   <br />
   ```

5. Validate the XHTML documents against the document type definition specified in Step 1. Use the W3C DTD validator at the following location: `http://validator.w3.org/`.

Note: For a description of an actual HTML to XHTML Web site conversion, visit:

`www.w3schools.com/xhtml/xhtml_howto.asp`

Topic C: XHTML utilities

Explanation

To facilitate the transition from older HTML versions to XHTML, and to convert sites automatically, the W3C provides compatibility guidelines (located in Appendix C of the XHTML 1.0 Recommendation), and access to three utilities.

W3C's HTML validation service

W3C provides a free service that checks HTML and XHTML documents for conformance to W3C Recommendations and other standards. By using their form at `http://validator.w3.org/`, you can validate a document by providing a URI for the document and then choosing validation parameters from the following:

- A selection of 33 character encoding schemes, from UTF-8 to EUC-JP (Japanese UNIX) to KOI8-R (Russian) and more.
- A selection of eight document type specifications: HTML 2.0, HTML 3.2, HTML 4.01 Strict, HTML 4.01 Transitional, HTML 4.01 Frameset, XHTML 1.0 Strict, XHTML 1.0 Transitional, and XHTML 1.0 Frameset.

As shown in Exhibit B-4, the validation service then examines the document at the URI you provide, in accordance with the options you've chosen.

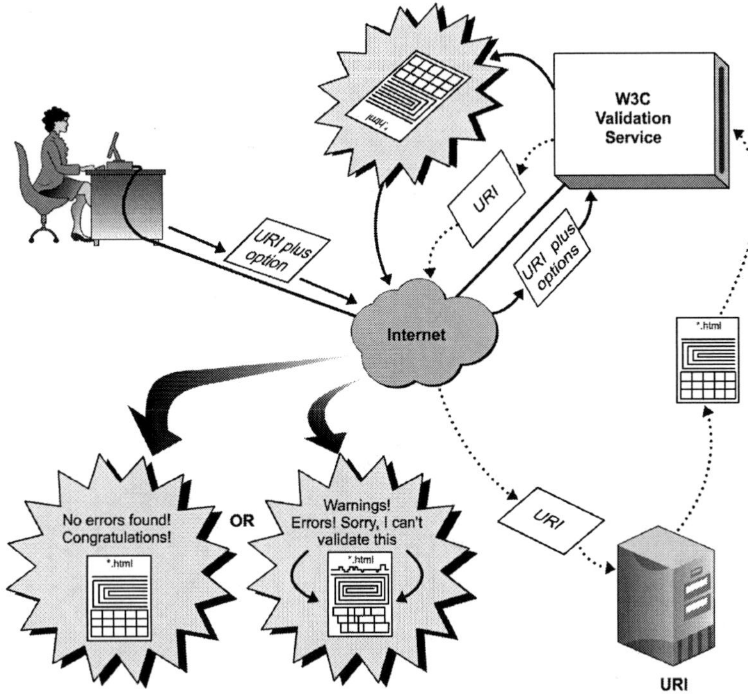

Exhibit B-4: W3C validation service: URL document check

Or, by using the W3C's related form at http://validator.w3.org/file-upload.html, you can validate documents on your computer by uploading them, as shown in Exhibit B-5.

You can find a summary of the most recent changes to the service by going to `http://validator.w3.org/`, and clicking "What's New."

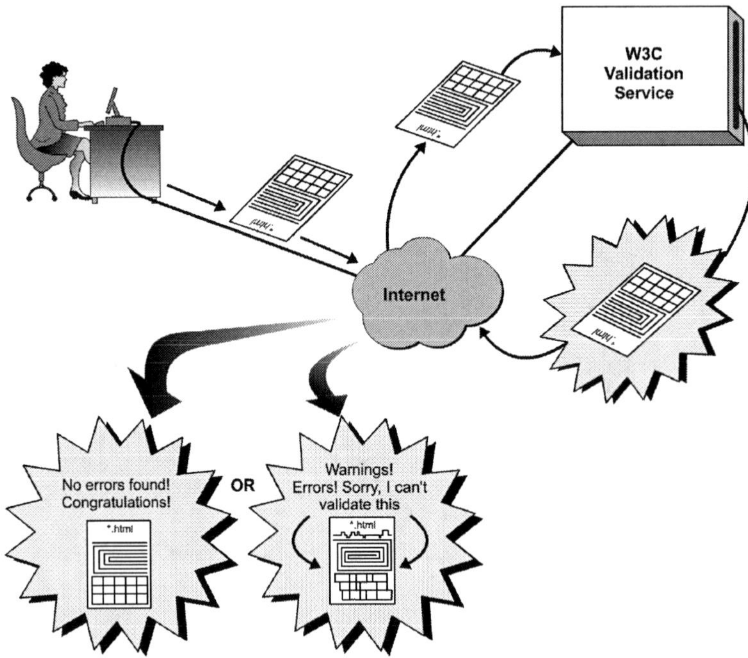

Exhibit B-5: W3C validation service: file upload

HTML TIDY

HTML TIDY is a free downloadable utility for editing HTML. Mistakes are fixed automatically and sloppy HTML editing is "Tidy'd" up into more easily understood markup. TIDY also converts existing HTML content into well-formed XML for delivery as XHTML. As shown in Exhibit B-6, Tidy can fix many problems automatically, but it won't fix errors. In those cases, Tidy brings those issues to your attention by logging them as errors and by offering suggestions.

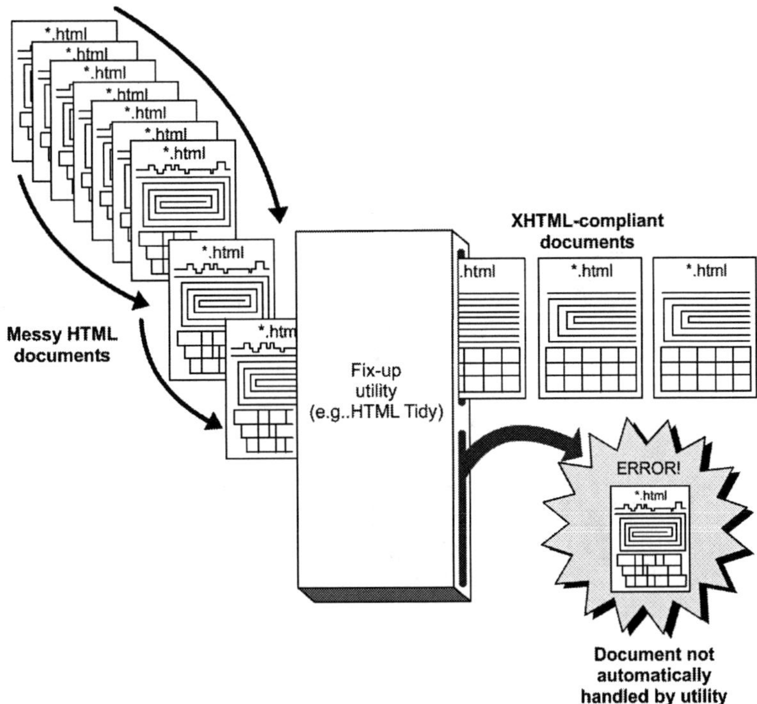

Exhibit B-6: HTML fix-up utility

Tidy can also help you determine how and where to make your pages more accessible to people with disabilities. Tidy is available for most platforms, and has been integrated into many authoring environments. For more information, go to:

`www.w3.org/People/Raggett/tidy/.`

Amaya: W3C's editor/browser

Amaya is an open source software project hosted by W3C. Amaya is a multipurpose active client that performs the following tasks:

- Retrieves documents from the Web and presents them to the user.
- Provides an authoring tool to edit existing documents and to create new ones.
- Publish these documents on remote Web servers.
- As both a browser and an authoring tool, it was specifically developed as a test bed client with which to experiment, test, and demonstrate a wide range of new developments in World Wide Web protocols and data formats, as well as new extensions to existing ones.

Both a client and a server are needed to test and demonstrate new Web specifications because the Web is based on client-server architecture. Within the realm of the W3C, Amaya plays this role on the client side; a product called Jigsaw plays the same role on the server side.

As an editor and authoring tool, Amaya correctly considers HTML to be an SGML application. It recognizes DTDs when manipulating the document structure, and it performs only valid operations. The advantage to this approach is that Amaya leads to well-structured documents, which facilitates safe processing by subsequent applications. Amaya is also available on both UNIX and Windows 95/NT platforms.

For more information on Amaya, check the following sources:

- The Amaya home page, at `www.w3.org/Amaya/`
- "An Introduction to Amaya"—the February 20, 1997, W3C Note document found at `www.w3.org/TR/NOTE-amaya-970220.html`.

XML

Course summary

This summary contains information to help you bring the course to a successful conclusion. Using this information, you will be able to:

A Use the summary text to reinforce what you've learned in class.

B Determine the next courses in this series (if any), as well as any other resources that might help you continue to learn about XML.

Topic A: Course summary

Use the following summary text to reinforce what you've learned in class.

XML

Unit 1

In this unit, you learned what XML is and how it functions as a **metalanguage** and a **markup language**. You observed a simple XML document and learned what **elements**, **attributes** and **tags** are. You also learned the basic rules needed to **write a simple XML document**. Next, you learned about **GML**, **SGML**, and **HTML**—the predecessors of XML. You learned why there is a **need for standards**, how XML evolved, and how it fits into the landscape of markup languages. You also learned how XML differs from SGML and HTML. Finally, you learned how **XML overcomes the shortcomings of SGML and HTML**.

Unit 2

In this unit, you learned about the **W3C XML 1.0 Recommendations**. You also learned that an **XML processor**, or **parser**, is a piece of software that reads XML documents and provides access to their content and structure. Then, you learned that the **application** is the major processing software module, and you learned that a **fatal error** is an error in the document that the XML processor must detect and report to the application. Next, you learned about the **physical structure** of documents. You learned that a document is made up of storage units called **entities** and a logical structure containing a **prolog** section. You learned that **elements** are the basic building blocks of XML, and you learned that the **root element** is the parent of all other elements. Finally, you learned how to use **attributes**, **entities**, and **CDATA sections** in an XML document, and you learned that a **valid XML document** is a **well-formed** XML document that also conforms to the rules defined in a DTD or an XML schema.

Unit 3

In this unit, you learned that **DTDs** and **schemas** facilitate XML **document modeling** by declaring a set of permissible elements, defining the content model for each element, and declaring the permitted attributes. You learned that a document might contain a stand-alone **internal DTD**; a reference to an **external DTD**; or a combination of an internal DTD plus a reference to another, external DTD. Then you learned how to **create a simple DTD** in XML Spy. You learned that a **content model** defines what an element might contain, and that there are several types of element content: **parsed character data**; **elements only**; **mixed content** (character data plus elements); **empty elements**; and **elements with no content restrictions.** Then, you learned about the **operators** used to define element content, and you learned how to declare **elements**, **attributes**, **entities** and **notations** in a DTD. Finally, you learned about **namespace declarations**, how to undertake **document analysis**, and how to **create and validate an XML document**.

Unit 4

In this unit, you learned some of the **limitations of DTDs**. You learned that document models are described in terms of **constraints**, and you learned that **schemas** provide more **XML namespace support** than DTDs. You learned that **element types** determine the appearance of elements and their content in instance documents, and that **compositors** define groups of elements and attributes within the schema. You also learned that **XML inheritance** comes in two forms—**restriction** and **extension**—and that schemas provide the ability to declare **empty content elements** and **mixed content elements**. Then, you learned how to define data more precisely by using **facets**. Finally, you learned how to **create schemas**, how to **convert an existing DTD to a schema**, and how to **add global components** to a schema.

Unit 5

In this unit, you learned the **advantages** and **limitations** of using **CSS** to style XML documents. You learned how to **create an external style sheet** and **link an XML document** to it. Then, you learned the **syntax of CSS rules**, and some fundamental **CSS properties**. You also learned about the principle of **inheritance**, and how to set an element as a **block** or **inline** element. Finally, you learned how to apply a **class style**, and how to include the **class attribute** in the attribute declaration list of a DTD.

Unit 6

In this unit, you learned about **XML data transformation**. You learned that XML data transformation is done in two phases: **structural transformation** and **structural formatting**. You learned how and why data is transformed, and how **XSL**, **XPath**, and **XSLT** transform data. Next, you about various **elements of XSL**, and you learned how to **transform an XML document to HTML** using XSLT. Finally, you learned how to use basic **conditional processing statements**, and use XSLT to **change the grammar** of an XML file.

Unit 7

In this unit, you learned about **XLink**. You learned there are two types of XLinks: **simple links** and **extended links**. You also learned about link traversal and how to use **resources**. Next, you learned how to **identify restrictions** and basic **XLink syntax**. You also learned about XLink's **global attributes**, and you set up and reviewed an XML document containing an XLink. You also learned how to **validate XLinks** and **create a simple XLink**. You reviewed examples of a **resource-type linking** element, a **locator-type linking** element, **inbound link arcs**, and an **extended-type linking** element. Finally, you learned about the **XPointer language**. You learned about **XPointer axes, node tests, predicates, location set functions**, and XPointer **points** and **ranges**.

Unit 8

In this unit, you learned about **XML APIs**. You learned the difference between **object-based interfaces** and **event-based interfaces**. You learned that an object-based interface creates a **document tree** in memory while an event-based interface **generates events**. Then, you learned about two of the most common XML APIs: **DOM** and **SAX**. You learned about different **DOM objects** and their **methods** and **properties**. Then you learned **how to add an element to an existing XML document** by using DOM. You also learned **how to extract attribute names and values**. Finally, you learned that DOM and SAX each have specific **advantages and limitations**, and you learned some **typical scenarios** where it's preferable to use the DOM over SAX, and vice-versa.

Unit 9

In this unit, you learned about **data binding** and **data consumer elements**. You learned how to **bind data** by using **HTML data consumer elements** and **extended attributes**. You also learned how to use the `<div>`, `<span>`, and `<table>` elements for **data set binding**, and you learned how to **integrate XML data sources with HTML documents**. Next, you learned how to apply **internal** and **external data islands**, and you learned how to use tables as binding agents. You also learned how to work with **data source objects**, and how data source objects return data. You also learned about **data nesting** and the **two-level rule**. Finally, you learned how to **create a simple navigation component**.

Topic B: Continued learning after class

It is impossible to learn to use any software effectively in a single day. To get the most out of this class, you should begin working with XML to perform real tasks as soon as possible. Course Technology also offers resources for continued learning.

Next courses in this series

This is the only course in this series.

Other resources

You might find some of these other resources useful as you continue to learn about XML. For more information, visit www.course.com.

- *New Perspectives on XML- Comprehensive*
  ISBN: 0619101881
- *Learn XML In a Weekend*
  ISBN: 1-59200-010-X

Glossary

Archetype
A reference where the element being referred to is declared within the schema element and not within any subelements. Also called global reference.

Attributes
Specify information about elements in the form of name-value pairs, and appear inside an element's start tag, immediately after the element name.

Block-level elements
Elements that create a line break.

Cardinality
Number of times an element might occur in an instance document.

Chameleon namespace
Namespace design where the supporting schema adopts the namespace declared in the main schema document.

Character data
Data containing plain text with no markup symbols.

Character-points
Origin node containing only text but no child nodes.

Child element
Element contained within a parent element. Also called a subelement.

Compositors
Specialized XML Schema components that define groups of elements and attributes within the schema and, thus, within the related XML documents.

Constraints
Define what can appear in a given language or document.

Content model
A pattern that indicates what elements or data can be nested within other elements, the order in which they appear, their cardinality, and whether they are required or optional.

Data binding agent
Establishes and maintains the synchronization of data values to the HTML document.

Data consumers
Elements in a Web page that are designated to receive and render data.

Data content elements
Elements containing character strings only.

Data islands
Distinct data storage elements.

Datatype constraints
Describe the units of data that the schema considers valid.

Declaration identifier
Combination of the start indicator (<!) and the uppercase keyword.

Document analysis
Process of determining the effectiveness of XML document development.

Document type declaration
The statement within the prolog of an XML document that specifies what type of document it is and sometimes refers to a document type definition.

Document Type Definition
A file that identifies all the elements in its respective XML document(s) and indicates the structural relationships among them.

Element
The basic building block of an XML document. It represents a piece of data, identified by a tag.

Element declaration
A statement that specifies the names of elements and the nature of their content.

Entities
Storage units that hold strings or blocks of parsed data such as text entities, and unparsed data such as graphics, audio files, or video files.

Entity declaration
A statement that specifies a name for the entity and defines what the entity represents.

Extended link
Offers full XLink functionality, including inbound and third-party arcs, and arcs that can simultaneously connect a local resource to several remote resources.

External data islands
XML data elements in a separate document.

Formal public identifier (FPI)
The code appearing immediately after the PUBLIC keyword in a document type declaration.

Formatting transformation
The transformation of an XML document into another format (e.g., HTML, PDF, DB2, Oracle, etc.).

Globally declared elements
Elements that are declared in the <schema> element. See also local elements.

Inline-level elements
Elements that do not create line breaks.

Instance documents
XML documents that conform to a particular schema.

Instantiation
Creation of a data structure with its own set of subroutines, which operate on specific data.

Internal data island
XML data elements nested in an HTML document.

Internal DTD
Listing of elements, attributes, entities or other types of declarations within the confines of a document type declaration in an XML document.

Links
Explicit relationships between addressable units of information or services in XML documents.

Local elements
Elements in a schema that are declared in subelements of the schema element, but not in the scope of the schema element itself.

Metalanguage
Language used to create a formal description of another language.

Nesting
The concept of placing one element inside another.

Notation declaration
A statement in a DTD specifying types of non-parsed binary data and occasionally text data.

Parameter entities
Entities that are used in an XML document's DTD.

Parsed entities
Entities containing text that might represent markup or content data.

Processing instructions (PIs)
Instructions passed by the XML processor to the application.

Range
Consists of all the XML content between two points: a start point and an end point.

Restriction
A form of XML inheritance used to restrict the content model of the base type.

Root element
Parent element of all other elements.

Schema
A model for an entire class of documents. The model describes the possible arrangement of elements, attributes, and text in a schema-valid document.

Schema element
First element of the schema; equivalent to the root element of an XML document.

Set binding
Inserting more than one value at a time during data binding.

Sibling elements
Elements that are at the same level and share a parent element.

Simple link
Associates exactly two participating resources, one local and one remote, with an arc traversing from the local resource to the remote resource.

Simple type elements
Elements containing only character data and no attributes or subelements.

Structural transformation
Transformation phase in which the data is converted from the structure of the incoming XML document to the structure of the desired output.

Unidirectional link
A link with only one source and one destination.

Unparsed entity
Resource whose contents might or might not be text, and which might be in formats other than XML.

Index